# SHOOTING
## THE MESSENGER

### Also by Paul L. Moorcraft

*African Nemesis:*
*War and Revolution in Southern Africa, 1945–2010*

*The Anchoress of Shere* (fiction)

*Axis of Evil: The War on Terror* (edited with Gwyn Winfield and
John Chisholm); the updated American edition is *The New Wars
of the West: Anglo-American Voices on the War on Terror*

*Chimurenga! The War in Rhodesia: A Military History* (with Peter
McLaughlin); forthcoming in an updated edition as
*The Rhodesian War: A Military History*

*Guns and Poses: Travels with an Occasional War Correspondent*

*A Short Thousand Years: The End of Rhodesia's Rebellion*

### Also by Philip M. Taylor

*British Propaganda During the First World War, 1914–1918*
(with M. L. Sanders)

*British Propaganda in the Twentieth Century: Selling Democracy*

*Global Communications, International Affairs*
*and the Media Since 1945*

*Munitions of the Mind: A History of Propaganda from the*
*Ancient World to the Present Era*

*The Projection of Britain: British Overseas Publicity and*
*Propaganda, 1919–1939*

*War and the Media: Propaganda and Persuasion in the Gulf War*

# SHOOTING
## THE MESSENGER

*The Political Impact*
*of War Reporting*

PAUL L. MOORCRAFT *and* PHILIP M. TAYLOR

Potomac Books, Inc.
Washington, D.C.

**Library of Congress Cataloging-in-Publication Data**

Moorcraft, Paul, 1948–
 Shooting the messenger : the political impact of war reporting / Paul Moorcraft and Philip M. Taylor.— 1st ed.
     p. cm.
 Includes bibliographical references and index.
 ISBN-13: 978-1-57488-947-5 (hardcover : alk. paper)
 1. War—Press coverage—History. 2. Press and politics—History. I. Taylor, Philip M. II. Title.
 PN4784.W37M66 2008
 070.4'33—dc22

                    2008004615


Printed in the United States of America on acid-free paper that meets the American National Standards Institute Z39-48 Standard.

Potomac Books, Inc.
22841 Quicksilver Drive
Dulles, Virginia 20166

First Edition

10 9 8 7 6 5 4 3 2 1

# CONTENTS

# PREFACE

This book probes a deep-rooted struggle: the continuing contest between the media and the military in which one side waves the banner of freedom of speech and the other trumpets the security of the state. Is this a result of a clash of cultures, or are the high-profile problems that sometimes occur in military-media relations the result of other pressures? The political environment in which soldiers and reporters have to work obviously influences both, but their respective institutional frameworks are also key factors influencing the way they operate. As a much older institution, the military sometimes—often—resents the way the more modern mass media covers military activity. In peacetime, the media seems uninterested—unless there is a barracks murder, a scandal over women at sea, a homosexual rape, or some other "bad news." While soldiers are training for war, enduring in the process what few other human beings have to undergo physically and psychologically, journalists seem to be anarchic, antiestablishment, skeptical, disrespectful of authority, competitive to the point of "dog eat dog," and what Kurt Vonnegut described as "voyeurs of strangers' misery." When war breaks out—a phenomenon that modern societies regard as a last resort and a failure of peacetime politics—the reporters rush to the scene like packs of wolves, reveling in the killing fields. Then, from the military point of view, you have civilians on the battlefield where reporters are a bloody nuisance, ignorant of what soldiers have been training for, and ill versed in the art of war. The military preoccupation with secrecy and OPSEC (operational security) clashes with the journalistic necessity for publicity and even sensationalism. The resultant tensions seethe over into postconflict relations until the next war, when the cycle of resentment and mutual incompatibility begins once again in debates over the need to know versus the media's claims to a right to know.

Behind the rhetorical flourishes, however, war correspondents and frontline officers, often despite themselves, are frequently similar in temperament and sometimes even in patriotic objectives. They share many of the psychological characteristics that come with experiencing the reality of combat. This distinct band of brothers experiences what the rest of humanity usually only observes—from a distance—through the "prying lenses" of television. Interestingly, radio correspondents and newspaper reporters tend to attract less opprobrium; we live in a visual society in which the camera is king, the "camera never lies," and "seeing is believing." Of course, in our modern society, characterized by digital technology that disseminates all sorts of information and images instantaneously and globally, 24/7, we know that in the kingdom of the blind, the one-eyed man is really the king. And journalists are the Cyclopes of a kingdom so saturated with information that ordinary observers can barely make sense of the world they live in. In the shared zones of danger, far from the norms of civilian culture, death is a common denominator. Both soldiers and journalists accept the possibility of death. Indeed, upon it they build their careers.

Wars are the ultimate audit of a state, although Western democracies no longer fight each other. For all its faults, so far the European Union has achieved its primary purpose: to outlaw war among member states. Previously, in the two World Wars and then in the Cold War that overflowed from them, governments forced citizens to accept censorship in exchange for the promise of national survival. The fall of the Berlin Wall—and UN peace *enforcement* in particular—introduced the so-called wars of choice, and critics demanded to know precisely what their soldiers were doing in their name. Ten years after the collapse of the Soviet Union, the "global war on terror" reintroduced ideological warfare between different belief systems, the purported clash of civilizations characterized by constant war abroad and heightened alert at home, while draconian antiterrorism measures prompted increasing evasion and secrecy in Washington and London.

All Western governments pay lip service to the theory that the media can audit their warriors and the politicians who send them off to war. The publicity surrounding the Abu Ghraib prison abomination showed that sometimes theory becomes practice. This study examines how military forces, sometimes under government orders, have circumvented democratic accountability. They have done so for a number of reasons that include instinctive military secrecy, reflex aversion in the defense ministries to public disclosure by civilians, and downright political chicanery, as well as the purported rationale of disguising vital information from the "enemy." The evidence comes mainly from wars fought by Western states, particularly the United States and the United Kingdom, although sometimes comparable examples are taken from more authoritarian polities.

This book covers various elements of the media, including print, radio, television, film, and still photography. For a generation after the Crimean War, correspondents and war photographers served complementary but different roles. By the 1890s, new technology, especially more portable cameras and better printing processes, allowed them to merge into a single profession: the photojournalist. While soldiers took cover, the photojournalists had to keep their heads up and take pictures—the closer, the better. Some of the best of them, such as Robert Capa, were killed in the process. For most of the twentieth century, journalists tended to specialize: snappers (photographers) and scribblers or radio and TV reporters prided themselves on the demarcation lines between them. But more recently cost cutting and technology (especially ultralight digital cameras linked to laptop computers) have again fused the different crafts of the wordsmith and the image maker.

Since modern war reporting began in the mid-nineteenth century the central question has always been: how much should be told? And when? At one extreme is the American censor who said: "I would tell the people nothing until the war is over. Then I would tell them who won." Conversely, it could be argued that TV viewers *should* be permitted to see the "splatter shots"—blood and gore, smashed bodies, bayonetted babies, raped women—in order to expose the wrongdoers and excite sufficient moral indignation to prompt NATO or the United Nations (UN) to deploy forces, as happened in the Balkans during the 1990s. In the final analysis, war correspondents, and their editorial bosses at home, must forge their own individual compromises between evading censorship and wallowing in total license. They walk the tightrope between voyeuristic war pornography and the dangers of "compassion fatigue," or desensitizing audiences to what real war can do to real people.

Striking this balance is crucial for the simple reason that the war correspondent's job is quite different from domestic reporting, not only because it is so personally dangerous and professionally demanding nor even because only a small minority of journalists graduate into the profession by being good (or crazy) enough to cover conflicts effectively. Rather, war reporting can have a dire impact on the numbers of lives lost—or saved. Domestic reporting may sometimes topple governments, but it rarely kills.

In the face of such moral burdens, how should journalists deal with military and political authorities who may try to suppress information that should be disclosed to the electorate? Jeremy Paxman, one of the most hard-nosed of British television journalists, famously remarked that a broadcaster's attitude towards politicians should display the same degree of respect that the dog reserves for the lamppost. That's fine for the decorous rancor of a TV studio, but it wouldn't always be recommended with, say, a Chechen or an Afghan warlord. Flying bullets, the crump of mortars, or even a punch in the nose teach rapid lessons in interview etiquette. In war zones, facing mutual dangers and sharing information, journalists and soldiers often learn to compromise. To survive, they must strike a deal. Correspondents frequently self-censor their reports to keep their vital military sources "on-side"; news is fudged. The individual tactics of war reporting are often as complex as the strategy of national propaganda campaigns. War is often hell, and war correspondents are not angels, despite the former fashion of white suits and the current one of pious rhetoric.

This book describes how democracies report wars. First, it provides a narrative account of how the media has covered all the major and some minor wars of the twentieth century. Second, it offers a frontline analysis from the perspective of soldiers and of humble "hacks" (as journalists call themselves). The story frequently zooms out from the front line and into the corridors of power to consider the vantage point of generals and government ministers. Third, and more implicitly, it evaluates the current debate over the impact of media coverage on foreign and defense policy.

We will also explore some media myths. Ever since the Vietnam War in the 1960s and 1970s, the military has tended to display open hostility to journalists (even though war correspondents were by and large "on-side" during that conflict, as indeed in most previous conflicts). More recently, however, journalists have become a crucial element of war planning, not least because of extensive "embedding" and new military doctrines such as information operations. Public affairs, or what the British call "media operations" (media ops), has become a key part of contemporary military doctrinal thinking and war fighting.

This shift is, in fact, a return to historical norms. In the nineteenth and twentieth centuries, military-media relations were generally cooperative, not conflicting, especially during wars of national survival. Provocation of public anger and dissent at home were the exceptions, although the father of all war correspondents, William Howard Russell, and his critical coverage of the British army's conduct during the Crimean War might appear to have established the norm. More contemporary exceptions are the Suez Crisis of 1956 and the Iraq War of 2003, which deeply divided public opinion, especially in Britain and Europe.

If cooperation is generally the rule, what are the reasons for this, bearing in mind the intrinsic dichotomies of media disclosure and military secrecy? How does the interface between the reporter's right to know and the military's almost knee-jerk commitment to "operational security" actually work? Does this create a gap between images of war and the harsh realities of the battlefield? Is modern embedding a Faustian pact for journalists? Reporters trade off freedom to say what they like for security and access to dangerous, newsworthy places. In the process, do journalists become more than simple observers and become actual participants? Usually, three or four days under fire can turn individuals into the best of buddies (and occasionally worst enemies). How has modern technology—especially live, satellite broadcasting from the front line—influenced journalism, military conduct, and even the public's perception of what is occurring?

A warning is necessary here. Journalists are more prone to subjectivity than most professionals precisely because they believe they are uniquely immune to its seduction. Of course, total objectivity is clinically impossible, especially after witnessing a massacre or two, but journalists should strive for it and reject the temptations of advocacy journalism. War correspondents may bond (or pretend to bond) with the warriors who share their food or armored vehicle. Ultimately, however, hacks must refuse to take sides, especially when they are covering wars fought by their own nationals. This is the prime imperative of war reportage.

The authors need, therefore, to inject a personal note. Paul Moorcraft worked as a freelance war correspondent for print, radio, and TV networks in many of the conflicts of the last thirty years. He also worked inside the military machine during various separate stints in the UK Ministry of Defence: as an inmate of the Royal Military Academy Sandhurst, later at the UK Joint Services Command and Staff College, then in Whitehall, and also in media operations in the field. Philip Taylor has researched in the area of military-media relations and the dreaded field of propaganda for more than thirty years. He firmly believes in the need for academics to interact with their subject matter and has worked, for half that time, with military forces engaged in psychological operations, information operations, and media operations (described as "public affairs" in the United States and "public information" in other NATO countries).

We hope this extensive firsthand experience brings a fresh perspective to this latest examination of war and the media. And, with all the keyboard courage we can muster, we shall both attempt to apply Paxman's dictum not only to deserving politicians but equally to journalists and military personnel.

# ACKNOWLEDGMENTS

We started this book a long time ago, so some of the people who helped may well have forgotten about their contributions. Professor Gary Sheffield, formerly of King's College, London, helped with the section on World War I. Chris Ashton, an Australian freelance journalist and old Africa hand, checked the section on Rhodesia. Irwin Armstrong, who filmed the Troubles in Northern Ireland, read the relevant section. Tim Lambon, deputy foreign editor of the United Kingdom's Channel 4 News, provided a variety of valuable insights. His colleague Lindsey Hilsum, the international editor and Beijing correspondent, helped, as ever, to raise the level of intellectual debate.

In the United States, Dr. Caroline Ziemke should be thanked for her intellectual generosity, likewise Justine Redman of CNN and writer Sam Dealey, for their guidance through the Washington labyrinth. Nik Gowing was always a source of inspiration. Though they did not, and could not, help with this book, we would still like to thank various denizens in the UK Ministry of Defence, North Atlantic Treaty Organization (NATO), Supreme Headquarters Allied Powers Europe (SHAPE), and the US Department of Defense who would like to remain anonymous. Tony Denton provided IT advice. We also appreciate the patience of our editor, Don McKeon.

Thanks, finally, to the busy hacks who found time to reply to our questionnaire, especially Allen Pizzey (CBS, while based in Baghdad), Mick Smith (*Sunday Times*), Chris Hughes (*Daily Mirror*), Jonathan Kapstein (*Business Week*), and Alex Thomson (Channel 4 News).

Despite this galaxy of advisers, we have, no doubt, committed numerous infelicities of style and content, for which we apologize in advance. We hope they can be rectified in future editions.

# 1

# THE ORIGINS OF WAR REPORTING

The history of mankind, as the famous British war correspondent Charles à Court Repington once remarked, is the history of war. Warfare has been a permanent condition of human existence rather than a temporary aberration from the supposed "normality" or ideal of peace. Yet a fundamental point to remember is that the experiences of those who actually fought in battles and of those who merely read about them or watched them from afar have been quite different. The gap between image and reality is huge. In the process of description, the sheer brutality of the experience of warfare goes through a process of mediation that turns it into something quite different—an epic poem, a painting, or, more recently, a film, a television documentary, or a news report. Of course, modern journalism is a relatively recent phenomenon. An eventual by-product of the invention of the printing press in the fifteenth century, newspapers, as we understand them today, began to appear several hundred years later. The mass circulation of newspapers is really a twentieth century phenomenon as, of course, is broadcasting and the cinema. Indeed, the arrival of these truly *mass* media is what distinguishes the twentieth century from all periods before it. However, that the gap between image and reality has narrowed somewhat does not mean that it has been eradicated.

Nonetheless, nothing springs from nothing, and it is important to understand the historical antecedents of contemporary war reporting, not least because so many aspects of today's military-media relationship were experienced long before the century of "total war."

## SHOOTING THE MESSENGER

According to some ancient sources, the Greeks disliked bad news so intensely that the runners carrying it from one point to another were sometimes killed. Thus began a long history of "shooting the messenger," a history that extends to the modern–day media that thrives on bad news. It is frequently said that history is written by the victors, and, of course, victory in war is the source of national celebration and commemoration of those who have lost their lives. In the classical Greek period, scribes recorded wars rather than reporting them, often many years after the event. As such, the accounts we have are riddled with myth and propaganda and are based on oral accounts passed down through generations by storytellers. Written five hundred years after the event, Homer's *Iliad* devotes more than half of its space to depictions of battles and the heroes who fought them. Together with his other epic poem, the *Odyssey*, Homer tells us less about the actual events of the Trojan War (indeed we are not certain it even happened) and more about how later Greeks used this "event" as the historical moment that defined their unity, culture, and character. Writing about the history of war is often more about the present than the past, and, until the arrival of the war correspondent in the mid-nineteenth century, it was less a matter of record and more a matter of myth.

Virgil, writing in Latin at the height of Roman power, followed the Homeric tradition in his famous masterpiece, the *Aeneid*. The Asian equivalent, the *Mahâbhârata*, reworked between 400 and 200 BC, describes the tremendous struggles that resulted from the Aryan invasion of the Indus Valley more than one thousand years earlier. Its one hundred thousand couplets make it probably the longest poem ever written. The *Mahâbhârata*, is also one of the greatest surviving accounts of primitive war, fought almost exclusively by foot soldiers armed with bows and arrows.[1]

But these were poetic interpretations of military history and popular myths, not factual reporting; they lack the authenticity and stylistic immediacy of eyewitness accounts. The Athenian historian Thucydides was a general who was exiled from Athens following his failure to prevent a city falling into Spartan hands. Although his *The History of the Peloponnesian War* must also be treated with some caution given his own background and the collection of firsthand accounts he personally collected during the rest of the conflict, his history of the Athenians' disastrous war against Sparta in the fifth century BC can legitimately be seen as a compelling forerunner of modern war reporting.[2]

Military commanders themselves have written some of the most powerful and immediate war records. In 401 BC, Xenophon led his army of Greek mercenaries in an epic retreat.[3] His detailed description of directing his troops through the snows of modern Kurdistan contains "human interest" details reminiscent, for example, of accounts of the siege of Stalingrad.[4] Likewise, Julius Caesar's understated style contains many of the elements of modern war reportage. For instance, in his description of his landing on

2

British soil in 55 BC, he adds what journalists today would call a "sound bite." The Roman landing force, accustomed to fighting on land, encountered stiff resistance from the natives massed on the beach. Caesar records the standard-bearer of the tenth legion shouting: "Jump down, comrades, unless you want to surrender our eagle to the enemy; I, at any rate, mean to do my duty to my country and my general."[5]

The Jewish historian Josephus, who sympathized with the Romans, indulged in what nowadays would be termed sensationalism. In his portrayal of the siege of Jerusalem in AD 70, he writes in almost tabloid style of a woman, driven by hunger and anger at her inevitable death, committing a crime against nature: "Seizing her child, an infant at the breast, she cried, 'My poor baby, why should I keep you alive in this world of war and famine?'" Then she kills her baby son, roasts him, eats half of the body, and keeps the rest for a later meal.[6] Although Josephus is considered an unreliable witness by modern historians, and the contemporary parallels should not be overdone, there are nonetheless elements of continuity not only in the abiding fascination with the detailed horrors of war but also in the overall aims of the stories. Right from the outset, epic poems and prose chronicles of war had a political purpose: to bolster the authority of the current ruler, which, for both Virgil and Josephus, was the Roman Empire.

After the collapse of the centralizing power of the Roman Empire, myths and legends of military prowess became even more integral to the survival of warrior societies in the flux and chaos of the so-called "Dark Ages." A central core of early medieval war stories centered on the various versions of *La Chanson de Roland*, based on Roland's defense of the rearguard of Charlemagne's army as it marched through the pass of Roncesvalles in the Pyrenees in AD 778. Roland's self-sacrifice became the prime motif of chivalric literature. In Anglo-Saxon and Celtic tradition, bards accompanied warriors into battle to add firsthand piquancy to their prose and poetry. In an illiterate tribal society, the oral traditions recorded genealogical and political legitimacy as well as flattering princes with praise-poems. From these stories and myths emerged the Arthurian legends, which later melded into chivalric traditions based on Roland and other knights. In a historical example from a later period (1400–1409), Owain Glyn Dŵr led the last major Celtic rebellion against English rule in Wales, while his faithful bard Iolo Goch proclaimed his lord's prowess.[7]

From Charlemagne to the time of Owain Glyn Dŵr, "war reporting" consisted largely of heroic combats between individual knights or sagas of noble leaders spearheading competing armies. One of the last flowerings of this tradition was the papal propaganda to support the crusades in the

Holy Land from 1095 onward. The church fused religion and reportage to buttress Christendom's wars with the Muslim world.

As the honor of individual swordsmanship gave way to the more mechanical and massed warfare of the bullet and cannonball, the annals of war became less heroic, and the literature began to present more realistic portrayals of combat. In 1609, for example, Samuel Daniel wrote of "artillerie, th' infernall instrument, new-brought from hell" in his account of England's Wars of the Roses in the fifteenth century.[8] His readers were perhaps as appalled by his detailed descriptions of the human impact of the latest engine of war, artillery fire, as modern generations were affected by written and photographic accounts of the nuclear attacks on Hiroshima and Nagasaki.

Improving technology was bound to influence not only warfare but also the means of reporting it. In the mid-fifteenth century, Johann Gutenberg pioneered printing by movable type, and this revolution, by initially producing more accessible Bibles, changed not only religion but also government and commerce. Printing prompted the Reformation and the beginnings of the press. The first newspapers written in English appeared in the 1620s. Spurred by demand for news during the English civil war, fourteen newspapers were on sale in London by 1645. Many of the early newspapers were highly polemical, and successive governments imposed restrictions on them. A tax on paper limited many eighteenth century newspapers to four pages; there was also a tax on advertisements and a stamp duty.[9] Some of the local information was founded on gossip and imagination or copied from rival publications. Writers lifted international news from foreign journals or based their accounts on travelers' letters and reports.

If sometimes newspapers said too much, editors were fined and imprisoned; at other times they said too little. The British forces' defeat at the Battle of New Orleans in January 1815 received little coverage in British papers, and the few that did mention it declared it an English victory. Some journalistic ignorance might be excused, however, as news then traveled at a slow pace. Soldiers fought this bloodiest battle of the Anglo-American War of 1812 more than two weeks *after* a peace settlement had been concluded in Ghent. English newspapers were too concerned with the escape of Napoleon and the events that culminated in Waterloo to be diverted by embarrassing American victories in faraway places. As ever, the press processed news that immediately concerned its readers.

Continental Europe enjoyed a period of relative peace for the rest of the nineteenth century. True, there were revolutions and shorts wars but nothing to compare with the upheavals of the French Revolution and

Napoleonic conflicts. This "Long Peace" and the spread of the industrial revolution spawned a series of media advances. In the newspaper industry, mechanical typesetting was developed in 1838, and the rotary press in 1846. These technologies, combined with linotype composition, devised in 1844, would allow thirty thousand copies of a newspaper to be printed in one hour. Early newspapers were composed of dull, dense columns, although magazines were spiced by artists' impressions of wars. In the late 1830s, Louis Daguerre developed photography; John MacCosh, a surgeon in the Bengal Army, used an improved process known as the calotype. MacCosh was one of the first war photographers, managing to take small portraits of officers and men during the Second Sikh War (1848–49), but it was technically impossible to reproduce these pictures in newspapers. It was not until 1880 that a photograph printed by the halftone method (in the *New York Daily Graphic*) allowed the slow phasing out of the laborious process of engraved wood block and line drawings.[10]

Rapid printing was all very well, but how could foreign news be transmitted more effectively from far-away war zones to newspaper offices? Previously, messages depended on the fastest horse or sailing ship. However, balloons had been tried, and in 1832 an English paper, the *True Sun,* carried news of French troops moving on Antwerp with the headline of "Just arrived by a carrier pigeon." Pigeons could travel at 35 miles per hour, but the newly invented steam trains were reaching speeds of 50 miles per hour. What accelerated communications in the nineteenth century in a way similar to how computers would affect the late twentieth century was a process that could send information at 186,000 miles per second—the telegraph.

In 1844, Samuel Morse, an artist and portrait painter, opened the first telegraph line, between Baltimore and Washington. One early witness of the first telegraphic transmissions declared: "Time and space are now annihilated."[11] In 1851 a submarine cable linked Britain and France, and a line spanned the Atlantic successfully in 1866. Surprisingly, many of the early war correspondents seemed extremely reluctant to use the telegraph; the same could be said for Alexander Graham Bell's invention of the telephone in 1876. Besides, most of the colonial war reporting in the second half of the nineteenth century took place far away from telegraph lines and certainly far from the newfangled telephone. Journalists either undertook long journeys on horses (or camels) or used dispatch riders. This, of course, added much color to their often highly personalized accounts of colonial warfare. And by the end of the century, radio developed from the wireless telegraph invented in 1896 by Guglielmo Marconi.

Allied to inventions in printing, photoreproduction, telegraphy, and radio were important social developments in Europe and North America: urbanization, compulsory education and, hence, literacy, and the extension of the franchise. The expansion of rail networks and later development of the petrol engine enhanced distribution of newspapers. The age of mass newspaper circulation had arrived. So, too, had an electorate, especially in Britain, that was highly sensitive to the political nuances of the imperial wars that fascinated the Victorian press.

Military defeats had presaged the collapse of governments and rulers throughout history, but it was not until the mid-nineteenth century that colonial battles could be dissected so quickly in the metropole because of improvements in communications technology. The disastrous defeat of an army at the Battle of New Orleans could be almost ignored in London, but seven decades later the killing in the Sudan of one man, Major General Charles George "Chinese" Gordon, could actually threaten the British government's survival. The advent of the modern war correspondent—the so-called specials—would play a role in bolstering or undermining the stability of governments. Whereas chieftains used to kill messengers bearing bad news in the Greek tradition, democracies resorted to censorship. Although formalized military censorship was not introduced until late in the nineteenth century, the key issue—whether to withhold military information in the perceived national interest or allow the Fourth Estate to tell the general public—predates the revolution in mass communication.

## THE RISE OF THE SPECIALS

At the beginning of the nineteenth century, war reporting consisted of official dispatches, travelers' tales, diplomatic gossip, direct copies from foreign periodicals, and occasional, usually self-serving, letters from officers in the field. The *Times* of London then came up with a revolutionary idea: why not employ someone to actually visit "the seat of war" and send back eyewitness reports as rapidly as possible? The man the paper chose was a barrister, Henry Crabb Robinson. He was also a student of German culture. In 1807 he was sent to report on Napoleon's campaigns along the Elbe. Robinson set a template for indolence by never visiting any battlefields, but he sufficiently satisfied his employers for the *Times* to send him in the following year to report on the Peninsular War, where he read local papers and picked up some tittle-tattle while again staying well away from the battlefield. His dispatches even managed to omit the famous Corunna victory in 1809 and the death of British Commander Sir John Moore. Although he did set a journalistic precedent for hype, absenteeism, and lack of curiosity, the *Times* failed to reemploy him. Nevertheless, the future doyens of war reportage were destined to work at the heart of the battlefield. As the distinguished combat photographer of the twentieth century Robert Capa used to say: "If the picture wasn't good enough, you weren't close enough." Whereas Capa was killed on assignment, Robinson wisely returned to legal practice and died in his bed at the ripe old age of ninety-two.

In 1809, the *Morning Chronicle* smuggled a journalist onto a warship that was accompanying a British expeditionary force to Antwerp, but Lord Castlereagh (soon to become foreign secretary) had him removed. In revenge the irate journalist, Peter Finnerty, lambasted the politician, an outburst that earned Finnerty a year in prison for libel.[12] Newspapers continued to rely on letters from serving British officers until the commander in chief, the Duke of Wellington (as he later became), clamped down on the practice, claiming that even the much-delayed appearance of such news could provide information to the enemy. Nearly eighty-five years passed before Military Intelligence formally censored such letters, but Wellington's actions had established a precedent for military suspicions of the press. The "Iron Duke," however, did make one concession: he allowed civilians to act as official war artists.

From 1815 to the mid-nineteenth century, there were numerous small imperial wars and revolutions in Europe where foreign correspondents worked harder at securing eyewitness accounts. The *Morning Post,* for example, sent its music critic, Charles Lewis Gruneisen, to cover the civil war in Spain (1835–37). Gruneisen did well, penetrating and reporting on the battle zones, but he was eventually captured and almost shot as a spy. This was more like it as far as the late Victorians' romantic image of the war correspondent was concerned. And this image was fashioned largely by one man: William Howard Russell.

## RUSSELL AND THE CRIMEAN WAR

Russell, born in Ireland in 1820, had wanted to be a doctor but couldn't stand the sight of dead bodies. Presumably he overcame his phobia because, after training to be a lawyer, he eventually became the father of all modern war correspondents or, as he dubbed himself, "the miserable parent of a luckless tribe." Like many of his tribe, Russell was deeply insecure, but he was fortunate in securing the constant support of the youthful editor of the *Times*, John Delane. For decades Delane massaged his employee's ego and encouraged him to develop a crisp, accurate, frontline style (although it might appear a little too flowery for modern tastes). Russell reported on the conflict over Schleswig-Holstein in 1850, but he first made his name in the Crimean War.

Britain and France had allied with Turkey to prevent the feared expansion of Russia into the Dardanelles region. Britain sent an expeditionary force—57,000 strong, the largest force deployed to a war overseas to date—in 1854. The British army, however, had changed little since its victory over Napoleon; indeed, the genial commander in chief, Lord Raglan, was seriously handicapped by his inability to grasp the notion that the French were now his allies, not his enemies. British troops also had little love for their secondary allies, the Turks. As one officer put it, "Everybody would rather go over to the Russians and help them" fight against the "wretched" Turks.[13]

If the grand strategy of the war appeared confused so were the logistics. Poor planning meant that supplies were lost or totally inadequate. It was a standing joke among the ordinary soldiery that, of the three thousand miles between the British armies and Plymouth, the most difficult were the last six. Poor food and unsanitary accommodations invited disease; after a year's campaigning less than 50 percent of the men were fit for duty. Russell and other correspondents described the makeshift hospitals for the diseased and wounded: "[T]here was not the least attention paid to decency or cleanliness—the stench was appalling . . . the sick appeared to be tended by the sick and the dying by the dying."[14]

Russell carefully noted the conditions of those who could still fight: "Hundreds of men had to go into the trenches at night with no covering but their greatcoats, and no protection for their feet but their regimental shoes. The trenches were two and three feet deep with mud, snow and half-frozen slush."[15] British troops were unquestionably brave, but no amount of courage could compensate for the appalling leadership, most egregiously the disastrous charge of the Light Brigade against Russian guns inspired by a poorly communicated order. Russell recorded the event with great panache in the *Times* of November 14, 1854:

> With diminished ranks, thinned by those thirty guns, which the Russians had laid with the most deadly accuracy, with a halo of flashing steel above their heads, and with a cheer which was many a noble fellow's death cry, they flew into the smoke of the batteries; but ere they were lost from view, the plain was strewn with their bodies and with the carcasses of horses.[16]

Although the fighting came to an inconclusive end in 1856, it had many long-term repercussions. Already the political shock waves had toppled the British government. As the Duke of Newcastle remarked to the *Times* correspondent when he visited the Crimea, "It was you who turned out the government, Mr Russell."[17] The *Times* had also set up a fund to support a team of nurses led by Florence Nightingale, who had been sent to reform the hospital system. More important, Russell's revelations of the "fatal cocktail of indifference, incompetence and senility" in the military command led to demands for the reorganization of the army.[18] In the longer term, the medical and military reforms benefited the ordinary soldier, but the reactions among many of the senior officers toward what the press had done were extremely hostile. Despite his bluff Irish charm, which won over his fellow journalists and some of the officers, Russell suffered all sorts of petty harassment from the military, including personal jibes that he was a "mad-dog Irishman" who hated the English, and he suffered constant "mishaps" to his supplies and baggage.

The generals in the Crimea took up what was to become the perennial complaint of the British military, namely that newspaper reports undermined national security. Lord Raglan wrote, "the enemy need spend nothing under the heading Secret Service . . . that enemy having at its command through the English press and from London to his Headquarters by telegraph every detail that can be required."[19] The military establishment was so incensed that Sydney Herbert, the former secretary of war, wrote: "I trust the army will lynch the *Times* correspondent."[20] After the war it became clear, not least from Russian sources, that the claims of security breaches by the *Times* were almost entirely groundless.

The military and government supporters exerted great pressure on the *Times* to silence or recall Russell, but the editor of *The Thunderer*, Delane, stood by his correspondents in the field, even in the face of an ultimate snub by the London establishment (several leading gentlemen's clubs banned the newspaper from their smoking rooms). Russell had always crosschecked the facts in his reports and based them on careful interviews with officers, men, and verified eyewitnesses, but he also offered to have his dispatches cleared by the military. This voluntary system of censorship was, however, rejected. Russell, acutely sensitive to the security dilemma, wrote, "Although it may be dangerous to communicate facts likely to be of service to the Russians, it is certainly hazardous to conceal the truth from the British people."[21] In February 1856, the high command in the Crimea issued an order that was to set an important precedent for military censorship: it banned the publication of any details that might benefit the enemy and authorized the expulsion of any transgressors.[22] This was the embryo of a censorship system that was later to crush almost all independent reporting during World War I. Throughout the twentieth century Western governments would parade what became known as "operational security" as an all-purpose device to stop pieces of information from being inadvertently released by journalists and later to rely on accusations of deliberate espionage to muzzle correspondents.

Russell, however, had simply been doing his job in the Crimea. It was the first time that a British military campaign had been subjected to continuous and close scrutiny by a civilian reporter. He had uncovered incompetence that had cost many lives. Revealing what he saw was surely in the public interest and the very foundation of the investigative reporter's task in a democracy. In addition to his role as an unintentional reformer, Russell also pioneered the essentials of all good journalism: energy, curiosity, bravery, accuracy, compassion, and an eye for detail. And he was lucky in finding an editor who was equally as determined and prepared to back him despite the furor his reports created. Yet Russell was no crusading radical. In professional terms, for example, he was initially reluctant to use the telegraph that (for a time) connected London to Varna in Bulgaria. Nor was he a radical in the social sense. Despite his moving portrayal of the ordinary soldier's hardships, he did not generally condemn those whom he regarded as his own class, the officers. (He did, however, occasionally refer to their "aristocratic hauteur.") Despite his detailed analyses of the abysmal conditions of the rank and file, he did not elaborate on the lavish lifestyles of the commanders, which even included a private yacht and accompanying wives. Indeed, he saw himself as part of the military establishment, rarely criticizing the strategic weaknesses of the war.

Later, in conflicts in Africa, India, and Europe, "Billy" Russell earned five campaign medals and even an Iron Cross, awarded personally by Prussia's crown prince. The correspondent became a close friend of the Princess of Wales, was awarded a knighthood, and, after he died in 1907, a memorial to him was erected in St. Paul's Cathedral. Despite Russell's earlier role as a hate figure for the military, Field Marshal Sir Evelyn Wood, who had served in the Crimea, declared many years after the war that Russell "incurred much enmity, but few unprejudiced men who were in the Crimea will now attempt to call in question the fact that by awakening the conscience of the British nation to the suffering of its troops, he saved the remnants of those grand battalions."[23] Regardless of the initial calumnies he endured from the military and politicians, the final verdict on Russell must be that he pioneered the role of informing the British public of the harshness of wars waged in their name. His career started with accusations of treason, yet in the end he was praised as a patriot. His obituary in the *Manchester Guardian* noted, "he was an honourable and patriotic journalist."[24] His successors would aspire to that ideal, but few were to match Russell's achievement.

Russell was not the only talented journalist in the Crimea; another *Times* man, Thomas Chenery, ably assisted him. In addition, there were French correspondents, who were closely censored by their military. There were also *Times* correspondents, including an admiral with the Baltic Fleet, which was enforcing a crucial economic embargo of Russian ports. But this aspect of the war has received little attention, partly because of the Royal Navy's order in February 1854 that stopped journalists sailing with the fleet and prevented serving officers from contributing to newspapers. So, in Britain's "first newspaper war," the traditionally "silent service," the Royal Navy, which did so much to weaken Russia's economic power, received few public accolades, while the army, which reluctantly allowed journalists, garnered many brickbats.[25] The campaign also witnessed the advent of the first war photographers, in particular Roger Fenton, another lawyer and the royal photographer, who was sent to record "a clean, ordered war in which the troops looked happy and healthy."[26] Comparing Fenton's photographs with the overwhelming body of critical press coverage should raise alarm bells about that old axiom that the camera never lies. Fenton's royal connections made him *persona grata* with the military, unlike Russell. When he dined with the commander in chief, Fenton was placed on Lord Raglan's right. Because he was thus "embedded" in the system, Fenton—despite his many private criticisms of the military mismanagement—practiced rigorous self-censorship in public. Fenton's pictures were exhibited throughout Britain and were made into postcards, with images designed to counter Russell's critical dispatches.

The war will always be associated, however, with Russell because of the impact his dispatches had on British public opinion. Although he did not stint on the heroics, he displayed the war's brutal horrors in a way that Fenton's anodyne photographs did not. In making a historical judgment, Russell's investigative achievements perhaps partly compensated for the war frenzy—whipped up by the press—that had helped to precipitate the war in the first place. Even then it must also be noted that his independent approach to reporting was subsumed within a hidden political agenda: the *Times* took up an antigovernment stance that was distinct from the issues of the Crimea.[27]

For much of the nineteenth century, the press was allied with jingoism and wartime nationalism: "Reporters functioned as frontline poets, scratching the first impressions into the culture's consciousness."[28] The extent to which this contrasts with the approach of the ancient Greeks can be debated. How much of the realities of war actually reached the public, even after Russell's breakthrough dispatches, must also be open to debate. Perhaps it would be fair to say that the major difference was the speed with which these mediated reports reached their audience. The military expected journalists to be patriots first and to keep their negative comments to themselves. So, in the immediate aftermath of the Crimean War, the military thought that it had made a grave mistake in tolerating the presence of Russell and his colleagues. In particular, many officers regarded his criticisms of Lord Raglan as grossly unfair, especially as the commander in chief had waged a ceaseless war with the London bureaucracy to ameliorate the logistical crises.[29] Raglan had never allowed Russell to interview him; indeed they never met. Raglan's situation illustrates a perpetual paradox for military leaders: was it better to work with war correspondents, especially the elite members of the tribe, and secure their tacit approval and perhaps printed praise or ignore and ban them and possibly risk harming one's military career? Throughout the age of new imperialism, British generals were to adopt different, often idiosyncratic, solutions to this conundrum.

Meanwhile, Russell's popular acclaim had established a new, distinct breed of journalists: a special group of men, and later women, who became fascinated by the stark challenges of combat. The era of the modern war correspondent had arrived as hundreds of specials flocked to the American Civil War. William Russell was among them.

## THE AMERICAN CIVIL WAR

In the first great American war, its struggle for independence from Britain, press objectivity was not at a premium: "The pens, like the muskets . . . were driven by passion and pamphlet."[30] There were no formal correspondents; the American press relied on rumors or letters from what today would be called "stringers" (i.e., freelance, occasional contributors). Opinion, not news, was the media currency. War reporting improved immeasurably, however, during the war with Mexico (1846–48). This time professional newspapermen entered the fray while regular army officers also doubled as correspondents. The penny press (so-called because the papers cost one cent) took full advantage of the telegraph and even hired small ships to speed the news from the south. The New Orleans *Picayune* even installed a typesetter aboard its hired vessel.[31] And, according to John Keegan, the first-ever war photograph was produced: a daguerreotype of American cavalry in a Mexican street.[32] In terms of comprehensive and adequate press scrutiny, the Mexican war paralleled the novel British coverage of the Crimean campaigns.

The American press was also active in the war at home against the Indian tribes. Humanitarians, led by the Quakers, were vocal in their criticism of military methods used against Native Americans. Conflict between the army and Indian Bureau agents was a permanent feature of civil-military relations in the "Wild West."

The American reporting of the Civil War (1861–65) reverted to the partisan style of the War of Independence because it was also seen as a mortal struggle for national survival, unlike the successful and relatively minor war against a weak Mexican adversary. Reporters from the Confederacy went to battle as propagandists, describing the North as "the cursed, cowardly nation of swindlers and thieves" that fought "drunken with wine, blood and fury."[33] The Northern papers, swept up in frenzied circulation wars, were almost as bad: the *Chicago Times* editor ordered one of his reporters to "telegraph fully all news you can get, and when there is no news, send rumors."[34] When William Russell accurately reported on the Northern defeat at the Battle of Bull Run in the London *Times*, there was uproar. He was extensively libeled and received numerous death threats. The *New York Times* described military-press relations as "a little side war going on between the newspaper correspondents and the military."[35]

Both sides in the real war indulged in crude propaganda. The North alleged "Johnny Rebs" made necklaces of Yankee eyes as gifts for their womenfolk, while Southern propaganda asserted Union soldiers played football with Confederate heads. The propaganda extended to the United Kingdom, where both sides curried favor. The Confederacy even secretly financed a British paper, the *Index*. Despite the relative objectivity of Russell's reportage, the *Times* tended to be pro-Confederacy, while the *Daily News,* for example, tended to support the North. Harriet Martineau, possibly the first woman in Britain to become a professional journalist, supplied the *Daily News* with regular articles.[36] There was no shortage of American war correspondents; five hundred worked on the Northern side alone. On both sides, however, the quality was poor. As one of the exceptions, Henry Villard, put it, "Men turned up in the army as correspondents more fit to drive cattle than to write for newspapers."[37] Journalists were incompetent, biased, poorly paid, and often corrupt; some took bribes from officers who wanted to see their heroics hyped in print. Although Russell, frustrated with his loss of accreditation from both sides, left America at the height of the war, some local journalists carried on his investigative tradition. In the South, for example, Peter Alexander, a lawyer from Georgia, campaigned for better medical attention for the troops and castigated the drunkenness of some officers.[38]

In 1862, Union secretary of war Edwin Stanton set up a formal system of censorship. He had already tried informal means—arresting editors, threatening to shoot journalists after a court-martial, banning correspondents from the front, and manipulating casualty figures. Having exhausted these indirect methods, Stanton began to report the war himself by issuing daily war bulletins circulated through the Associated Press. For this striking innovation in media manipulation, perhaps Stanton deserves the title of "father of spin-doctors."

Union Gen. William T. Sherman was best known for fighting with the press; on one occasion he court-martialed a reporter. It would appear that Sherman's campaign was a personal vendetta resulting from press reporting of his financial failures in San Francisco in 1858.[39] Others such as Union Gen. George B. McClellan positively courted the press in order to receive favorable coverage to enhance their careers.

The war witnessed many innovations: the widespread use of breech loading, repeating small arms, and the machine gun, as well as the first clash between iron-clad ships. The most notable media developments centered on the telegraph and photography. Possibly as many as 250,000 images were taken, including the first combat photographs. Some, however, were faked or doctored. Mathew Brady, America's most famous photographer, set out to document the whole conflict (despite being almost blind). To this end the *New Yorker* fielded and equipped Brady with his own small army of twenty camera-reporters. The wooden darkroom vans of "Brady's Photographic Corps" became a common sight on the battlefields. Soldiers eventually came to regard them as an ill omen, a sure sign that fighting was imminent.[40] Both the military and pressmen used the telegraph (including mobile field telegraphy) widely, though the *New York Daily Tribune* described telegraphed news as "the great mother of false intelligence, windy rumours and sidewalk stories."[41] Access to the telegraph created intense competition between journalists: on one expensive occasion, Joseph Howard of the *New York Times* telegraphed the genealogy of Jesus Christ to prevent his rivals from the using the wire. The extensive use of telegraphy transformed the written style of reportage. First, despite the famous exceptions, messages had to be short because of the high cost. Hence a new sharp prose style with brief sentences was required. Second, because of breaks in transmission, a story might end in mid-sentence. In reaction, the "inverted pyramid" evolved, where the bottom line was sent first; the punch line, as it were, led the article. Editors taught journalists to put the basics—who, what, when, how, and, if possible, why—in the first paragraph. Russell's lengthy narrative style, leading eventually to a classical denouement, had become outmoded.[42]

Despite the technical advances in technology and style and the popular appetite for frontline news, generally the war was poorly reported. The blame for this rested on the partisanship of most journalists and editors as well as the intervention of the censors. Formal censorship tried to control the news from the battlefield, while more informal propaganda worked insidiously on public opinion. The Civil War is also significant because it was the first time that the media was extensively used to win over hearts and minds in foreign countries, especially Britain. The press had become a vital military flank. Outmatched by the industrial resources of the North, the Confederacy soon realized that political and logistical support from Britain could save the South. Accordingly the North, aware of British sympathies for the rebels, played on the emotive issue of the abolition of slavery rather than the original casus belli of states' rights versus federalism.

The Civil War confirmed the press's pivotal position, even if in America it was cowed by censorship and enfeebled by partisanship. Fundamental questions were now being asked: did the press merely report wars or did newspaper campaigns actually inspire conflicts and even make them more savage once they had started? These issues became acute as the age of imperialism dawned. From the end of the Civil War to 1914, it was a golden age of romantic wars in far-off places for the specials, a chance to chronicle, usually without censorship, numerous little wars before the big one that promised to end all war.

## THE IMPERIAL WARS

During the second half of the nineteenth century, there was scarcely a year when the British army was not fighting a campaign, however small, somewhere in the world—a fact that undermines the nineteenth century's reputation as the century of peace. There was a curious development of what the German military thinker Karl von Clausewitz had called the "trinity" of the military, the people, and government. British administrations were sometimes reluctant to annex further chunks of empire, but in general a sense of manifest destiny underpinned imperial expansion. The colonial army was transformed from, in Wellington's terms, the "scum of the earth" to the noble warriors of Rudyard Kipling's verse. The increasingly educated public grew accustomed to colonial exploits: the British, it is said, had become a "newspaperised people."[43] And the glue that held the trinity together was the corps of specials. As John Mackenzie has suggested:

> The war correspondents had indeed glorified atavistic war. In their entente between the sword and the pen they had written of war in the "grand old style," of Homeric combats, of informal war in which they themselves participated and featured as celebrities. Moreover, they heightened the devilry of the pre-colonial regime, offering up a repeated moral justification for their colonial wars.[44]

The French, too, were busy "pacifying" rebels throughout their empire. The media stories were uncannily reminiscent of today's headlines. For example, French General Joseph Gallièni and General Louis Lyautey developed in Morocco the *tache d'huile*, or "oil spot," strategy (the exact same phrase used in Iraq and Afghanistan in 2006). This was a slow and methodical expansion of pacified areas that had been given protection and social services to create a large area under French control. It encouraged occupied populations to rally to the occupier by granting benefits of security, trade, and prosperity. The imperialists also had their own terrorists. In Algeria in the 1830s, French officers were keen to create a single enemy, a unified conspiracy against the glories of Western civilization. Abd el-Kadr, the head of a loose confederation of resistance leaders, became that figurehead. The officers' plan backfired because choosing this shadowy group as scapegoat prevented the single decisive victory that the imperialists craved. General Shamil fulfilled a similar function for the Russians as they advanced into the Caucasus.

Likewise, after the Indian Mutiny of 1857, the British hunted two of the resistance leaders, especially Nana Saheb, for decades. In perhaps the first example of a major photographic cover-up, few pictures of Indians swinging from gibbets were published, although Billy Russell wrote movingly of the executed Indians who festooned the trees along the Ganges. Many, he suspected, were innocent.

The newspapers followed the flag, and circulations boomed, as did the profits of the telegraph companies. The specials were everywhere, even with Custer at the Battle of Little Big Horn and with Gordon at Khartoum. They needed to be tough, displaying the physical and psychological fortitude of successful soldiers. They also had to be "competitive, assertive and relatively unscrupulous, able to deceive the authorities as well as rivals."[45] They were required to show constant initiative, even audacity. Bennett Burleigh, in one celebrated example shortly before the Boer War, actually stopped General Joubert's train to request an interview. Burleigh had already been mentioned in military dispatches (the first time a war correspondent had been honored in this way) when writing for the *Daily Telegraph* during the Sudan campaign.[46]

In imperial wars, there were fewer restrictions on the specials' derring-do, but in campaigns between so-called civilized powers, such as the Franco-Prussian conflict that broke out in 1870, the correspondents were expected to carry identity cards and wear brassards. Journalists usually reported from one side and would rarely venture to cover the opponent for fear of arrest as spies. The specials tended to self-censor their reports to avoid offending the host armies, which were prone to withdrawing cooperation. The French, sensitive as ever to perceived slights, exerted almost complete censorship, evaded dramatically by journalists' use of hot air balloons to send out copy during the siege of Paris. The Germans, however, recognized the need for good publicity, especially in England. Both Russell and Archibald Forbes, who was to inherit Russell's mantle as the premier British special, were invited to follow the rapid German advance into France. Such a speedy and stunning victory needed little German media management anyway. One of the noteworthy aspects of this war was the introduction of a pool system whereby the *New York Tribune* and the *London Daily News* arranged to share the dispatches of each other's correspondents. In the future, the military would develop this ad hoc cooperative mechanism and turn it into a formal means of control.

The specials soon turned to Africa. In 1873–74, the British launched a typical punitive expedition to crush the Ashanti in what is now Ghana. Its commander was the preeminent imperial troubleshooter Sir Garnet Wolseley. When he decided to destroy the Ashanti capital, Kumasi, he declared that the purpose was "to leave marks of our power or vengeance."[47] A number of well-known journalists accompanied Wolseley, including the famous African adventurer Henry Morton Stanley who reported for the *New York Herald*. The British had become engaged in West Africa to curb the slave trade, to secure gold, and to keep out other European imperialists, especially the French. But writers such as Stanley played up the humanitarian role of British intervention, not least the ending of human sacrifices. The British army fought five campaigns against the Ashanti, quelling the final uprising in 1900.

The Zulu, however, were a more determined foe. The Zulu War of 1879 comprised a pattern that became almost compulsory for the later military campaigns of the empire: the opening tragedy, the heroic redemption, and the final crushing victory.[48] The tragedy was the Battle of Isandhlwana, the worst British military disaster since the Afghan retreat of 1842.[49] The heroic redemption came at Rorke's Drift where 110—mostly Welsh—soldiers gallantly warded off waves of charges by four thousand Zulu warriors. Eleven Victoria Crosses were awarded to the defenders, more than for any other single engagement. Six months later the British commander, Lord Chelmsford, determined to redeem his reputation after Isandhlwana, staged a crushing victory at the Zulu capital of Ulundi. The imperial forces formed up in the classic hollow square, four deep with fixed bayonets, with Gatling guns at each corner. There was no digging in. "They'll only be satisfied," said Chelmsford, thinking of his critics in London, "if we beat them fairly in the open."[50] Archibald Forbes was in the square to record the details for the many erstwhile critics of the war. This time, except for one brief rush, the

17

Zulus did not approach within thirty yards of the redcoat square because of the disciplined rifle fire. When the courageous Zulu *impis* finally faltered, Chelmsford unleashed the cavalry, the 17th Lancers. The British broke Zulu power, and Forbes had a great story. He left the battlefield immediately, taking a sketch hurriedly drawn by the *Illustrated London News*'s Melton Prior. Forbes rode through 120 miles of largely hostile territory to reach a telegraph station to send his dispatch, which was soon read to both houses of Parliament. "A proud moment," declared the *Times*, "for the confraternity of special correspondents."[51]

The British, however, were about to face an African foe that could break the redcoat square: the Mahdists in the Sudan. In March 1874, Colonel Charles Gordon, who had made his reputation in China, was installed as governor of the region, which was technically under Egyptian suzerainty. After making strenuous efforts to stamp out the slave trade and to improve the oppressive and corrupt Egyptian administration, Gordon left the Sudan in 1879. A revolt, led by Mohammed Abdullah, then erupted with the aim of purging the territory of foreign rule. Abdullah declared himself the *Mahdi*, or promised Islamic messiah. In 1884, Gordon, promoted to major general, was asked to return to organize the evacuation of Egyptian forces, but he insisted on remaining in the capital, Khartoum, where Mahdist forces besieged his position. Gordon was a national hero, and British newspapers encouraged the prime minister, William Gladstone, to sanction a relief expedition. The British-led relief forces arrived but two days too late. After 317 days of siege, the Mahdists captured Khartoum and slaughtered the inhabitants. Despite the lack of reliable eyewitnesses, varying—but always lurid—press accounts of Gordon's death created a national scandal. This tradition was later maintained in the Hollywood version of events (*Khartoum*, 1966) in which Gordon, played by Charlton Heston, is beheaded on the steps of the governor's palace. In the 1990s, journalists had to ascend the same steps to secure their press passes from the radical Islamic regime.

The public blamed the British government for Gordon's murder or at least the slowness of the rescue expedition. Despite the clamor, it was not until 1898 that imperial honor was restored in the second Sudan war. The reconquest was led by Major General Sir Horatio Herbert Kitchener, the last British soldier to have remained in contact with Gordon during the siege. His campaign, portrayed as national revenge, culminated in the Battle of Omdurman, which included one of the last British cavalry charges. The young Winston Churchill, who had inveigled himself into the campaign as an officer-correspondent—despite Kitchener's initial rebuffs—took part in the charge.

Unlike Raglan in the Crimea, Kitchener's personality dominated the war in the Sudan. Although he made a few exceptions, the general usually detested journalists, famously calling them "drunken swabs." One of the exceptions was the *Daily Mail*'s George Warrington Steevens, a 28-year-old Balliol man, who had described the general in glowing terms: "His precision is so inhumanly unerring, he is more like a machine than a man."[52] Nevertheless, the commander did not want any journalists to accompany him. Later, because of massive popular interest in the war, he was persuaded to allow a small contingent, which had to submit brief reports (two hundred words per day) to military censorship before they were sent on the military telegraph. Kitchener remained hostile to the press, as did one of his subordinates, a young cavalry officer named Douglas Haig, who would later exercise total control of media coverage of World War I.

The military not only controlled the press but also manipulated it to gain national and international support for imperial policy in the Sudan (and elsewhere). Many of the journalists in the Sudan, most notably Churchill, hardly needed media management because they were as jingoistic as the military commanders themselves. But some in London raised voices of protest at the triumphalism following the defeat of the dervishes (as the followers of the Mahdi were called). Critics noted that the Sudanese had fought a modern army while wearing chain mail and using ancient weapons. As Steevens conceded in the *Daily Mail*, "It was not a battle, but an execution."[53] In addition, liberals at home excoriated the practice of killing the wounded, while the military explained that the Mahdists fought on even when severely wounded. Lieutenant Colonel Charles Townsend, a witness of the final battle, noted, "The valour of those poor half-starved Dervishes in their patched jibbahs would have graced Thermopylae."[54] And, in his poetry, Rudyard Kipling later immortalized these same "Fuzzy Wuzzies" for breaking the British square. Churchill's own account of the famous charge explained that the cavalry fought with equal weapons, the sword and the lance (though Churchill used a Mauser pistol). When describing the rest of the battle, he referred to British discipline and machinery triumphing over the most desperate courage, and the fanaticism of the Middle Ages colliding with the organization of the nineteenth century.

In September 1898, Kitchener completed his act of vengeance by ordering the destruction of the Mahdi's tomb at Omdurman by Gordon's nephew and the Mahdi's skeleton to be thrown into the Nile. (The Mahdi had died earlier of smallpox.) Only public protests, including murmurings from Queen Victoria, prevented Kitchener from sending the Mahdi's skull to London as a trophy.[55]

Few photographs survived from the period of the siege, partly because the Royal Engineers' camera team perished. When the avenging British returned a decade later, many of the officers carried Kodak box cameras, which had been developed in America in the 1880s. Seven journalists had lost their lives during the second Sudan campaign, while others, such as Winston Churchill, had made their reputations. The young Churchill had sidestepped the censor's regulations by sending stories disguised as personal letters; he also wrote an "instant book" on the campaign. Steevens's book, *With Kitchener to Khartoum,* was published within weeks of the end of the war. These accounts helped to transform Kitchener (later Lord Kitchener) into an imperial icon—despite his dislike of the "drunken swabs."

Steevens had written about the poor quality of army boots during the campaign, a peculiar if understandable obsession that was to reappear even in the more recent Falklands and Gulf wars, but Steevens had also played down criticisms of Kitchener, particularly the allegations of his men killing wounded dervishes on the battlefield. Bennett Burleigh, however, was not so discreet. Thoroughly annoyed by Kitchener's open hostility toward him, he published the story in the *Contemporary Review.* Self-censorship, it seems, had as much to do with personality (and potential book royalties) as patriotism.

The wars in Europe and Africa had honed the skills of the British specials, and U.S. journalists had been left somewhat behind. The Spanish–American War gave them a chance to catch up. At its start (1898), it appeared to be a minor conflict, but in retrospect it was a highly symbolic struggle between the oldest European imperial power and the emerging superpower of the New World. The Americans had sympathized with Cuban unrest under Spanish rule, and U.S. investments were also at risk. The popular press clamored for intervention, especially after a mysterious explosion sank the U.S. battleship *Maine* in Havana harbor. Under the slogan of "Remember the Maine! To hell with Spain!" America surged toward war.

This war "was bred, not born," according to one American historian: "With the assistance of the New York papers, a small rebellion became a full-scale revolt."[56] Mass-circulation newspapers were now big business, and powerful newspaper proprietors, such as William Randolph Hearst and Joseph Pulitzer, were accused of warmongering to boost circulation. Indeed, a few months before the war broke out, Hearst sent Frederic Remington (the pictorial historian of the American frontier) to sketch the insurgents in Cuba. Witnessing no skirmishes of consequence, a bored Remington cabled his boss from Havana: "Everything quiet. No trouble here. There will be no war. I wish to return." Hearst famously cabled back: "Please remain. You furnish the pictures and I will furnish the war."[57]

Another Hearst man in Cuba was the flamboyant Richard Harding Davis, who took intervention to new heights by competing with Stephen Crane, author of *The Red Badge of Courage*, to lead the capture of a Spanish-held town. James Creelman, also reporting for Hearst, even offered to lead a bayonet charge. In those days, long before political correctness, papers encouraged specials to be part of the stories they covered. Their proprietors paid well for their stories and for their bravery. No expense was spared: for example, the Associated Press chartered a flotilla of small ships to carry dispatches to the nearest cable station.[58] Hearst's newspaper empire grew with the American victories, even when the war against Spain spread to the Philippines where, in a prequel to Vietnam, U.S. troops indulged in large-scale and indiscriminate killing of the local inhabitants.[59]

In South Africa, Britain was about to face its own version of the Southeast Asian tragedy. As a historian of military-media relations commented, "the Boer war can be seen to have preceded the Vietnam war in its cynical pattern of jingoism, patriotism, questioning, and then doubt within the home nation, as the Boers turned the conflict into an unpopular protracted war of insurgency."[60] Unlike the United States, however, the imperium was doomed the moment the Boers showed how a professional British army could be outwitted by a small number of farmers turned guerrillas.

In 1899 imperial forces marched into the first twentieth-century war ready to fight with nineteenth-century tactics. The mounted, highly mobile Boers with their magazine-loading Mausers and their devastating "Long Tom" artillery soon drove the British into siege positions at Ladysmith, Kimberley, and Mafeking, which was defended by forces led by Robert Baden-Powell. The later founder of the Boy Scouts was lionized by the press despite his abysmal behavior (even by standards of the day) toward the garrison's black people, whom he reduced to starvation and death by keeping the whites reasonably fed. Or at least this was the judgment of Thomas Pakenham in his definitive study, *The Boer War.*[61] Although other historians, notably Tim Jeal, have disputed this verdict, at the time nearly all the journalists pandered to the jingoistic version of the siege.

George Warrington Steevens, the *Daily Mail* man in Ladysmith, died of fever during the siege. On his deathbed, in true war-correspondent style, he drank a hoarded bottle of champagne, surrounded by his fellow specials. One of them said: "What Kipling did for fiction, Steevens did for fact."[62]

The empire fielded more than 450,000 men, while the Boers, or Afrikaners as they later were known, could never muster more than 35,000. Lord Kitchener, the hero of Omdurman, smashed into the two Boer republics and captured the main towns. In reply, the Boers resorted to guerrilla tactics. Kitchener responded with a scorched-earth policy of burning down farms and herding Boer women and children into refugee camps, called "concentration camps" after the *reconcentrado* camps used by Spain in her Cuban colony. Disease killed thousands of these noncombatants, especially children, which prompted activist Emily Hobhouse to carry the cause to the British public. International criticism finally stung the imperial government into negotiating a peace settlement, which was signed at Vereeniging in May 1902—a moderate peace to end a savage war. In money and lives, no British war since 1815 had been so prodigal. And what was it all for? "For the gold mines," was the verdict of one British soldier.[63]

Richard Harding Davis, though an Anglophile American, felt impelled to cover the war from the Boer side. A handful of his compatriots, as well as U.S. journalists, rode with the Boer commandos; they joined the guerrillas usually out of pre-existing anti-British sentiments. The Boer riflemen reminded Davis of the Minutemen who had fought the British in the American colonies in 1775. Many Americans and Europeans felt sympathy for the Boer underdogs resisting the world's strongest empire.

Despite the significance of the war and the size of the press corps—three hundred European and U.S. correspondents—it was inadequately reported. The glorification of Baden-Powell serves to suggest a partial explanation: British journalists were all too keen to turn a blind eye to British malfeasance. Another reason was military censorship. In a style reminiscent of the Falklands armada, soldiers on the troop ships initially sent out to South Africa were forbidden to speak to the press. Later, however, the commander in chief, Field Marshal Lord Roberts, a self-publicist of some genius, adopted a more media-friendly attitude. According to Miles Hudson and John Stanier, he was "probably the first British general to fully realize the importance of public relations, even in one case delaying the entry of his soldiers into a town so that the media could film his triumphal entry. He himself wrote many of the reports sent home."[64] But media-military relations turned sour when Roberts returned to London, and his chief of staff, Kitchener, assumed overall command. The new commander imposed strict military censorship in the field and also at headquarters on all telegraphed dispatches although longer "color" features could be sent, uncensored, by post. This was not unreasonable, as telegraphic news was being monitored in Europe, and immediately information was sent back to the Boers. Kitchener also made it an offense for soldiers to discuss the conduct of the war with accompanying pressmen. His justification was that precipitate press reporting had compromised details of British attempts to relieve Kimberley.

The specials moaned, of course, about the censorship. Churchill complained that the censor had altered one of his reports to the *Morning Post* to read "small parties" of Boers instead of two thousand.[65] On the other hand, the correspondents often went out of their way to outwit the censors, who held one of the least popular jobs in the army. One military censor, writing of the Sudan campaign in 1882, noted: "Of all the thankless positions in an army, the press censor has the worst. Abused by correspondents at the seat of the war, maligned by editors at home and continually found fault with by his superiors in the army for allowing too much to pass."[66]

The Boer war attracted a host of literary figures, including Edgar Wallace (soon to turn his hand to fiction, or *continue* to write fiction, according to many pressmen in South Africa). Arthur Conan Doyle served as a volunteer in a field hospital, while Rudyard Kipling edited a local newspaper. Churchill achieved further fame in his (ambiguous) role as soldier-special, especially when he was captured by the Boers (and almost shot) and then made a well-publicized escape. Wallace, writing for the *Daily Mail*, espoused ultraimperialist views but fell foul of Kitchener when he used a clever subterfuge to discover the outcome of the 1902 peace talks. The site of the peace agreement in Vereeniging was heavily guarded and journalists were strictly excluded, but Wallace bribed a former army colleague to signal the final agreement by using a colored handkerchief while the journalist went past on a scheduled train. Wallace had the scoop of a lifetime—and a lifelong ban. Kitchener had him arrested and removed his accreditation, a punishment that lasted even through World War I. Hell hath no fury like a general outmaneuvered.

In addition to stills photography, recently invented movie cameras also covered the war. The Biograph Company of London had recorded the departure of troopships at the outset of the war, and the Warwick Trading Company was set up to film its actual course. Audiences at home queued to see the newsreels, especially one showing a dramatic incident in which Boers attacked a British Red Cross ambulance team while it was helping wounded men. This would have been astounding journalism if the film had not been faked on London's Hampstead Heath and used as government propaganda.[67] Indeed, although the Boer War was technically the first to be filmed, most of the footage was taken in Britain. However, this didn't stop movie audiences from flocking to the cinemas and theater houses to display their jingoistic support.

Despite the censorship and propaganda, the specials did manage to send copy that revealed the incompetent generalship and tactics of the British. Bennett Burleigh, for example, leveled the (now obvious) criticism of troops advancing in line rather than by small squads rushing from cover to cover. He also emphasized how Boer snipers picked off the officers because of their conspicuous swords and Sam Browne belts. He even dared to suggest that Highlanders should wear khaki kilts.[68] Many of these lessons were tragically relearned at the start of World War I.

Military controls constrained the specials, especially the threat of expulsion from the country, but they used a two-step policy of sending their more critical comments by letter for home-based journalists on their papers to use in editorials or features. Nevertheless, the press failed to present the real exposé of the war, namely the largely inadvertent genocide of the Boers in the camps and the grossly inadequate medical conditions, especially during the Bloemfontein typhoid epidemic. Possibly as many as 28,000 Boers died in the camps, of whom 22,000 were under sixteen years old, while a further 14,000 black Africans died in segregated camps.[69] The Boers might have forgiven Britain's heavy-handed treatment in the Cape Colony, their expulsion from Natal, the shifty seizure of the Kimberley diamond mines, even the notorious Jameson raid, but the bodies of concentration camp victims were to be dragon's teeth, sowing a fierce and bitter xenophobia among those Afrikaners who would later establish the apartheid state. The media heritage was almost as ghastly. A detailed study of the conduct of war correspondents in the South African war concludes:

> Although the conditions did improve in the camps, this was more the work of concerned individuals rather than of the Government. In stark contrast to *The Times'* reporting of the scandal of medical care in the Crimean War, this time *The Times* was instrumental in the covering up of the scandal.[70]

At one stage there were twenty-four *Times* reporters covering the war, but they all turned a blind eye. Some British-based journalists (most notably W. T. Stead) took up the hue and cry, but it is Hobhouse, as well as concerned politicians such as David Lloyd George, who will be remembered for their humanitarian stance in defiance of blind patriotism.

The Darwinian notions of racial supremacy that were part of British press coverage of wars in Africa extended to concurrent conflicts in Asia. In 1900, the Boxer Rebellion broke out in China. The Boxers were a secret society dedicated to purging China of foreign influence, particularly the humiliating treaty concessions enforced by European powers and the United States, indignities intensified by Japan's military success over the Chinese in 1895. An international force was sent to suppress the uprising and to defend Westerners and their commercial interests. Most of the famous correspondents were busy in South Africa, but a rather diffident Italian journalist, Luigi Barzini, covered the war in an impressively detached fashion. He loathed the concept of journalists securing campaign medals because it implied a loss of objectivity. He also disdained Western stereotypes of Asians.[71]

In 1904, Barzini returned to the Far East to cover the Russo-Japanese war, the first time in modern history that an Asian state defeated a European power. Since Japan did not have a free press, it had no idea how to handle correspondents and so resorted to a strategy that became commonplace later in the century: it denied visas to all but a handful of Western reporters. Culturally xenophobic, the Japanese authorities regarded all Westerners as spies, and not without reason. As Phillip Knightley has shown, there is a substantial history of the British government deploying journalists, especially on the *Times*, as part-time intelligence agents. A *Times* man, Lionel James, with the connivance of Japanese intelligence, used radio for the first time to send reports on the naval war.[72] In the land war, the Japanese fought on a front of over ninety miles, and the few journalists allowed to cover the fighting were dependent on military transport as well as communications. This set a pattern for future wars. Since it was impossible for one journalist or even a small team of correspondents to cover such a large-scale war properly, it has been suggested that this helped to create the home-based armchair military analyst such as Charles à Court Repington, who covered World War I—with some success—from London.[73]

Britain had sent a team of military observers to Japan. "The policy of censorship by absolute denial, and the freedom of action it afforded the commander, was not lost on them."[74] This lesson was applied in World War I and, arguably, also in the 1991 Gulf conflict. Certainly in the Japanese precedent, the policy of exclusion seemed to have worked: only three foreign journalists stayed the course of the war. Of these, Barzini was the only one to move outside Japanese military headquarters and then only with a military minder.

The Russo-Japanese war marked the finale of the more freewheeling age of international reporting. It had been a golden age for the specials but a bloody period as well: "Life had counted for little when measured against empire, glory and mass circulations."[75] The general public, especially in Britain, had responded enthusiastically to the adventures in far-off countries. Usually they were small, "safe" wars against natives: colorful epics of swords flashing and cavalry charges against "rebel" Māori, Ashanti, or dervishes. In Britain's shortest war—forty minutes—hundreds of people died in Zanzibar on August 27, 1896; it was little more than mass murder using the latest military technology, although the British used their determination to stamp out slavery as a partial explanation. Occasionally there were depictions of defeats, such as in Afghanistan or Zululand, but soon afterward the empire would secure a heroic redemption and glorious resolution. Some journalists became successful novelists-cum-patriots. A good example is G. A. Henty, while Kipling became the undisputed bard of empire.

Journalism, as well as poetry and fiction, clearly influenced and was influenced by the muscular, imperial Christianity of the times. More specifically, newspapers played a role in exciting popular support for the Spanish-American and Boer wars, although that is not the same as saying that the media had a measurable impact on government policy. There is little evidence, however, to indicate that journalism spawned antiwar sentiments. Knightley provides only two definitive examples in the whole imperial period.[76] In the first case, during the mid-1870s, British Prime Minister Benjamin Disraeli sympathized with Turkey in its long conflict with Russia, while William Gladstone, his eternal nemesis, supported the rebellions in the Turkish-controlled Balkans. A series of brilliant reports by an American, Januarius MacGahan, revealed the extent of Turkish atrocities against the Bulgarians. This helped sway British opinion against supporting Turkey, as it had done in the Crimean War twenty years earlier. The second example is the Japanese invasion of Manchuria in 1894. James Creelman, a Canadian who had made a name for himself in the Spanish-American War, reported on the sacking of Port Arthur. In a famous report he wrote: "The Japanese troops entered Port Arthur on November 21 and massacred almost the entire population. The defenseless and unarmed inhabitants were butchered in their houses and their bodies were unspeakably mutilated."[77] Knightley has argued that American public opinion, until then friendly to Japan, changed overnight.

A direct cause and effect of the political impact of foreign reporting is difficult to prove, although Russell's coverage of the Crimean War undoubtedly influenced the fall of Lord Aberdeen's government. But this is one of the few indisputable examples. Nevertheless, war correspondents did cause governments serious embarrassment. There are two well-known examples that occurred in a single month, May 1885. These were Bennett Burleigh's articles in the *Daily Telegraph* about the poor quality of the cartridges and bayonets for the Martini-Henry rifle, which caused a scandal, as did the ponderous preparations for the relief of Gordon.

More frequently, British journalists empathized with the officer class and tended to self-censor potential military embarrassments. For example,

Archibald Forbes declined to report on the British troops he had seen panicking during the Zulu War.[78] Many correspondents were ex-officers, while a few were serving officers, Churchill being the best-known example. They were awarded campaign medals and sometimes even led troops in battle. During the Russo-Turkish war of 1877, the eighty journalists on the Russian side were put on their honor as officers and gentlemen not to reveal details of impending maneuvers, and, as a result, censorship in the field was abandoned.[79] Such practices, allied with a shared imperial ideology, created a mutual esprit de corps that discouraged exposés. This applied especially to sexual scandals, a leitmotif of military life not entirely absent in the contemporary armed forces. Such reticence had little to do with Victorian taboos; the press had a field day with the sexual scandal that caused Irish leader Charles Stewart Parnell's downfall.

It is likely that some British specials connived to ignore what could have been the biggest military and imperial scandal of the age. Maj. Gen. Sir Hector Macdonald had been a national hero; arguably his generalship had saved the second Sudan war from disaster. He had, however, a major weakness: he liked small boys. So had General "Chinese" Gordon, and in the mid-twentieth century there were two field marshals with the same problem, but they were all protected by the absolute loyalty of their staff and perhaps the indulgence of well-informed specials.[80] Macdonald's peculiar sexuality eventually became impossible to ignore when he was made commander in chief of Ceylon in 1902. This furnished the general with "a lethal combination of a military command which was inactive and uninteresting and a community of boys who were interesting and very active."[81] After a famous denouement in a railway carriage in Kandy, the general was discovered. Although Gen. Sir Claude Auchinleck was (in a later period) sanctioned with a high-level warning, Macdonald was probably told directly by the king to leave and shoot himself—which he did. The establishment showed no mercy to this war hero.

It has long been argued that the enmity toward Macdonald can be traced to his status as an outsider, a working-class Scot who had climbed through the ranks. In establishment terms, he was not a "real" officer and certainly not a gentleman. Two similar establishment figures guilty of similar offenses at the same time (the Canon of Westminster and the seventh Earl Beauchamp) both escaped prosecution. But Field Marshal Roberts had insisted on a court-martial for Macdonald, and suicide was the only way to avoid dragging the army further into disrepute. As the example of the Boer War suggests, there was a tendency for establishment figures—both in the army and in the press corps—to cooperate in shared imperial goals. In addition, a strong sense of class solidarity countered against unsavory revelations, whether military or sexual. Macdonald was an exception. Not only was he a class outsider, but he went completely beyond social tolerance by indulging in pederasty on a vast scale.

## ENTENTE BETWEEN PEN AND SWORD

Throughout the imperial age, media-military relations consisted of much mutual contempt, hostility, and conflict. Journalists often sought military allies to exclude press rivals, and officers sometimes used the specials to gain preferment over officers they disliked. Despite this opportunistic crossing of demarcation lines, commanders generally assumed that journalists had a tendency to be inaccurate and to exaggerate. Also, they naturally disliked criticism in the field and so resorted to censorship and exclusion. During the Afghan war of 1879, Gen. Frederick Sleigh Roberts expelled the *Standard*'s Hector Macpherson for alleging atrocities and for altering dispatches after they had been censored. In the 1885 Burma war the military expelled a *Times* man, E. K. Moylan.

Journalists would retaliate, however, and opposition politicians could make it difficult for a general who excluded the specials. Accordingly, many commanders adopted a posture of private loathing and, when the occasion demanded, public cordiality toward the specials. A good example is Garnet Wolseley, who published the controversial *Soldier's Pocket-Book for Field Service* in 1869. He wrote of the press in a way that many later commanders would emulate:

> These gentlemen, pandering to the public taste for news, render concealment most difficult, but this very ardour for information a General can turn to account by spreading fake news among the gentlemen of the press and thus use them as a medium by which to deceive the enemy.[82]

Field Marshal Roberts tended intuitively to cooperate with the specials, except when he felt personally aggrieved by media misrepresentation, but even Kitchener and Wolseley, who shared a deep-seated hostility to newspapermen could make exceptions for individuals whom they respected for their military knowledge or whose favorable reports could enhance their own promotion opportunities. Famous quotations, endlessly repeated, have tended to distort the ambiguity of the relationship, for example, Kitchener's "drunken swabs" and Wolseley's depiction of "those newly invented curse to armies, who eat the rations of fighting men and do not work at all."

It is true that specials were sometimes arrested or expelled, but these were the exceptions. Most war correspondents shared instinctively the same imperial ideology of the officer class. In 1911, an experienced journalist and editor observed, "Throughout the Victorian Age the relations between the journalist and the general were on the whole those of mutual goodwill and reciprocal assistance . . . the new *entente* between the sword and the pen worked in the interests of all concerned."[83]

This coziness had been predicated on imperial victories in small wars. Within a few years, Britain was to risk strategic defeat on a grand scale. The erratic media restrictions of the golden age were transformed into a formidable propaganda machine. This continued in the next world war, and thereafter, with Wolseley's advice on deploying the media to deceive the enemy reaching an apogee over a century later in the 1991 Gulf War. Nonetheless, 1914 was the watershed year in military–media relations, ushering in the modern epoch of government press controls and media spin.

# 2

# THE WORLD WARS

Popular literature whipped up nationalist fervor long before 1914. A new genre of bestselling books about imaginary future wars was enthusiastically received throughout Europe; publishers released nearly two hundred books in the main European languages in the decade before 1914. Arthur Conan Doyle predicted with some accuracy the threat of unrestricted German submarine warfare, while German novelists foretold the conquest of England. The biggest seller of all, William Le Queux's *The Invasion of 1910*, was issued in 1906 and sold more than a million copies. At the turn of the century, British authors still depicted the French as their favorite enemy, but Erskine Childers's 1903 story about a German invasion plan, *The Riddle of the Sands*, shifted popular demonization to the Kaiser. These books later helped to feed the hatreds engendered by the professional propagandists of World War I.

## THE GREAT WAR

It is difficult to find much nobility in the mass slaughter of 1914–18, except for individual acts of bravery. For four devastating years, the unholy trinity of trench, barbed wire, and machine gun provoked a deadlocked war of attrition, albeit largely hidden from the general public by censorship and propaganda. Indeed, one of the most tragic legacies of the war was how the British press connived to keep this carnage from its own readers. Journalists became both victims and perpetrators of a labyrinth of lies, but millions of soldiers knew that the newspapers were not reporting the truth because they had personally experienced the reality of war in the mud of Flanders. One MP even wrote after the war, "there was no more discreditable period in the history of journalism than the four years of the Great War."[1] If these words seem too strong or retrospectively judgmental, Lord Rothermere, the newspaper baron and brother of Lord Northcliffe, confessed as much at a private dinner party in November 1917, during the battle of Third Ypres:

We're telling lies, we daren't tell the public the truth, that we're losing more officers than the Germans, and that it's impossible to get through on the Western Front. You've seen the war correspondents shepherded by [General] Charteris. They don't know the truth, they don't speak the truth, and we know that they don't.[2]

From the start of the war almost to the finish, false proclamations of constant success generated a suspicion of the media that lasts to this day. Moreover, many of the wartime shackles imposed on the media also still exist.

On the outbreak of war in August 1914, persuading the small professional British army to fight was no obstacle, although the top brass needed some persuasion tactics to make sure they fought the Germans, not the French. The war was, after all, supposed to be over before Christmas. At first, a flood of volunteers responded to posters of Lord Kitchener's outstretched finger with the words "Your King and Country Need You." Notice that this famous poster did not say "*Our* King and Country," reflecting the disdain resulting from deep class divisions that still existed within British society. In 1914, only one third of the male population had the right to vote and no women had the franchise as yet. However, this initial tide of patriotism began to ebb, and, coupled with mounting casualties of "cannon-fodder," the need for conscription became imperative in 1916.

All belligerents publicized heroes, as though there was a collective need to promote the individual warrior in a time of mass often-indiscriminate slaughter. In 1916 a British pilot, Lieutenant William Leefe Robinson, shot down a zeppelin; his photograph appeared almost daily in the newspapers. Acclaimed Royal Flying Corps pilots in France started appearing on cigarette boxes and postcards, although only one ace, Manfred von Richthofen (the Red Baron), has survived to the present day as a household name. Much later, in 2006, Hollywood lionized the thirty-eight volunteers from the United States who flew with the French air force. *Flyboys* told the story of the brave young Americans who called themselves the Lafayette Escadrille.

Individual tales of bold exploits could not hide the increasingly industrial levels of human destruction on the battlefields. A compelling question by then was how could the population be mobilized for total war without revealing how abysmal things were on the fighting fronts? Britain's intellectual and creative elites as well as its government responded by instituting a disinformation machine that was subsequently to earn the praise of Adolf Hitler in *Mein Kampf* and provide many lessons for Josef Goebbels's propaganda ministry from 1933 onward. The Fourth Estate was not unduly concerned with news: "The real work of the Press," as a lecture by literary critic and historian Sir Walter Raleigh to Eton College in March 1918 made abundantly clear, was "to help to hold the people together."[3] The press had already succeeded before the war in focusing on the German "menace" by publishing stories of invasion scares and serializations about German spies. When the war erupted, cheering crowds gathered throughout the capital cities of Europe. World War I would prove to be the end of a genuine "age of innocence."

In Britain, before the war, a scheme was proposed to encourage newspaper editors to take responsibility for censoring themselves, but internal disagreement festered in the press hierarchy, and so a complex system of government censorship was introduced and enforced. Many of the powers centered on the Defence of the Realm Act (DORA), which in August 1914 drastically increased the state's right to regulate news. Editors could be prosecuted for publishing stories that were "not in the national interest"—even if they had been given the information by official sources. The government introduced similar restrictions throughout the British Empire. All letters and telegrams of a private, press, or commercial nature could be vetted, both in London and in the field. (What DORA was to British writers, "Anastasie" was to their French counterparts: the personification of wartime media manipulation.)[4] A War Press Bureau was set up, headed by F. E. Smith (later Lord Birkenhead), supposedly to issue war news. On August 7, Churchill informed Parliament that the War Press Bureau would ensure that "a steady stream of trustworthy information supplied both by the War Office and the Admiralty can be given to the press."[5] The bureau quickly earned the nickname of the "Suppress Bureau." In September, the bureau was moved to the Royal United Services Institution (RUSI) where it remained for the rest of the war.

The War Office dropped initial plans for the management of war correspondents (which magnanimously allowed each reporter to take one servant and one horse) when Lord Kitchener, replicating the French ban, ordered the withdrawal of all correspondents without explanation—a move that poisoned the cooperative spirit that had been built up during the prewar years.[6] The British Expeditionary Force (BEF) consequently deployed to France without a single reporter in tow.[7] Indeed, news of the BEF's arrival in France took three days to be released by the press bureau. Kitchener, whose dislike for journalists was well known, issued orders stating that any correspondent found in the field was to be arrested and have his passport withdrawn, although some independent British pressmen did manage to write about the BEF's early debacles.

The reactions to this independent reporting—especially a story about the BEF's retreat from Mons by Arthur Moore in the *Times* headlined "Broken British Regiments Battling against the Odds"—led to demands for almost total control of the press. For instance, despite his own background as a war correspondent, Winston Churchill, now the First Lord of the Admiralty, wanted the *Times* to be commandeered and turned into an official British gazette.[8] His friend, F. E. Smith, could have suppressed Moore's story, but Smith let it go to strengthen the mounting argument for troop reinforcements, revealing how politicians were prepared to use the newspapers for their own political agendas.[9] Eventually a compromise was reached, "the kind of compromise the British always introduce when faced by conflicting claims. It neither provided a supply of news nor did it clear away the question of censorship."[10]

Col. Ernest Swinton, an occasional author and an officer in the Royal Engineers, was to provide accounts from France for use in the British papers. His dispatches were officially titled "Eye-Witness" and were immediately derided as "Eye-Wash" by soldiers and pressmen alike. The colonel and his small staff produced 103 turgid articles between November 1914 and July 1915, but even these were vetted by a series of military busybodies. Finally, the British press barons, via the Newspaper Proprietors' Association, demanded a more effective and independent system.

As a result of this pressure, from mid-1915 to the end of the war, selected correspondents were attached to British forces on the Western Front, in the Middle East, and at Gallipoli. They wore officers' uniform without insignia, except for a green band on their right arms, but were accorded the privileges of army captains. At first, the genuine officers treated them as though they were "criminals let loose."[11] Later, the military gave the accredited journalists better access to the fronts, but it cranked up the system of government supervision to restrict what correspondents could actually say. In 1917 the press bureau was subsumed under the Department of Information, which was turned into a full ministry in 1918 headed by Lord Beaverbrook, owner of the *Daily Express*. Also in 1918 a specific Department of Enemy Propaganda was set up at Crewe House under the direction of Lord Northcliffe, owner of the *Daily Mail* and the *Times*. The government by then felt that it was far better to harness the power of the press by making it part of the government rather than risk becoming a critic of it. These ennobled press barons drew other newspaper proprietors and editors, as well as historians and literary figures, into their propaganda web. For example, in 1917 the novelist John Buchan headed the Department of Information and was immediately responsible to the prime minister. Buchan echoed an earlier sentiment of Napoleon when he admitted, in so far as Britain was concerned, "the war could not have been fought for one month without its newspapers."[12]

It has been suggested that the British are culturally averse to lying even though they proved to be World War I's best propagandists. Perhaps this is a self-deception, and the French, who for centuries had labeled Britain as "Perfidious Albion," would certainly have scoffed at it. However, moral repugnance was certainly a major factor in the 1918 decision to shut down all the British government's propaganda sections except for a small branch in the Foreign Office.[13] Fear that the press barons had become too powerful for normal peacetime government was another.

This unwieldy and morally debatable system did, however, achieve three significant objectives: it largely hid the military failures from the British public; it besmirched the enemy; and it helped to persuade neutrals, notably the Americans, to join the crusade against the "barbarous Huns." A further element was the development of psychological warfare techniques in Crewe House whose head, Northcliffe, was to claim after the war that "good propaganda saved a year of war . . . and at least a million lives."[14] Indeed, official propaganda eschewed lies that might be found out by the enemy: "A point was made of telling the enemy only the truth. The truth was being concealed from them by their leaders. Nothing could be more effective in depressing their spirits than a daily dose of unpleasant fact."[15] That, at least, was the theory, although it has to be said that the majority of atrocity propaganda published in the British press tended to be generated by the newspapers themselves to sell more copies and bolster morale, rather than being the product of an official campaign. The government could have stopped press excesses if it wanted, but they did, in fact, help the government to justify why the fight had to go on, Christmas after Christmas, to the bitter end.

The first British and French military disasters went almost entirely unreported. In two days of the initial fighting, the Germans caused nearly three hundred thousand French casualties, and the British lost more officers in the first few months than the combined total from all their wars of the previous century. On the Russian front, the Germans annihilated three army corps at the Battle of Tannenberg in August 1914. Later, in the 1916 Battle of the Somme, the Allies lost six hundred thousand men. Cultural historian Paul Fussell wrote, "The Somme affair, destined to be known among troops as the Great Fuck-Up, was the largest engagement fought since the beginnings of civilization."[16] Yet French and British newspapers did not report the defeat at Tannenberg at all, while they often portrayed catastrophes such as the Somme as successes or, at best, minor setbacks. Pictures as well as words were ruthlessly suppressed. The most famous

British "documentary" film of the war, *The Battle of the Somme*, contained some fake footage among relatively innocuous images of what the Western Front battles were actually like. Besides the official war artists, the British allowed only two photographers near the front, both army officers. Anyone else found with a camera risked facing the firing squad, although a handful of British soldiers did hazard furtive snapshots of the battles.

The British largely triumphed in the propaganda war against the Germans. In particular the immediate casus belli, the invasion of "poor little Belgium," was brandished to disseminate ceaseless, though often unfounded, accounts of German atrocities against women and children. Such allegations of German brutality secured official approval with the 1915 publication of the Bryce Report and set the tone for why the public should support the troops throughout the war. The most long-running canard, the allegation that Germans used British corpses to make glycerine for munitions (or for lubricants, pig food, and manure) was a lie, although Germans did process dead horses. The German execution of Edith Cavell, a nurse at a Brussels hospital, was a boon to British denigration of the Second Reich. The Germans shot her because she was helping Allied servicemen escape, which Cavell knew to be a capital offense. The French had already shot one woman for the same crime (and went on to shoot another eight), but the Germans were forever damned as the murderers of an angel of mercy. The British troops who were in the field saw none of these alleged atrocities.

The Central powers, of course, conducted extensive propaganda campaigns of their own. Their take on the Belgian war crimes, for example, was rather different. German stories had "priests, armed, at the head of marauding bands of Belgian civilians, committing every kind of atrocity."[17] But Berlin was never as effective in the black arts as the British. In both World Wars, London waged a sustained and subtle campaign to seduce the Americans into becoming combatants. This was achieved by a highly coordinated campaign within the United States that predisposed Washington to support Britain, despite the large German–American population. Berlin issued orders to sink American merchant ships as part of the attempt to break the strangling Allied blockade. Together with German meddling in Mexico, these were more tangible factors, but the cumulative creation of a psychological climate in which such events as the sinking of the *Lusitania* were perceived as further acts of Hunnish barbarism played a significant part.

The British also influenced American reporting on the Western Front. The army gave a distinguished American correspondent, Frederick Palmer, special privileges. An Anglophile who represented all three major

American news agencies, Palmer was the only non-British journalist accredited to the BEF in 1915. Palmer played the game of self-censorship, but he eventually became deeply disillusioned with the news process when the Americans finally entered the war in 1917. "The war correspondent as a news-bearer is dead," he confided to his diary. "He survives only as a writer who can give human expression to what the military staff utters in its laconic and matter-of-fact way."[18] The U.S. commander, Gen. John Pershing, thought highly of Palmer and persuaded him to turn gamekeeper by becoming, in effect, chief censor with the U.S. forces in France. Palmer had already advised, before the United States became a belligerent, that Washington should appoint a chief civilian censor with army and navy officers as assistants "so that all possible details of the war could be released to the public that was footing the bill."[19] Palmer failed in his task, partly because American journalists, then far less deferential than their Allied counterparts, had become accustomed to the more balanced coverage they had been permitted as neutrals. When Palmer tried to apply the harsh constraints of the British system, his erstwhile colleagues shunned him. Nevertheless, the same pattern of deception was imposed, although the American Expeditionary Force (AEF) was one of the worst-armed and worst-supplied U.S. armies ever fielded. The United States finished the war without forwarding a single aircraft to the battle zone, and of the 4,400 tanks contracted, only 15 reached France—after the war had ended.[20]

American war reporters were more successful than their government's military logisticians. For example, William G. Shepherd of United Press evaded censors in April 1915 to report on the Allied casualties of the first German gas attack on the Western Front. He also covered the first zeppelin raid on London on September 8 of the same year. Another memorable American scoop was the German torpedo attack on the Cunard liner *Laconia* on February 25, 1917. A passenger, Floyd Gibbons of the *Chicago Tribune*, recorded the sinking of the ship, which occurred within twenty minutes. He helped rescue fellow passengers and then managed to send one of the most powerful dispatches of the war when he arrived back on dry land in Ireland. Read from the floor of Congress, it caused a national sensation.

The press coverage of the first months of the war was much better and more accurate in the neutral United States than in the combatant countries. But, despite the influx of a small army of American correspondents, America's entry into the war led largely to a repetition of the old British and French propaganda and censorship. Men of the caliber of Richard Harding Davis despaired at their inability to cover the frontline fighting, and returned home rather than compromise their integrity.

Conversely, the first Pulitzer Prize for reporting went to Herbert Bayard Swope of the New York *World* for his dispatches from the Western Front.

While censorship forced the press to peddle fantasies, the media often ignored the real stories, such as the chronic mismanagement of some generals, poor training of the rank and file, appalling loss of life, and large-scale mutinies in the French army. Nevertheless, important stories sometimes surfaced. Charles à Court Repington, a professional soldier whose career had been ended by a sexual scandal and who then wrote for the *Times,* deployed his excellent political and army contacts to sidestep censorship and report on the shortage of shells in 1915 as well as the withholding of reinforcements in 1918. In his memoirs, Repington commented on the so-called Battle of the Shells by confessing that he was armed with "enough high explosive to blow the strongest Government of modern times into the air."[21] Not only did he break the story, he also provided additional confidential information to the parliamentary opposition. The public uproar caused by the *Times*'s disclosure helped to precipitate the formation of a new coalition government under Lloyd George in 1916. Repington, however, rejected the accusations that he was intriguing against the previous Herbert Asquith administration by simply following the orders of his employer, Lord Northcliffe. "It is not an intrigue," he wrote, "to endeavour to save an Army from defeat by a necessary public exposure when all official representations have hopelessly failed."[22] Repington was here putting patriotism above not only censorship but also, perhaps, professional ethics (by meddling in party politics). The majority of correspondents used the same patriotic rationale to *suppress* information. When Repington later left the sanctuary of the *Times* to join the *Morning Post,* he continued to criticize the management of the war effort. Despite his connections, he was eventually prosecuted under the Defence of the Realm Act and fined over a story that had, in fact, already appeared in the French and German press.

The long arm of the British censor did not always extend to the more unruly colonials. Charles Bean, an indefatigable Australian, had visited every area where his countrymen were fighting and reinforced allegations that the British were not utilizing efficiently the troops from the Dominions. Bean, however, was writing an official history, not news stories. Fellow Australian Keith Murdoch, the father of media tycoon Rupert Murdoch, ignored the censors and revealed the abysmal conduct of the Dardanelles campaign, sourced mainly from data gathered by Ellis Ashmead-Bartlett of the *Daily Telegraph*. This information, reinforced by the intervention of the Australian government, led to a Royal Commission of Enquiry.

Murdoch's and Repington's experiences were exceptional, however.

Both managed to drag their revelations into the open because of quite extraordinary political pressure to transcend the norms of military censorship. The general rule was print nothing unless the censors had approved it. The official justification was that no information should be published if it might assist the enemy, but, as Kitchener confessed in November 1914, "it is not always easy to decide what information may or may not be dangerous, and whenever there is any doubt, we do not hesitate to prevent publication."[23] And the attitude of military censors toward the "writing chappies" whom they were forced to endure was best indicated by a remark of Gen. J. V. Charteris, chief of intelligence, when asked by a new correspondent about the extent of press freedom: "Say what you like, old man. But don't mention any places or people."[24] So vague were many of the censored end results that the correspondents were sometimes left with only their descriptions of the weather, and even then some in the military felt that too much mention of rain and mud might discourage recruitment.

Nor was British censorship confined to the battlefield. The government also suppressed publications by Irish nationalists, pacifists, and socialist groups, as well as school magazines that mentioned details of old boys fighting in France. Even railway timetables were confiscated because of allegedly sensitive information about the transport system. Plays and novels were also banned. Niall Ferguson, in his controversial book *The Pity of War*, alleged "wartime Britain became by stages a kind of police state. In 1916 alone, the Press Bureau, assisted by the secret service department MI7(a), scrutinized over 38,000 articles, 25,000 photographs and no fewer than 300,000 private telegrams."[25] Nevertheless, the image of a supremely efficient and draconian British propaganda machine has been overdone, partly because of later Nazi praise and imitation. General Erich Ludendorff's and Hitler's accolades were based on the presumption that the Germans would have won in a "fair" fight. Hitler's delusion was that the lesson of World War I was to lie repeatedly and to do so on a grand scale. But, as Ferguson suggested, Anglo-French propaganda was more successful because it was sometimes based on a more truthful version of events, especially accounts of German treatment of civilians in occupied areas and on the high seas.[26]

Moreover, much of government and military invigilation of the media, while innovative, was also ad hoc and ramshackle—the truly British way of fighting. Although the war correspondents were certainly sickened by the lies they were forced to tell, it would be wrong to place the blame solely on a paranoid alliance of inept generals and shifty politicians. The silence of the Allied correspondents was not simply a result of the censors' diktats. Many journalists were psychologically numbed by the vast landscapes of horror caused by total war. Repington was one of the few who grasped the massive scale—not only geographically but also technologically—of mechanized war in the air and undersea. The military did feed secret information to favored correspondents, but many journalists, traduced by a sense of duty, patriotism, and frontline bonding, succumbed to the most corrosive dictatorship of all: self-censorship.

Editors and proprietors back home further enforced correspondents' shameful perjury. Here Ferguson contradicted his own description of the British "police state" when he characteristically overstated the argument: "At times Britain seemed to be heading for a Press Government."[27] This is much more credible than the notion of a police state. Some of the newspaper proprietors were megalomaniacal meddlers in politics, especially the archetypal press barons, Northcliffe and Beaverbrook (the latter satirized as Lord Copper in Evelyn Waugh's *Scoop*). Stanley Baldwin (later to become Conservative premier) had them in mind when he said—repeating a phrase suggested by his cousin, Rudyard Kipling—that the press lords were concerned only with power, "and power without responsibility—the prerogative of the harlot throughout the ages."[28]

Northcliffe did use his newspapers to destabilize Kitchener in 1915 and Prime Minister Asquith in 1916. In August 1914, only the *Times* was eager for war, but the rest soon followed suit. Northcliffe's papers campaigned for an intensification of the war, most notably on the issue of conscription. The politicians found these pressures highly irksome. Press magnates had traditionally used their newspapers as levers of power *within* the political parties, but now they had become independent instruments of power *against* political parties at a time of national crisis. Churchill was not the only political leader to advocate that the *Times* be nationalized. Asquith ignored this advice, but he later had cause to regret his more liberal approach to press freedom. As Ferguson noted, "Though Northcliffe was not the sole architect of [Asquith's] downfall as Prime Minister—Beaverbrook also played a part—there is no question that the press lords hastened it."[29]

Thus, the conventional image of a totally supine wartime media must be modified. The press barons did play an influential role in the management of the war. No doubt the proprietors were sometimes led by their own personal convictions, but in the final analysis they were also pandering to and generating popular support for the war among their readers. Although a few brave intellectuals publicly opposed the fighting (such as Bertrand Russell, who was imprisoned for his conscientious objection), the majority of poets and writers and especially filmmakers willingly mobilized themselves. This response was mostly freelance and motivated by patriotism, not directed by government. Many well-known writers prided themselves on the fact that they were not paid (much to the anguish of their literary agents). The spontaneity was exemplified by the fact that the *Times* received approximately one hundred patriotic poems every day in August 1914. Most of this flood of creative talent was focused on antipathy toward the Kaiser and all his works. It became necessary, as Robert Graves put it, "to make the English hate the Germans as they had never hated anyone before."[30] When the government established a highly secret War Propaganda Bureau at the start of the war to conduct a propaganda campaign in the still neutral United States, most of Britain's leading writers and editors were consulted. The list is a galaxy of creative talent: J. M. Barrie, Arnold Bennett, G. K. Chesterton, Arthur Conan Doyle, John Galsworthy, Thomas Hardy, John Masefield, Gilbert Murray, G. M. Trevelyan, and H. G. Wells. Rudyard Kipling was noticeable by his absence; he was hated by Sir Edward Grey, the foreign secretary, under whose direction this group was to work. Kipling later went to France, Arnold Bennett joined the Ministry of Information as Beaverbrook's assistant, and John Masefield went to Gallipoli. John Buchan wrote propaganda tales before he became what was, in effect, Lloyd George's spin doctor (despite their mutual antipathy). H. G. Wells poured scorn on "Frankenstein Germany" and even briefly headed Crewe House's German section. In the first month of the war, Wells had written a seminal pamphlet, *The War That Will End War*, which was so finely tuned to American sentiment that it helped to inspire much of President Woodrow Wilson's pious rhetoric.

In short, the war was very popular, especially in the beginning when victory was assured and "before the leaves of 1914 turned brown." But if a modern lightweight video camera had captured the nightmare that was Flanders and then broadcast to the masses at home, how long would the war have lasted? In a sense, such counterfactual questions are pointless because the footage would never have passed the censors. In 1917 Lloyd George admitted to a newspaper editor: "If the people really knew, the war would be stopped tomorrow. But of course they don't and can't know."[31] But most people most of the time believe what they want to believe, especially during wartime. The farther away from the actual fighting, the more blindly optimistic the patriot becomes.

There is little doubt that propaganda played a vital part in galvanizing support against the Germans but, interestingly, very little propaganda was aimed at the fighting men. This is partly because any kind of formal political indoctrination has been anathema to the British army. The front-line soldiers treated most of the half-hearted attempts at political propaganda, such as newsreels, with complete derision. Both British and French troops preferred to trust their own trench newspapers (often produced by noncommissioned officers, and enlisted personnel). Siegfried Sassoon, the highly decorated antiwar poet, called the official material "intolerable twaddle."[32] The men in uniform had little chance to voice any dissidence or to vote with their feet; deserters, even those traumatized by shell shock, potentially faced a firing squad. But, at home, the newsreels and press stories on the war found an avid and credulous audience, especially among children.[33]

From this perspective, it may be necessary to rethink the popular conception of British journalists buying into a military-imposed conspiracy to hoodwink an innocent public. Admittedly, the war correspondents betrayed the suffering of the fighting men while subscribing to the government's fight for national survival. After the armistice, William Beach Thomas of the *Daily Mail* and the *Daily Chronicle*'s Philip Gibbs publicly confessed their shame at their limp descriptions of epic battles such as Passchendaele. As Gibbs put it, "We identified absolutely with the Armies in the field. . . . There was no need of censorship in our despatches. We were our own censors."[34] Gibbs was knighted, as were many of his fellow journalists and editors for their services to the war effort. They had done their duty to their country but not to their profession. Their justification during the war was that some description was better than none; full and accurate reporting would have resulted in swift eviction from the front. This meant that when occasional exposés did surface, they were greeted with popular outrage and disbelief. When the *Daily Mail*, Northcliffe's sister paper to the *Times,* ran a more sensationalized version of Repington's revelations about the shell shortage under the headline "Lord Kitchener's Tragic Blunder," there was a massive groundswell of popular support *for* the military leadership. Members of the London Stock Exchange burned copies of both Northcliffe newspapers, decried as "Allies of the Hun."[35]

In Britain today, World War I is often viewed entirely negatively, especially when compared to the assessment of the "good war" against Hitler or from the ingrained cultural and literary stereotypes inspired by the war poets, movies, later television series such as *Blackadder*, or bestselling novels, particularly Sebastian Faulks's *Birdsong*.[36] Popular works such as Alan Clark's *The Donkeys* and A. J. P. Taylor's *The First World War* have also influenced the dominant British perception of World War I as a pointless series of disasters and not an eventual British military triumph.[37] More recently, academic historians have revised the notion of an accidental conflagration and interpreted the conflict as a just war, conducted with some skill, to prevent German hegemony of Europe.[38] Unsurprisingly, the work of these revisionists has not infiltrated the popular consciousness in the way that films such as *Oh! What a Lovely War* have done. It can be argued, however, that most Britons fought the war because they believed it to be just (although obviously other factors were instrumental, ranging from cultural conditioning to the anticipated benefits some groups, such as women rights' movements and profiteers, gained from the war):

> The British home front supported the nation's participation in a war not because they were blissfully ignorant about the death and destruction that it caused, but because they thought it was a war worth fighting.[39]

Additionally, to the general public in 1918, Field Marshal Haig was a national hero, not a donkey. The latter is a late-twentieth-century reinterpretation.

Even with unified allegiance among themselves, the war correspondents and proprietors would have found it almost impossible to sail against this tide of national fervor. Hugh Cecil has aptly summarized the paradox: "It was the Great War correspondents' tragedy that they were forced to hide the truth—which men at the front found hard to forgive. The general staff regarded them as lackeys of the popular press, fit to be bullied or manipulated; the home front public wanted only patriotic news and plenty of it."[40]

If the agonies of the Somme, for example, had been shown in full in Britain's cinemas, and if the war correspondents had presented a truer, nastier picture of the war, would it have resulted in a quicker end?[41] British society was perhaps the least divided of all the combatants. Unless the army had totally collapsed under the strain of total war, the general public "would have rejected accounts of soldiers drowning in mud or killing prisoners as 'defeatist.'"[42] Moreover, even if Britons had relaxed their military censorship or toned down their propaganda campaigns, would the Germans have done the same? If not, would that have boosted the chances of a German victory? Despite the million dead from the British Empire, there is little evidence of widespread contemporary criticism of the general war aims in 1918, either in the ranks or on the home front.[43] Too much has been made, for example, of the growing tide of pacifism surrounding the letter that the 5th Marquess of Lansdowne (after circulating in government circles his ideas for a negotiated peace) published in the *Daily Telegraph* in 1917.[44] A few British newspapers welcomed the letter, as did the German press and some senior politicians in Washington. Later research has suggested, however, that Germany's minimum peace terms involved extensive territorial claims in Europe and elsewhere. The Western Allies could never have accepted these terms.

Although not on the scale of the Nazis, the verified German maltreatment of Belgian civilians and the harshness the treaty of Brest-Litovsk imposed on the Russians in 1918 allowed the British to believe they were waging war on behalf of liberal democracy against a Prussian war machine that would have extinguished emerging democratic values in Europe. Those same liberal instincts meant that Machiavelli's dictum was ignored: either pamper or crush your defeated enemies. The Versailles Peace Treaty of 1919 did neither; German militarism soon reconstituted itself.

The year 1914 inaugurated a mass killing process that World War II brought to a merciless consummation. World War I destroyed the socialists' cherished concept of class solidarity, and nationalism triumphed everywhere, especially among the proletariat. Just as with the notion of "the end of history" after the Cold War, Edwardian meliorism—the belief in the inevitable liberal democratic progression of humankind—was annihilated in the trenches. War had been transformed from a series of actions into a culture, as Paul Fussell so brilliantly explained; moreover, it was a thoroughly debased culture. Language itself had been devalued, he argued. One maxim had become ingrained: you can't believe a word you read. "A lifelong suspicion of the press was one lasting result of the ordinary man's experience of the war."[45] The ridicule later heaped on Allied propaganda claims regarding atrocities in Belgium led directly to skepticism about real abominations. The reluctance to believe in the Jewish Holocaust until it was fully realized was one fatal legacy. So was the U.S. reticence to stand alongside Britain in 1939 after British propaganda efforts in America in the previous world war had been (partly) revealed.

Media management had almost totally excluded correspondents from British sections of the Western Front until May 1915. When access was then granted, the selected few saw little and could report even less. In the last year of the war, especially as the fighting became more mobile, the military cooperated more closely with the writers who had become merely an adjunct of the propaganda machine. In a statement prefiguring the late twentieth century concept of the "media flank," one key participant noted in 1921: "the Press has to be treated as an arm [of the armed forces], like tanks or aeroplanes, suitable for defence or attack."[46]

Any moral judgment about the draconian media controls in World War I somewhat depends on an assessment of whether the 1914–18 war was both just and necessary. Allied victory was a close-run affair, but the British and French empires survived—for a while longer. And a part of the cost was not telling their populations the true price of the great struggle they were waging in their name. Propaganda and the subversion of professional war reporting did undermine liberal values among the Allies, but the "thought police" of the communists and, later, the Nazis were far more dangerous threats to European security. The year 1918 did not end the continent's self-flagellation: "Totalitarianism was the political continuation of war by other means."[47]

The 1914–18 conflict was a war of the worlds: thirty-two nations across the globe took part. The war was prompted more by the participants' fears than calculated ambitions, and soon all gave way to the tyranny of events and terrain. What original war aims there were became obscured as the ever-rising cost of the military means inflated the political ends. The ideas of Karl von Clausewitz were turned on their heads. Yet in the Western democratic states, politicians dictated the strategy. As far as Britain was concerned, it was a parliamentary war, a war of amateur strategists. The military historian Major General John Fuller suggested that London behaved similarly in 1775 against the American colonies.[48] James Morris, making a similar comparison, said that Gallipoli was the greatest reverse of British arms since the American Revolution.[49]

Bursting through the Dardanelles was an attempt to escape the stalemate in the West, but that too became bogged down. At Gallipoli, "eating a meal on the body of a dead Turk too heavy to lift out of the trench," summarized conditions.[50] On the Western Front, offensive attrition became a policy of exhaustion, of troops chewing barbed wire or sunk into holes in the ground: "rain, mud, 'rats as big as cats,' lice—'a real menace'—the stench of horse carcasses."[51] The Eastern Front was a war shaped by German strength, Austrian weakness, and Russian determination, and conditions were often just as terrible, although it was a more mobile conflict.[52] Only toward the end of the war when the Central powers were facing defeat did rapid offensives reintroduce mobility to the fronts. French-led operations in the Balkans and British advances in Arabia combined the oldest and newest instruments in a war of movement: cavalry and aircraft. General Edmund Allenby's Middle East invasion was arguably the last great cavalry campaign of history. Allenby crushed the Turks at Megiddo in one of the most absolute victories of imperial history—and the British did see this as imperial expansion, despite what the Americans thought. Ironically, the British triumph at Megiddo, the Armageddon of the Bible, later comforted the "end-timers" of the American right in the twentieth century. For many fundamentalist Christians in the United States, the Megiddo battle fulfilled the description in the book of Revelation about the timing of Christ's return.

After November 1918, what did the combatants think all the fighting accomplished? When the British struck their victory medal for issue to all those who had served, they provided one answer: "For Civilisation" it said on the medal, just as today the West claims it is fighting for its civilization in the "war on terror."

Yet Britain's imperial civilization had been undermined. Edward Elgar "sang no more of the bayonet's clash"; having lost his only son in the war, Kipling never again wrote a lay of empire.[53] In 1929 Erich Maria Remarque published his original German version of *All Quiet on the Western Front*, which revived the flagging market for war books. Yet it was not a glorification of war; rather, its theme was of shattered illusions. Frederic Manning's *Her Privates We*, an often overlooked masterpiece also published in 1929, fatalistically presented the conflict as a horrible but unavoidable part of the human condition. Few held on to the belief that the 1914–18 war was the war to end all wars. Hitler confirmed the fears. Since then, historic fashion has venerated writers who condemned World War I but "at the same time condemned those who embraced appeasement, the logical corollary."[54] Antiwar literature and appeasement both derived their appeal from the same basic liberalism that inspired the peacemakers' ideals, especially the Americans, at Versailles in 1919. Liberalism failed in the interwar years—failed to enforce its own standards, especially via the new League of Nations—because that determination had been sapped by the horrors of the trenches. World War I broke the empires of Germany, Russia, Austria-Hungary, and Turkey, but it also broke the spirit of liberal interventionism in the United States and Britain until it was far too late.

Both World Wars had similar causes: the drive of German-speaking peoples to improve their international position, with the more immediate catalysts being disputes between a German-speaking ruler and a Slav neighbor. In 1939 the war that ostensibly began to secure Polish freedom ended with her bondage. But the conflicts between the World Wars, most notably the Russian and Spanish civil wars, were to produce even more tragic ironies, not least for those correspondents who formed "the brotherhood of the press agents of Mars."[55]

## THE WARS BETWEEN THE WARS

The postwar newspapers carried stories and pictures of soldiers coming home, the surrender of the German fleet, and statesmen at conference tables, but they also reported on the revolutions of disintegrating empires. "Interwar years," the common phrase, is a misnomer: wars there were in abundance for journalists to cover. And, usefully, a new camera came on

the market in 1925: the 35mm Leica. This was a more compact camera with an automatic range finder, which dramatically improved the capability to capture the fleeting images of combat.[56] But what dominated the political columns was whether these wars would turn into a global conflict, a replay of World War I. The key word was "appeasement." The term is usually associated with British and French attempts to appease Adolf Hitler and Benito Mussolini, although the concept is very old. Whenever nations do not regard warfare as the main ingredient of resolving disputes, the door is open for compromise—a lesson that could be applied to the so-called long war following the 9/11 attacks on the United States. The problem is that appeasement has now acquired a negative connotation.

Appeasement, after the traumas of World War I, was logical, not—to use a contemporary analogy—the antics of "cheese-eating surrender monkeys." (The phrase, taken from a character in *The Simpsons*, was applied by some Republicans to the French opposition to the 2003 war in Iraq; in Britain, opponents of the war retaliated by describing Americans as "burger-eating invasion monkeys.") Prime Minister David Lloyd George could be dubbed the first appeaser in that he sought a lenient peace for Germany. Britain tried to reconcile Franco-German differences throughout the 1920s. Ending the occupation of the Rhineland and the virtual scrapping of reparations—important elements of the 1919 Versailles Treaty—cleared the way for future appeasement. Until 1933, the policy made sense. But Hitler's insatiable demands were not amenable to logical compromise. Anglo-French policy also sought security via alliances, hence the desire to placate Mussolini, detach him from Germany, and yet not antagonize the Italians too much over their colonial ambitions, especially in Abyssinia (now Ethiopia). The invasion of Ethiopia in 1935 ruptured the collective security system of the League of Nations because there was no desire to go to war to preserve an African state.

The United States had not joined the League and remained aloof, even though it was the one country strong enough to tip the balance in favor of collective security against the Fascist states. The Spanish Civil War, which began in 1936 shortly after the end of the Italian conquest of Ethiopia, gave new opportunities for the dictators to flaunt their power. Military aid flowed from Germany and Italy to support the Fascist side in Spain, ill balanced by Soviet support for the Madrid government. When Neville Chamberlain became British prime minister in 1937, he was as disposed as his predecessors toward the appeasement policy. The League was bust, France was defeatist, and British rearmament had hardly begun. It made sense to seek out the dictators, determine their demands, and—within reason—to satisfy them. Much of the press debate centered on the Munich crisis of 1938, especially concerning the need for extra time for military preparation by Britain and France. Hitler's violation of the September 1938 Munich agreement and his takeover of the whole of Czechoslovakia the following March effectively undermined the logic of appeasement, though hindsight informs us that Hitler should have been stopped much earlier. Munich was the last great settlement in which the fate of Europe was decided without the participation of the two future superpowers, the United States and the USSR. Despite their world interests, leaders in Washington were committed to neutrality. Walter Lippmann, the great American columnist, perched at the *Herald Tribune* for more than three decades, wrote very little about Ethiopia or Spain and concluded Chamberlain was making the best of a bad job. From today's standpoint, appeasement was a policy of weakness, but to a generation that had endured the slaughter of World War I and the hardships of the Great Depression, it made sense to most people, most of the time. The alternative was simple: another war of even greater destructive potential thanks to the arrival of a new weapon—the bomber aircraft.

The press barons played a more than active role in the debate over appeasement. Lord Rothermere supported fascism and—in alliance with Lord Beaverbrook, the champion first of isolationism and then of appeasement—formed his own political party, the United Empire Party. Beaverbrook used his newspapers to contest by-elections, which suggested that "the Fourth Estate was sabotaging the Third Estate."[57] A detailed analysis of the quality British weekly magazines and Sunday papers, especially in the crucial years 1935–38, shows that fear was the essence of the debate,[58] specifically fear of air power. The Italian military theorist Giulio Douhet had argued that future wars could be won by air power alone. The vogue phrase was "the bomber will always get through." Though the limited bombing campaigns against cities in World War I had caused relatively few casualties, Hitler believed that his new Luftwaffe could break the Royal Air Force and civilian morale with a concentrated blow.[59] Britain feared a three-front war (without alliances with the United States or the USSR) against Germany (in Europe), Italy (in the Mediterranean and Africa), and Japan (in the Far East). Understanding the concerns about air power and Britain's military weakness during the 1930s, the policy of appeasement—discussion of which permeated the intellectual weeklies and the quality Sunday papers—becomes more intelligible to a modern audience. Despite calls in some of the left-wing press for collective security and a "popular front" against fascism, appeasement made military and political sense at the time. It was consensus politics across the intellectual spectrum in the United Kingdom. Hitler's occupation of Prague in March

1939, Britain's new fighters, and the secret development of radar ended appeasement. Soon most of the media decided "right about turn," to use Winston Churchill's phrase.

## THE RUSSIAN REVOLUTION AND ITS REPERCUSSIONS

With a few honorable exceptions, the press failed to effectively cover the Russian Revolution and the ensuing civil war. During World War I, Western newspapers largely ignored the massive casualties suffered by the Tsarist armies. Of course, a propaganda problem intruded: how do you fight a war for democracy by allying with a savage autocracy such as Russia? As in 1941, such moral squeamishness had to be subsumed in the practical need for a two-front war to defeat the common enemy, Germany. With the exception of the *Manchester Guardian*, the British press swallowed the line that Russia would fight on indefinitely. When the first revolution came and Alexander Kerensky emerged in 1917, temporarily, as perhaps the kind of social democrat with whom the West "could do business," it made it easier for Western, especially American, propaganda.

Bolshevism, however, was much more difficult for most editors to comprehend. Churchill described Vladimir Lenin's historic journey from exile across Germany thus: "transported in a sealed truck like a plague bacillus from Switzerland into Russia."[60] Most Western analysts expected the revolution to collapse quickly, a misperception that lingered for decades. American John Reed, later immortalized by Warren Beatty in the Hollywood bio-epic, *Reds*, covered the revolution of October 1917 for a number of newspapers. His dispatches were made into a classic book of instant history, *Ten Days That Shook the World*. (Reed died of typhus in Russia in 1920.)

Journalists such as Arthur Ransome of the *Daily News* (who later became famous as the author of *Swallows and Amazons*) tried to explain that Bolsheviks believed the Western Allies were deliberately allowing the Germans to advance in the east so as to strangle the revolution at birth (a suspicion that fed Josef Stalin's paranoia in World War II). The *Times*, however, conjectured that the silent majority of moderate Russians would welcome Allied intervention to remove the hated Bolsheviks. Soon followed one of the greatest acts of folly associated with World War I: Britain, France, Japan, and the United States entered the civil war, poisoning relations with Russia until the end of the Cold War seventy years later. Thus began the "Red Scare." Fueled by the Russian imperial family's murder, Bolshevism generated fear (and hope) throughout Europe.

Leon Trotsky, the commissar of the Red Army, released to Morgan Philips Price of the *Manchester Guardian*, later *Daily Herald*, details of the secret deals between Moscow and the Allies. For example, Trotsky revealed British plans to split Persia with Russia and the infamous Sykes-Picot agreement that carved up the Middle East between the French and British despite the many promises made to the Arabs, not least by a guilt-ridden T. E. Lawrence.[61]

The armies of intervention allowed some newsmen to accompany them, while the Bolsheviks also had their own cameramen who managed to create a partial photographic record of the fighting despite a chronic lack of film supplies. As the loose federation of anti-communist forces, the White armies, converged on Moscow and the Western press daily predicted the end of Bolshevik Russia, pictures of Trotsky rallying Soviet troops became common. Trotsky himself was a rarity, an amateur strategist who displayed military genius in the field. Each of the White armies was defeated in turn, though the Red Army overreached itself when it advanced on Warsaw and was overcome by the revitalized nationalism of the Polish army.

The Russian revolution merely survived, but at great costs—not least of which was widespread famine. Vladimir Lenin decided that publicity could prick the conscience of the West, which might send food rather than armies. In 1921, Floyd Gibbons, a one-eyed photographer who worked for the *Chicago Tribune*, was granted permission to film in some of the stricken areas. Gibbons's photographs, especially of skeletal children, allied with Lenin's show of political and economic moderation, triggered an Anglo-American aid package.[62]

The generally biased reportage of the revolution and its aftermath, coming on top of the constant cover-ups in World War I, displayed war correspondents at their worst. The misreporting engendered a distrust of journalism that lingers to this day in the West, and in the East the behavior of correspondents (especially their occasional dual role as intelligence agents) soured relations with Russia for at least two generations. It was not a good war for the correspondents.

## ABYSSINIA

Evelyn Waugh's *Scoop*, probably the best-known and funniest book on journalism, was based on the far-from-amusing tragedy in Ethiopia. In the summer of 1935 tensions along the border between the Italian colonies of Somaliland and Eritrea and the independent state ruled by Emperor Haile Selassie prompted an influx of journalists. In the dusty capital of Ethiopia, Addis Ababa, Waugh joined 120 hacks, including the Australian Noel Monks, the gloriously made-for-a-byline H. R. Knickerbocker (of the Hearst chain), and the young Bill Deedes, destined to be a Fleet Street legend. Most journalists disliked the bombastic dictator Mussolini and supported the underdog emperor. Corralled in Addis on the emperor's orders (on the grounds that his tribesmen, often portrayed as homicidal maniacs, could not distinguish them from Italians), they grew restless and inventive. The media hyped up the Ethiopians' fighting potential, not least because they had fought the British, with temporary success, and had beaten the Italians before, in 1896, at Adowa. But the Italian army had since been well blooded by World War I. It should have been obvious that a modern army, even an Italian one, would overwhelm the spears, daggers, and muskets of the Ethiopians. Yet such was the hype that it was generally held that "the Abyssinians would conduct a brilliant guerrilla campaign, trapping the advancing Italians in lion pits, and, if given guns, would, according to a widely held view in the United States, be able to fire them both with hands and feet."[63]

While the Addis contingent was hemmed in, Italian journalists embedded with the advancing Fascist troops rarely crossed swords with the strict censors. George Steer, of the London *Times*, who later, as an officer, became a pioneer in British media-military operations, thought that the Italians were winning the hearts of minds abroad. Italian propaganda, he wrote, "flickered dully across sham-pacific newsreels" showing the war "as a series of submissions, non-resistance, ceremonial occupations, road building . . . a political parade without horrors."[64] The result was that many of the numerous atrocities on both sides went unrecorded. The Ethiopian government did provide what is now called a photo opportunity when the Italian air force bombed a Red Cross dressing station at Dessye. The emperor posed with one foot on an unexploded bomb and also stationed himself on an anti-aircraft gun. The Italian bombing techniques were notoriously inaccurate, so the Red Cross bombing may have been an accident, not a war crime. Moreover, the Ethiopians frequently abused the Red Cross flag (which also happened to be a local symbol for a brothel). Elsewhere in the area of Adowa (where the Italians had been thrashed forty-five years earlier), the invaders used mustard gas. George Steer, then a twenty-six-year-old correspondent, witnessed the results. In an emotional and historically inaccurate account—the British army used gas shells against rebel tribesmen in Mesopotamia in 1920, while the air force prepared, but did not use for technical reasons, aerial bombs with poison gas—he wrote: "For the first time in the history of the world, a people supposedly white used poison gas upon a people supposedly savage. . . . Some were blinded."[65] Journalists took powerful photographs during the war, although it has been estimated that 99 percent were faked.[66]

It was a war fought with increasing barbarity by both sides, and the press missed most of it. "The Ethiopians took only five Italian prisoners, while the Italians literally gassed their way into Addis Abba early in the summer of 1936. . . ,"[67] so much for the League of Nations and its ideals of collective security. Ethiopia fell to fascism; the emperor, the Lion of Judah, was left to roar in exile; and the war correspondents trooped off to Spain, where the Fascists would be defeated this time, or so they thought.

## THE SPANISH CIVIL WAR

The Spanish Civil War (1936–39) did almost as much harm to journalism as it did to the country. Churchill later told Stalin: "In wartime, truth is so precious that she should always be attended by a bodyguard of lies." In Spain, truth died and the bodyguard became king. On July 18, 1936, military garrisons in twelve cities in Spain and five in Spanish Morocco rebelled against the left-wing Spanish government. The revolt would have failed without rapid and generous military support from Germany and Italy. The USSR later sent smaller amounts of military aid. France and Britain were officially neutral, but thousands of French and British flocked in as foreign volunteers to join the famous "International Brigades." In the United Kingdom, left and right divided in society as a whole, and especially in the press. British intellectual opinion was as inflamed as it had been by the French Revolution. Publisher Victor Gollancz set up his Left Book Club to publish a book each month against "Fascism and the war"; a Right Book Club was established in opposition. For Cecil Day-Lewis, future poet laureate, the war was a battle of "light against darkness." W. H. Auden talked about passionate "poets exploding like bombs." Most writers were committed to the left, the Republic. As Auden said, "the struggle in Spain has X-rayed the lies upon which our civilization is built."[68] In France, opinion was even more bitterly divided. Spain was seen as a testing ground for fascism; if it triumphed there, France would also be pincered by the dictators in Germany and Italy. Many intellectuals saw Spain as a warm-up match before the big game throughout Europe. In this they were essentially correct (although Spain remained neutral in World War II). It explains why so many writers were so determined to drop their objectivity in pursuit of what they saw as a far greater cause.

Most traveled to Madrid, the seat of the socialist republic. Ernest Hemingway was the most famous, and his fictional *For Whom the Bell Tolls* brilliantly captures the mood of the times. The third Mrs. Hemingway, Martha Gellhorn, also recorded the tragedy. Her husband may have written the greater novels, but she created greater journalism. Eric Blair—later to change his name to George Orwell—went there to fight and write. Arthur Koestler's assignment was as a correspondent for the London *News Chronicle*, but he was also a spy for the Comintern; Kim Philby worked there for the *Times* and the KGB. A young Hungarian, Andrei Friedmann, later to become known as Robert Capa, set out with a 1925 Leica to freelance. In October 1936, *Vu* published in Paris his photograph "The Falling Soldier," which purported to capture the actual moment that a bullet entered the head of a Republican militiaman. This has become perhaps the most controversial photograph ever taken, spawning a complete subgenre of photographic studies. Long held to be a reenactment, there is some recent evidence to suggest otherwise.[69]

Capa's masterwork may have been arguably genuine, but Claude Cockburn's most famous dispatch was a fake. Cockburn was the editor of a radical journal, *The Week*, and a staff journalist on the Communist Party's *Daily Worker*. After briefly serving as a combatant, he became a propagandist for the Republicans. He fabricated a report of fighting in Tetuan, in Spanish Morocco, the original base of the Falangist leader, Gen. Francisco Franco. Concocted in Paris with the help of Comintern agent Otto Katz, Cockburn provided "a tip-top, smashing eye-witness account of the great anti-fascists revolt which occurred yesterday at Tetuan, the news of it having hitherto been suppressed by censorship."[70] The aim was to persuade the French government that Franco had suffered a major defeat at a crucial time when Léon Blum, the French prime minister, was dithering about sending critical arms supplies to hard-pressed Republican forces. A Parisian newspaper published the story on the day Blum met the desperate Republican delegation, and the fraud seemed to have worked. Believing the tide was turning against Franco, Blum's government transported the guns to Spain. Historians have argued that Blum was planning to allow the shipment anyway and that the spurious report merely confirmed that he was right to do so. Cockburn in his autobiography, and also when confronted by outraged colleagues, was unrepentant that he had used the press to achieve a political goal. It is interesting to note that in the modern debate about the effect of war reporting, it is a totally fabricated story that may lay claim to being one of the clearest examples of a war correspondent's single story having a major political impact. Cockburn's later defense was that his report was no different from the many other false propaganda stories and subterfuges (for example, "Monty's double" or cardboard invasion armies in 1944) designed by the British government during World War II. In his seminal work on war correspondence, Knightley takes Cockburn to task: "If readers are to have no right to facts, but only to what a war correspondent feels it is in his side's best interest to reveal, then there is no use for war correspondents at all."[71] Even Orwell, who repudiated modern ethics of journalism by taking up arms as well as writing, noted that the propaganda conjured up by both sides was often too incredible to be taken seriously. He said newspapers of both the left and right had dived into the "same cesspool of abuse." "I saw great battles reported," he wrote, "where there had been no fighting and complete silence where hundreds of men had been killed."[72]

The Republicans were "media savvy" in providing regular and frequent (though often sanitized) reports and inducting as propagandists many of the talented writers who flocked to the International Brigades. They were also fortunate in that they had control of the principal international telephone and cable lines, and so their version reached the world first. The Nationalist side adopted a much more rigid style akin to the early days of World War I and suffered because of it.

Both sides replayed 1914–18 atrocity stories: barricades were constructed from human bodies, Muslim Moroccan soldiers ravished naked Catholic nuns, and infants were torn limb from limb. The *Daily Mail* carried a headline that read, "Reds Crucify Nuns," while the *Daily Worker* claimed Franco's Foreign Legion comprised "murderers, white-slavers, dope-fiends and the offal of every European country."[73]

Censorship and the fog of war prevented any major advance in media technology during the conflict, despite improved telephone and cable services. Radio began to play a role, though there is little evidence of its coherent use as a propaganda tool. Cinema newsreels had credibility and much more effect. Posters and, indirectly, novels had a longer-term impact. Photography was important, though perhaps the most long-lasting pictorial icon is Picasso's painting of the suffering at Guernica when the German Condor Legion bombed the town. The source and intention of Guernica's immolation was much debated by propagandists at the time and by historians since, but the responsibility for the massacre must lie with the German Fascist forces, whether or not the Spanish Falangists ordered it and for whatever reason. George Steer reported firsthand from Guernica, where civilians became the front line, establishing a new benchmark of horror, a precedent for Hiroshima and 9/11.[74]

Reportage of Spain was, and in many ways still is, a hall of mirrors. Nonetheless, by 1939 the Fascists had won. But even though Franco's long dictatorship (he survived until 1975) was called Fascist, the description was not entirely correct. His party, the Falange, was one of several factions and institutions that rallied to support the officers who rebelled against the elected Spanish government in 1936 and emerged victorious a half million lives later. In addition, the Church and two rival monarchist groupings backed Franco.[75] Likewise, the Madrid government forces comprised communists, anarchists, socialists, and trade unionists, among others.

Perhaps more than any other twentieth-century conflict, the Spanish Civil War inspired an indelible passion in those who reported it firsthand. This explains but does not excuse the fact that objective reporting reached a nadir there, mainly because so many first-class writers and journalists became mere mouthpieces for their chosen sides. Ironically, perhaps because Hemingway was the most apolitical of the famous writers (despite his comical attempts to instruct in military tactics and drill), he created fiction that so effectively captured the Zeitgeist. The more committed Orwell had a wider political vision than Hemingway; he could see that totalitarian instincts were to be found on the left as well as the right. When he wrote about fratricidal aspects of Stalinist influence, the *New Statesman* rejected his dispatches. Even Victor Gollancz turned down his *Homage to Catalonia*. When it was finally published in the United Kingdom, it sold only six hundred copies in Orwell's lifetime.[76]

For the left, Spain was a lost crusade, although many still carried the flame despite the defeat of the Spanish republic and the signing of the Russo–German pact in 1939. Cockburn, though he was appalled by Russia's deal with Hitler, never recanted his Tetuan fake. The establishment was to have its revenge. When Cockburn applied for accreditation as a correspondent in World War II, the Ministry of Information rejected him on the grounds that, as a communist, he was likely to whip up agitation among British troops. Maybe that decision was a mistake. He had failed abysmally as a war correspondent, but he could have been hired by the ministry as a propagandist of some genius.[77]

## THE GATHERING STORM

Utter war weariness after 1918 seduced a generation of politicians into advocating appeasement; anything was better than another pan-European conflagration. This was also the psychological mood in Europe in 1945, and it led to a successful antiwar machine—the United Nations and, more recently, the European Union. But the League of Nations set up in the wake of World War I failed definitively in the area of world disarmament and on the battlefields of Manchuria, Ethiopia, and Spain. After 1919 a strong tide of pacifism swamped Britain. The armed forces were wound down and the small army returned to its former role as an imperial police force. The British government reduced the Royal Navy, which connected the far-flung empire, to a capability that would not allow it to do this historical job in the future.

Initially the policing was done at home, when the regular army and the irregular Black and Tans fought the Irish Republican Army. The one-eyed privateer, Floyd Gibbons, was there and his pictures of tanks in Dublin streets and British troops corralling civilians with barbed wire helped to persuade the American press that London was an oppressive occupying power. In December 1921 the Irish Free State was born. A free Ireland resulted, except for the six mainly Protestant counties of the north.

The journalists were also busy in the Raj, especially after Maj. Gen. Reginald Dyer ordered his men to fire 1,650 rounds at point-blank range into a crowd of men, women, and children at Amritsar on April 13, 1919. Dyer subsequently became known as the "Butcher of Amritsar." The Amritsar massacre fueled a nationalist propaganda campaign that eventually led to independence for India and Pakistan. The correspondents were also busy in the Far East. In China, warlords, nationalists, and communists were destroying the country. It was similar to the Balkans in the 1990s, except it was bloodier, longer, and more brutal. The Japanese advanced through Manchuria, and in January 1932 landed a seventy-thousand-strong army in Shanghai. The Nationalist Chinese Koumintang fought back hard but then concentrated on their war with the communists led by Mao Tse-tung. Edgar Snow spent four months with the communist leader and was deeply impressed by what he saw. In 1937 Snow published *Red Star Over China*, a book that introduced Mao to revolutionaries worldwide, revealing that Mao was preaching a new kind of war.

In Britain few strategists had learned much from old wars. Many of the lessons so painfully learned in the mud of Flanders or the deserts of Arabia were cast aside. While the potential for air power was inflated, crucial innovations on land, especially the tank, were not developed. An exception was Capt. Basil Liddell Hart, an infantry officer who had been gassed on the Western Front. After retiring from the army in 1927, Liddell Hart, along with Major General J. F. C. Fuller, advocated the modernization of the British army as a fully mechanized force that could fight a rapid war of movement. Liddell Hart also expounded the same gospel in his capacity as the military correspondent of the *Daily Telegraph*. What he said was accurate and vital, but he was largely ignored in Britain. However, the military writer's point was not lost on Germany, where generals of the caliber of Heinz Guderian imbibed the message and as a result developed the concept of blitzkrieg. In the four years of World War I, German advances were sometimes measured in yards and sometimes at the cost of tens of thousands of men per day. When the German army returned to France in 1940, the new blitzkrieg strategy was to win them the whole country in six weeks and with comparatively minor casualties. It was, however, to be a false dawn for Hitler's Third Reich.

# WORLD WAR II

Fifty-five million people were killed in this war, most of them civilians. If the trenches of the Western Front composed the essential image of World War I, then bombed cities were arguably the equivalent in World War II. Historians have debated whether strategic bombing—largely the killing of civilians in cities—was an effective war-winning tactic, especially in undermining morale and crippling the economy. The mass killings at Dresden and Hiroshima, however, were not judged at the postwar Nuremberg trials of the chief surviving Nazis. One-third of British military energy was funneled into the bombing offensive against the German war machine. According to iconoclastic historian Norman Stone, "It would be cruel, but not inaccurate, to say that the British war effort consisted of taking American dollars to pay for Russians to kill Germans, while the British just dropped bombs on civilians."[78]

One of the most controversial views of World War II can be found in A. J. P. Taylor's *The Origins of the Second World War*. He argues convincingly that the Germans fought the second war to reverse the verdict of the first.[79] Germany certainly struck the first blow. It was a total war for militaries, economies, and propaganda. Despite the North African campaigns, Britain fought essentially a naval war, supported by aircraft, until 1944. In the U.S.-Japanese battles in the Coral Sea (May 1942) and at Midway (June 1942), the naval conflicts were decided by aircraft that kept the surface fleets at arm's length. At Midway, the Americans sank the entire Japanese carrier force. In 1943–44 Japanese shipyards supplied a further seven aircraft carriers; American shipyards produced ninety.[80] This was a true symbol of U.S. economic and military power and the rise of the "American Century." But the 1939–45 war was won and lost on the steppes of Eastern Europe. The Red Army destroyed 607 divisions of German and Axis forces; two-thirds of German tank losses were on the Russian front.[81]

The major combatants considered World War II a total war for national survival, and journalists, almost to a man and woman, threw their lots in with their government propaganda machines. Often little coercion or censorship was needed: nearly every journalist packed away his or her professional principles "for the duration." The year 1918 ran into 1939 for the hacks: it was "more of the same," although better technology and more sophisticated dictatorships forced even greater media subservience.[82] Wartime propaganda is typically aimed at four fronts: the enemy, neutrals, allies, and the domestic audience. In all areas, governments weighed in, especially in Germany and Britain, utilizing everything at their disposal, including cinema and radio. Unlike the summer of 1914, little pan-European patriotic enthusiasm for war was apparent. Memories of the savagery

**57**

of the trenches and disillusionment over the Spanish Civil War were especially influential in Britain.

Journalists, Albert Camus once wrote, are "historians of the moment." In London and Berlin, the censors were already writing the first drafts of history. The Germans set up a sophisticated system to woo the neutrals, especially the Americans. But every branch of German media suffered from excessive state control, hence the satirical slogan "*Ein Volk, Ein Reich, Eine Zeiting*" (One People, One State, One Newspaper). During the so-called phony war in the West, the British way of war was as ever ad hoc; that was certainly true in the field initially in France. But two days before the war commenced, a Ministry of Information was created that was given almost unlimited powers to control every press, commercial, or private message leaving Britain by mail, cable, wireless, or telephone. Nevertheless, the Ministry of Information accepted that with a more skeptical and informed British public a fuller explanation of why and what Britain was doing in the war was required. The problem was the armed forces, especially the Royal Navy, which was adamant that nobody would know the location of their ships. (It may not be apocryphal that nervous naval censors even deleted references to HMS *Pinafore* and the *Marie Celeste*.)[83] They were extremely reluctant to share any news with the ministry; defeats and victories—Dunkirk and the Battle of Britain—were reported equally optimistically. It was not until 1941, when Brendan Bracken, a friend of Prime Minister Winston Churchill, became minister of information that the grip of the armed services and the censors was loosened.

Some newspapers had been critical of the excessive censorship and of the government's mismanagement of the army, particularly after Dunkirk. Generally, papers could voice critical opinion, but any negative facts—especially if they could in any way help the enemy—could be subject to review. The press dogs could bark but not bite: Editorial comment was usually allowed. Hard news on the early British disasters was not. A censorship directive was often advice, not an order, and editors did use their own judgment. "D [Defence] Notices" provided information on what was illegal. D Notices were first used in 1912 and are still in force today, although they are called DA Notices now—the more politically correct "defence advice." Occasionally editors published articles that were not submitted to censor's advice and so risked prosecution, though few prosecutions actually occurred. Mostly the system was based on bluff, goodwill, and the old-boy network. Ultimately, though, "behind all the velvet gloves, lurked the mailed fist of coercion."[84] No editor wanted to help the enemy, and if the semivoluntary system broke down, a more draconian enforce-

ment would have ensued. The newspapers, denuded of many of their reporters as a result of call-ups, practiced a large degree of self-censorship.
Besides, the papers wanted to give their readers what they wanted—more
upbeat stories. And with tight government restrictions on newsprint and
the large public information advertising budgets, it also made business
sense to toe the official line.

Unofficial censorship of British Broadcasting Corporation radio was
much tighter. Four censors were permanently stationed at the BBC's Broadcasting House. But serious attempts at objectivity were maintained and
many people believed—especially abroad—that BBC news, the "voice of
freedom," was uncensored. Both Germany and Britain had the same level
of radio ownership in their homes: 75 percent. (There were 23,000 TV
sets in the UK, though television was shut down for the duration.) Radio,
"wordy warfare," was to play a vital role in the war: a German newspaper
described the BBC's broadcasts as a "spiritual danger, intellectual poison,
and a weapon more paralyzing and deadly than cannon and machine
gun."[85] No wonder the Nazis took extreme measures to stop people from
listening to the BBC throughout occupied Europe.

Rumors and urban myths of course abounded. Britons spoke in hushed
tones about a German bomb so advanced that it could chase you around
corners, although the world didn't see those until the appearance of cruise
missiles in the 1991 Gulf War. The most famous wartime myth was of a
failed German invasion of England in the summer of 1940; stories circulated widely about thousands of German corpses washed up on the coast.

War correspondents could not report the truth of Dunkirk. Only one
amateur naval writer was a brief eyewitness of the withdrawal, which
was accordingly transformed from a colossal military disaster into a
"miracle." Then came the Blitz, the aerial bombardment of Britain, which
was seen as a prelude to German invasion. American correspondents, most
famously Edward R. Murrow, covered the dramatic events on radio. Known
for his opener "This is London," Murrow's style was stark and simple, and
increasingly pro-British. In one report in summer 1940, a month after the
Blitz had started, Murrow said:

> It's a beautiful and lonesome city where men and women and
> children are trying to snatch a few hours' sleep underground. . . .
> Today I went to buy a hat—my favorite shop had gone, blown to
> bits. The windows of my shoe store were blown out. I decided to
> have a haircut; the windows of the barbershop were gone, but
> the Italian barber was still doing business.[86]

This was emotive stuff for an American audience. Ed Murrow, working with William Shirer, had pioneered live radio broadcasting as CBS correspondents on the spot in European capitals before the war. Their reports stood in stark contrast to the stuffiness of the BBC's reported speech. Almost without exception, American foreign correspondents soon became pro-British and anti-Nazi.

America's entry into the war—and without it Britain would have been defeated—was an event Churchill had "dreamed of, aimed at and worked for."[87] Until that happened, Lend-Lease, especially fifty rusty old U.S. Navy destroyers, would help Britain survive (although only nine were immediately usable). Because of Americans' wariness of crude British propaganda to seduce the United States into the first war, Britain now waged one of the most diverse, extensive, and subtle propaganda campaigns ever directed by one sovereign state at another. The Blitz spirit, shared history, and the battle for Christian civilization were aimed constantly at getting the American people to stand "shoulder to shoulder" with their "cousins" across the Atlantic. President Franklin D. Roosevelt needed time, and help, to win over his electorate. Unfortunately for Churchill, many Americans thought that Britain, a "museum piece," was doomed. "Let God Save the King" summed up the views of many isolationists or pro-Germans.

Americans may not have liked British politicians, but they did like British actors. In Hollywood the Jewish moguls (despite some caution in the Jewish community because of British policy in Palestine) were determined to help and offered to launch a series of anti-Nazi films, but the British Treasury turned them down, and in the beginning the censors in London also gave American correspondents the bureaucratic runaround. Despite the gremlins of British interdepartmental rivalry, Foreign Office hauteur, and downright myopia in the War Office, eventually the British refined their propaganda campaign, which involved forgery, rumor-mongering, loans of the Magna Carta, and royal visits, all to promote the "hands across the sea" campaign.

Films such as Charlie Chaplin's *The Great Dictator* had a profound impact on American opinions of Hitler and Mussolini. Hollywood did make a series of anti-German films with the help of British directors such as Alfred Hitchcock (*Foreign Correspondent*, for example). Many of the films encouraged by London—*Mrs. Miniver,* starring Greer Garson, is the best known—portray wartime Britain as Mary Poppins meets Biggles. Although *Mrs. Miniver* was distributed after Washington entered the war, some earlier films fashioned a popular image of a plucky, fellow English-speaking people. Pro-British documentaries, inspired by pioneers such as John Grierson, provided more accurate portrayals than the saccharine caricature of Mrs. Miniver. Gradually opinion in the United States shifted from neutrality to acceptance of war. Sherlock Holmes (Basil Rathbone) was pitted against Nazi saboteurs; the "Invisible Man" (played by John Hall) parachuted into Berlin as *The Invisible Agent*. Even Tarzan and Lassie did their bit. Real-life secret British propagandists ranged from the matinee idol Leslie Howard to Oxford philosopher Isaiah Berlin and society photographer Cecil Beaton. The most durable link, however, was forged by Bill Stephenson (the "man called Intrepid") who helped set up what became the Central Intelligence Agency.[88]

The British also made their own domestic films despite opposition, often from the military. Air Marshal Arthur "Bomber" Harris loathed Terence Rattigan's play *Flarepath* and discouraged films about Bomber Command. Churchill, despite being a movie fan, tried to stop the screening abroad of *The Life and Death of Colonel Blimp* (1943), which is regarded as one of the best productions of that period. Despite the public skepticism of propaganda entertainments, many were popular. The RAF got in first during the phony war with the patriotic *The Lion Has Wings,* but the navy sponsored what is still considered a masterpiece, *In Which We Serve*, starring Noël Coward. The army's equivalent, *The Way Ahead,* opened to coincide with D–Day (1944).[89] But nothing rivaled the greatest wartime hit, Tommy Handley's *ITMA—It's That Man Again*. The half-hour BBC radio program was full of dotty British humor. It used to be said that if Hitler invaded between 8:30 and 9:00 p.m. on a Thursday, he would have had an easy job. Handley was more of a morale booster than any government propagandist.

The British media initially concentrated on the desert war, especially when the Italians were being thrashed. This was a more flexible campaign of movement, easier for war correspondents to operate in. Censorship was moderate, and some first-rate writing emerged, especially from Alan Moorehead, an Australian of ruthless charm.[90] Another successful Australian correspondent was Chester Wilmot. Wilmot and Moorehead were key figures in the ninety-two-strong Allied press corps that was effectively embedded with the British army in North Africa. They wore officers' uniforms with green epaulettes and their cap badge was a gold-lettered "C" (although the War Office had originally proposed "W.C.," maybe without irony).[91] They had the rank of captain, although real officers complained they sometimes behaved like field marshals. One senior officer told Moorehead sourly, "The only time I want to see anything about my men in print is when the Honours List comes out."[92] However, this opinion was not the norm. When the Americans entered the war, Gen. Dwight Eisenhower treated his "warcos" (war correspondents) as staff officers. Shortly before the landings in Tunisia in November 1942, he said: "As staff officers your first duty is a military duty, and the one fact you must always bear in mind is to disclose nothing which would help the enemy."[93] Wilmot, for example, was treated in the same way by Field Marshal Montgomery. Like Eisenhower, "Monty" treated senior warcos, especially in the BBC, as military men. He trusted them and, in turn, won their respect and commitment.

The fluid conflict in rugged terrain, in a land almost designed for war, made censorship difficult. The military commanders preferred reporters to operate their own system of self-censorship, a psychologically astute method of handling war correspondents. Working closely with the very armed forces that provided them with all their information and, in most cases, protection, food, accommodation, and transport, made the warcos members of the fighting team. Often correspondents were armed, and occasionally they took part in the fighting, just as in the period of imperial reportage in the nineteenth century. One journalist even shot down an enemy fighter while taking over for a wounded rear gunner. So they went along with the team message and self-censored the awkward truths. If a hack told the complete truth, he was out in the cold, accused of damaging morale, and sent out of theater. Still, the current crop of World War II journalists' freedom of reporting and movement in the desert would have astounded their World War I predecessors. The war was reported in almost romantic terms. General (later Field Marshal) Erwin Rommel, the "desert fox," was lionized as the new Hannibal. Italians were portrayed as though if not brave then at least chivalrous. And the British generals, most notably Monty, worked astutely on what would now be called their "media images."

Chester Wilmot, who worked for the Australian Broadcasting Corporation and then the BBC, honed his strategic skills in the desert. Many warcos concentrated on immediate tactics or local color; Wilmot had a great talent for seeing the broader picture (displayed in his best-selling book, *The Struggle for Europe*). In the North African campaign, he evolved two basic rules: go on your own and always establish, and keep, contact with the senior commander.[94] In the modern era of media packs and herd mentality, this is still very sound advice for new journalists.

The fighting in China before 1939 was covered as if it were the good old freebooting days. Bulging with expense accounts, British and American correspondents rushed to cover the bombing raids, the use of poison gas, and in 1937 the Battle of Shanghai ("the world's greatest drama") as well as the "rape of Nanking" (when over 300,000 Chinese civilians were slaughtered by Japanese troops). Farsighted writers such as Edgar Snow warned that the Japanese advance would soon encroach on the Western colonies, as well as American interests. Meanwhile, the United States, despite leaning toward Britain in 1940–41, was still reluctant to enter World War II. As the *Wall Street Journal* noted, "The principal difference between Mr. Hitler and Mr. Stalin is the size of their respective moustaches."[95] Then came Pearl Harbor and new American rules for correspondents. The Japanese surprise attack was a U.S. intelligence disaster, the 9/11 of its day. If Operation Barbarossa, the German attack on Russia, was the neutralization of a superb intelligence service by Josef Stalin's arrogant stupidity, and if the Normandy landings were a triumph of deception over an efficient German intelligence system, then Pearl Harbor represents the folly of not having a functioning intelligence service at all. The United States had all the information and nearly all the key intelligence indicators, but failed to recognize them or take action on them.[96]

Militarily, the United States was equally unprepared: its army ranked nineteenth in the world. But the propagandists were in better shape, though they never reached the levels of British cunning. In World War I, censorship and propaganda had been combined into one department, but in 1942 President Roosevelt set up a big-budget Office of War Information and a separate Office of Censorship. The Americans adopted a much more scientific and controlled approach to censorship. As one senior journalist observed: "The official censors pretty much succeeded in putting over the legend that the war was won without a single mistake by a command consisting exclusively of geniuses."[97] The U.S. propaganda machine built up heroes, just like the British. A good example was Gen. Douglas MacArthur, despite his defeat in the Philippines. Hollywood-style publicity surrounded his promise to return (and when he did, he was filmed and photographed during repeated re-takes of his landing). He was described as "a hell-to-breakfast baby, long and lean" using "ten-dollar words delivered in a million-dollar manner."[98] Another very PR-conscious U.S. general was George Patton, a natural for a later Hollywood biopic (*Patton,* 1969, starring George C. Scott).

Despite the fact that the Allied invasion of Europe rested on a knife's edge, the Normandy landings, by sea and air, included 558 correspondents. But many correspondents couldn't get on the first ships to cross. Brig. Edgar Williams, Gen. Bernard Law Montgomery's intelligence staff officer, tried to placate them. One complained: "But this is the biggest story since the Crucifixion!" To which Williams replied, "Yes, but they managed very well with four correspondents."[99] *Time* magazine's Charles Christian Wertenbaker described the naval forces as "a floating island of men and metal."[100] The military had helpfully provided eight gross of condoms, which were "guaranteed to render photographers' negatives watertight if closed with a rubber band."[101] Any spares would come in handy when Paris was liberated. Distinguished American journalist Ernie Pyle, who had made himself famous by portraying the "grunt's-eye" view of the fighting, summed up the mood of the city: "Anybody who doesn't sleep with a woman tonight is just an exhibitionist."[102] Like Murrow's, his prose was direct and simple. (A sinewy "American" style had been popularized by Hemingway and Gellhorn, and reached its zenith in John Hersey's reporting on Hiroshima.) In the hard fighting that followed the breakout from the Normandy beaches, Pyle deployed this highly effective prose style in his powerful reports for the Scripps-Howard wire service. Pyle, who was nicknamed "the G1 journalist," won a Pulitzer, but—with his last column still folded in his pocket—he was killed by sniper fire on April 18, 1945, alongside the U.S. Marines on Ie Shima, west of Okinawa.

So-called hometown copy, stories about individual GIs for local newspapers, was sometimes difficult to get. At one point, Victor O. Jones of the *Boston Globe* was having trouble finding soldiers from Massachusetts. Following the example of Gordon Gammack of the Des Moines *Register Tribune*, who put up a big sign saying "Iowa" on the windshield of his jeep, Jones did the same with a notice saying "Mass"—"only to be besieged by penitent Catholics pining to confess."[103] Thus correspondents kept the folks back home happy without telling them too much about the effects of determined Nazi resistance, especially "the honey-on-herring stench of death."[104] Since 1898 there had been an embargo on publishing photographs of dead American soldiers, however, after a decree by President Roosevelt, *Life* magazine was allowed to show three American military bodies on the beach at Buna on September 20, 1943. But this picture caused outrage.

By 1944 close proximity to the army, especially in hard fighting in Africa, Italy, and Normandy, had made the media many military friends. They were no longer meddlesome civilians in a kind of khaki fancy dress. They were men of the army who just happened to have a rather specialized job. And, in particular, "the army accepted the BBC correspondents as an informal extension of its own public relations system."[105] How cozy— and a portent of things to come.

Moorehead described the final push into Germany as the greatest and most tragic European spectacle since the collapse of Napoleon. But Western correspondents had not endured the years of savage fighting on the Eastern Front. Perhaps the most able Russian war reporter was Vasily Grossman, who worked for the Red Army newspaper, *Red Star.* Grossman, later a brilliant, if banned, novelist, covered the German advance, where Heinkels and Junkers flying at night, "spread among the stars like lice." It was at the turning point of the war, Stalingrad, that Grossman honed his powers of description: "the usual smell of the front line—a cross between a morgue and a blacksmith's."[106] He continued to report until the final Battle of Berlin.

Field Marshal Montgomery tipped off his select band of media acolytes, especially Wilmot, about the details of the German surrender on May 4, 1945. Wilmot got his radio scoop for the BBC with the details of the end of the war in Europe. The last days of the war also produced some classic photographs. Margaret Bourke-White's photographs of Buchenwald managed to capture much of the horror of the Holocaust. On April 30, the day Hitler killed himself, Russian soldiers had climbed to the top of the Reichstag to hang a huge improvised Soviet flag over the city. The moment was captured, or rather reconstructed, by the Red Army photographer Yevgeny Khaldei. It was vital that the picture be in Moscow for political celebrations on May 1.[107] Perhaps the most famous American photographic icon of the war—perhaps of any war—was Joe Rosenthal's picture of five Marines and a Navy corpsman raising the Stars and Stripes on top of Mount Suribachi on the island of Iwo Jima in March 1945. This picture was also reconstructed, as Clint Eastwood's 2006 film, *Flags of Our Fathers*, made clear. Before the television age—from this photograph of Old Glory to the dome of St. Paul's rising above the ruins of London—the work of photojournalists had bequeathed a rich pictorial heritage, far more than the newsreels. Meanwhile, magazines such as *Life, Picture Post*, and Germany's *Signal* were the 1939–45 equivalent of contemporary television.[108]

But much of the real war was unreported. British correspondents failed to report disasters such as the Dieppe raid or the "bridge too far" at Arnhem. The fall of Singapore was hushed up. There, in February 1942, a British army with sufficient ammunition surrendered to a Japanese force barely one-third its number and down to its last one hundred rounds per man. It really was the end of empire as its later chronicler, James Morris, lamented: "The Royal Navy had failed; the British armies had been outclassed; white men had been seen in states of panic and humility; the legend had collapsed in pathos."[109] True, as Morris also noted, for the British World War II also assumed a heroic quality. The British Empire, with eleven million marching under the same flag, fought the three great enemies—Germany, Japan, and Italy—first to last. But they did so at great cost, not just in lives and treasure and, eventually, territory, but also in truth. Much was missed, not least at home, where racketeering, draft dodging, shelter fever, chronic grumbling, and, especially in the beginning, antiwar sentiment were rife. It was more than sixty years before the antiheroic, anti-British bulldog underworld of spivs, fascists, and opportunists was popularized in Independent Television's *Foyle's War,* a program about a fictional detective fighting these nonpatriots.

If the warcos missed stories by accident, or more often spiked them because of the iron hand of the censor, they also over-egged others, especially the role of "the dam busters," which was immortalized in the 1954 film of the same name. They also overdramatized the role of Orde Wingate and the Chindits in Burma while generally avoiding the story about the large number of Indian army prisoners who had joined the Japanese-sponsored resistance army. India was the jewel in the crown of empire; suggesting that it would be lost (as it was by 1947) was too sensitive in wartime. Oddly, when the most brutal and yet largely unreported story during the war, the Nazi Holocaust, was finally recorded for broadcast on April 15, 1945, by the BBC's Richard Dimbleby, the first correspondent into Belsen, the corporation refused to believe his emotional dispatch until it had been verified by newspaper reports. Martha Gellhorn, one of the first journalists to reach Dachau, said that practically every German she met at the time claimed to have opposed Hitler and/or to have taken in Jewish refugees. Ed Murrow was first through the gates of Buchenwald alongside liberating American soldiers. On April 15, he delivered one of radio's most evocative broadcasts. It was as bare as Gellhorn's prose and as quietly agonized as Dimbleby's. "For most of it, I have no words," Murrow said simply.

With the exception of feisty individualists such as Gellhorn and Murrow, many American correspondents perhaps took their initial cue from the Washington military censor who was alleged to have said: "I wouldn't tell the people anything until the war is over and then I'd tell them who won." The American media, for example, largely went along with the propaganda line on the Chinese nationalists' bold fight against the Japanese. It is perhaps more understandable for the detailed facts about disasters such as Pearl Harbor or the impact of kamikaze planes to be cloaked, but keeping secret decisive victories, such as the Battle of Midway, makes far less sense.

Both British and American media chose to avoid the initial disasters of the Battle of the Atlantic. Nor did they expound on the secret U.S. submarine offensive that had cut off oil to Japan. The Japanese homeland was defeated long before the immolation of Nagasaki (where the special torpedoes used at Pearl Harbor had been made) and Hiroshima in August 1945. On September 5 in the London *Daily Express,* Australian Wilfred Burchett, a determined correspondent but alleged by many to have been a KGB agent, broke the story of Hiroshima's destruction and radiation caused by the atomic bomb. It was a year before John Hersey published a powerful book, *Hiroshima*, based on his report for the *New Yorker*.

Censorship about history's most powerful weapon is certainly comprehensible, but the dismal reporting of the Russian front is less so. An exception was Margaret Bourke-White's presence in Moscow when the Germans invaded. "Maggie the Indestructible," as her colleagues on *Life* magazine called her, had the lucky knack for a journalist of always being in the right place at the right time. Soviet media was muzzled by a brutal dictatorship, and Moscow assumed, often correctly, that Western correspondents were also spies. So the epic siege of Leningrad, for example, was grossly unreported; the greatest battle of the war, Kursk, barely rated a mention in the Western press. That nearly one million citizens of the USSR, most notably in the Ukraine, put on German army uniforms was practically ignored. The British handover for elimination by Stalin at the end of the war of tens of thousands of Cossacks who had fought alongside the Germans was also hushed up. Nevertheless, over 20 million Russians were killed in their "Great Patriotic War" against Nazism. Many British and American schoolchildren are still being taught that the Western democracies won the war without very significant Soviet contributions.

War correspondents in World War II often displayed great élan. Early in the war, it had been assumed that correspondents, as noncombatants, could not receive medals. But General MacArthur defied precedent by awarding the Silver Star to AP's Vernon Haughland. Soon journalists from United Press and other organizations received awards. British reporters were mentioned in dispatches for bravery under fire. On a number of occasions at the end of the war in Europe, Jeep-loads of armed correspondents accepted the surrender of towns. Many were living their vocations, their lives, and events to the full, especially such pioneering female correspondents as Gellhorn and Bourke-White. Few, men or women, were as indefatigable, however, as the French adventurer, writer, and novelist André Malraux (though he has been criticized for mythmaking about his own extraordinary career). Besides writing brilliant prose, in his personal war on fascism he flew over sixty missions as a combat pilot, was a bold tank commander, and fought in the French resistance. After the war, President Charles de Gaulle made him a government minister. Such armed participation in conflict would not accord with modern media ethics.

During World War II great writing, photography, films, and radio reports emerged, but in nearly all cases they were shackled to patriotic goals. Journalists showed immense courage and their casualty rate was very high, but they rarely produced independent work that changed policy. They broke the ethical rules of their profession, from minor infringements (for the period) such as carrying guns to gross racism, especially in U.S. and British reports on the fighting in Asia. Censorship, self-censorship, terrain, and the fog of war all played a part in this. But the key factor was loyalty to the cause. Correspondents wanted their side to win, almost regardless of the facts. These patriots with pens and cameras were cheerleaders, not objective reporters. It was total war, which demanded total commitment. Knightley quotes Charles Lynch, a Canadian correspondent, who said: "It was crap—and I don't exclude the Ernie Pyles or the Alan Mooreheads. . . . It wasn't good journalism. It wasn't journalism at all."[110]

William Howard Russell generated a freebooting style of enquiry that sometimes influenced the imperial and small nationalist wars of the nineteenth century. Occasionally this freedom enabled correspondents to influence political policy at home and, even in one or two celebrated examples, to bring down governments. The perceived war of survival in 1914 stopped this style of journalism in its tracks. In the interwar period, campaigns outside Europe allowed more freedom of maneuver for enterprising correspondents. But again in 1939, the Fourth Estate had to bow its knee to the dictates of national survival. That nobody wanted to help the enemy in any way was the leitmotif of even the most cynical war correspondent. Modern technology, especially the "wireless" and the cinema, as well as modern transportation (particularly the airplane) gave more flexibility to journalism, but the military and government propaganda machines quickly monopolized these advances.

After VE Day and VJ Day, no worldwide peace emerged; the Cold War and the clash of ideologies dominated the media. Europe was frozen in the glacis of competing systems, so shooting wars were exported to the perimeters that saw proxy combat in former imperial possessions, especially in Asia and Africa. These wars mattered to the new superpowers of America and the USSR, but they were not wars of survival for their homelands. It meant that Western populations were afforded "the luxury of opinion without patriotic penalty."[111] Television would soon make itself felt globally, not least by bringing fire and flame, death and gore, in full color, to the homes of voters in the West.

In both World Wars, correspondents had been transformed, or transformed themselves, from chained watchdogs to docile lapdogs. After 1945 would they be able to deploy the new power of live television, and later live satellite transmission, to break their chains?

# 3

# THE COLD WAR (OF WORDS)

"The onrush of the barbarians" was Gen. Sir Bernard Montgomery's description of the arrival in 1945 of the Red Army in Berlin; these same "barbarians" would within a matter of years acquire nuclear weapons.[1] For a millennium, wars in Europe had either been about religion, secession, or the balance of power. The Cold War, initially about German secession, was inspired by a combination of causes: balance of power and an ideological rivalry that spanned the globe for forty-four years. The two great successors to the European state tradition, the United States and the USSR, fought perhaps the last and greatest of Europe's wars.[2] And, as with the two previous World Wars, the cold version soon spread. Some of the conflict was focused on Europe—for example, the Berlin Blockade, the Hungarian uprising, and the erection of the Berlin Wall—but all the actual fighting took place on the peripheries.[3] The wars of independence and "national liberation," especially in the Middle East, Asia, and Africa, were essentially proxy wars for the new superpowers in a bipolar world.

Two European camps were formed on either side of the Iron Curtain, each led by an overarching military alliance that was aimed at the external rival, but they were also protection rackets to dominate the internal coalitions as well. Yet the American bomb and the dollar also saved Western Europe for democracy. The military doctrines of nuclear deterrence became a form of global insurance against Mutual Assured Destruction (MAD). The MAD insurance came closest to breakdown in the eyeball-to-eyeball Cuban Missile Crisis in 1962. Devout theorists developed a Dr. Strangelove-like doctrine of thinking about the unthinkable—how to actually fight a nuclear war. Military writers immersed themselves in the arcane details of these doctrines, while conventional war correspondents were kept busy too. If the Northern Hemisphere was dominated by the threat of atomic Armageddon, then the south was frequently engulfed in the reality of insurgency.

Most of these wars of insurgency were perceived, and reported, through the prism of the Cold War. Meanwhile, in many Western European universities, two generations of arts and social science students were exposed to Marxist thinking. Later few dons, if any, apologized or recanted when after 1989 the USSR imploded and revealed what a Potemkin village the whole edifice had been. Battalions of journalists were also conscripted by the Marxist tradition, though it was never quite as divisive or subversive of media ethics as the Spanish Civil War. Both Moscow and Washington set up numerous covert fronts as media organizations to wage propaganda war, often staffed by talented journalists. Neither did many of these recant afterwards, though those that did were more likely to be found in Eastern rather than Western Europe, and barely at all in the United States.

The type of correspondents who liked to "get their boots dirty" was busy in the period 1945–53, when the rivalry between the West and the Soviet Union was especially intense. American journalists were primarily concerned with the triumphant communist victory in mainland China, though others were fascinated by the collapse of the British Empire. Associated Press's Max Desfor, for example, photographed the massacres that resulted from the partition of India in 1947. Another British retreat was from Palestine. Stories from the *Herald Tribune*'s Homer Bigart and photographs by Frank E. Noel of Jewish girls being taken prisoner by British police, and of soldiers turning back desperate Holocaust survivors trying to disembark from the American-owned ship *Exodus,* influenced American popular opinion against the British. This pressure helped to precipitate the imperial scuttle from the Holy Land and elsewhere.[4] Although Britain's retreat from empire was in many respects less traumatic than others such as the French, its legacy—in Israel and in Pakistan especially—survives in many of today's dangerous crises. Additionally, the propaganda wars that engulfed the reporting of these events goes on. Britain itself was about to launch into the first limited war of the nuclear age.

## THE KOREAN WAR

On June 24, 1950, the West assumed the Cold War was suddenly turning hot when communist North Korea invaded South Korea. For three years, under the banner of the United Nations, the West fought the most important campaign of the Cold War, which was essentially an American war. It was led by commanders who threatened atomic weapons but who in the end did not use them. Although Washington feared that the fall of the pro-Western, corrupt South Korea would constitute a domino that would

70

tip other Asian states into the communist camp, it was not a war of survival to parallel World War II. Journalists assumed that, freed from the dictates of patriotism, they could report this war with little censorship. The U.S. military soon thought otherwise. As American correspondent Hal Boyle remarked, this was the worst-reported war of modern times.[5] Part of the reason was the actual request by some reporters for greater guidance from the military as to what they should or should not say.

Some 270 correspondents were in theater by the end of 1950, with only Wilfred Burchett and Alan Winnington covering the communist side. Most stayed at headquarters and out of the field; less than a fifth were on the frontline, and many of these were Australians. The harsh terrain and weather, and the chaos of the disastrous first stage of the war when the American-led forces were trapped in the small Pusan pocket impelled journalists to rely on food, transport, and, above all, communications supplied by the U.S. armed forces. All copy required routing through army headquarters in Tokyo, which resulted in the opportunity for selection, delay, or deliberate "loss" of unfavorable material. Initially, however, there was little deliberate censorship, especially since most Western correspondents adhered to the propaganda line of an anti-communist crusade.

The combined Allied commander was Gen. Douglas MacArthur who, besides spending two years as a press liaison officer in Washington in his early career, had enjoyed being in the spotlight in his glory days at the end of World War II. He also deployed the media for his own purposes. He even encouraged *Life* and *Newsweek* magazines to publish pictures of the bodies of soldiers who had been killed by North Korean troops.[6] But there were atrocities on the UN side too, particularly the South Koreans, and the military situation was worsening. In December 1950, MacArthur imposed strict military censorship. The voluntary "staff officer" style of Eisenhower and Montgomery was discarded. Journalists who didn't "join the team" were ejected from theater; seventeen suffered this fate. The new medium of television had already penetrated 65 percent of American homes, but there was no means to send the signal directly to the viewer. So censored film footage slowly reached the stateside television audience days after events occurred.

In September 1950 MacArthur decided to try to turn the war around with an ambitious but risky amphibious landing at Inchon. With 262 ships, it was the largest naval task force since 1945. Journalist James Cameron was in one of the assault ships with a group of other correspondents. He observed wryly that the ship had been "full of agitated and contending correspondents, all trying to appear insistently determined to land in Wave One, while contriving desperately to be found in Wave Fifty."[7]

After the successful landings, South Korean forces treated prisoners appallingly. Cameron, a bloody-minded and determined Scot, complained to the UN command to no avail. Cameron reported on the atrocities and, along with photographs by Bert Hardy, sent the material to Tom Hopkinson, the editor of *Picture Post*. After much cross-checking and the inclusion of a photograph of North Korean atrocities, the story was set to be published when the proprietor of the magazine, Sir Edward Hulton, pulled it. Hopkinson protested and was fired. It became a cause célèbre on Fleet Street. This famous case demonstrates that censorship can stem from all sorts of causes. Hulton spiked the story not because of any official pressure; his own personal political views stopped the publication. Also petty personal factors may have intruded: Hopkinson objected to Hulton's wife trying to install herself as fashion editor of the magazine. The proprietor subverted the truth about an important story and his editor was sacrificed. Nonetheless, Hopkinson went on to edit *Drum* in South Africa and to be knighted for his services to journalism.[8]

I. F. Stone was as determined as Cameron or Hopkinson to dissect the truth behind the official lies about the war. When his classic work *The Hidden History of the Korean War* was published, many journalists and the U.S. government were quick to condemn it as Soviet propaganda.[9] He had made himself almost unemployable in the era of McCarthyism, so he started the famous *I. F. Stone's Weekly*, which became a financial success and an icon of the antiwar movement in the 1960s.

Many reports about atrocities and racism in the war were hushed up, as well as many acts of military incompetence. One long-delayed story was of the amazing collapse of morale among U.S. prisoners of war, especially compared with the successful stoicism of Turkish POWs. Nearly every major newspaper in Britain and the United States supported the war. This was the period of Sen. Joseph R. McCarthy's anti-communist witchhunt in the United States. No one wanted to be accused of giving succor to the red peril, which now consisted, it was claimed, of a monolithic communist bloc in the form of both the Soviet Union and China. After Inchon, UN forces pushed up to the Chinese border, whereupon—after many warnings—the Chinese People's Liberation Army intervened and propelled Western forces back down the peninsula. Hence the famous comment by a Marine general: "Retreat, hell! We're just attacking in another direction." Another Marine told a correspondent, "Remember, whatever you write, that this was not a retreat. All that happened was we found more Chinese behind us than in front of us. So we about-faced and attacked."[10]

The war ended in a negotiated stalemate in the summer of 1953. The border between North and South Korea was roughly where it had been in the summer of 1950. No peace, merely an armistice was the result. Technically, more than five decades later, a highly belligerent, and now nuclear-armed, North Korea was still at war with the South. Perhaps the intractability of the conflict explains why the war came and went with much bloodshed but precious little glory and left no mark on American imaginations though nearly as many Americans died there as in Vietnam.[11] The Korean tragedy produced few films or novels in the heroic mold. The movie *M\*A\*S\*H*, the most popular televised icon of the war, was actually made during the Vietnam era and bears little reference to the harsh realities of the Korean situation at the time.[12] British war correspondent and historian Max Hastings concluded, "The war seemed an unsatisfactory, inglorious, and thus unwelcome memory."[13]

However, many Asians did not want to forget the war. "Where America paid a price," according to Henry Kissinger, "was among revolutionary leaders of Southeast Asia and elsewhere, who discovered a method of warfare that avoided large-scale ground combat yet had the ability to wear down the resolve of a superpower."[14] Korea, of course, was largely a conventional war where the Western industrialized powers had a marked advantage, but it spawned alternative, Maoist-style insurgencies that played to the strengths of weaker and more patient opponents.

Unlike later in Vietnam, Britain had joined in this fight reluctantly. The British were wary of MacArthur and played a part in encouraging President Truman to fire him. They feared, rightly, that the maverick military genius was trying to incite an all-out war with China. Not for the first time, the British showed better judgment than their American allies. During World War II, the Americans had insisted that Chiang Kai-shek was the leader who would save China and that French military leader Charles de Gaulle was insignificant. In each case, London took the contrary view and was proved correct. In Korea, Prime Minister Clement Attlee displayed good sense in helping to dissuade Truman from using nuclear weapons. The British were also more skeptical about the anti-communist ruler of South Korea, Syngman Rhee.[15]

Korea was a disaster for the profession of war correspondence. The frontline cadre often showed great physical courage but did not display the same moral courage in questioning the overall purpose and conduct of the war. As James Cameron said, it was a "prep school for Vietnam." But would journalists do any better in the next Asian war?

## FRENCH INDOCHINA

If General MacArthur had underestimated the capabilities of his Asian foe, Gen. Henri Navarre was to do the same in French Indochina. Leaders in Washington had supported Ho Chi Minh's resistance to Japanese occupation of the French colony. They were to regret doing this in the same way that they rued their support in the 1980s for Osama bin Laden's contribution to the war against the Soviets. By 1950, Ho Chi Minh's campaign against the French was splitting domestic opinion along political party lines. The Francophone Vietnamese intellectuals could appeal directly to the growing communist and socialist forces in the metropole. French journalists in Indochina were likewise split in their loyalties.

Frustrated with a nine-year guerrilla war, the French commanders, especially Navarre, wanted to win an outright victory in a single, major, pitched battle. They chose Dien Bien Phu on the Laotian border, situated in the middle of the anti-French Viet Minh supply lines. After a fifty-five-day siege, the French surrendered on May 7, 1954. Morale in Paris collapsed. The French withdrew from their Far East empire, leaving the Americans to defend the corrupt pro-Western regime in the south. But Vietnam's division would not endure like Korea's.

Three weeks after the fall of Dien Bien Phu, the most distinguished war photographer of the time, Robert Capa, visited Nam Dinh in the Red River Valley. He was killed in action, still clutching his camera in his left hand.[16]

## SUEZ: NO END OF A LESSON

For the British, according to one historian, "Suez was an imperial cataclysm."[17] In 1956, two-thirds of Europe's oil went through the Suez canal, giving Gen. Abdul Nasser, the Egyptian leader, a "thumb on our windpipe," to use Prime Minister Anthony Eden's phrase. (Thirty-five years later, two-thirds of the West's oil came from a region menaced, it was argued, by Saddam Hussein: "Same windpipe; different thumb," according to a well-known British columnist.)[18] Acting in collusion with Israel, in the autumn of 1956 Britain and France (which was anxious to curb Egyptian meddling in Algeria) sent their largest and most publicized punitive expedition to topple Nasser and so protect, it was believed, the canal and access to Middle East oil. Such old-fashioned gunboat diplomacy did not work in the American century. The canal was becoming irrelevant anyway as a new generation of giant oil supertankers was unable to pass through it. Anglo-French imperial hubris looked back rather than forward. The United States stopped supporting the pound, and France could not proceed on its own. Both nations were forced into a humiliating withdrawal. The Suez Crisis split Britain and its press in a way that foreshadowed the divisions over the 2003 Iraq War. With fewer than five million British television viewers in the first half of the 1950s, heavily read British newspapers cheered on the invasion, led by a particularly aggressive London *Times*. The *Manchester Guardian*, the *Observer*, and the *New Statesman* opposed it.[19] *The Daily Mirror* demanded the resignation of Prime Minister Anthony Eden, which he did two months later. France never again trusted the United States, while for London the lesson was not to wage war without the Americans. The military strategy worked, but the political policy failed.[20]

In 1956, the Soviets took the opportunity to crush the simultaneous Hungarian uprising. For nearly a decade, the U.S.-funded Radio Free Europe had urged the subjugated peoples of Eastern Europe to throw off their chains. This was in fact against the spirit, if not the law, of Article 2.7 of the UN Charter, which forbade interference in the internal affairs of sovereign nations, although Moscow allowed the Hungarians precious little sovereignty. When they did rise up, and they were ruthlessly suppressed by the Soviets, America did little but protest.[21] (The same mistake was to be made in the 1991 Gulf War when U.S.-generated, covert propaganda broadcasts encouraged the Shias and the Kurds to overthrow Saddam Hussein, even though "regime change" was not yet part of official U.S. policy.)[22] In 1956 the Soviets arrested American photographer Georgette "Dickey" Chapelle and held her for three months, but not before she was able to smuggle out stirring photographs of the uprising.[23] The BBC's Charles Wheeler was in Hungary reporting for the flagship *Panorama* program. When the Hungarians heard about the Suez invasion they were horrified. "As they saw it," wrote Wheeler, "London and Paris were throwing away the moral authority that might have deterred Moscow from committing aggression in Hungary."[24] If the Soviets used Suez as a convenient cover to suppress a revolution, the Anglo-French imperial ignominy helped to fire up the revolutionary war in Algeria.

## ALGERIA: A SAVAGE WAR

The French may have helped Algeria as a nation but not most Algerians. "In this admirable country in which a spring without equal covers it with flowers and its light, men are suffering hunger and demanding justice," in the poetic words of writer Albert Camus in 1958.[25] The war for independence in the French territory lasted from 1954 to 1962. Paris, humiliated by the German occupation,[26] the fall of Indochina, and the Suez fiasco, was determined to hold on to Algeria, which was regarded as part of France, *La Patrie*, and not a colony. In Indochina, there had been a steady erosion of local control: *pourissement* (rotting) was the term used. But in Algeria, the French army held firm and fought the nationalists (whom they perceived as communists) with their own *guerre révolutionnaire.* This soon became a dirty, not a revolutionary, war.

The conflict ended the careers of six French prime ministers—prompted the rise and nearly the fall of President de Gaulle—and twice led France to the edge of civil war at home. When it ended, after unspeakable mutilations and torture, a million Algerians had died and a similar number of French settlers had fled. The Algerian revolutionary struggle was the most pitiless of the European colonial wars.

As in Indochina, Francophone Algerian intellectuals could influence socialist and communist supporters in the metropole. In addition to newspaper campaigns, radio stations in Tunisia, Cairo, and Damascus stirred up the many illiterate followers of the Algerian Front for National Liberation (*Front de la Libération Nationale,* or FLN).[27] After Suez, General Nasser's support for the FLN intensified, while Soviet propaganda focused effectively on Algeria as a symbol of Western imperialism. Unwilling to be seen opposing noncommunist national aspirations for independence, Washington allowed an Algerian Office of Information to be set up in the United States, a significant media victory for the Algerian provisional government. The French authorities controlled the radio stations and French-language newspapers in Algeria. The divisions in France, however, and the antipathy of the pan-Arab press could not be disguised.

In military terms, the French army fought an effective counterinsurgency war, especially in the countryside, despite its pervasive sense of racial superiority and willful confusion of nationalism with communism. Then the FLN stepped up its bombing campaign in the capital, Algiers. Foreign Legion paratroopers went in hard and the bombing declined rapidly, but thousands of Algerians simply disappeared, while many others were tortured. The savage countermeasures fueled the antiwar lobby, aided by revelations in *Le Monde* that confirmed torture was a central feature of French policy. The FLN's strategic information operations on torture influenced French and Muslim audiences as well as public opinion in the United States and at the UN. (The campaign had echoes in the criticisms of the U.S. treatment of suspects in its war on terror after 2003.)[28] The media exposure of "the loss of the moral compass" as shown by tireless Dickey Chapelle's photographs, particularly of French air raids on villages, reverberated around the world. Using a ploy extensively copied in the twenty-first-century wars, she had dressed as a veiled Muslim woman to gain access to the killing zones.

The French Fourth Republic collapsed, and de Gaulle returned to power and offered self-determination, which was eventually achieved after a failed French military coup in Algeria. It is arguable whether the limited

Western war reporting in theater, in a conflict that was difficult to access, was a primary factor in the French defeat. France was severely divided politically by other factors, not least by the ideological chasm of the Cold War. The assaults on the morality of war by leading intellectuals (such as Jean Paul Sartre), trade unions, and political parties greatly influenced public opinion. Whether the domestic media generated and led, or simply followed, these intense divisions, is a debate that became characterized more clearly in the U.S. involvement in the Vietnam War, which started to gear up just as the Algerians achieved independence.

## BRITAIN'S COLONIAL WARS

Until Suez the tone of British reporting, especially in the still popular cinema newsreels, was that of a great power, one of the "Big Three" alongside the Soviet Union and America. Despite the dramatic reduction in imperial land holdings, journalism often remained couched in an old-fashioned jingoistic, nation-superior style. British war correspondents were active, for example, in Cyprus from 1954 to 1959, when Gen. George Grivas waged a guerrilla war for union with Greece.

A much longer campaign was fought in Malaya (later Malaysia). Particularly for Americans, this became a beacon to counterinsurgency experts, being the one major communist insurgency in Asia that was defeated, although it was a special case. The insurgency, which ran from 1948 to 1960, was rooted in the Chinese, not Malay, population. The Malayans were largely Muslim and intrinsically suspicious of godless communism. The British initiated an effective hearts-and-minds campaign (the term gained its popularity in this war) and were ready to grant independence quickly—the one thing the French so long resisted in Algeria. The British could still be heavy-handed, not least in the resettlement program, though it was often welcomed by the locals as an improvement in the quality of their lives, and not merely a case of being herded into fortified villages. Nevertheless, in a replay of the scandal in the camps of the Boer War thousands died of disease. British soldiers did commit atrocities, but the practice was not a sustained policy in the way that torture had been used in Algeria. The worst example was the murder of twenty-four Chinese villagers by the 2nd Battalion of the Scots Guards at Batang Kali in Selangor in December 1948. A cover story was concocted alleging they were guerrillas trying to escape. The truth did not come to light until an investigation by the *People* newspaper led to an admission of guilt in the House of Commons twenty-two years later.[29]

Malaya was not well covered by war correspondents, not least because it was a virtually inaccessible jungle war, which required walking long distances, especially in tropical heat with an over-abundant supply of leeches and snakes. Every contact with the enemy required an average of 1,800 man-hours of grueling foot patrols; only tough and lucky reporters witnessed or photographed a contact. Most correspondents who covered the war went to Malaya on press facility trips and filed "color" pieces about being on "patrol with the Jocks in the jungle."[30] Even so, some correspondents who participated in such managed forays gleaned a story. The *Daily Mirror* reported on the army's "league table" of kills, which prompted questions in the House of Commons (though the army carried on with the practice anyway). This was an interesting precedent for the American military's later obsession with body counts in Vietnam.

Malaya was an example of both successful counterinsurgency *and* decolonization. The military had deployed effective media operations in both its propaganda campaigns inside the country as well as largely deflecting a less-than-inquisitive British press. The overall commander, Gen. Gerald Templar, claimed that the British had simply reversed Mao's doctrine and won the hearts-and-minds campaign. But he had demography on his side, and—like all successful commanders—he had more than his share of good fortune, not least with the media. In particular, Templar was lucky because there were no photographers like Dickey Chapelle in Malaya to take incriminating pictures.[31] Dramatic photographs of the occasional atrocities or the frequently dismal conditions in the coastal resettlement camps could have derailed the effective police, army, and intelligence elements of the war.

Malaya became independent in 1957. In 1963 British territories in Borneo, Sarawak, and Sabah joined the renamed "Federation of Malaysia," while Singapore was later encouraged to leave. The new government soon asked the British army to return to assist in a confrontation with Indonesia over a disputed border with Borneo. Conscription had ended in Britain in 1960, and the Borneo confrontation was the first major operation in Malaysia by regular troops, often supported by the Special Air Service. Excellent leadership and first-rate UK, Gurkha, and Commonwealth troops deterred a major escalation, which—in the opinion of one senior participant—could easily have become another debacle like Vietnam.[32]

Malaya was an exception in the imperial recessional: it was a genuine communist revolt. That didn't stop the "Reds-under-the-bed" paranoia in many UK newspapers, most notably the *Daily Express* and the *Daily Telegraph*. Any instance of an African nationalist visiting Moscow or Beijing or showing the mildest interest in Marxism convinced some editorial writers that the whole empire (now Commonwealth) was under siege from the worldwide communist conspiracy.

The "emergency" in Kenya, which started in 1952 and continued until 1960, was definitely not a communist revolution. It was about a desire of some Kikuyus to regain their land by force from the white colonial settlers, a war of decolonization. But it was also a civil war between the Mau Mau rebels and the Kikuyu loyalists who supported the colonial administration. The alleged leader of Mau Mau, Jomo Kenyatta, was demonized by the British; many senior colonial officials thought they were in the presence of the devil when they dealt with him.[33] But the blood oaths and murder by machetes roused the media in Britain and prompted equally primitive reprisals by the colonial administration. Despite exaggerated reports of machetes in the night, the total figure for white settlers killed was thirty-two. In response, more than 1,000 Kikuyu were hanged, and perhaps 12,000 rebels were killed in police and army actions. Thousands more died in detention camps. Additionally, many atrocities associated with the police and army counterinsurgency units were hushed up. Missionaries protested, questions were asked in parliament (especially by Barbara Castle, a future Labour minister), and the left-wing press waged a campaign, but none of these actions ignited public interest. James Cameron, reporting for the *Daily Mirror*, saw among the settler community "the death of colonial liberalism, and the loss of the moral order that gave empire its only possible justification."[34]

Historically, the British boasted that their empire was uniquely benign in its mission to spread civilization and freedom, and that, unlike the French, their decolonization was dignified. This may have been largely true, but not in Kenya. Yet nearly fifty years passed before the real story emerged. Two recent authoritative studies (by David Anderson and Caroline Elkins) showed that Kenya was turned into a police state and that the number hanged, 1,090, was more than the number executed by the French in Algeria (though far fewer "disappearances" occurred in Kenya).[35] Far more were killed because of a routine culture of beatings, starvation, and torture. Alsatian dogs were used to terrify prisoners, and men were forced to sodomize one another. Racist savagery created a primitive psychopathology sometimes matching the Mau Mau abominations that were so regularly featured in conservative newspapers such as the *Daily Mail*. If Kenya was Britain's Algeria, London was nevertheless successful in easing the erstwhile devil into a pro-Western presidency of independent Kenya. President Kenyatta was equally eager to erase the past in the interests of national and pan-tribal unity. It was perhaps similar to South Africa's "truth and reconciliation," after 1994, but without the truth.[36] With some honorable exceptions such as James Cameron, journalists failed to expose this absent truth.

Britain continued to fight far more secret campaigns. In 1957 the Sultan of Oman asked Britain to help contain a rebellion in the great mountain massif known as Djebel Akhdar. This was post-Suez era, but nevertheless, Britain had long-established treaty obligations with Oman as well as a string of colonies and protectorates in the area, from Aden on Oman's border to Kuwait, Bahrain, Qatar, and the Trucial states north of Oman. All would perceive failure to support Oman as a further indication of British weakness. So a typically deniable British compromise was arranged: British army officers and NCOs were seconded to the Sultan's army. The RAF was quietly sent in as well.

The Djebel Akhdar campaign was clandestine, but the problems in nearby Aden were widely covered in the media. In the late 1950s, Aden was one of the busiest harbors in the world and a vital element of British security. By 1967 the most densely occupied quarter of Aden, Crater, had become a restricted area for British troops, even though London had promised to leave by the following year. Col. Dick Blenkinsop worked closely with the press in the final period of British rule. He said that the British press and the BBC were "extremely helpful. I found it was always enough to say, 'Gentlemen, I don't want you to repeat what I'm saying but let me bring you into the picture, off the record,' and I was never let down once."[37] As the tally of military deaths mounted, the British press transformed Lt. Col. Colin "Mad Mitch" Mitchell into something of a national hero because of the way he complained about "prowling journalists" and "squeamish politicians" who prevented him from "sorting out the Arabs."[38] Mad Mitch was told to wind in his neck by his superiors, and the British soon left. Far from sorting out the Arabs, the campaign was disaster for the departing empire. The Aden protectorate was renamed the People's Democratic Republic of Yemen and became a wholehearted Soviet satellite. The journalists who had been reporting British military failures in 1967 were now firmly kept out.

The British army also excluded the press—and parliament—from the top-secret five-year war fought in Dhofar in the 1970s. Three hundred officers and NCOs plus an eighty-strong SAS squadron fought in a territory the size of Wales in the western part of the Sultanate of Muscat and Oman. No pressmen were allowed in by the Sultan. And so the military thereafter liked to point out that this might have been a factor in winning the war, one of the few examples where a communist insurgency was decisively defeated.

## AMERICA'S WAR ON THE DOORSTEP

In December 1956, a small group of revolutionaries led by Fidel and Raul Castro and a young Argentinian doctor called "Che" Guevara landed in the south of Cuba. The band was soon dispersed by government forces. For two years the revolutionaries, through force of circumstances in the Sierra Maestra mountains, developed the concept of *foco* insurgency. Later developed in Guevara's book *Guerrilla Warfare*, it suggested that a dedicated armed revolutionary group could cause a shift in mass opinion, which would precipitate a social revolution. This foco theory was a handy shortcut for those who did not have the patience to engage in Mao's concepts of protracted war. Moreover, it could perhaps work in cities in the West, not just in Third World jungles or bush. The vital qualities were moral rather than ideological.

Fidel Castro was a romantic socialist. Only after he had taken power in the face of extremely hostile U.S. opposition did he become a hero of communism. In his time in the mountains, Fidel Castro offered the *New York Times* exclusive rights to cover his revolution. Soon television crews were clamoring to film the long-haired wild bunch. One CBS investigative reporter, Robert Taber, stuck with Castro throughout the fighting and later produced a minor classic on guerrilla warfare, *War of the Flea*.[39] The pro-American dictator of Cuba, Fulgencio Batista, sent more and more troops into the Sierra Maestra and many defected to the rebels. On January 1, 1959, Castro's army entered Havana.

A photograph or poster of Che soon became compulsory in nearly every European student's bedroom, as the Cuban revolution promised to spread, especially in Latin America. An American economic blockade and a failed U.S.-sponsored invasion pushed Castro further into the arms of the USSR. Another photograph, this time from a U-2 spy plane, showing the construction of Soviet missile sites in Cuba, pushed the two superpowers to the brink of a nuclear war in October 1962. In the U.S. perspective, Moscow blinked and pulled back. Dramatic TV aerial shots of the Soviet ships approaching and then stopping at the U.S.-imposed "quarantine" line around Cuba captured an attentive and anxious worldwide audience.

The Cuban war established a romantic guerrilla legend that many tried, and failed, to imitate. Guevara himself died in the Bolivian jungle in 1967. Rural guerrilla insurgencies did spread to Guatemala, Venezuela, Colombia, and Nicaragua, with varying degrees of success. The concept of the urban guerrilla became fashionable, especially in Western Europe, inspired by the theories of Carlos Marighela: that gangster-like action in the cities—bank robberies and kidnappings—could provoke the government into repressive countermeasures that in turn would antagonize and mobilize the people. Governments, however, often proved effective in labeling would-be urban guerrillas as mere "terrorists." This happened in Uruguay where the Tupamaros, after initial popular success with their

Robin Hood tactics, were crushed, not least by a massive swing of public opinion to the right. In the words of a French writer and sometime revolutionary, Régis Debray, the insurgents had become "the gravediggers of liberal Uruguay."[40]

Nevertheless, the lives and works of revolutionaries such as Guevara and Debray, as well as Franz Fanon, a doctor from Martinique who wrote *The Wretched of the Earth*, had a profound influence on literature and journalism, especially on the left. The arch apostle of the New Left revolutionaries was Herbert Marcuse, a philosophy professor based in California, who encouraged disaffected students to apply Guevara's teaching to the streets of the West rather than the jungles of the Third World.

Other insurgencies in Latin America inspired numerous headlines later, especially the revolution in Nicaragua and the U.S.-backed counterrevolution of the 1980s. The funding of the Contras created at least two major scandals. The Iran–Contra affair of 1986 and 1987 rocked the Reagan administration. Secondly, in 1996 Gary Webb wrote in the *San Jose Mercury News* a three-part series, "Dark Alliance" (later made into a book), which linked CIA support of the Contras to the distribution of crack cocaine in Los Angeles.[41] Amid the national furor and attacks from major national newspapers, the *Mercury News* backed away from the story, and Webb's career as a mainstream journalist was ended.

But the financial and drug scandals in the 1980s and 1990s media were light-years away from the ideological passions of the New Left in the 1960s. The media stars of the "alternative society" are now almost forgotten: Stokely Carmichael, Eldridge Cleaver, Angela Davis, Abbie Hoffman, Timothy Leary, and Jerry Rubin, to name but six. The radicals in the 1960s student movements and the left-wing media in Europe and the United States were soon to coalesce on one issue that has not been forgotten: Vietnam.

## VIETNAM

Vietnam utterly polluted contemporary military-media relations by creating a myth that the media lost the war. Especially in the United States, the military credo for officers became "duty, honor, country, and hate the media."[42] Much of the argument hinges on the coverage of the 1968 Tet offensive, a major military defeat, but an accidental propaganda triumph, for the North Vietnamese and Viet Cong. The reporting was to leave

an ineradicable grievance in the US military mind against the lies, incompetence and self-seeking ambition of journalists in particular and the media in general. It remains to this day. In the words of one Vietnam veteran: "We lost the war at Tet. When those lying sons of bitches showed American boys fighting and dying in Saigon and Hue. . . . Hell, what did they expect real combat looked like? A cat fight in the ladies' room? But they never showed what was happening to the VC [Viet Cong] in the [Hue] Citadel and what they were doing to those Vietnam civilians. They never explained just how we was whuppin' those NVA [North Vietnamese Army] bastards' ass. . . . I'll never, ever, trust the press again. . . . They lied."[43]

Much of the current debate about media power is founded on the assertion that television lost the Vietnam war. The Tet Offensive, however, was mounted by the North Vietnamese and Viet Cong, not CBS. Journalists do not lose wars, even though the PR–media–marketing strategy may often be a vital ingredient in starting and even sometimes in winning them. No matter how streetwise public affairs specialists might be, if democratic governments are losing a war, or have just lost one, war correspondents—blinkered as they may be sometimes—will eventually notice. More importantly, so will the voters at home.

The Vietnam War, like the Iraq War of 2003, was fought without understanding anything about the country beyond a few clichés.[44] Americans simply did not comprehend the Vietnamese peasantry in their "black pajamas," and they certainly underestimated them. The harder Americans attempted to win this war, the more injury, disruption, and chaos it brought to a society that had a long tradition of repelling foreign invaders. Washington did not grasp the complexities. When it started to, frustration set in, and eventually the public demanded to get out, under a fiction of "peace with honor." The cultural gap was immense, not least because of foreigners' bewilderment with the Vietnamese language. The sung vowels and glottal stops were, according to the one correspondent, "like listening to ducks fucking."[45] As Daniel Ellsberg, of Pentagon Papers' fame, once put it, "No American in Washington or Saigon could have passed a term paper on Vietnamese history" at the start of the war.[46] Despite this cultural ignorance

the United States dispatched its greatest ever land army to Vietnam, and dropped the greatest tonnage of bombs in the history of warfare, and pursued a military strategy deliberately designed to force millions of people to abandon their homes, and used chemicals in a manner which profoundly changed the environmental and genetic order, leaving a once bountiful land petrified.[47]

That was veteran Australian journalist John Pilger's take on the war. Another old hand, Richard Beeston of the London *Daily Telegraph*, tried to explain in his memoirs the reasons for the war:

> Shortly before leaving Vietnam I met a rather drunk CIA agent, who was a specialist in Indochina. "What the f*** are we doing here?" he said over a bottle of scotch. "This is a civil war between the North and the South that's been going on for centuries, it's nothing to do with us." How about the "Domino Theory"— the then fashionable theory that an American pull-out would deliver South-east Asia to the communist bloc—I asked. "It's all a load of balls," he replied. "The moment we leave here, China and the Soviets will be at each other's throats." He was absolutely right—but no one was listening.[48]

How important was the war to U.S. security, and could it have been won at an acceptable cost? Those questions have inspired thousands of learned tomes since the war ended in 1975. Was the war a deliberate crime or merely a catastrophic mistake? The Donald Rumsfeld of his day, Robert S. McNamara, has contributed a number of belated mea culpas.[49] Others have suggested that the war could have been ended earlier or that it could it have been fought more forcefully, or that the final years were not the military disaster often described.[50] And yet the best insight into the war is still to be found in the gonzo classic, Michael Herr's *Dispatches*. Here he is describing some of the hard men sitting around the bar of the Rex in Saigon:

> This is where they asked you, "Are you a Dove or a Hawk?" and "Would you rather fight them here or in Pasadena?" *Maybe we could beat them in Pasadena,* I'd think, but I wouldn't say it, especially not here where they knew that I knew that really they weren't fighting anybody anywhere anyway, it made them pretty touchy. That night I listened while a colonel explained the war in terms of protein. We were a nation of high-protein, meat-eating hunters, while the other guys just ate rice and a few grungy fish heads. We were going to club him to death with our meat; what could you say except, "Colonel, you're insane"? It was like turning up in the middle of some black loony tune where the Duck had all the lines.[51]

Vietnam hosted at the war's height up to 1,000 senior war correspondents and many would-be reporters. The prevailing view has been that Vietnam was a media free-for-all and that enterprising journalists used this freedom to crusade against an arrogant civil-military elite's unwinnable war. In reality the South Vietnamese applied censorship and American self-censorship abounded, practiced not least by editors in Washington and New York. Above all, journalists, especially in the United States, generally supported the mindlessly optimistic authorized version of the U.S. government. Pulitzer Prize–winner Philip Caputo, in his memoirs *Means of Escape*, used the phrase "Great American Delusion Machine." As Peter Arnett, later a correspondent for the Cable News Network (CNN) and also Pulitzer Prize–winner, summed it up: "Supporting the official American policy of concealment was the politically repressive Vietnamese regime that was distrustful of all comers, and all too willing to bully and intimidate the foreign press."[52] Arnett also quoted a colleague who suggested that the censorship was worse than the Kremlin's.[53] It is true that free transport, usually by helicopters, was often readily available. Indeed, the chopper crews were often lionized by the media. It was this access that prompted Max Hastings to comment: "The Americans may not tell you the truth, but they provide the means for you to go and find out the truth for yourself, if you can be bothered."[54]

Until the Tet Offensive, the vast majority of Western correspondents backed the Cold War strategy of the conflict, though they questioned, sometimes, the tactical means to achieve victory. Even after Tet, when many foreign correspondents became much more skeptical, they did not conspire to dethrone the U.S. military. By instinct, journalists do cock-ups, not conspiracies. The profession is too anarchic and sometimes too inebriated to spawn effective mass organizers. Few outside journalism can comprehend just how competitive top correspondents are. Even the best and the brightest in Vietnam spent much of their time squabbling with one another. Associated Press, for example, was locked in bitter ground combat with United Press International. And Saigon's increasingly cynical resident press corps waged a silent and sullen war against their usually more hawkish colleagues and editors safe in newsrooms back home.

After 1968, television criticism of the war intensified, especially after the great Walter Cronkite famously lamented during Tet, "But I thought we were supposed to be winning." This led President Lyndon Johnson to confess; "If I've lost Cronkite, I have lost the war." Cronkite's own statement was classically moderate: "We did our best; we must get out."[55] Yet such criticisms tended to *follow* and *echo* the breakdown of political consensus in Washington. Moreover, quality newspapers probably had more direct impact on policymaking elites than television did.[56] Television did not lose Vietnam, but many U.S. decision-makers, especially in the military, *believed* it did.

In the longer perspective, it is the iconic still photographs that have been scorched into the collective memory. A Buddhist priest, Tich Quang Duc, burned himself to death in June 1963 to act as a catalyst for change. History did not disappoint him. On February 1, 1968, Eddie Adams, a thirty-five-year-old AP correspondent, caught the instant Brigadier Gen. Nguyen Ngoc Loan put a gun to the head of a young prisoner and pulled the trigger. It won Adams a Pulitzer. On June 8, 1972 came the pictures by Nick Ut of AP that broke the hearts of the most hardened war correspondents: young children running with their flesh alight after South Vietnamese aircraft had mistakenly napalmed the village of Trang Bang. Some of the best photographs of the war were captured by a cantankerous and garrulous Welshman, Philip Jones Griffiths, who wrote and designed the famous book *Vietnam Inc.*, published in 1971.[57] Photographers won prizes and many, such as Tim Page who worked for *Time* and *Life*, became addicted to war, but they also paid a high price. Early in the war, on October 18, 1965, Dickey Chapelle was killed by a landmine, the first American female photographer to be killed in action. She was given the last rites by a kneeling chaplain. She wore, as usual, small pearl earrings, and there was a flower in the band of her bush hat. After experiencing many wars, her last words were reported as "I guess it was bound to happen."[58]

Vietnam may have been called the first "television war," but television played a relatively small part in deciding its outcome. Possibly the still photographs explained more. Perhaps the war was not entirely explicable. As Michael Herr suggested, conventional journalism could no more reveal this war than conventional firepower could win it. He called it "a communications pudding." And this was a deliberate policy of the U.S. government's public relations campaign. Herr said:

> At each stage of the escalation, the United States tried either flatly to deny what it was doing or to minimize the effects or to conceal the results behind a torrent of questionable statistics, a bewildering range of euphemisms, and a vocabulary of specially created words that debased the English language.[59]

The American military found it hard to understand why journalists, although by and large sympathetic, would not treat Vietnam as they had World War II and the Korean Conflict. The war corroded the reputation of both professions. Journalists often fell prey to racist stereotypes and failed to uncover the massive corruption endemic in U.S. support for Saigon.

Indeed, some journalists were accused of being black marketers themselves, especially regarding foreign currency transactions. And they backpedaled too: Arnett admits that it would have been "professional suicide" for journalists in AP to have suggested that the North Vietnamese opposition was generally superbly trained and well-motivated to believe in their revolutionary cause. Good and honest journalists such as Arnett were effectively dissuaded by home-based editors that it was best to ignore the fact that the conflict was in many respects a civil war, not just one of U.S. technology versus communist ideology.[60] In-country journalists made some major mistakes, including missing stories such as the My Lai massacre, which was picked up by a diligent home reporter.

Yet a few journalists established durable reputations in Vietnam by proving that government and military personnel alike lied to the correspondents, perhaps deliberately or because they were deceiving themselves. David Halberstam won a Pulitzer in 1964 for his reporting. Like Neil Sheehan, he followed the charismatic Lt. Col. (later a "civilian general") John Paul Vann into action. Halberstam came home and wrote a classic book, *The Best and Brightest.*[61]

Sheehan worked for UPI and then the *New York Times.* His diligent journalism won him many admirers, not least in the U.S. Army. Such was his reputation that military analyst Daniel Ellsberg decided to entrust his famous *Pentagon Papers* to him. Ellsberg, an ex-Marine, was highly placed in the Pentagon. In 1969, he came across a 7,000-page top-secret history of the war going back to the initial U.S. involvement. He was appalled at the mendacity of the public position on the war and became convinced that his country was wrong to continue waging it. Over the years he photocopied the papers. In March 1971, he decided to entrust the papers to Vann. Their secret meeting went awry, and Ellsberg turned to Sheehan. Their decision to publish led them and the *New York Times* (and *Washington Post*) to the Supreme Court, where they were vindicated. Later Sheehan wrote a bestseller, *A Bright Shining Lie: John Paul Vann and America in Vietnam.*

Other correspondents such as James Cameron went to Hanoi. So too did the most famous American antiwar intellectual, Noam Chomsky. They both wrote intense accounts of the suffering and courage they saw there. But the overall accusation embedded in military folklore—the so-called guilty media thesis—has shown to be wrong-headed. To summarize one recent and persuasive analysis of the debate, "The notion of a feckless, irresponsible and oppositional media is therefore misplaced."[62] Another authoritative study succinctly suggested that the media "reflected public opinion rather than formed it."[63] As the war worsened, the U.S. military became more obstructive and administered "news with an eye-dropper."[64] But the extent of U.S. casualties could not be hidden. Whereas in the Korean War, television was in its infancy, by the Vietnam War, casualties were shown on the nightly news. With both the Korean and Vietnam conflicts, public support dropped when casualties mounted. The collapse of the will to fight in Vietnam resulted from "a political process in which the media were only one part."[65] The editors and op-ed writers in the United States shifted along with their constituency and source of authoritative information, the government.[66] As befits a mature democracy, there is evidence that from the beginning of the war, whatever the efforts of the press or the government, the American public made up its own mind.[67]

The U.S. military returned home but not as heroes. Those most emotionally bound to the failed U.S. policy fixed their anger on the most visible elements of the society that had rejected them: the media. In 2006 Britain's leading military historian, Sir John Keegan, still subscribed to the guilty media thesis in Vietnam and warned that it might happen again over Iraq.[68] The Vietnam/Iraq debate has rekindled all the old wounds, although there are obvious differences. Nevertheless, by 2007, four years after the impressive military victory in Iraq that toppled Saddam Hussein, America was again preoccupied with an unwinnable war, started on false pretences and with little cultural understanding of the country it was occupying. Despite mounting casualties, atrocities, and no clear exit strategy, so far, this time, the media has not borne the brunt of blame. Perhaps this is because it has not replicated President Nixon's infamous claim that the Vietnam War was "the first in our history during which our media were more friendly to our enemies than to our allies." Nixon of course would say that, given that his own downfall was precipitated by the famous investigative journalism of the *Washington Post* that exposed the Watergate scandal.

## THE EMPIRE STRIKES BACK

On March 19, 1982, a detachment of Argentinean soldiers posing as scrap-metal dealers raised their country's flag on the uninhabited rocky island of South Georgia in the South Atlantic Ocean. They sparked a conflict that proved to be a watershed in the military-media relationship. Although Argentineans previously had no claims over the sovereignty of South Georgia, they took Britain's nonreaction as a signal to launch, two weeks later, a full-scale invasion of the adjacent islands, which they claimed as their own Malvinas. With 1,800 islanders involved in a change of regime they did not want, the British government, led by Margaret Thatcher, proved determined to retake the Falkland Islands by force if necessary.

The UN condemned the Argentinean action and had the justification for doing so from the international community—despite centuries of disputes over the islands' true sovereign owners.

It was the last war in which the military could guarantee control over the flow of information going into and out of a theater of operations. The media problems of the war also caught the UK Ministry of Defence (MoD) by surprise, and anything that could remotely be described as its media "policy" was more backward- than forward-looking, deriving from an age of secrecy and operational security rather than proactive media relations. This was personified by the MoD's spokesman, Ian MacDonald, whose briefings in London earned him the nickname of "The Speak-Your-Weight Machine."

As for the war itself, fought 8,000 miles from Britain, the rapidly assembled task force somewhat reluctantly took with it twenty-nine correspondents and their support crews. They were all British; the foreign media were to be supplied with news by the Reuters correspondent. One of the reporters, Robert Fox, described the information and press policy as "chaotic,"[69] while the MoD subsequently admitted that there was a "degree of improvisation about all the arrangements."[70] Although this was largely because of the speed with which the task force was assembled, the navy retained its wariness of dealing with the press. The army had learned through its Northern Ireland experience that it could forge a working relationship with reporters; the navy relented only under pressure from 10 Downing Street.[71]

As the task force sailed south, it was clear that many people doubted the outbreak of an actual war. *Time* magazine published an incredulous cover under the headline, "The Empire Strikes Back." Indeed, the traveling correspondents took little with them. They had been chosen by their editors because they had either simply been available or because they were only expecting a "boating holiday."[72] Although many did become quite famous subsequently—Brian Hanrahan and Robert Fox, for example—the reaction to those selected by the military was "what the hell do they know about war?"[73] They were given the *Green Book*, the MoD handbook for media operations based on World War I guidelines and hence woefully out of date. This in itself revealed how seriously the British military regarded media relations at the time, perhaps because it had become so accustomed to patriotic media coverage of its activities. The hacks were then allocated to ships where the attitude toward them varied greatly according to the prejudice of the senior staff. Officially, there was no censorship, merely "guidelines" as to what they could and could not report to which they had to adhere as part of their accreditation. The no-go areas related largely to OPSEC (Operational Security) matters, such as troop sizes and locations, equipment capabilities, and so on. For the most part, the journalists cooperated: this was epitomized by Hanrahan's famous report of Harrier aircraft returning from a mission with the words: "I counted them all out and I counted them all back."[74] However, two of the most infamous breaches of security—often recounted in staff colleges as an example of how the media cannot be trusted—were the result of leaks from troops and officials rather than the media. The loss of two Wessex helicopters on South Georgia became public only when a young sailor on HMS *Antrim* wrote about it in a letter home,[75] and the BBC's broadcast in advance of the Goose Green Operation was possible only because an MoD official in London had told about it. Other information came from "armchair strategists" in the UK. This was usually lucky or clever speculation and had nothing to do with any leaks from the corralled journalists in theater.

Aboard the ships, the reporters found that they had military "minders" allocated to them. These public relations officers had traditionally been regarded as having dead-end careers, effectively going nowhere in the military. Not only was the media suspicious of them but often their military comrades had little time for them. While the minders saw their own role as "security review," the press saw them as censors, and other soldiers saw them as colluding with the media.

The war took place just before the age of portable satellite communications equipment; task force reporters were completely dependent on the military for communicating their copy and images back to Britain. Additionally, the task force was dependent on U.S. satellite technology for its intelligence gathering and communications with London. The reporters, however, were clearly quite low down the priority order for use of the military communications systems, especially television images requiring high bandwidth. The navy insisted that live television coverage was impossible owing to technical reasons, so the reporters were forced to send their dispatches and tapes to Ascension Island before being flown on to London, which could take as many as three weeks. Indeed, one ITN report took longer to reach London in 1982 than Russell's dispatches from the Crimea 130 years earlier. Most reports of the war's events went public days or even weeks after the event and not, in fact, "as they happened." And it is sobering to reflect that the eventual surrender of the Argentineans at Port Stanley went "completely unrecorded" by the media.[76] As Robert Harris noted, "for the bulk of the Falklands war, the camera might as well not have been invented."[77]

When words or images did reach London, they were subjected to a second scrutiny at the MoD. Further delays caused further tension. Indeed, because the Argentineans had allowed their reporters to accompany their troops, both the BBC and ITN, starved of current images from their own reporters, broadcast "enemy" footage—causing the Thatcher government to fume. This in turn reflects how much warfare was on the cusp of a new information age. The unique nature of this particular war may have enabled Adm. Sandy Woodward to conduct his campaign to retake the Falklands within a virtual information vacuum from the media's point of view, yet beyond the theater of operations news was getting out via Argentina and feeding the global village. But old-fashioned values still prevailed in London. Prime Minister Thatcher even objected to BBC reports referring to the "Argentineans" rather than the "enemy," and she considered using reports from "enemy" television stations as unprofessional conduct.

Back with the task force, any attempts by reporters to remain impartial were proving difficult after weeks of spending time aboard ships with the men who faced the possibility of death in combat. One reporter noticed that "I began by saying 'the British' and within a few weeks I was [saying] 'us' or 'we.'"[78] This kind of bonding is perhaps inevitable in such circumstances, but the lesson was not lost on the MoD when planning media access for future campaigns. Reporters accompanying troops for prolonged periods soon begin to identify with them. As Robert Fox testified: "If the Argentineans had shown any sign of counter-attacking and overrunning our positions . . . I would have grabbed the nearest weapon to hand and used my limited knowledge to make it fire back."[79] This kind of statement causes fury in journalism ranks, but it is difficult for those who have not served as war reporters to understand the pressures that frontline reporters face when they accompany military personnel into war— especially if the war is popular as this one was, with around 80 percent support in Britain. Back home, the tabloids in particular reflected this public support with excessive headlines such as "Up Yours Galtieri!" and "Argie Bargy." Perhaps the most infamous of all was the *Sun*'s headline over the report of the sinking of the *Belgrano*: "Gotcha!" This seemed heartless in light of the fact that almost a thousand Argentinean sailors drowned in the sinking. When questions were asked about this in the House of Commons, the government stated that the ship was sunk because it was steaming toward the task force, which subsequently turned out to be untrue. Twenty years later, Martin Howard, director-general of communications at the MoD at the time, commented on the episode:

> On some occasions, the thing to do is just simply say, "We don't know." It's very hard for government departments to say "we

don't know" because it sounds as if we don't know what we are talking about, but that is very frequently the reality of the situation. The second thing is to correct things which have been said and which turn out to be wrong . . . the information given to us [about the *Belgrano*], by the naval staff, at the time was, quite honestly, wrong. It was used as an answer to a PQ [parliamentary question] and as a result became part of the accepted wisdom. The Government made a huge mistake there, because when it was discovered in fact that the *Belgrano* hadn't been steaming towards the task force, what should have happened is that a minister should have gone to the House of Commons and said, "Sorry, the information was duff, but it actually made no difference—it was a threat to the task force and we were justified in sinking it."[80]

This was partly because the news operation was centered in London rather than in the field. As a result, news reports were bound to become caught up in Whitehall bureaucracy and Westminster politics.

The politics of the Thatcher government had set the tone for the nationalistic media coverage that followed. The Falkland Islanders, hitherto forgotten and recently made British citizens (albeit second-class ones) under the 1981 Nationality Act, were suddenly portrayed in terms of national self-determination against a brutal invasion by a fascist dictatorship. The prime minister talked of "British sovereign territory . . . invaded by a foreign power . . . unprovoked aggression by Argentina against British sovereign territory . . . not a shred of justification, and not a scrap of legality."[81] Four days later, the *Sun* was referring to "a black moment in our history . . . a wound we cannot forget. But now our troops are on the way to wipe out that memory and free our loyal friends."[82] The Falkland Island sheep farmers became "British bulldogs" defiantly resisting their "criminal" invaders with such songs as "Land of Hope and Glory."

Having established the "just war" tone for the coverage, the lack of timely news from the theater of operation, along with the censorship arrangements, meant that "hard news" about the war's progress was lacking. Setbacks, such as the sinking of HMS *Sheffield*, could be minimized in such a news-starved, speculation-rich environment. Sir Frank Cooper, the undersecretary of state for defense at the MoD, told a post-war enquiry into the media "coverage": "You will never have it easier than the Falklands. There is no doubt about that."[83]

The war was a disaster for the British media; it was also an intelligence fiasco.[84] The Ministry of Defence, especially the Defence Intelligence

Staff, blamed the Foreign Office—"that hotbed of cold feet" was the memorable expression used. Added to the infighting in Whitehall and between government and the civil service, many disputes within the armed forces abounded. The media also fought among themselves—the navy started calling the onboard reporters the "fourth form."[85] The problems of communications over 8,000 miles, abused by the MoD's censors, plus the restraints of the correspondents' self-censorship and often gung-ho patriotism, created a very one-sided coverage of the conflict. The task force journalists felt that they had been misled by the MoD, but a general coalition of the willing emerged: military, media, and government immersed themselves in a patriotic desire to win. Opposition in the UK was generally drowned out or ignored.[86]

Despite, or perhaps because of, the British casualties caused at the battle of Goose Green by unnecessary political intervention, the Ten Weeks War proved a massive vote winner for Prime Minister Thatcher.[87] The correspondents' anger at the MoD was, therefore, somewhat misplaced. "The MoD achieved *exactly* what its political masters wanted it to do, and its role in the Falklands campaign will go down in the history of journalism as the classic example of how to manage the media in wartime."[88] And many in the media, especially at home in London, connived with the MoD to wave the flag. "If it was rape," concluded Phillip Knightley, "then it was rape with contributory negligence."[89]

Perhaps the sole example of reporting that had unintended political consequences was the Argentinean coverage of the Royal Marines surrendering at the outset of the invasion. The prisoners were forced to lie on their stomachs on the road outside Government House in the capital, Stanley. When the photographs were published in the UK, they provoked outrage—ending the possibility of a negotiated settlement.

The war established the reputation of one correspondent above all—Max Hastings—the first reporter to reach Port Stanley. In his memoirs he wrote: "No big feature film has ever been made about the Falklands war, because the imperialists won and no Americans took part."[90] The Americans, however, played a key intelligence role in the war. Initially Washington appeared to side with the Argentinean junta, which it was wooing in its campaigns against left-wing insurgencies in South America, especially in Nicaragua. Eventually the special relationship, particularly between Ronald Reagan and Margaret Thatcher, kicked in, and vital satellite and munitions data were passed to London. But most crucially the American military became intrigued by the media lessons of the war. The Falklands was an atypical colonial-style war fought at the ends of the earth. It was short and, for Britain, successful. Above all, the UK MoD had a communications monopoly over the British correspondents. The Pentagon decided that Britannia had waived the rules as far as the lessons of Vietnam were concerned. Next time, Washington would fight according to the new Falklands rulebook.

## GRENADA, PANAMA, AND HAITI

American forces invaded Grenada in 1983 and Panama in 1989 on the grounds that elements in those countries had threatened U.S. lives, endangered Washington because of the expansion of communism (Grenada) or drug trafficking (Panama), and were generally not practicing democracy. The reasons were largely spurious, but the issue here is the political decision to exclude, censor, and manipulate the media during these examples of closed expeditionary warfare.

Like the Falklands, Grenada was relatively remote and lacked a sophisticated media infrastructure. Grenada was also a former British colony, which had gained independence within the British Commonwealth in 1974. Neither London nor White House spokespersons were informed of the invasion. Prime Minister Thatcher refrained from public criticism, mindful of her recent debt to President Reagan during her own military adventure.

The United States launched Operation Urgent Fury on October 25, 1983. The military were allowed almost complete exclusion of the media, both American and foreign, especially in the first few days after the invasion. Under the guise of a multinational operation (including 300 troops from Caribbean states who saw no action), the United States deployed overwhelming strength against the lightly armed Grenadian forces, which numbered about 1,000. At the UN, U.S. Ambassador Jean Kirkpatrick fulminated about Grenada's secret military deals with North Korea, Cuba, and the USSR. In fact, some largely unfit and relatively old Cuban construction workers on the island did put up a good fight during a U.S. operation that was largely a fiasco, though few correspondents could attest to that because of the news blackout. Years passed before the full story seeped out, but at the time military stills and video gave the impression of a new efficient American military, which had fully recovered from the traumas of Vietnam.

On the second day, despite an official "quarantine" of the island, enterprising journalists hired boats and landed to attempt independent coverage, but they were intercepted and transported to the U.S. flagship, the USS *Guam*, for their "own protection." On the third day, the military accepted the first press pool, which was soon expanded but still heavily controlled. The number of journalists eventually reached more than 300, but "by that time the fighting was over and there was nothing to report except the fact that they had not been able to report."[91] The media also resorted to amateur radio operators in the region, but the military jammed the frequencies.

Journalists complained about the military operating a "mad dog and pony show."[92] Some television stations, when using military footage, used the superimposed caption "cleared by the Defense Department" to imply censorship. That was more than the UK MoD allowed in the Falklands: the term "censorship" had been censored on UK broadcasts. Nevertheless, Grenada was a public relations triumph, and initial U.S. opinion polls indicated that the public supported the post-Vietnam restrictions on the media. The only legal challenge to the media restrictions came shortly after the invasion from an unlikely source: Larry Flynt, publisher of the pornographic *Hustler* magazine.[93] There followed eventually a movie (*The People vs. Larry Flynt*, 1996) that touched on the case, though in 1984, a court case had already ruled that restrictions on the press in theater were the responsibility of the military commanders in the field.[94] The military's perspective emerged in more traditional terms in the 1986 Clint Eastwood film, *Heartbreak Ridge*.

The patriotic surge and controlled media manipulation of the invasion of Grenada, cynics alleged, may well have been timed to drown out the bad news from Lebanon. Two days before the invasion, Hezbollah insurgents drove a truck loaded with explosives directly at the U.S. Marine Corps barracks at Beirut airport, killing 241 Marines and sailors. The French were also hit: seventy-one French troops died. British sentries stopped the truck aimed at their base, and no British casualties ensued. Photographs of the American disaster were circulated around the world. Grenada, however, boosted Ronald Regan's domestic approval rating.

Just as the Falklands media fiasco prompted the Franks Report in the UK, the American media criticism also prompted a report by Maj. Gen. Winant Sidle (ret.) that recommended a continuously updated accredited pool system, proper communications for media use, and transport to, and within, theater for the correspondents. The military realized that exclusion and media monopoly worked effectively only for a short time and in conditions of rapid U.S. success. Although the Sidle report was generally welcomed by the media it would lead to much greater control, under the cover of apparent access via pooling. Control of the pool led eventually to the "embedding" principle and to manipulation in longer and far less successful wars.

On December 20, 1989, 24,000 U.S. troops invaded Panama to remove a former CIA "asset," Gen. Manuel Noriega. He had been demonized by the U.S. government as a drug dealer on a massive scale, providing official protection for the growing, processing, and transportation of drugs into the United States.[95] Noriega was also accused of nullifying elections and democracy, as well as threatening the lives of U.S. citizens. The U.S. claimed the right under the existing Torrijos–Carter treaties to intervene militarily to protect the canal. Sidle's work was completely sidelined in the invasion, dubbed Operation Just Cause, Washington's biggest military operation since Vietnam, as news was controlled by exclusion and manipulation. The Pentagon's aim was to portray the war as clean, swift, and efficient—to create, in the words of a British academic, an "illusion of bloodless battlefields."[96] Again, the selected pool hacks, as well as senior public affairs specialists in the military, were kept out of the loop. Accredited journalists who accompanied the military were cooped up and soon sent home. "William Boot" defined the Defense Department pool as "a select group of combat journalists that is never permitted to see combat."[97]

The military achieved its aim: the media were silenced and the administration had apparently met its real goal—the security of the crucial Panama Canal Zone, with its bases, installations, and, of course, its canal. A few hours after the invasion began, Guillermo Endara, who would probably have won the elections nullified earlier in the year, was sworn in as president. Much of Latin America criticized the United States, accusing it of wanting to reestablish military bases and even renege entirely on Torrijos–Carter treaties whereby the administration of the canal had to be returned to the Panamanian government on December 31, 1999. From the U.S. perspective, the security of the canal had been restored (and Washington fulfilled its treaty obligations in full and on time).

The combat was over quickly and Congress, except for Democratic stalwarts such as Edward Kennedy, was silenced. The publicity triumph stalled, however, once the media managed to get into Panama. First, Noriega had not been captured. Instead he retreated to the papal nunciature in Panama City. U.S. forces laid siege and, under the orders of Gen. "Mad Max" Thurman, "they bombarded the embassy with loud and violent rock music including songs with messages such as "Nowhere to run" and "I fought the law and the law won."[98] Noriega was believed to be an opera buff who hated pop music. Other embassies were besieged and diplomatic rights violated. Then the invasion was revealed to have been rather less bloodless than depicted by the Pentagon. Spanish-language newspapers report that up to 400 civilians had been killed and 2,000 wounded. Photographs of the destruction emerged. The "cocaine" reportedly found in Noriega's quarters proved to be talcum powder. The disclosures got worse; Gen. Colin Powell, the chairman of the Joint Chiefs of Staff, admitted: "The Press ate us alive, with some justification."[99] But General Powell was wrong—what mattered was the initial impression of the invasion—successful and bloodless. That had been the headline news on TV. The truth, dribbling out over months on the inside pages of newspapers, mattered far less, especially once U.S. troops returned to their bases. Another inquiry followed (the Hoffman Report) the following year, but that too was sidelined.

The invasions of Grenada and Panama were to prove practice runs for the Gulf War of 1991. The strategy for media management was clear: secrecy in planning; demonization of the enemy; destabilization of the target; search for legitimacy; build up and deployment; and declaration of victory, rapid pull out, and the truth to filter out slowly thereafter. In this process, the media were to be used where appropriate. Even the trusted and vetted pool correspondents were to be excluded from planning but would be useful in demonization. Noriega was lambasted in the U.S. press: he was called everything from a child molester and sexual deviant and Satanist to, inevitably, a latter-day Hitler. The target country would be softened up by economic sanctions and other pressures. And the media could then be used again in the search for legitimacy. While diplomats worked on the UN, the American media could help woo friendly states. Once the war was won, journalists' infamous short attention would soon move elsewhere and leave deeper investigation to reporters such as John Pilger, who remains critical of the manipulation of mainstream journalism. The strategy would vary slightly according to the geographical and political factors, but what remained constant was a "secret agenda by the military and government to ensure maximum exclusion and containment of the media, while paying lip service to the public's right to know and the duty of the media to keep them informed," according to one definitive analysis of military-media relations.[100]

As experience in Vietnam indicated, and Grenada confirmed, American-based journalists had a remarkable tendency to accept government information as basic truth rather than consider its strategic value as propaganda, as happened in Grenada (and to a lesser extent Panama). In 1983 the faction with the Reagan administration that advocated a strict control of the media prevailed.[101] In 1983 there had been muted Democratic Party attacks of the invasion, but by 1989 President George H. W. Bush won bipartisan support in Washington for his actions in Panama. It is true that the wind-down of the Cold War allowed the United States, as the only effective superpower, to act more aggressively and more unilaterally. But a more important factor was probably the Democrats' increasing desire to seem less soft on defense and foreign policy issues in a period of Republican dominance. It has been argued that just one segment of the electorate was crucial: Southern swing voters, who favored a hawkish posture. Without these votes the Democrats could not recapture the White House.[102]

Both major U.S. political parties soon found Cold War hawkishness defunct. But the government once more used old-fashioned methods on its own doorstep, in Haiti in 1994. The country had witnessed, 200 years earlier, the only successful slave revolt in history and then became the world's first black republic. In 1991, the Haitian military overthrew democratically elected President Jean-Bertrand Aristide. U.S. propaganda had previously painted the former priest as a Marxist psychopath, but soon he was transformed into a latter-day champion of civil rights because Washington liked the military junta even less. President Bill Clinton decided to restore democracy, though his action may have been motivated by cutting the flood of Haitian refugees into the United States. The usual tactics were employed: demonization, the search for legitimacy, and destabilization via sanctions. After the softening up would come the application of force. The Marines had invaded before, in 1915, and stayed for nineteen years. Washington later backed the voodoo-expert tyrant, Francois "Papa Doc" Duvalier, and subsequently his son, Jean-Claude, presumably because— for all their faults—they were at least not communists like Castro. Prior to the 1994 UN-sanctioned invasion, U.S. military psychological operations (PSYOPS) teams had been stationed on the island and were known to have sent information to the American media as well. This enabled American television news crews to anticipate the invasion and so reach the island before the troops. The threat that news sources could transmit the invasion live spurred the Pentagon to establish some guidelines, but the TV networks had the upper hand. They were already in Haiti and could not be excluded. The disorganized, ill-equipped Haitian troops were not prepared to offer resistance, and the Americans landed almost completely unopposed. This was an easy victory for the Pentagon in a no-risk war, and the media got their pictures. Haiti's politics remained much the same as before, and Aristide was ousted, with U.S. help, ten years later.[103]

## END OF HISTORY?

In 1989 popular efforts brought revolution to Eastern Europe and to Western television screens. "Parliament on the streets" prompted the non-violent "Velvet Revolution" in Czechoslovakia, the collapse of the Berlin Wall, and the bloody events that ended Romania's dictatorship by Nicolae Ceausescu. Similar and simultaneous "people power" events in Brazil and Chile (in defiance of American interests) received minimal television coverage. The retreat of the Soviet army from Afghanistan and dramatic pictures from the revolt at Tiananmen Square in Beijing were couched in implicit Cold War terms. How else could they be interpreted, after so many years of a media framework of ideological conflict between capitalism and communism? Ever since the Russian revolution, most of the media most of the time took for granted the master pattern of good versus evil. Sometimes it was modified by détente or later glasnost, but it was still a case of "friendly enemies." Many correspondents had spent years studying the arcane nuances of nuclear weapons' technology and strategy, as well as the complexities of arms control; the peace movements and the Campaign for Nuclear Disarmament received far less attention. Gradually, especially with the arrival of Soviet President Mikhail Gorbachev, the harsh media images of the Russian Bear softened. This was a man "we could do business with," in Margaret Thatcher's famous words. With the end of the Soviet Union and the media shorthand of the Cold War, journalists groped for new guidelines.

What would replace the national security directive, NSC-68, which became the fundamental document of the psychological war in Europe? The original command post of the Cold War *Kulturkampf* was the CIA's International Organizations Division, set up in 1950 by Tom Braden, a disciple of the legendary spy-master Allen Dulles. NSC-68 was meant to win over not just journalists, but novelists, painters, and musicians—the cream of the intelligentsia. Many were ex-communists—who better to fight the not dissimilar cultural war waged by Moscow? Many of the greatest thinkers, some unwittingly, were involved. Stephen Spender, Arthur Koestler, Raymond Aron, and W. H. Auden were invited, sometimes paid, to join fronts such as the Congress for Cultural Freedom or to write for journals such as *Encounter*. John Updike's Bech novels caught the atmosphere of this period—the radical American writer wanders Europe on cultural tours, meeting a CIA operative here, a Communist functionary there. When *Ramparts* magazine blew the story amid the anti-Vietnam protests in Europe, the American cultural bubble was burst, leaving a legacy of strong suspicion and resentment among the intellectuals of Western Europe. Especially in France, this hostility grew intense as the chattering classes in Paris perceived the cultural domination of Europe as being transformed into commercial globalization of the continent, and indeed the planet.[104]

This had been the deployment of what came to be known as "soft power." There would be little cultural freedom in Western Europe if the Soviet tanks rolled in. Naturally, most war correspondents—they included intellectuals in their ranks too—concentrated on the hard power. After 1945, the West intervened militarily in the Third World, but success was rare. The French army lost in Indo-China and Algeria. The British bogged down in guerrilla wars in Greece, Cyprus, Malaya, and Kenya during the

1940s and 1950s, in Aden and Malaysia in the 1960s, and the longest counterinsurgency in Europe, containing the Irish Republican Army for thirty years. The United States was traumatized by its defeat in Vietnam.

The Cold War had conditioned the mind-set, morality, and careers of nearly two generations of foreign correspondents. The West also contended with international terrorism, but that was an intellectual construct that did not play well with ambitious journalists who wanted to get their boots dirty in "real" wars. But when conventional wars were fought, the side with the best-trained forces generally won. The professional British army defeated the largely conscript Argentinean forces in the Falklands, although distance and terrain made it a close-run affair. The Israelis established themselves as masters of the art of rapid mobile war and air combat. It was easier, and much safer, for hacks to work with well-disciplined modern armies. When both sides were incompetent, as in the eight-year Iran–Iraq War, the campaigns could be long and indecisive. But very few Western correspondents were permitted to cover the battles between Iran and Iraq. Nonetheless, the well-trained and highly armed modern states were deterred by the threat of nuclear war, the continuous paradigm, and by the increasingly effective new forms of insurgency: a Maoist war that humbled the Americans in Vietnam, the Jihadist success against the Soviets in Afghanistan, and the quagmire of Israeli forces in Lebanon.[105] South Vietnam was well-populated with journalists, and Lebanon, though more dangerous and unpredictable, was often accessible to the hacks. Saigon and Beirut had hotels and bars. Afghanistan, especially the wild interior, long marches away from the Pakistan border, was largely terra incognita to all but a small band of determined journalists who had to be tough, fit, and able to do without alcohol for long periods.

After 1919, the United States withdrew from Europe. In contrast, in 1945 American vision helped to create the Marshall Plan, the North Atlantic Treaty Organization, and global financial institutions. Central to this was the rebuilding of Germany and Japan, both of which became stalwart allies of Washington. Some military correspondents devoted the majority of their time analyzing the arcane intricacies of the defense systems which did not fire a single shot in anger. When it came to shooting wars, nearly every time the West fought after 1945, it lost or at least failed to win (British counterinsurgency in Malaya was an honorable exception). While it suffered reverses on the battlefields of Korea, Dien Bien Phu, Suez, and Vietnam, the West constructed regional economic success stories in Europe and Asia, which were to prove more decisive in the long run.[106] "By the last decade of the Cold War," according to a senior journalist-turned-historian, "the supreme irony had emerged of the Soviet Union steadily diluting its ideological commitment, while the Reagan and Thatcher governments promoted their own counter-ideology of free markets and private property with proselytizing fervor."[107] Reagan, however, was only partly responsible for the arms build-up that helped to precipitate the fall of Soviet communism. The USSR was indeed, in economic terms, Upper Volta with nukes. When the Berlin Wall came down, many correspondents indulged in bouts of triumphalism about an event nearly all of them failed to predict.

After the fall of the Berlin Wall, Washington for the third time in the century had the chance to step in and make a "new world order," though it was not the "end of history" as some had hoped. Still, the hacks jumped on the bandwagon; their articles were frequently infected by the new world lexicon that was cranked out by Washington. The United States had to strike a balance between its twin instincts—that the U.S. must slay every "distant monster," to use John Quincy Adams's phrase—or to succumb to its latent tradition of isolationism. For a while, however, the media generally reflected the optimistic engagement and hopes for a "peace dividend." The Soviet collapse brought knock-on effects around the world, for example, in Cuba, Angola, Cambodia, and the Horn of Africa. If Soviet withdrawal encouraged the old nationalisms in Eastern Europe, in the developing world it helped to display the fragility of the nation state itself. Somalia was a classic example. And this now provided the adventurous hacks with lots of opportunity to dirty their boots and please their editors. Even in the Soviet Union, hopes of rapid liberal democratic advance soon faded; nevertheless, the correspondents could now poke around in a post-glasnost society previously closed to outsiders. In spite of its Marxist pretensions, communism was not intrinsically different from traditional Russian despotism; rather it was a particularly vicious and destructive manifestation of it.[108] In its "heroic" phase—the Soviet Union in the 1930s and China in the 1950s and 1960s—communism inflicted catastrophic damage on its own people, though little was reported to the outside world. "The United States and its allies killed tens of thousands of people defending freedom; the communist countries killed tens of millions in promoting socialism," according to one assessment of the Cold War.[109] The difference is not fortuitous; it was a matter of open versus closed systems of thought, politics, and free speech. And a key element of the last quality is the ability of Western foreign and war correspondents to report on the closed societies despite the intrinsic difficulties, not least lack of access. Overall, journalism largely failed to report on the monstrous conditions in the Soviet Union and China during the Cold War, as well as their reflections in the numerous proxy wars elsewhere. The failure to report on major tank battles in Angola is one egregious example.

At the beginning of the 1990s the United States found itself in a unique position. It was the sole superpower, yes, but—to paraphrase Kissinger—America could neither dominate the world nor withdraw from it, when it found itself both all-powerful and totally vulnerable.[110] Soon the country was to enter another long war—accompanied by big battles in the media, especially as the occupation in Iraq became a quagmire— where it would have to relearn the lessons of the Cold War: that military strength, when misused, could be highly counterproductive. When the collapse of the USSR and its satellites came, it was partly with delicious irony because of the weight of communism's own internal contradictions. Yet, as Michael Burleigh has persuasively argued, it was also because of the resilience and eventual resurgence of a competing ideology, Christianity. The first government of the newly liberated German Democratic Republic boasted four Protestant pastors, for example. Evangelicalism flourished in the United States, while Orthodox Christianity dramatically resurfaced in Russia itself. But did this renaissance of faith help to inspire the hatred of the Occident in an even more implacable and violent form of totalitarian philosophy, Islamic extremism?[111] Just as most media pundits failed to anticipate the imminent collapse of the Soviet system, likewise few predicted the rise of religion as a key factor in modern warfare.

# 4

## AFRICAN "SIDESHOWS"?

The central antagonism of the Cold War may have been couched in ideological terms of the West versus the USSR and China but, as earlier chapters have shown, the hot war actually took place elsewhere. Often the conflicts were mingled with existing nationalisms, as in Vietnam for example. The Cold War forced many states into accepting the imperative of Washington, Moscow, and Beijing: "you are either with us or against us." Thus, in sub-Saharan Africa, longstanding racial, tribal, and nationalist issues were often couched inaccurately in communist and progressive versus imperialist and reactionary frames. This breakdown of us versus them also happened in Latin America. In the Middle East numerous preexisting political and religious fault lines centered on the Arab-Israeli dispute were also dragged into the Manichean disputes between the USSR and the USA.

In these regions, Western correspondents, even from the sanctified BBC, often cut their way through thickets of local prejudices, starting with the location and political orientation of their media organization, before they could begin covering a story. Even before they dealt with the usual problems of censorship, access, terrain, transport, temperature, bullets, bribery, language, and nagging calls from editors at home, they were afflicted with their editors' patronizing confidence in received wisdom or political correctness. This was especially true of Africa.

The decline of good news reporting on Africa can be blamed on many factors. Cost-cutting has removed most of the hard-bitten, grizzled journalists who had spent decades on the same foreign beat. They could return time and time again to the same story and provide context and continuity. For the Americans, U.S. troops need to be involved for continuous coverage. The market impacts on nearly all media: people read or watch what they want. A foreign subject on a *Newsweek* cover will usually result in a 25 percent drop in newsstand sales,[1] which influences editors to stay within certain parameters when covering news. Constant news stories about disasters also foster what Michael Ignatieff has called a generalized misanthropy, meaning the world has become too outrageous to deserve serious attention.[2] The misuse of aid too has played a role.[3] "One man's humanitarian relief is another man's aid to the enemy."[4] And raising funds through constant atrocity and famine images can become counterproductive, not least by damaging images of Africa and its people.[5] Journalists too are human. A constant diet of the same depressing story in the same cycle of famine and war, with natural disasters occasionally added, wears down even the most resolute of news appetites. Repeated exposure to the "dying skeletons"—the cynically named "stick action"—can corrupt the hardiest correspondents.[6] Journalists, as well as audiences, suffer from compassion fatigue. Old hands will say that the continent is full of great Africans and truly awful leaders. Most of Africa's calamities are man-made and largely the product of corruption, greed, and short-term thinking. African leaders, not the Western media, must bear most of the responsibility for the bad news out of Africa.

Frank Barton, in his seminal work on the press in Africa, was of the opinion that "As political freedom came to the continent, so did press freedom disappear."[7] He qualified this assertion, made in the late 1970s, by arguing that the African media were less corrupt than Western newspapers in their early days. Many of the post-colonial states inherited a cornucopia of censorship laws. President Robert Mugabe of Zimbabwe, for example, maintained and then intensified nearly the same media restrictions as the white Rhodesian regime. & trashed the economy so no one can live well

In the 1960s most African states achieved independence. The new governments were soon transformed into one-party or military regimes. Their leaders frequently argued that indigenous independent media could exacerbate internal tribal divisions especially when encouraged by outside correspondents. Particularly with radio, they claimed media should be used to build up the unity of the post-colonial societies, an approach sometimes called developmental journalism.[8] This journalism ranged from "good news" propaganda diktats to encouraging rural community projects. Western academics debated the need for a New World Information Order—a concept that the Western capitalist systems were ignoring or misreporting news from the "Third World." African governments lambasted Western media for their obsession with news stories about wars, coups, and famine. Unfortunately, most of the news was indeed bad. Wars and natural disasters dominated African news in the Western media, when Africa was covered at all. Generally, Africa took up less than two percent of annual international reporting. The headline exceptions were usually the dramatic coverage of whites slaughtering blacks or vice versa: the Congo massacres in the 1960s, the Rhodesian war of the 1970s, and the struggle against apartheid South Africa in the 1980s.

The Mau Mau rebellion in Kenya was extensively, if not always accurately, reported. In March 1960, the police shooting of black demonstrators in Sharpeville, South Africa, and the banning of the African National Congress (ANC), prompted much media attention, while the killing in June 1960 of more than 500 protestors in Mozambique by Portuguese security forces garnered far less coverage. In the following year, insurgencies began in two other Portuguese colonies, Angola and Guinea-Bissau. But the long bush wars in the Portuguese territories were poorly covered by the English-language media. An honorable exception was the indomitable South African war correspondent, Al J. Venter.[9]

The early 1960s was a time of madness in many parts of Africa, especially in the former Belgian Congo. Rapid decolonization, secession of parts of that vast mineral-rich country, and UN military intervention resulted in tabloid stories of massacres of whites and rape of nuns.[10] These stories, and the actual flood of white refugees from the Belgian Congo into Northern Rhodesia (soon to be Zambia), helped fuel white fears of black rule in Southern Rhodesia and prompted its unilateral declaration of independence.

In 1967, British correspondents were drawn to another civil war, this time in Nigeria, a former British colony. Despite a long and emotive press campaign to assist the breakaway region of Biafra, the British government—irritated by France's support for the secessionists and concerned about Nigerian oil supplies—connived at a federal victory and thus allowed the Nigerian military to starve its unwilling compatriots into submission. One historian termed the three-year conflict "Black Africa's first major war fought with modern weapons in which all the generals were Africans."[11] Its disorganization matched the ethnic brutality and financial corruption. The only saving grace perhaps was the behavior of the devoutly Christian federal head of state, Gen. Yakubu Gowon. He ordered that there should be no reprisals or medals and that oil profits should be channelled into the reconstruction of Iboland (Biafra). According to one military historian, "It was a bizarre war. Its ferocity as extraordinary as the magnanimity of the victor."[12] The often partisan war reporting—not least by the young Frederick Forsyth—to aid "plucky Biafra" had little or no impact on the oil politics of the British government.[13]

## RHODESIA: ARGUING WITH ARITHMETIC AND HISTORY

With the complicity of British companies, oil also reached sanctioned Rhodesia, which soon became a major diplomatic headache for the UK government. Ian Smith, the Rhodesian Front leader, had declared illegal independence at 11 A.M. on November 11, 1965. The timing, the anniversary of WWI's armistice, was to remind the British of Rhodesia's major contributions in both World Wars, and the wording of the declaration was to remind the United States of its own rebellion against the British Crown.

Rhodesia was a well-armed suburb masquerading as a country. How could 250,000 whites, outnumbered by blacks by twenty-five to one and ostracized by most of the world, think they could retain power? After the Portuguese colonies collapsed by 1975, Rhodesia's sole reliable ally was South Africa, but even Pretoria refused to recognize the rebel state formally. Soon the media witnessed in southern Africa the equivalent of a "moral panic" as Rhodesia and especially South Africa almost ceased to be geographical entities. To the outside world they were more a *condition,* a disease. South Africa was no longer a country but a map of the mind, in which anyone could find his own place.[14]

The Unilateral Declaration of Independence (UDI) in 1965 was a bluff and a blunder. Except for a few hotheads, the Rhodesian armed forces would not have resisted a British military intervention.[15] (The British had intervened to stop *black* army mutinies three times during the year before in Tanganyika [Tanzania], Kenya, and Uganda.) Harold Wilson, the British premier, however, fretted about his small parliamentary majority, as well as the kith-and-kin factor in the British armed forces. Wilson then renounced the use of force—his ace card. Instead he threatened to "throw the book" at the rebels, yet he only flicked a few pages, one at a time. Sanctions were a gesture, never a concerted policy. Until 1974 they boosted rather than undermined the rebel economy. Britain kept supplying oil, making more than enough money to pay for a useless naval blockade supposedly to stop the oil getting there in the first place. It arrived via South Africa.

In the greatest paradox of the Rhodesian war, Ian Smith, a RAF pilot whose wartime heroics had been celebrated in the British tabloids, broke away from Britain to avoid black rule, only to have the white regime become totally dependent on the South African government. This government was eventually more determined than London to forge a moderate black leadership in the capital, Salisbury (later Harare). Pretoria wanted to distance itself from Rhodesia's failing white government, but it also wanted to show that sanctions did not work and could not be seen to abandon a white ally publicly. Until 1976 Anglo-Rhodesian diplomatic history was a long melodrama punctuated by angry encounters on ships and trains, foolish estimates, and inane postulates (especially Smith's "there will never be black rule in a thousand years"). The country's fate would be decided largely on the battlefield. Had the British-sponsored 1979 Lancaster House talks not intervened, military defeat for the regime would have soon followed.

Journalists were rarely allowed near the fighting. There were few actual battles; most were in cross-border raids into Mozambique and Zambia, where the two guerrilla organizations, the Chinese-backed insurgents loyal to Robert Mugabe and the Soviet-sponsored army led by Joshua Nkomo, were based. For the guerrillas, the war was characterized by fleeting ground skirmishes and helicopter firepower. Short of enlisting or accepting conscription (some local journalists served in the part-time police reserve), few correspondents witnessed actual military action. An exception was the dashing Lord Richard Cecil, who had served with distinction as an officer in the British army. The Rhodesian military establishment had been attracted to his derring-do style of filmmaking. Ironically, he was the only white correspondent killed in the war when a single guerrilla shot Cecil in a surprise attack. He had been unable to defend himself because his rifle, inexplicably, was not working—he had not checked if it was functioning. It is further ironic because Richard Cecil was a member of the Salisbury family; the capital was named after a former British prime minister, Lord Salisbury.[16]

Seventy-five percent of whites voted for Smith during the UDI years and *after* independence in 1980.[17] This sincere but narrow-minded Rhodesian leader accurately represented the best and worst of white society. Rhodesian culture, such as it was, was based on a siege mentality: UN harangues, the war, and sanctions galvanized the spirit of white nationalism. Rhodesian propaganda had little effect on blacks (even when the air force deployed "sky-shouts" to broadcast messages from long-dead spirit mediums), but it did work on the whites—proof of the old adage that people believe what they want to believe. The majority of whites accepted the Rhodesian Broadcasting Corporation's view of the world: that the Beatles, international finance groups, and colonial freedom agitators were all agents of a communist plot to dominate the world. As in most wars, patriotism distorted perception. Television and radio harped on a few basic themes: the chaos in black states, disorders elsewhere in the world (especially in countries such as Britain that attracted southern African émigrés), and, always, the monolithic communist threat. Smith claimed to have "the happiest blacks in the world," bar a few troublemakers misled by professional

Moscow-trained agitators. Few whites acknowledged that they too would fight if they were deprived of an effective vote and given inferior schooling, medical services, and land, as well as treated as second-rate "kaffirs."

Relatively few whites had access to world news (except for the BBC World Service) or the reports from foreign correspondents working in Rhodesia. Because of local censorship and the pitifully small holiday and emigration allowances, many whites were captives rather than supporters of the Rhodesian Front government (although some were true believers). Rhodesians seemed to understand little of the modern world and heartily disliked what they did understand. This dislike often extended to white South Africa. Many Rhodesian whites believed they were battling against communism to preserve a civilized, Anglo-Saxon, Christian order, not merely to protect a privileged lifestyle. Though the whites did fight long and hard, and despite the ubiquitous weaponry and uniforms, Rhodesia was not a militaristic society. They much preferred beer and barbecues to military parades. Later, as black rule became imminent, the whites looked back with sorrow and resignation rather than anger; with bruised pride at having survived so long against the odds.[18] Perhaps they would have fought even harder if they could have known that Smith's worst (perhaps self-fulfilling) prophecies would come true: that Robert Mugabe would destroy the country.

This tragedy, however, was yet to unfold. In 1979 and early 1980, a racial Armageddon seemed possible, and the foreign press corps—dubbed "the vultures" by Rhodesians—trooped in to cover the one-person, one-vote elections. (The first election, in 1979, was not internationally recognized whereas the second, in 1980, which included the "external" guerrilla organizations, was.) Because in the first poll Smith's interim government wanted maximum publicity, the government more willingly granted press accreditation. While most of the indigenous white males were on call-up "in the bush," the predominantly male press corps, flush with foreign currency, attracted hordes of local women, which did nothing to improve the relations between the Rhodesian military and the foreign media. Relations were strained with the police as well, though the Special Branch officer attached to the press bar at the Quill Club had his expense account dramatically increased to cover drinks with friendly journalists. Never had so many journalists been shown so much affection in one place. Paul Ellman, a prominent British journalist, complained that he couldn't obtain a phone for his apartment because of wartime exigencies. "How can you bug me if I don't have a phone?" he logically asked the Special Branch man permanently attached to the Quill Club. Ellman's phone was installed the next day.[19] Access to the war suddenly improved for journalists. Even the air force's overstretched supply of old Alouette helicopters was switched to ferry the press around the country.

Though the Rhodesian government regarded the 1979 election as a political success, the sheer number of guerrillas pouring in from Mozambique swamped white power. As one member of the elite Selous Scouts said after a major raid into Mozambique, "We knew then that we could never beat them. They had so much equipment and there were so many of them. They would just keep coming with more and more."[20] Nevertheless the white-dominated regime of the short-lived Zimbabwe-Rhodesia (June 1 to December 12, 1979) fielded more than 70,000 military and police personnel to secure a victory for Bishop Abel Muzorewa, the most popular of the "internal" leaders. The externally based guerrilla armies refused to accept the outcome of the election, which they had largely boycotted. In the jargon of the time, *a luta continua*—the war went on.

Short of additional South African military support, the Muzorewa-Smith regime could not survive once the newly elected right-wing British conservative Margaret Thatcher rejected the election results. The war also beggared Rhodesia's black neighbors, Mozambique and Zambia. These two countries forced their warlike guests to attend the Lancaster House conference in London mediated by Lord Carrington, the foreign secretary. Compromise was finally reached after much haggling and a firm hand by Carrington as well as information from British intelligence service MI5 (which had bugged the hotel rooms of all participants). Attendees also agreed on a new constitution and a ceasefire. In December 1979, Lord Soames took over as governor, which was the first time that a white colonial official had replaced an African president.

New elections were scheduled for February 1980, and 350 foreign correspondents flocked into Salisbury. More than 1,300 troops in the British-led Commonwealth Force tried to monitor the ceasefire and elections, while rival marauding armies and militias, as well as the security forces, ravaged the country. More than 30,000 people were killed in the fifteen-year civil war, although fewer than 1,000 were white civilians and servicemen. However, this latter figure was proportionately very high for the small close-knit white community. The whites were now more bitter, particularly in the security forces, and the well-fleshed governor, the son-in-law of Winston Churchill, had to rely on them to run the country until independence. Lord Soames had no divisions, a position the Rhodesian military supremo, Gen. Peter Walls, understood. Walls and Soames remained calm while the country teetered on the brink of full-scale fighting. The white Rhodesians took solace in their belief that London had concocted the so-called ABM option—Anybody But Mugabe. Pretoria's officials were also certain that the Conservative British government wanted to assemble a coalition to isolate the Marxist Mugabe. Eventually, 2,702,275 men and women, under the watchful eye of 570 British police officers, voted in the middle of the rainstorms of February 1980. Would it be peace, coup, or all-out war in southern Africa?

Robert Mugabe won a stunning victory. The Rhodesian military came within hours of a coup, but General Walls insisted, "We will not copy the rest of Africa."[21] A rapid exodus of southern African troops and equipment followed. Ken Flower, head of the powerful Central Intelligence Organisation (CIO), burnt its files that detailed trade with the Soviet bloc and its links with the Vatican, and British and French intelligence. Files on the CIO's extensive network of secret allies throughout black Africa were shoved into the incinerator at the local crematorium. Cabinet papers were spirited away to South Africa along with the mess silver from Rhodesia's regiments.[22] Some whites panicked and headed south with only a few possessions. After these first waves of shock, many whites responded to Mugabe's calls for reconciliation and remained in Rhodesia.

On April 18, 1980, Zimbabwe became independent. Prime Minister Margaret Thatcher had unintentionally caused the first democratic electoral triumph of a Marxist in Africa. Many Rhodesians focused their loathing on Lord Peter Carrington. They claimed this was another Munich, an appeasement of dictators. The Rhodesians had spat into the winds of change.

The history of the Rhodesian security forces, which were manned 75 percent by blacks, was one of tactical and operational brilliance but also strategic political ineptitude. The initial aim of the war was to prevent the passing of power to any black government, no matter how moderate. The Rhodesian Front never articulated any clear political program for the military to follow beyond a vague preservation of the status quo. There was little faith in far-reaching reform as a war-winner; it would have undermined the very reasons for fighting the war at all. White Rhodesians struggled against what could have avoided the war: black African participation in national politics. Faced with their strategic weaknesses, the Rhodesians resorted to more and more desperate measures. They abandoned the policy of winning hearts and minds in the field precisely when the first moves toward a political strategy of a moderate black regime were coming to fruition. Political warfare gave way to slaughter safaris. As one senior officer admitted, "We relied 90 per cent on force and ten per cent on psychology, and half of that went off half-cocked. The guerrillas relied 90 per cent on psychology and only ten per cent on force."[23]

The insurgents' vision was to break the back of white supremacy and establish a black majority government. This gave them remarkable stamina and their cause the strength to weather numerous political crises and considerable military defeat in the field. In the pattern of all colonial wars, the Rhodesian settlers simply relinquished too little power too late for their political ends. More thoughtful Rhodesians now asked if South Africa would heed the lesson.

The Zimbabwean insurgents had deployed an intensive international propaganda campaign supported by African states, the Soviet bloc, the majority of the UN, and liberals throughout Europe. Though insurgents also had many supporters in the media, few journalists reported the war from the frontline guerrilla side. Jeremy Brickhill, later a filmmaker, was one of a handful of whites who joined the Zimbabwe People's Revolutionary Army, Joshua Nkomo's guerrillas. Brickhill later wrote a series of academic accounts based on his experiences.[24] Journalists David Martin and Phyllis Johnson penned a pro-Mugabe book soon after the war.[25] At the end of the conflict, Martin Meredith, a correspondent for the UK's *Observer* and *Sunday Times*, produced a dispassionate account of the saga.[26]

Australian journalist Phillip Knightley, however, argued that the coverage of the Rhodesian war was deeply flawed:

> How could any war correspondent give a balanced account of a war where one side was Anglo-Saxon, entrenched in the cities, with access to the resources and the techniques of public relations, and where the other side consisted of people of a different race and culture, operating in the remote countryside, and who had neither the means nor—and this many be more important—the inclination to compete in terms of propaganda? The answer is that no war correspondent could.[27]

In truth, the insurgents, particularly their political wings, waged an effective propaganda war internationally, as did their allies in the South African liberation movements.[28] The insurgents' success, however, was more a case of plugging into, rather than creating, a vast international network of supporters in the media, churches, political parties, and lobby groups. White Rhodesian propaganda, as well as the apartheid regime's, were ham-fisted by comparison when persuading international opinion and foreign correspondents. Knightley also pointed out that British newspapers could not admit they were denied access to the war and simply extract their correspondents. Thus, some relied on one man: a "multiple correspondent," Ian Mills, who filed under an array of pseudonyms for major UK papers and the BBC. Knightley accepts that Mills was competent but believes that having many journalists all (inevitably) agreeing on one story was highly undesirable. Mills could hardly argue with himself or challenge his own reporting.[29]

Mills was only one of many competent correspondents operating in Rhodesia, especially in the final years of the war. Knightley concedes the effectiveness of the *Daily Telegraph*'s Chris Munnion, a highly distinguished "old Africa hand." But many other foreign journalists worked diligently to cover the story: James McManus (the *Guardian*), Canadian Allen Pizzey (later of CBS), and Peter Sharp (later with Sky TV), Richard West, a freelance who wrote extensively for British magazines,[30] and Peter Jordan, a daring photographer for *Time* magazine. Some local Rhodesian journalists also unearthed stories or worked to help foreign journalists who had less to lose if they were deported. (That tradition has been maintained by Peta Thorneycroft who continued to report from Zimbabwe for the London *Daily Telegraph*, after nearly all foreign correspondents were banned.)

Nevertheless, the coverage of the war did not reveal the extent of the killings and atrocities on both sides, though by and large the Rhodesian security forces were true to their legacy inherited from the British army. The sanitized reporting tended to play to existing prejudices: the conservatives in the UK and United States backed the white Rhodesian anti-communist stance, and the liberal media continued to cry freedom for the black majority.

The transformation of Rhodesia to Zimbabwe was the replacement of an efficient, racist, white elite with an inefficient, tribal, black elite. It was inevitable and should have happened without bloodshed. The Rhodesian republic fell in 1979 and left South Africa as the last white-ruled bastion. White supremacy in Rhodesia, to paraphrase historian Robert Blake, was always a dubious and impractical expedient, but south of the Limpopo River apartheid was a religion.[31]

## SOUTH AFRICA: REPORTING APARTHEID

Unlike Rhodesia, South Africa was not a case of thwarted decolonization. The three million or so Afrikaners were a genuine white African tribe. The ruling Afrikaner National Party enshrined racism (much of it inherited from English colonial rule) in its constitution when it won power in 1948, three years after the fall of Hitler. Revolution and war were inevitable as long as the whites, 13 percent of the population, controlled 87 percent of the land. As with most authoritarian states, South Africa had an efficient security police, as well as the most effective army in Africa. The Soweto uprising of 1976 was quelled. The core of the banned African National Congress opposition, the South African Communist Party, predicted another Russian revolution. Unlike Russia in 1917, South Africa had not been defeated in war. It was a regional superpower, an economic giant with a military publicly (but falsely) denying the possession of nuclear weapons.

The apartheid regime boasted that it had the freest press in Africa. Nevertheless, from 1948 to 1990 media freedoms were increasingly restricted. Newspapers were banned, and foreign journalists were deported. But the Afrikaner government was reluctant to impose total media curbs on local and foreign media, because it was concerned with its image as a vanguard of Western Christendom's battle with Moscow's "evil empire" (as U.S. President Ronald Reagan named it). The Afrikaner government had a Ptolemaic view of the world: Pretoria, not Berlin, was the centerpiece of the Cold War. Pretoria, therefore, had to allow a semblance of media freedom as integral to its defense of Western values. Additionally, it was required to curb Moscow's total onslaught aided wittingly or unwittingly by the local and foreign media. Pretoria desperately wanted to be treated as part of the West and as a result continually explained that problems with terrorists also existed elsewhere, not least in Europe.

Democracy, however, presents special problems in Africa: South Africa was First World and Third World, like Australia dumped on Nigeria. The rich white Johannesburg suburb of Sandton was in close proximity to the impoverished black township of Alexandra. For the comfortable whites, the problems were not happening in the next township, which they rarely, if ever, visited, or in the dustbowls of the black homelands hundreds of miles away. The starvation and turmoil were another *world* away, in other words, the Third World.

The Afrikaner government continued its attempts to squash investigative journalists' coverage. Some newspapers, such as the *Rand Daily Mail,* fought the government before they were forced to close. In the infamous Infogate scandal (also known as Muldergate), Pretoria secretly bought large shares in media outlets abroad and took control of the *Citizen* in Johannesburg.[32] Some of the newspapers read predominantly by blacks (but owned by whites) had been banned. Literature sympathetic to the African National Congress and the resistance in general was rigorously suppressed until 1990.

Despite the media restrictions, the government's banana-republic "goonsquadism" failed to completely stamp out news of apartheid crimes (unlike Pretoria's covert wars in neighboring states).[33] "This is not a society where it is possible to cover up major events, major atrocities, for any length of time," according to John Battersby, who covered South Africa for the *New York Times* and the *Christian Science Monitor.*[34] Newcomers to South Africa were surprised to read virulent attacks on the government in newspapers such as the *Star*, Africa's largest English-language daily. Liberal white journalists, both in Afrikaans- and English-language papers, often purported to speak for the oppressed black majority.[35] For example, Donald Woods, the former editor of the East London *Daily Dispatch*, helped expose the inhumanity of apartheid. His writing and later the film of his friendship with the murdered black leader Steve Biko, *Cry Freedom*, attracted worldwide attention.[36] Although, in the 1980s, an alternative press—independently minded and independently owned newspapers such as the *Weekly Mail*—adopted a much more populist, pro-ANC line. Experienced foreign correspondents also played a key role in helping local South African journalists break their stories abroad, though these correspondents often took the credit, or the opprobrium, for the scoop. Locals risked imprisonment while foreign journalists, such as the BBC's Michael Buerk, were simply ordered to leave. After the 1976 Soweto uprising, white society relaxed back into what novelist Nadine Gordimer called "a dreadful calm" in *A World of Strangers*. The war was far off, a thousand miles to the north on the Angolan border. The increasing political influence of the military under President Pieter W. Botha ensured that external military operations were kept from public view.[37] South Africans were virtually unaware of the battles to control Namibia (South-West Africa), the wars of destabilization in Angola, Mozambique, Zimbabwe, and other neighboring states, and even the details of the 1975 invasion of Angola, which stopped on the outskirts of their capital, Luanda. The long devastating civil war in Mozambique was barely treated by Western journalists.[38] The biggest tank battles in Africa since World War II also went largely unreported when they erupted in Angola in the late 1980s. Relatively small forces of South African troops backed Jonas Savimbi's rebel National Union for the Total Independence of Angola (UNITA) in tough conventional battles against Angolan government troops as well as extensive formations of Cuban soldiers and Soviet advisers. A British journalist, Fred Bridgland, and a South African correspondent for *Jane's Information Group*, Helmoed Römer-Heitman, did publish detailed accounts in 1990, when media restrictions were eased.[39]

The high point of international media attention was the so-called "unrest" of 1984–86, as the young lions in the black townships across the country erupted in a revolt that took the ANC leadership in Lusaka by surprise. The fighting was also emblazoned across television screens in Britain and America. The Afrikaner government believed that the television crews sometimes created rather than recorded the grim events. There was a ring of truth to this supposition that the presence of reporters could alter the course of events. For example, crews setting up cameras in a township could prompt youngsters to start throwing stones at the police, who would often overreact with their firepower. Pretoria's decision to ban all media coverage was unsurprising; more remarkable was the year or so it took to implement. It was a cynical gesture that seemed to work. Perhaps Pretoria had adequately sized up the attention span of Western viewers. But their political leaders, even President Ronald Reagan, had been alerted to the moral crisis.

Until the television ban in 1985, images of boycotts, rent strikes, demonstrations, riots, police retaliation or provocation, single shots, tear gas, panic, confusion, concentrated automatic fire, funerals, and more funerals were endlessly recycled. At the burial services, one of the few legal outlets for the outpouring of political and personal grief that too was eventually restricted, ANC, Soviet flags, and wooden replicas of AK rifles were openly displayed. Arson and murder of suspected informers, black councilors, and black policemen, was perceived to be the main, and available, local representative of apartheid. The necklace execution, where a tire was placed around the neck of the accused, filled with gasoline, and then ignited, became a trademark of the young comrades in their war against collaborators. For television viewers abroad, South Africa was in flames. On the censored local television, little of this was shown, except the occasional necklacing to emphasize black barbarity. The new alternative press and English-language stalwarts such as the *Star* and the *Cape Times*, particularly Ken Owen's blistering editorials and columns in *Business Day*, spoke out, playing Russian roulette with the censorship laws.

President Botha, nicknamed "The Great Crocodile," was a man possessed of a strange mixture of "sentimentality and intolerance."[40] Previously he had usually opted for military solutions, hence his Afrikaans nickname "Pieter Weapon." His reforms began to include, though far too slowly, mixed-race and Indian South Africans in a "new dispensation," though this "tricameral parliament" amounted to a declaration of war against the African majority. Botha was destined to illustrate the truism that a government is most at risk when it is trying to reform itself. The government modified some of the harsher social aspects of apartheid, and on August 15, 1985, Botha promised to satisfy world leaders in his famous Rubicon speech. As unrest increased, he decided, however, to declare a prolonged state of emergency. South Africa's currency, the rand, fell to an all-time low. Foreign investors deserted in droves. Market-led sanctions became much more important than official government-enacted UN sanctions against the regime.

The government continued to blame all the bloodshed on the ANC as well as the South African Communist Party (SACP). The SACP checked the *Umkhonto we Sizwe*, the ANC's military wing, which wanted to hit soft white targets. In June 1985, however, the ANC adopted a strategy of people's war intended to take the struggle into the comfortable and relatively untouched white suburbs. Despite this threat, President Botha still refused to speak with the ANC, who insisted that the freedom of their imprisoned leader, Nelson Mandela, be a precondition for serious talks. The rollercoaster of repression and occasional reform appeared mutually exclusive. As veteran South African journalist Stanley Uys noted, "Botha's reformism in South Africa today is like a lift going up in a building that is coming down."[41]

By mid-1986, the liberation mania in the black townships appeared to have dissipated. After two years of repression, sheer physical exhaustion and frustration with the excesses of disciplined comrades, roving bands of young thugs, and psychopathic elements had taken their toll. Chaos in the townships was not the same as people's power. In June 1986, George De'Ath, a freelance cameraman who had grown up in Rhodesia and was working for the BBC, died. He had been mortally wounded during the fighting among vigilantes, the police, and the comrades in Cape Town, making him the first foreign correspondent to be killed while covering the civil war. In the same month the state of emergency, which had been lifted in March, was reimposed. By the end of 1986, more than 23,000 people, including 9,000 children, were jailed under the June decrees. The South African Defence Force (SADF) smashed the pretensions of the liberated zones in the townships. Pretoria was back in power. With a new dose of strict press controls again, the powerful if not ludicrously named Bureau of Information handed out official reports. At daily press briefings in Pretoria, police brigadier and former journalist Leon Mellet conveyed his thoughts on what the government wanted the press to know about the insurrection. He insisted on being called Mr. Mellet in case anyone should think the police was running the country.

Despite the military defeat of the comrades, a psychological corner had been turned. It would take time, but belief in ultimate victory was now implanted in the popular psyche. In 1989, President Botha, enfeebled by a stroke, reached a political dead end: the Rubicon disaster, the curt dismissal of a Commonwealth peace mission, and the public humiliation of his "Coloured" and Indian allies lit up his tricameral parliament as a ship of fools. His successor, F. W. de Klerk, finally dragged the party out of its bunker and across a real Rubicon on February 2, 1990: the African National Congress and the Pan-Africanist Congress were unbanned. Days later Nelson Mandela was freed after twenty-seven years in jail.

De Klerk and Mandela managed an uneasy rapport for four years of constitutional horse-trading between the ANC and the ruling National Party. The international media were less interested now because of the virtual absence of large-scale violence. The local journalists were thereby responsible for covering the continuing killing, often tribal, between the Zulu Inkatha Party and the PAC, ANC, and Black Consciousness supporters, which was dubbed "black on black." This phrase, however, was as useful as deeming the Second World War "white on white." The years 1990 to 1994 were no longer a tale of good versus evil. Some American journalists had analyzed the complexities of the region in superlative style, for example, Joseph Lelyveld in the Pulitzer Prize–winning *Move Your Shadow.* No one, though, captured the country with so much brio as South African journalist Rian Malan in *My Traitor's Heart.*[42] Certainly, after Mandela's freedom, the conflict could no longer be refracted through the prism of the civil rights movements for American audiences, as it had been. Some U.S. journalists struggled to interpret the atrocities—for example, those committed by Mrs. Winnie Mandela's personal followers in her "football team"— or the socialism of most and the communism of many in the ANC coalition, by way of the simple analogy of the Mason-Dixon Line. Many gave up. Local journalists could not. For example, Max du Preez and Jacques Pauw, of the *Vrye Weekblad,* took extraordinary risks in their exposure of the death squads within the South African Police.[43] Most famous were the four young photographers who comprised the Bang Bang Club—Ken Oosterbroek, Kevin Carter, Greg Marinovich and Joao Silva. They risked their lives daily covering the inter-black fighting in the townships. Oosterbroek died after he was shot by a stray bullet, with camera in hand. A few weeks after winning a Pulitzer Prize for his photograph of a starving child stalked by an expectant vulture in Sudan, Carter committed suicide. The two survivors, Greg Marinovich and Joao Silva, wrote their harrowing story in *The Bang Bang Club.*[44] Here is an excerpt on war correspondents' guilt:

> At times, we felt like vultures. We had indeed trodden on corpses, metaphorically and literally, in making a living; but we had not killed any of those people. We had never killed anyone; in fact, we had saved some lives. And perhaps our pictures had made a difference by allowing people to see elements of other people's struggles to survive that they would not have otherwise known about.[45]

The days of political haggling drew to a close and an election was set for May 1994. Ultra-conservatives in the white community, especially in the neo-Nazi *Afrikaner Weerstandsbeweging* (AWB), prepared for a last stand or perhaps a retreat to some white-ruled redoubt. Some right-wingers, including AWB men, poured into the tottering homeland of Bophuthatswana to back the apartheid puppet, Lucas Mangope. The date was March 17, 1994, the day that awe for white South Africa died. Three armed neo-Nazis, travelling through Mangope's dusty capital in a dilapidated green Mercedes, threw racial taunts at a group of blacks. A local black policeman fired at the car, fatally wounding the driver. The two whites with him stumbled out of the car, their hands in the air, but they still used the term black bastard to nearby journalists. Two minutes later both whites were killed, shot in the head by other black policemen. That picture was flashed around the world: a black man in uniform pointing a rifle at the head of white man prostrate in the dirt. Such pictures had not been widely seen since the Congo massacres in the early 1960s and never in South Africa, still cocooned by the sputtering racism of apartheid's last days.[46]

The old Africa hands among the resident press corps had expected the Afrikaner tribe to fight as the Rhodesians had, especially when remembering the *bittereinders* who had campaigned to the last in the Boer War. The two lawyers, Mandela and de Klerk, however, managed to control their respective sides.

Thousands of international correspondents flocked in for the elections, expecting a bloodbath. The last-minute decision of the Inkatha leader, Chief "Gatsha" Buthelezi, to take part was a key factor in keeping the peace. The promised Zulu rising in Natal and Johannesburg did not materialize. Nelson Mandela's ANC won an expected landslide victory in a largely free and peaceful poll. As a result, the long-ruling National Party began to implode.[47] Many whites accepted black rule as inevitable, while others thought in cosmetic terms: they would allow the ANC into parliament in exchange for the resumption of international rugby tours. One cynical journalist observed: "South Africa was a first world dictatorship, now it's a third-world democracy . . . for a while."[48]

South Africa had been a difficult conflict to cover. It was fiendishly complicated, never a simple morality tale. It was a statesman's hell and a sociologist's paradise and demanded high standards of journalism. The apartheid philosophy was demonstrably evil, but the question remained if it had been uniquely evil. Some journalists argued it was a special case, a special evil. Others found it tempting to take sides after witnessing a massacre or two. It was no wonder Pretoria accused foreign journalists of incitement. Afrikaners used to say that many overseas journalists displayed a "Jericho complex": one more trumpet blast and the whole edifice would collapse. As in Vietnam, suggesting a conspiracy by foreign correspondents in the field is utterly fanciful. Correspondents were still as fiercely competitive and disorganized as ever, though the Western media organizations that paid them may have had their own political agenda or skewed editorial policies. Most foreign correspondents in South Africa did not crusade against Pretoria, despite the siren calls of the advocacy journalists ensconced in newsrooms at home. Still, the vast majority, even the crusty old Africa hands, were frequently appalled by Pretoria's inept manipulation of the media.

For journalists, balancing moral convictions with professional standards in Africa is difficult. A legitimacy could be created, by default, by giving a rough balance—say 50 percent blame to Mugabe and 50 percent to Smith. It is perhaps better to sponsor this practice than yield to one-sided advocacy journalism. For once journalists accepted apartheid as a special case, they would have to accept such exceptions as Papa Doc's abominations in Haiti, Idi Amin's buffoonery and butchery in Uganda, and the Khmer Rouge. Arguments could be formulated for a raft of special cases. Those journalists who did take up cudgels for the ANC should recall that revolutions tend to devour their kind. For example, were partisan foreign journalists who crusaded for Mugabe prepared to stay in Zimbabwe and live under a dictatorship that destroyed an economy relatively vibrant in 1980 despite sanctions, war, and no foreign aid? Mandela became a secular saint, but what if he had inadvertently played Russian leader Alexander Kerensky to a future despot? Should journalists judge Africa by Western standards, or should they, patronisingly, make allowances, as in the case of Frank Barton?

In terms of conventional war reporting—witnessing battles and campaigns—the wars in southern Africa were generally poorly covered, especially with the apartheid's "second front" where neighboring countries were destablized. Here the terrain was difficult and reporting the wars often required feats of endurance, determination, and at least basic military skills to survive. Above all, Pretoria went to great lengths to hide these wars from the public. While the fighting in Angola could involve thousands of combatants in a single battle, the guerrilla warfare and sabotage campaigns inside South Africa were poorly orchestrated with few white casualties. Sanctions, trade union militancy, and the churches all played a part in the downfall of white rule. Despite the clumsy propaganda of the government, which emphasized the external Cold War threats and not stark domestic inequalities, many whites followed along. As in Rhodesia, people tended to believe in what they wanted to believe, especially if it preserved the status quo.

In sixty years of mayhem throughout the continent, apartheid was the most popular running African story. This continued coverage could be because the media often portrayed whites, nearly always fluent in English, in conflict with blacks, whose leaders had mastered English sound bites. Greater slaughter in neighboring wars, such as the mass butchery in Rwanda, did not inspire sustained media interest perhaps because it could not be easily portrayed in stark moral terms, good versus evil, justice versus apartheid, black versus white. One other hypothesis is that Johannesburg, compared with most other African cities, was a comfortable place to be based as a journalist, in lifestyle and its access to modern communications and transportation. The frontline states in the struggle against apartheid—such as Zimbabwe and Zambia—did warn correspondents that they would have to move north to the Zimbabwean capital, Harare, or be banned from those states, but to no avail. Now Zimbabwe bans Western journalists and none of its neighbors dares whisper an official complaint because of misplaced regional, racial and "anti-imperialist" solidarity.

Did the many foreign reporters have any political impact on the demise of apartheid? Despite the self-image of truculent indifference, most South African whites, especially in the government, were concerned how the world viewed them. And, like most siege cultures, many whites were deeply religious, especially in the ruling Afrikaner elite. The constant worldwide drumbeat of moral condemnation and sanctions did have an effect.

Though foreign correspondents colonized affluent white suburbs, the dangerous streets of the townships, where George De'Ath and Ken Oosterbroek were murdered, were testing environments. No single story or event comparable with Vietnam's Tet Offensive doomed the regime. Rather, stories covered over a long period did cause political embarrassment for the Afrikaner rulers, including Steve Biko's death, corruption in the government, and the secret northern wars, especially when South African special force soldiers were captured. The often close cooperation between well-known foreign journalists and determined local correspondents, both black and white, sustained the pressure, even when the government banned television cameras. A few correspondents betrayed their calling by extreme partisanship, but the vast majority did not. Despite Pretoria's media management, the story was relayed to the public over decades. This triggered the international political and economic levers that eventually forced Pretoria to accept the inevitable. Although the South African military was still the most powerful on the continent, the political war had been lost.

Nelson Mandela eschewed bitterness after decades of unjust incarceration and preached reconciliation for the new rainbow nation of South Africa. Sanctions ended, exiles came home, and the Truth and Reconciliation process displaced calls for Nuremberg-style trials. For once, a good news story dominated reporting on Africa. Moreover, the recent collapse of the Cold War rivalry on the continent led many African journalists to examine their own one-party systems. They had all preached democracy for South Africa, yet could it not also be practiced elsewhere? Phrases such as Second Liberation and African Renaissance peppered political discourse. In southern Africa, Mozambique found peace and reconciliation partly based on the South African approach.

Sadly, after the encouraging turn of events, Africa was soon back to the cyclical crop of coups, famines, and killing fields. After a (temporary) ceasefire and some intense politicking in Angola, however, UNITA leader Jonas Savimbi was assassinated in 2002. As Mandela walked free, a long civil war in Liberia broke out. In the Horn of Africa, in Ethiopia, the famine of "biblical proportions" (to quote Michael Buerk's famous BBC documentary) and the civil war that had raged since 1974 died down in 1991, though Ethiopia and breakaway Eritrea would soon fight one of the most bloody wars over the most undesirable tract of desert. In the same region, the continent's longest war, in Sudan, Africa's largest country, was to rumble on for another decade; the savage rivalry between the Arab regime in Khartoum and the largely animist and Christian south of Sudan had started in the mid-1950s when the British were the effective colonial power. The Islamic revolution in Khartoum in 1989 did not end the war in the south, which had been rekindled by the 1983 imposition of Sharia law. A north-south agreement was not signed until 2005, though war in Darfur in western Sudan disrupted peace dividends in the oil-rich state. And, as South Africa marched towards democracy, another Islamic insurgency was tearing Algeria apart.

Nothing, though, matched the killing fields of Rwanda, where Hutu extremists killed perhaps 800,000 fellow Rwandans, mainly Tutsis, in 100 days. This extermination rate surpassed Hitler's. As with the Holocaust of the Jews, many of the world's officials chose to ignore Rwanda. It caught the UN and nearly all the veteran correspondents unprepared. The only British correspondent to report on the initial killings in Kigali, the Rwandan capital, was the gutsy and determined Lindsey Hilsum, then with the *Observer* newspaper.[49] A few days later, American reporter Donatella Lorch reached Kigali in a Red Cross medical convoy. "Bodies lay everywhere," she wrote. "Several truckloads of frenzied screaming men waving machetes and screwdrivers drove by. At night, screams followed by automatic fire could be heard from the churches in Kigali."[50]

Rwanda's genocide was not a tribal frenzy, nor anarchy, but the work of an organized and obedient society—men and women who were convinced that mass annihilation was their *umganda,* their civic duty.[51] Because of the rapidity of the slaughter, it did not become a media circus. Additionally, the country's African neighbors and the Western powers chose not to recognize the atrocity. The U.S. State Department's spokeswoman was ordered not to use the term genocide, but deployed the slippery phrase "acts of genocide" instead.[52] The worst offender was the UN, however, which recalled all but a handful of peacekeepers who were currently in the country. "There were other episodes of mass murder in the twentieth century," according to one British filmmaker. "But—other than the Allied planes flying over the Nazi death camps—there has been no other such demonstration of the Contract of Mutual Indifference in a country where the onlooking world—in an age of mass media—has had a military presence."[53] Rwanda was framed as refugee crisis, which enabled, by default, many of the Hutu killers, the *interahamwe,* to evade punishment. These camps became humanitarian havens for the killers and a more telegenic means for some NGOs to portray a suffering Africa.[54]

"Never again" had happened and was soon to happen again elsewhere, in the Balkans and in Africa. Some of those Hutus responsible for the Rwandan massacre fled into Zaire (now the Democratic Republic of the Congo) after the Tutsi-led Rwandan Patriotic Front took control of Rwanda. The new Rwandan government sent in its troops to kill Hutu militiamen hiding in refugee camps in the Congo. This was partly the cause for Africa's first world war. Nine nations became embroiled in a long, complex ethnic and resource war in a vast land that has known little peace since the greedy and often cruel Belgian colonial administration quit in 1960. After five years and three million deaths, a shaky ceasefire was signed. Although there was television coverage of the refugee camps' conditions along the eastern borders of Congo, the absence of roads and the presence of dense jungle and armed anarchy, as well as the ritual military secrecy in Africa, prevented any effective international coverage. Moreover, it was a complex war and completely unlike the Western portrayal of apartheid.

Above all, media compassion fatigue about Africa intruded. The tragedy that was, and is, Somalia drew in compassionate Westerners and inspired a disastrous military intervention. The debacle in Somalia largely explained, but could never excuse, the moral blindness about, and the later reluctance to intervene in, Rwanda.

## SOMALIA

The intervention in Somalia is often portrayed as the classic example of the CNN effect. Pictures of starving people prompted armed UN intervention backed by the United States. Graphic pictures of U.S. soldiers' bodies dragged through Mogadishu's streets and Black Hawk helicopters downed drove the UN to bring U.S. troops home quickly. Of course the facts are far more complex.

Somalia was anarchic partially because of the fall-out from the Cold War. The Soviets had backed the Somali dictator Siad Barre. Emboldened by their support, Barre invaded neighboring Ethiopia and occupied its Ogaden region to create a greater Somalia. For a while Moscow supported Somalia and Ethiopia before solely supporting the more powerful Ethiopia. Similarly, in 1980, the United States provided military aid to Somalia. When President George H. W. Bush spoke of doing "God's work" in the initial humanitarian intervention in the early 1990s, he ignored the previous superpower rivalry that had poured guns into a country vitiated by clan rivalry. The intervention in Somalia followed U.S. triumphalism in the 1991 Gulf War. The intervention was also seen as deflecting criticism from America's failure to act in the Balkans wars following the break-up of Yugoslavia.

In the beginning, the media framed the Somali crisis as a humanitarian aid problem, not a civil war, with a particular emphasis on feeding starving Somalis. UN Secretary General Boutros Boutros-Ghali criticized the Security Council for being ethnocentrically distracted by the "rich man's war" in the Balkans. On December 3, 1992, the Security Council was stung into action: an intervention was authorized to secure humanitarian operations. Aid convoys would no longer be hijacked by Somali warlords riding their technicals—pickup trucks with machine guns mounted in the back. The enterprise was dubbed "shoot to feed." Washington officials offered to provide the core leadership of the Unified Task Force. On December 9, 1992, Operation Restore Hope opened with 1,600 American troops storming ashore at Mogadishu; waiting for them were hundreds of journalists and television cameras with full lighting sets. The journalist-to-combatant ratio was 1 to 4. (Peter Jennings of ABC News suggested that the SEALs were outnumbered 10 to 1 by reporters.)[55] This was pure Hollywood, *The Sands of Iwo Jima* revisited, and foreshadowed what was to come. Coverage exploded as journalists swarmed across the country, free of the restraints of the pool system that had plagued them in the Gulf and reviving, for the military, all the horror of the Vietnam War.[56]

Though pictures of emaciated Somalis may have prompted an intervention, this impression is misleading. U.S. government aid officials and NGOs had been working for over a year to persuade the media to take notice of the estimated 500,000 Somalis who had died by the summer of 1992.[57] The media was reluctantly following, not leading, the story about "the worst humanitarian crisis in the world today." The U.S. military airlift of food in August 1992 did spark viewers' attention, however. President Bush may well have wanted to leave office with a major humanitarian gesture and, after the Gulf War victory, depart in a blaze of glory as the foreign policy president.[58] The Bush administration perceived it as a quick win, with little cost. The administration was not concerned about an exit strategy, because soon President Bill Clinton would move into the White House. The elaborate planning to have television cameras in place for the spot-lit invasion only confirmed the administration's questionable motives. This coverage, however, sent American evening news ratings to the highest levels since the Gulf War.[59]

As in previous interventions, there had been careful secret planning in Washington. The main enemy—the Somali warlords, particularly "General" Mohamed Aidid—was demonized. The UN provided legitimacy and the Powell Doctrine in the Gulf War was reapplied: overwhelming superiority of force to achieve a quick objective and then a speedy exit was the aim.[60] But it was not to be. Military aid to humanitarian food distribution soon became nation-building amid a civil war. Mission creep became mission gallop. Soon, in some U.S. generals' perspective, the manhunt for General Aidid switched from professional to personal imperatives. When President Bush visited Mogadishu in January 1993, violent interclan fighting erupted. UN peacekeepers and journalists alike were massacred. The United States brought in the deadly AC-130H Spectre gunships to attack Aidid's strongholds. His popularity soared among the Somalis. UN troops fired on a civilian crowd, killing fifty, mainly women and children. (Aidid's guerrilla fighters regularly merged with civilian crowds to discourage UN fire.) This was still, though, a shocking example of a civilian massacre by UN forces, many of which were ill-equipped troops. Infighting within the UN military high command resulted, with even an Italian general sent home to Rome for alleged insubordination. The peace mission was now a limited war, with more than 28,000 UN troops. In June 1993, the UN ordered the arrest of Aidid for war crimes. A series of highly embarrassing military operations to capture him floundered. Another inadvertent killing of 100 civilians by UN troops occurred.

The infamous "Black Hawk Down" incident then ushered in the denouement for American prestige. In October 1993, fourteen U.S. soldiers were killed and seventy-seven wounded in a battle with Aidid's militia. Two American Black Hawk helicopters were shot down, and the pilot of one was captured by militiamen. Television images of the desecration of Americans' bodies shocked the country, which now demanded the return of its troops. The pity for the famished Somalis gave way to the anger against the gunmen in the technicals. As Republican senator Phil Gramm famously noted, the Somalis "don't look hungry to the people of Texas," drawing no distinction between the militia and their victims.[61]

This moment was supposed to be a classic CNN effect, live on prime time. The "Somali Doctrine," the successor to the Vietnam Syndrome was then born—that the United States should not get involved in faraway crises unless its own national security was directly threatened. The Black Hawk incident, however, was not actually live prime-time television. Most of the international press corps had vacated. A Somali stringer using a Hi-8 camcorder, left to him by the departing Reuters crew, had shot the dramatic footage soon broadcasted on CNN and other channels.[62] Evidence also suggests that the new Clinton administration had already considered scaling down and then abandoning the Somali intervention.[63] Black Hawk Down may well have been a useful exit strategy for the new administration in Washington, not one imposed by a crusading media.[64] Clinton could have invested political capital in staying in Somalia. Washington could also have spun out a delayed exit as efficiently as it had glamorized the Navy landings. Instead, U.S. troops were withdrawn, and by early 1995 the last of the other UN contingents departed, and the country dissolved once more into civil war and anarchy. The United States was again to deploy its Spectre gunships in January 2007 to attack al-Qaeda components of the Islamic Courts Union guerrillas. Aided by Washington, Ethiopian forces had pushed the guerrillas from Mogadishu.

Nevertheless, despite the Black Hawk humiliation, the essence of the Western media obituaries on Restore Hope was that of UN failure. The United States was seen as a victim of a failed and noble humanitarian gesture, in a situation in which Washington had had no strategic interest. During the Cold War, however, the United States government had many strategic interests in Somalia and the Horn of Africa. There is evidence that the humanitarian intervention in Somalia echoed the Gulf War: American oil giants Conoco, Amoco, Chevron, and others also had major interests in Somalia.[65] Although U.S. policy can easily be translated as straightforward oil greed, there is also evidence that President George H. W. Bush had genuine humanitarian concerns and had been deeply influenced by a visit, a decade before, to southern Sudan's refugee camps.[66] The president's motives may have been pure, but the Western media's role was perhaps less noble. The scenario of famine to Black Hawk is trite. Randolph Hearst's manipulation of the Spanish-American War through pictures was not going to be repeated. CBS anchorman Dan Rather argued, "It takes more than pictures to move the American people." He noted that the photos of Somalia had been around for a long time, worse were coming out of Bosnia, and the U.S. leaders had not (then) acted.[67] Rather than trail-blazing, the media had been led. Often their reporting was muddled, as few in the chancelleries of the West could fathom the clan mosaic. Moreover, much was patriotic tub-thumping for their boys in uniform. And, as ever in Africa, they walked away from the story as Somalia sunk into a morass of misery, out of the glare of spotlights.

After Somalia and Rwanda, a pattern emerged in reluctant Western involvement. They would step in to resolve a relatively small, correctable problem, similar to the British in Sierra Leone in 2000, the French in the Ivory Coast in 2002, and the Americans in Liberia in 2003. Really major long-term suffering, such as in Darfur after 2003, might have prompted U.S. or NATO involvement before 9/11. Iraq and Afghanistan, however, became distractions for Anglo-American policy. Darfur was left with an African Union (later hybrid AU-UN) force of peacekeepers who could not even organize their own pay corps. They were there, however, as witnesses to a mass tragedy, which few journalists managed to cover effectively.[68]

Yet there is an old saying that Africa is like a poison, that it stays in the blood and the infection is incurable. The politics appall, but the natural beauty is magical. After being wounded again, war correspondent Sam Kiley—born in Africa—wrote for the *Times* on the agony and ecstasy of reporting the continent:

> Africa is a world of absolutes. And the longer I live here, the less I understand. This continent's history keeps repeating itself as a farce and tragedy in ever tighter revolutions. But I draw strength from the staggering magnificence of Africa's vastness. . . . One cannot fail to be moved by a tropical rainstorm. Heavy, warm rain pours from the endless skies plumping into red dirt sending plumes of dust and a smell never to be forgotten.[69]

To those who know Africa well, that sweet-sickly smell is also redolent of the musty honey odor of fresh corpses.

# 5

# EUROPE'S INTRA-STATE CONFLICTS

European powers had long intervened throughout the world as a matter of imperial habit. Even during the 1960s and 1970s, Britain, France, and Portugal were still players in colonial and post-colonial conflicts, especially in Africa. Conflict, however, was also common within Europe itself. Some of these tensions were related to the Cold War. Terrorist groups in Italy and Germany spoke in Marxist terms of class war while emulating terror tactics developed in Latin America. Some were based on nationalism, as with the Basque separatists in Spain. Others were amalgamations of these tensions, as with the official Irish Republican Army (IRA) and later the Provisionals who adapted elements of Marxism, nationalism, and terror tactics. In addition, the politics of the Middle East intruded, with the deaths of 13 Israeli athletes at the 1972 Munich Olympics and Libyan arms supplies to the IRA that same year. Criminal gangs also became embroiled in European tensions as people and arms smuggling, as well as drugs, financed a large black economy. Afghan heroin, Russian weapons, and illegal goods provided by Albanian smugglers created an underworld in which the embryonic jihadist movement could operate clandestinely.

The consensual glue, the ideological framework of the Cold War, had allowed Western journalists an uncomplicated means of practicing their craft. With the collapse of the Soviet Union and the downfall of Marxism throughout Western Europe, however, journalists were confronted with many challenges. This included changes in their lexicon. From "Apparatchik" to "Zhivago," covering events in the USSR had popularized numerous concepts and phrases. Suddenly, "Big Brother" and the "Gulag" became less fearsome terms. Marxists no longer set the intellectual agenda for the chattering, let alone, the working classes. Monolithic communism had been easy to hate and, for most Western columnists, to fear and fight. "Glasnost," initiating a new era of peace, was good, they said, but suddenly conflicts were springing up throughout Europe. Now journalists had to grapple with an intimidating mosaic of supranational threats interwoven with a host of domestic conflicts. Globalization of the world economy, environmental threats, resource wars (for example, the "cod war" between the UK and Iceland in 1975–6), virtual wars (for example, Kosovo in 1999, which will be discussed later), and the impetus for the waves of immigration into Europe all demanded a new intellectual rigor from journalists. Correspondents were further impacted by the Afghan defeat of the Soviets in 1989, which marked a shift from the old communist threat to the new, Islamic extremism. Few in the media understood this crucial transition from the end of the capitalism–communism battle to the much bigger challenge from jihadism in the crucial years 1989–2001. A short analysis of three civil wars—Yugoslavia, Northern Ireland, and Chechnya—will help to explain this transition and outline how correspondents coped with this complex transformation in international relations.

## BALKAN WARS

Scarcely larger than Britain but with a population of twenty-four million, the Yugoslav federation comprised six republics and two autonomous regions, as well as different languages and various isms. It ranged from Slovenians and Austrians in the north, to the Kosovo Albanians in the south. The abundance of cathedrals, monasteries, and mosques reflected the variety of religions practiced in Yugoslavia. Although most Yugoslavs were Catholic or Orthodox Christians, the federation had Europe's largest Muslim community. Perhaps inevitably, the Balkans, as formed by the treaties imposed after World War I, began to unravel. Yugoslavia and the Soviet Union, with its recent implosion of communism, were linked: both enforced federations were on the point of economic and political disintegration.

Slovenia, or, in economic terms, the Sweden of the Balkans, was the first to break away from Yugoslavia. This declaration of independence sparked the Ten-Day War in June and July of 1991. Casualties were low, and surprisingly few Slovenians were killed when the federal Yugoslav planes launched air raids on their cities, the first such assault in Europe since 1945. This was a token spasm from the federal government in Belgrade. Because Slovenia contained a small minority of Serbs in its population of two million, it could gain its independence as long as Belgrade could secure a greater Serbia that encompassed all Serbs throughout the failing federation. In contrast, the independence of neighboring Croatia resulted in major combat.

As Croatia moved to independence, the Serb minority inside Croatia rebelled and declared the Republic of Serb Krajina. Serbia's traditional allies France and Russia were hostile to Germany and its push to recognize Croatia, a friend under Nazi rule. Because of these divisions within Europe, and the initial reluctance of the United States to intervene, especially after Mogadishu, the war escalated as regular Croatian and Serb forces joined the battle between their militias in eastern Croatia. Soon, Serbs controlled about a third of Croat territory. In September 1991, the UN imposed an arms embargo, which affected all involved except the heavily armed Serbs, who had inherited the bulk of the old federal army. The mainly Serb remnants of the federal army backed the Serb rebels in Croatia. Over ten thousand were killed in bitter fighting and hundreds of thousands were displaced in what became known as "ethnic cleansing." Heavy fighting continued from mid-1991 until a temporary ceasefire in January 1992. After intermittent combat, regular Croat armies in rapid offensives retook their occupied lands before the internationally imposed ceasefire in 1995.

Journalists portrayed Croatia as chaotic, where guns and slivovitz were used immoderately. The war created a media frenzy, because there were no pools in the anarchic conditions; this coverage would be more akin to that in Spain during the Spanish Civil War and Vietnam during the Vietnam War. As a historian of photojournalism noted, "Would-be Robert Capas and Margaret Bourke Whites, festooned with Nikons, swarmed into the war zone. Some were going to die, many were going back to 'proper' jobs, but a few would make it."[1] Despite some excellent work by professional photojournalists and filmmakers, lightweight video and audio recorders, or camcorders, proliferated among soldiers, victims, and voyeurs, as well as reporters. There were many pictures, but profound analysis was rare. Moreover, journalists often could not master the complex languages, where names were Tolkienesque, and where, as writer P. J. O'Rourke famously quipped, "the unpronounceables were killing the unspellables." "Ancient tribal rivalries" became the handy, if incorrect, shorthand for the opposing factions.

Ethically, it was difficult to decipher, in the beginning, who wore the white hats—the Serbians, the Croatians, or the Bosnian Muslims. Would the Western correspondents and government officials favor the side that suffered the most casualties or committed the fewest war crimes?[2] Soon, the media, in the main, opted to blame the Serbs—justly, because they did commit the most, and worst, atrocities. Serbia was dubbed the land of Mordor by the more literate journalists, in honor of writer Tolkien's dark vision of a fallen kingdom.[3] A few even explained Serbia's paranoid belligerence. Mark Thompson, in his book *Paper House: The Ending of Yugoslavia,* argued, "There is no understanding Serbia without fathoming its wounded self-righteousness, its perception of itself as more sinned against than sinning."[4]

By the spring of 1992, the civil war had spread to Bosnia (Bosnia-Hercegovina). Bosnian Serbs declared their own republic and, with federal (i.e., Belgrade's) forces, blockaded Sarajevo, the Bosnian capital. It came within a whisker of falling, but its inhabitants, including some Serbs and Croats, fought on for three years. It seemed a revisit to the siege of Leningrad during World War II, and was certainly the heaviest fighting in any European capital since 1945. The newest state in Europe appeared as though it would be the most short-lived. The UN estimated that in 1992 alone one hundred and thirty thousand soldiers and civilians were killed in Bosnia. Young men of military age who were not killed were often rounded up into Serb-controlled concentration camps. Ron Haviv, a twenty-six-year-old New York photographer, discovered a camp at Trnopolje; his pictures appalled the world by exposing the atrocities that may have never come to light without his reportage.[5] "Never again" had been the watchword after 1945, but death camps were once more a part of the European landscape. Sadly, while the United Nations Protection Force (UNPROFOR) was tasked with safeguarding humanitarian relief, it could do little about these massacres and atrocities because the UN force was so poorly equipped and under such strict mandates.

Sarajevo became the media cockpit of the Bosnian war. The UK Ministry of Defence was horrified of committing more British troops to the Balkan quagmire, partly because of the graphic images coming out of the region, and instead wished to withdraw its elements of the peacekeeping forces. Speaking for the ministry, Defence Secretary Sir Malcolm Rifkind energetically informed the Overseas and Defence Committee of the Cabinet that such a commitment could be endless and could risk a considerable number of British lives. As one intelligence expert argued, however, "Ministers like Rifkind were swimming against a tide of television images of suffering."[6] Many journalists stayed in Sarajevo only temporarily.[7] American journalist Janine di Giovanni of London's *Sunday Times*, however, endured the majority of the siege. She delivered some of the most powerful reporting and, in the process, came to understand Bosnians' perception of war. In her emotive book, *The Quick and the Dead,* di Giovanni observed that Yugoslavia was "like a wind tunnel, sucking in everything around it back in time, the century beginning and ending with a brutal and vicious conflict."[8] The fault lines in Bosnia did date back, arguably, to the division of the Roman Empire into East and West. Correspondents quoted variations on the story of a Bosnian Muslim combatant raving about a Serb crime in the dark medieval past. In utter exasperation the journalist would usually say, "But that was in the fourteenth century!" "Yes," the Muslim soldier would reply, "but I heard about it only last week."[9] Ed Vulliamy, in his book *Seasons in Hell: Understanding Bosnia's War,* also recognized this tendency and touched on Yugoslavs' interest in cartography, "The answer to a question to a Serb about a Serbian artillery attack yesterday will begin in the year 925 and is invariably illustrated with maps."[10]

Though the Bosnians may have attributed the war to factors rooted in another century, much of the antagonism was recent and artificial, stoked up by firebrand politicians and the local media in the new republics.[11] One exception was the remarkable Sarajevo daily, *Oslobodjenje.* The newspaper was unusual for two reasons. First, it was comprised of a multiethnic staff; Muslim, Serb, and Croat journalists worked together to deliver their stories. Second, the newspaper continued to churn out issues in the years of the Bosnian Serb siege, despite adverse conditions. During the winters, the office was bereft of heat and electricity and was eventually shelled out, forcing the staff to relocate to the building's basement. Tom Gjelten of National Public Radio covered the story of this courageous newspaper in his book *Sarajevo Daily: A City and Its Newspaper Under Siege.*[12] His book was a happy marriage from a tragic circumstance, where the subject, a newspaper under fire, and a journalist with a distinguished career, including authorship of a study on professionalism in war reporting, came together via a respected organization, NPR. Despite criticism from both left and right in the United States, Gjelten maintained high standards of public broadcasting in delivering the story. His coverage of the wars in the former Yugoslavia earned him the Overseas Press Club's Lowell Thomas Award, a George Polk Award, and a Robert F. Kennedy Journalism Award. Though other journalists earned Pulitzers for their heavyweight analysis, television attention was often focused on human-interest stories.[13] In July 1993, British television broadcasted the tragedy of Irma, a young girl wounded in Sarajevo. In a knee-jerk reaction, the British government flew her (and approximately forty other casualties) out of Sarajevo for specialist treatment in the UK. The Sarajevo UN headquarters cynically referred to Irma's case as "Instant Response to Media Attention."[14] Uncynically, others rescued children from Sarajevo. For example, Mike Nicholson, of Independent Television News, saved an eight-year-old Sarajevan orphan named Natasha and brought her back to England. He wrote a book on this experience, titled *Natasha's Story,* which later became the basis for *Welcome to Sarajevo,* a feature film starring Woody Harrelson and Marisa Tomei.[15] Marcel Ophüls, the director of *The Troubles We've Seen,* a film on journalists in besieged Sarajevo, described war correspondents as "today's resistance fighters."[16]

Despite the UN declaring certain towns in Bosnia, such as Sarajevo, safe havens, these towns were neither safe nor havens. In July 1995, the Bosnian Serb army overran one town, Srebrenica, with tragic and momentous consequences. Scornful of the UN, its four hundred inadequate Dutch peacekeepers, and the media, the Serbs massacred eight thousand male Muslims—the largest mass murder in Europe since World War II.[17] The failure of the UN to respond and its lack of preparation were blatantly obvious; the previous year the UN had abandoned the arms embargo, while on the ground NATO peace enforcers replaced UNPROFOR. In August 1995, the retrained and re-armed Croatian army, backed by NATO air power, rolled up Serb forces in the Krajina region. A heavy aerial bombardment of Serb artillery positions around Sarajevo finally lifted the siege and forced the Serbian government to accept an agreement negotiated in Dayton, Ohio. Nearly all the Western journalists cheered on the eventual NATO response. Their reaction was generally: the Serbs were getting the shit well and truly kicked out of them after three years of doling it out to everyone else. In the Balkans, NATO had fired its first shot in anger, but only after hundreds of thousands of killings in Croatia and Bosnia. In the Cold War, deterrence had created an alliance system; in the unipolar new world order, NATO compulsion was creating protectorates.[18] Bosnia duly became a de facto military protectorate of the West. The politics were still muddled, but large-scale killing in the former Yugoslavia stopped—at least momentarily.

For the international press corps, covering the Bosnian war had its advantages and disadvantages. It was difficult to cover for journalists because of the war's inherent dangers; at least seventy-five reporters were killed between 1991 and 1996. The Serb snipers did not check for press cards before pulling the trigger. In fact, they sometimes received bonuses for killing journalists. There were also no effective pools, though NATO and the UN offered accreditation and occasionally aid. In contrast, the Bosnian war was a long war in relatively favorable terrain, unlike the short and wide-ranging desert war in the Gulf, and in terms of access was easy to get into and to operate in. Since it was a UN humanitarian mission and, as so, officially transparent, journalists could switch sides, often by crossing a bridge, though perhaps under fire. The military, in short, could not dictate to them. As Gen. Sir Michael Rose, the UNPROFOR commander, said, "In a war environment, journalists cannot travel freely about the battlefield or talk to the enemy, and they are often obliged to depend upon the military structure for their information as well as their survival. In a UN mission, however, journalists owe peacekeepers nothing."[19]

Because of this transparency, journalists from larger organizations, such as the BBC, would travel in their armored vehicles to places many soldiers were not permitted or able to visit. In this sense, they were useful sources of intelligence for the military. Because of its reliance on journalists' access, the military was progressively friendlier and more helpful the closer reporters came to frontline fighting. Journalists railed against the local warlords, not the disciplined Western armies, though the French military was rarely popular with British correspondents because of its perceived bureaucracy. Journalists behaved more responsibly than they had in previous conflicts as far as the British army was concerned partly because of their sense of ownership. The journalists had called for Western intervention, and they had received it, albeit belatedly and piecemeal. It had become their war as well. The BBC's Martin Bell, perhaps the most distinguished British journalist in the Balkans, described this odd-couple tango in his book *In Harm's Way*:

> In peacekeeping, we in the press were engaged in an entirely new relationship with the military—that is the blue-helmeted military. Of course we had our differences with the UN—usually over interpretations of its mandate—but we were fundamentally its partners and not its antagonists. We shared its dangers and frustrations. We were to some extent responsible for its deployment in the first place. We wished it to succeed.[20]

Though good relations with the Western peacekeepers may have helped correspondents, the war itself was far more complex because of the tribal gridlock. This was a far cry from the recent Gulf War where most journalists could focus on one evil figure, Saddam Hussein. (Later in the Balkan imbroglio, though, NATO spin doctors demonized the Serbian president, Slobodan Milosevic, as a latter-day Stalin.) From the start, media images tended to conform to Cold War stereotypes: good and brave Slovenians and Catholic Croatian capitalists versus the big and bad communist Serbians. Furthermore, journalists tended to commonly refer to the Balkan people, as a whole, as "others," lost in dark myths and chasing ancient ghosts—not as fellow Europeans. If context was deficient, pictures were often far too powerful. In fact, many images were sanitized because of their anticipated impact on squeamish Western audiences. Why wars should be sanitized, except on the feeble grounds of good taste, has never been adequately addressed by anyone. The media satellite dishes in Sarajevo still pumped out daily horror pictures, though not from Mostar where conditions were even worse.

Journalists, most eloquently Bell in his regular BBC reporting, called for NATO powers to relieve the agony. He warned that unless the West intervened early, the problems would only worsen and be more insoluble in the long term. UNPROFOR, and then NATO, provided pseudo-action and alibis, not policies to end the war. Some journalists argued that humanitarian aid distorted the war and prolonged it.[21] Effective peace enforcement depended on American will and power. Only U.S. air power could push the contestants to what Karl von Clausewitz called the culminating point, which, in this case, was marked by the Bosnian Serbs' military defeat, the Dayton peace accords, and the deployment of sixty thousand NATO troops in 1995.

Most veteran Western journalists felt that they had acquitted themselves honorably. "We had our faults," confessed Bell, "but at least we were not inert in the face of genocide, and we did not run away."[22] How effective, though, were the journalists in influencing policy? Little to no policy existed in the beginning. Furthermore, correspondents tended to concentrate on the symptoms, not the causes of the war, and called for intervention, though the parameters for an intervention had not yet been determined. The Western European powers did not wish to intervene and only reluctantly embarked on a peacekeeping role. They did not accept peace enforcement until Washington was fully prepared to commit hard power to strengthen the relatively feeble European response. After being asked whether television coverage was blowing British policy off course, Lord Carrington, former British defense secretary, replied, "That always supposes that there's a course to be blown off."[23] The coverage, though, was extensive, with mass communication of the slaughter beamed by satellite into living rooms daily. Pictures such as the Sarajevo marketplace massacre in May 1992, and the appalling pictures of the Omarska Mine concentration camp soon after, were as graphic as Westerners could handle. The Irma rescue too played on popular sympathy, but it did not necessarily drive political change.

The drip drip effect of Bell's authoritative delivery seemed to have worked on the consciences of some British ministers. His regular reporting positioned Bosnia at the top of the government's agenda. Though the coverage may have also affected policy as it was crystallizing toward real intervention, it did not fundamentally change policy. The impact of the media on decision-making was incremental and tactical but not strategic, unless the decision-makers were caught unawares, as with the concentration camp pictures on the UK's Independent Television News in summer 1992. As it happened, Western intelligence agencies knew of these camps, yet politicians lacked the will to tackle the crisis openly. With pressure from the media mounting, Serbian officials sometimes shifted inmates out of Serb-controlled areas which indirectly suggested that television had enforced complicity in ethnic cleansing. This is, however, a convoluted argument. While the constant influx of pictures fed politicians' fear of intervention, their influence on editors and newspaper columnists opened politicians and their publics to the feasibility and necessity of real action.

In his memoirs, *In Harm's Way*, Martin Bell famously called for "journalism of attachment, journalism which cares as well as knows," despite his additional, perhaps contradictory, insistence on objectivity.[24] Many journalists had become personally involved in the Bosnian war, although few, such as Mike Nicholson, ventured as far as adopting orphans.[25] Whether or not their professional objectivity had been undermined by this exceptionally emotional and lengthy war, Western correspondents were clearly biased against the Serbs. To journalists, the Serbs, or rather their leader and his armies and militias, had been largely responsible for the destruction of the once-prosperous federation. Some journalists had even attacked the Sarajevo foreign press corps for abandoning objectivity by aligning themselves as propagandists for the Bosnian government and choosing to ignore Bosnian atrocities.[26]

Though it would seem that major wars in Europe should be of concern to a British cabinet, especially when an invasion force had been sent to the remote Falklands, the Conservative governments of the period were instinctively cautious about entering wars. With Tony Blair's appointment as prime minister in 1997, however, wars of intervention, usually shoulder to shoulder with the United States, became fashionable. And the first of the Blair wars was Kosovo.

## KOSOVO

In summer 1999 NATO turned its head toward Kosovo, determined to drive out Serb forces (Serbs accounted for only ten percent of the population), and to bring back 800,000 Albanian Kosovars who had been forced to flee. NATO also had other aims: notably stabilizing the Balkans and, by default, preserving NATO's credibility. Serb atrocities in the province—exaggerated by the Western media and NATO—encouraged the Alliance to bomb a resistant Serbian President Milosevic into submission. The Western allies believed that a short, sharp air war would dismantle the Belgrade strongman, maybe in less than seventy-two hours. "Air power," as Eliot Cohen noted in *Foreign Affairs*, "is an unusually seductive form of military strength because, like modern courtship, it appears to offer gratification without commitment."[27] This estimate proved to be modest; the actual bombing campaign lasted seventy-eight days. After the first twelve days, NATO had launched the same number of combat operations that it had ordered in the first twelve hours of the Gulf War. The Alliance, President

Bill Clinton in particular, was reluctant to commit combat troops on the ground. It became increasingly clear, though, that a ground offensive, in addition to the air campaign, might be necessary. This decision, however, became obsolete. Milosevic soon realized he was largely on his own; Russia, though anti-NATO, was not going to intervene and defend Serbia.

The Serbs capitulated, and the war ended on June 11, 1999, without a single combat fatality on the Allied side. Since there were no NATO casualties, the Western media concentrated on the impact of the bombing, especially on civilians. Milosevic survived long enough to finesse an arrangement: an international force was sent into Kosovo to maintain a UN protectorate that was autonomous but not officially independent. In fact, international peacekeeping troops, including Russians, were tasked with curbing the unruly Kosovo Liberation Army and its bandit partners in Albania proper. When Milosevic regime started to totter, the allies also had to pay millions of dollars for the repair of Serbia's bomb damage.

Although it was a short war, it was destined to be a long peacekeeping operation. The intervention had fulfilled one of NATO's aims by refashioning an alliance that had lost its rationale. Yet the alliance still had its flaws. NATO's British commander in Macedonia, Gen. Mike Jackson, had negotiated the initial peaceful withdrawal of Serb forces from the province, until the Russians sent a small armored flying column to Pristina, the Kosovo capital, where the local Serbs treated them as heroes. Ordered to send in British forces by helicopter to Pristina's airport to face down the Russians, Jackson refused to obey his NATO commander, U.S. Gen. Wesley Clark. "General, I'm not going to start World War Three for you," the Brit famously declared.[28] The race to Pristina could be seen as the last battle of the Cold War.

Unlike the long unruly wars in Croatia and particularly Bosnia, Kosovo was a heavily media-manipulated war. The first time since 1945 that so many European countries were involved in one war, it was clear from the start that the Serbs could not defeat NATO in battle. Milosevic's only chance of success was for Belgrade to break allied solidarity by launching a media war, or what journalist Peter Dunn dubbed "the first international conflict fought by press officers."[29] The Serbs controlled the small Western press corps in Belgrade, and NATO's HQ in Brussels micromanaged the initial reasons for intervention and the air war. The Serbs cleverly used propaganda, especially Serb and Kosovar civilian casualties, to trumpet the dichotomy between the failure of NATO's humanitarian mission on the ground and the additional casualties caused by air bombardment. Serbian propaganda was so prevalent and influential that British government ministers attacked the BBC, especially John Simpson, for reporting from Belgrade.

Simpson replied that it was "ludicrous and offensive to suggest that I was this glove puppet for Milosevic."[30]

NATO's media operation in Brussels began to fold under the Serb propaganda, especially after untrue accounts of NATO's air attack casualties came out. Overtaxed press spokesman Dr. Jamie Shea, who conducted the daily press briefing in Brussels, was responsible for relaying what military historian Alistair Horne called "the predigested spin that had been chewed over at length by a committee of NATO ruminants."[31] Tony Blair sent in spin doctor and eminence grise Alastair Campbell to Brussels to relieve Shea, reorganize the media process, and steady nerves.[32] On the ground, a new breed of British army media operations specialists was assigned to Pristina to manage the 2,700 foreign journalists following NATO's occupation of Kosovo. Depite better media ops personnel, the hacks still complained. "We were given lots of material but no information," said *Sky News* correspondent Jake Lynch.

NATO and its respective governments, especially in Washington, D.C., and London, were also subjected to media criticism. They were guilty of propaganda and gross exaggeration—especially about Serb atrocities and the accuracy of NATO bombings—in order to diabolize the Serbs, Milosevic in particular.[33] Phillip Knightley, in *The First Casualty*, accused NATO propaganda of being worse than the old Soviet propaganda "because there was no opposition to it."[34] Knightley, however, commented approvingly on the work of veterans such as John Simpson of the BBC who reported out of Belgrade, Christiane Amanpour of CNN, who was forced out of Belgrade by Serb threats, and Julian Mannion of ITN, also in Belgrade. He also cited the Kosovo endeavors of Maggie O'Kane of the *Guardian* and Marie Colvin and John Swain of the London *Sunday Times*, commenting as an aside on the high number and the quality of senior female correspondents covering Kosovo. Nonetheless, his overall conclusion on media coverage of Kosovo was stark, "The lies, manipulation, news management, propaganda, spin, distortion, omission, slant and gullibility of the coverage of this war, so soon after the media debacle in the Gulf, has brought war correspondents to crisis point in their short history."[35] The *British Journalism Review* noted, however, that when, compared with Desert Storm, the Falklands, Suez, and certainly the Korean War, "we must conclude that we have not been badly served" by the profession.[36]

Since this was a new kind of virtual war, journalists in the field, and out of the Brussels propaganda web, conducted themselves reasonably well. The Kosovo War had been termed the virtual war by Michael Ignatieff in his book *Virtual War: Kosovo and Beyond*. Because this war was a war without death, at least on the Western side, it ceased to be fully real. He argued that the victory was also virtual, particularly as the future status of Kosovo had not been resolved. In this new surreal conflict, all NATO citizens were mobilized "not as combatants but as spectators," with Western journalists turned willingly or otherwise into combatants in the media war, because so many swallowed the NATO line.[37] Assuming the role as combatants was not without danger. NATO launched an air attack on Belgrade's main Serb TV station in April 1999 that was also used by Western film crews. This was to set a pattern for later wars, not least in Iraq when TV stations, and even TV crews, were attacked by American aircraft and tanks. The editorial in the *British Journalism Review* on Kosovo had proven prophetic: "The media, and therefore working journalists, have now become prime targets for destruction as well as for influencing."[38]

Other writers attacked NATO's circumvention of international law. Left-wing critics admitted that they had failed to castigate the war. Diana Johnstone summarized this critique when she wrote: "Not since the Socialist Parties of Europe rallied to their governments' war programs in 1914 has the left's opposition to war collapsed so ignominiously and with such good conscience."[39] She admitted that the real challenge to the war came from right-wing analysts, often spurred by libertarian suspicion of official propaganda. Johnstone also noted:

> Media attention to conflicts in Yugoslavia is sporadic, dictated by Great Power interests, lobbies, and the institutional ambitions of "non-governmental organisations"—often linked to powerful governments—whose competition with each other for donations provides motivation for exaggerations of the abuses they specialise in denouncing. Yugoslavia, a country once known for its independent approach to socialism and international relations, the most prosperous country in Eastern Central Europe, is being systematically reduced to an ungovernable chaos by Western support to secessionist movements. The emerging result is not a charming bouquet of independent little ethnic democracies, but rather a new type of joint colonial rule by the international community, enforced by NATO.[40]

Given the Zeitgeist and the mood of humanitarianism via casualty-free virtual war throughout Western Europe—though Blair was prepared for major casualties in the British army—NATO governments and their electorates largely supported this war. It was about humanitarian impulses as much as power plays. Their involvement also reflected guilt about delayed intervention in Bosnia: perhaps the Kosovo intervention was partly an atonement for Srebrenica.

Though media critics such as Knightley and proponents of the left such as Johnstone may have overstated their arguments, the military, and their governments, undoubtedly dominated the media in Kosovo. Despite the new openness of the military's media operations, manipulation and misinformation were still rife. Army media specialists on the ground and the war correspondents in the field were both victims of the intense propaganda campaigns of NATO's political leaders, and not only in London and Washington. Most of the media in Western Europe and the United States joined the campaign and quickly moved to promoting war and pressing for violent action to maintain credibility instead of providing reasonably objective information that would contribute to public debate.[41] Though it is a gross distortion to accuse the BBC of being a "de facto public information arm" of NATO, it is true that most media outlets bought into the demonization of the Serbs once more.[42] Like the Kosovo conflict itself, it was also, as later wars were to prove, merely a virtual victory for the democracies. Unfortunately for the Serbs, their sophisticated external media propaganda war over Kosovo, especially their use of the Internet, was not matched by a greater self-awareness of their own political deficiencies at home.[43]

In December 2004, more than six thousand EU troops replaced NATO in Bosnia. By spring of 2007, the number was reduced to twenty-five hundred. That March, the remaining British troops departed after having served fifteen years in Bosnia. Based on these figures, Defence Secretary Sir Malcolm Rifkind had been justifiably concerned about the length of commitment reinforcing the Balkans would require after the Bosnian war. UK and other NATO casualties, however, were actually much lower than forecasted. The same is not true for the civilian casualty rate. Compared with other battlefields, Bosnia's are still the most densely mined, and, with luck, it may take another seventy-five years to clear them.[44]

By 2007, the Kosovars and the Serb government had not reached agreement on the status of the province. A senior mediator proposed that the UN allow Kosovo its independence, setting the stage for further diplomatic tensions between Russia and the West.[45] Russian diplomats argued, inter alia, that recognition of Kosovo would give Moscow leverage over pro-Western Georgia by suggesting that the breakaway provinces of Abkhazia and South Ossetia could follow Kosovo's example. Conversely, the lure of EU membership has brought much peace to the Balkans. Slovenia, for example, had joined the EU. Prompt Western military and political intervention largely resolved the highly explosive region of

Macedonia. Montenegro peacefully voted for independence in May 2006. Even Serbia underwent major reforms, and, in the same year, NATO granted Belgrade Partnership for Peace status—the first steps to joining the alliance that had expelled it from Kosovo seven years earlier. The Balkans now fell into the category of "good news" journalism because of its progress and, as such, was guaranteed to earn far less airtime than when its states had been at war. "If it bleeds, it leads" was still true of most news editors.

## NORTHERN IRELAND

Northern Ireland (Ulster) was a classic case of a protracted war—over thirty years—in a liberal democracy. The origin of Ireland's "Troubles," as the recurrent bouts of fighting were called, can be traced back hundreds of years. An American journalist of Irish extraction, P. J. O'Rourke, provides the pithiest summary in *Holidays in Hell*:

> The Brits arrived [in Ireland] somewhat tardily, in 1169, and proceeded to commit the unforgivable sin of having long bows and chain mail. For the next 819 years (and counting) the English stole land, crushed rebellions, exploited the populace, persecuted Catholics, dragged a bunch of Scottish settlers into Ulster, crushed more rebellions, held potato famines, hanged patriots, stamped out the language, taxed everybody's pig, crushed more rebellions yet and generally behaved in a manner much different than the Irish would have if it had been the Irish who invaded England. . . .[46]

In short, this partisan view expresses the defense that enough barbarism had been inflicted on the Irish to excuse all barbarities later committed by the Irish.[47] More recently, though, Ireland and its relationship to England has not been the sole reason for its conflict. Instead, internal religious tensions, albeit indirectly involving England, has caused strife. This intra-Christian feuding has been likened to the Sunni-Shi'a divisions in Islam.

Surfacing again in the 1960s, the conflict centered on the Protestant majority's desire to remain part of the UK and the Catholic minority's determination to join the Republic of Ireland in the southern twenty-six counties. Up until the 1970s and 1980s, the Catholic minority suffered discrimination over housing and employment. In 1969, civil rights marches by Catholics and counter-demonstrations by Protestant loyalists (loyal to the British Crown) led to violent unrest in Belfast. The British government sent troops to support the police who were losing control over the crowds.

Greeted warmly at first by the Catholics, the army soon was challenged by their Provisional Irish Republican Army. As a result, Northern Ireland's regional parliament was suspended and direct rule was imposed from London. In an act of rebellion, the IRA pioneered the car bomb attack and continued bomb, mortar, rocket, and gun attacks in Northern Ireland, England (but not the fellow Celtic nations of Scotland and Wales), as well as military installations in mainland Europe. Loyalist paramilitaries targeted Catholics in tit-for-tat killings.

After years of intermittent fighting, broken ceasefires, and hidden deals, the Good Friday Agreement was signed in 1998, after much effort by Prime Minister Blair and some help from President Bill Clinton. A power-sharing executive was set up, backed by referendums in Ulster and in the Irish Republic, which gave up claims to the north. Power-sharing devolution broke down, partly because of the slow progress of arms decommissioning by the IRA. On March 26, 2007, the two opposing hardliners, Gerry Adams of the IRA/Sinn Fein and Ian Paisley, the leader of the largest Protestant party, finally sat down together. They did not shake hands then, but they agreed to share power in a devolved assembly. Though a few extremists on both sides opposed the settlement, the vast majority of the citizens of Northern Ireland welcomed the change and the peace, prosperity, and employment that followed it. For them, regressing to the Troubles was unthinkable.

The British media had taken a battering during the Troubles. Much of the coverage of the conflict had been one-sided. As one experienced British journalist articulated, "Reporting a war on one's own doorstep is always more difficult than reporting someone else's war."[48] The nationalist/republican newspapers in the province were expected to be partisan. The BBC and the quality English newspapers were not. Much of the time, however, the English media failed the Irish as well as their own professional standards (though the reporting of the indefatigable Robert Fisk was an honorable exception). Initially, the British army was to blame for the BBC's bias. Its response to the media was secretive, unreliable, and hostile. Gradually, it improved as it realized that the IRA and its political wing, Sinn Fein, were winning the propaganda war in the province and in the United States, with its large Irish-American community. Successive British governments treated the unrest as a wartime emergency and put great pressure on newspapers and broadcasters to avoid publishing the views of the terrorists. In particular, Prime Minister Thatcher was determined to cut off what she called the "oxygen of publicity" to the IRA.

The government used an array of existing legislation and some specially devised for Ulster to keep the media's focus away from the IRA. The government also was guilty of cover-ups, with the 1972 "Bloody Sunday" killing of fourteen civilians by British paratroopers as the most infamous example. Spasmodically, the serious UK newspapers would return to issues such as "Bloody Sunday" and prod the authorities. A series of expensive government enquiries eventually demonstrated that the army's report of the deaths was inaccurate, though one military expert argued that it was caused by "an undisciplined cock-up, not a conspiracy."[49]

The British government's relations with the media further deteriorated with the aftermath of the Milltown cemetery killings. The BBC and ITN had taken pictures of two slain undercover British soldiers who had mistakenly passed through an IRA funeral at Milltown cemetery in March 1988. The government forced both broadcasters, after serious protest, to hand over their tapes after news editors were threatened with arrest under the Prevention of Terrorism Act. Though the BBC accepted that it had to abide by the law, it recognized that complying was not only against media ethics, but also meant that its film crews could be targeted by IRA gunmen who did not want television footage in the hands of security forces.

Relations between the government and the media reached its lowest point with the 1988 ban on the direct airing of IRA representatives, though there had been relatively few television interviews with them. The broadcasters found a loophole in the legislation (which was based on similar existing laws in the Irish Republic): Sinn Fein spokespeople were broadcast, soundlessly, with their words subtitled or spoken by actors. This only drew attention to what the IRA had to say. "There is a no more ludicrous sight on television than the lip-synched soundbite," in the words of John Simpson, then the BBC's foreign editor.[50] The ban survived until September 1994, shortly after the IRA announced a ceasefire. More effective was the secret arm-twisting by government officials, especially on the BBC, which was inevitably sensitive about its status and funding, particularly during the Thatcher premiership. This has been called the "British way of censorship": self-censorship and filtration of news stories up the chain of command, notably in the highly bureaucratic BBC.[51]

Although Northern Ireland was, and is, officially part of the United Kingdom, the military counterinsurgency sometimes acted as it would in a Third World country. Laws were ignored, bent, or reinvented, such as internment without trial, harsh treatment of internees, and the alleged "shoot-to-kill" policy. There was initial justification to IRA publicity in the United States that described "an army of occupation out of control." The army soon learned, however, that it was not at war, but providing aid to the civil power, particularly as it "Ulsterized" the conflict by working alongside the Royal Ulster Constabulary and the Ulster Defence Regiment. It refined its techniques, not least in dealing with the media. After 1977, all army units had to field a press officer. This hard training ground would later prove useful for the army and its peacekeeping missions in the Balkans and elsewhere.[52] And, in the secret war, the army was highly successful in the use of "supergrass" informants and moles, which reached to the top of the IRA. The IRA was determined to sap the will of the army in the province, but the heavy-handed preliminary responses were replaced by sophisticated containment over the three decades. During this time, army officers patiently understood they were "holding the ring" for politicians in Belfast, Dublin, and London to reach a political solution. At the same time, the IRA/Sinn Fein maintained a successful propaganda war, especially in hiding its retributions and fund-raising activities, which echoed the Mafia's.[53] The IRA manipulated the freedoms that a liberal democracy offered, though some of these were eroded by government legislation and covert means of pressure on the media. The National Union of Journalists, particularly during the ban on hearing IRA voices, regularly accused the government of emulating the apartheid regime in South Africa.

Especially in liberal democracies, the longer the conflict and the greater the lack of success in quickly ending the war, the more determined the media will become in circumventing restrictions.[54] Yet, the media generally failed its audience on the English mainland. Except when the IRA staged a "spectacular" by bombing British cities or assassinating a Cabinet minister or a member of the Royal family, the electorate tried to forget the Troubles.[55] If there had been a UK-wide referendum on withdrawing from the province, the vast majority of the population would have been in support of it (as they would to the return of capital punishment). No major British political party, however, could be seen to surrender in the province, especially the Conservative Party, which was constitutionally committed to the Union with Northern Ireland (and Scotland and Wales).

Italy and Germany also brought the media, by persuasion and legal pressure, into a centralized response to their homegrown terrorists, the Red Brigade and the West German Red Army Faction. West Germany effectively imposed a news blackout after the kidnapping of a prominent West German industrialist in 1977. Italy was less successful in controlling its media after the kidnapping of Aldo Moro, the twice-elected prime minister. In both cases, the hostages were murdered. As with the IRA, whether deprivation of publicity had a direct impact on the terrorists' goals is difficult to prove. Political redress for long-running grievances, such as Basque separatist group ETA's demands for autonomy and independence, are in the long term the key, not short-term media tactics. A historian of media-military relations summarized the debate thus:

Withholding the "oxygen of publicity" may suppress some outward manifestations of terrorism, although such repressive measures . . . force "terrorists" to resort to yet more spectacular atrocities in order to pierce the veil of censorship. . . . But bans on media reportage are most unlikely to suffocate terrorism altogether, for this prescription tackles only the symptoms, not the underlying malady, and treats terrorism as essentially a problem for journalists, not politicians.[56]

The civil war in Northern Ireland was often treated as a form of IRA psychosis. Tabloid headlines screamed variations on "murdering mad bastards." The military, in the beginning, bungled operationally in military and media terms. On occasion, the government behaved, particularly under Thatcher, as though the English media was in cahoots with the IRA. The media also tended often to take the path of least resistance, even censoring itself. Moreover, the Irish seemed unpredictable. Even traffic wardens, Catholic and Protestant alike, were friendly to visitors in Ulster. A few square miles of Belfast looked like conventional war zones, where young street kids would ask cheekily, "Would you be needing a sound-bite, sir?" and then criticize the journalist's choice of shutter speed on his Nikon. Even in South Armagh, amid the serene countryside that constituted the majority of the province, stood the British army observation towers, gangling, soaring contraptions of guy wire and pipe that looked like Heath-Robinson building scaffolds had cross-bred with the Martian war machines of H. G. Wells.[57]

Underneath the superficial charm of the IRA and the loyalists lurked intense emotions: a passionate anger of the IRA men who could starve themselves to death in prison protests, and the deep allegiance of the ultra-loyalists who would fight anyone, including the British, to remain British. Except for a few Fleet Street veterans of the Troubles, the English media were often bamboozled by the Irish people, as much as by their government or the army. In London it was easier to adopt the Basil Fawlty mantra: "Don't mention the war."[58]

## HIDDEN WAR: CHECHNYA

In 1858, after decades of tough resistance, Chechnya was conquered by Russia. This followed the defeat of Imam Shamil, whose fighters had vowed to establish an Islamic state. During the chaos of the Russian revolution, the Chechens briefly secured independence. Germany's invasion brought renewed hope of freedom from the Soviet yoke. When World War II ended, Josef Stalin sought vengeance by wholesale deportation of the

Chechens, mainly to Siberia. They were allowed to return in 1957, after Stalin's death.

When the USSR collapsed in 1991, the Chechens again declared independence. In 1994, the Russians bungled a poorly planned bid to regain control. They attacked, as they had in Afghanistan twenty-five years before, at Christmas time, to dilute Western protests. Perhaps a tenth of the population was killed in the onslaught, especially in Grozny, the capital. David Loyn, of the BBC, observed, "For the first time since the Second World War thousands of shells were fired into a city in a single day. The snipers of Sarajevo seemed almost gentlemanly by comparison."[59] The main resistance leader, Gen. Aslan Maskhadov, fought well and hard. Former British army officer and co-founder of Frontline TV News Vaughan Smith commented on the widespread support that the Chechens gave Maskhadov, "If you were a fighter, you didn't get a shag from the missus that night unless you killed a Russian."[60] Amid growing public concern in a Russia that had grasped at media freedoms, Moscow withdrew its forces after heavy losses. Chechnya achieved substantial autonomy but not full independence. It did not achieve stability either, as warlordism and organized crime proliferated. In August 1999, Chechen fighters crossed into the neighboring Russian republic of Dagestan as part of a planned Islamic insurrection in the region. The following year, the Russians blamed the Chechens for a series of explosions in Moscow apartment blocks. Others, including ex-KGB officer Alexander Litvinenko (who was famously assassinated by radiation poisoning in London), suspected that the Russian security services had bombed them to create a pretext for war and the reelection of President Vladimir Putin in 2000.

The assertive and autocratic president ordered a brutal campaign to re-conquer the rebel state. Putin used the Second Chechen War to instigate Russian xenophobia and to curb his domestic media. There had been Western coverage in the First Chechen War, although it had been sporadic. Because of this coverage during the first war, Russia imposed a total ban on journalists in the second. In February 2000, the Russians captured and destroyed much of Grozny. This time, however, the Russians combined the reconstruction, especially in the capital, with gross violations of human rights. After 9/11, Putin projected his Chechnya adventures as part of the wider war on global jihadist terror to mute criticism from Washington and London. As John Pilger opined, "Having demonstrated his ability to keep post-Soviet Russia under control, Putin was Washington's and London's man, and in return received carte blanche in troublesome Chechnya."[61] If the Cold War had not ended, the Chechens would probably have been armed by the West in the same way that the Afghan fighters had received support in the 1980s. Journalists covering the war generally admired the Chechens' courage in fighting the Russians, but understood why their struggle had been sacrificed to the politics of the new world order.

Chechen rebels seized a Moscow theater in October 2002 and held 800 people hostage; 120 of the hostages were killed when Russian troops stormed the building. Moscow then damned the Chechens for organizing the siege at North Ossetia's Beslan school, which ended in a bloodbath. The fighting by dissident Islamic fighters continued against the pro-Moscow Chechen leader, Ramzan Kadyrov. The anti-Russian forces were still trying to widen the conflict to include the whole of the Caucasus, where a kaleidoscope of conflicts smoldered, not least in Georgia.

In the early days of the Chechen independence wars, Western journalists could gain access to the region, though it was dangerous. The BBC's Jeremy Bowen produced powerful television footage in 1995 and succinctly described in his memoirs the Stalingrad-like conditions in Grozny.[62] Since Putin's crackdown, it became increasingly difficult for foreign journalists to operate freely in Chechnya. A few Russians were allowed entry, and they reported the war from the official Moscow standpoint. A brave exception was Anna Politkovskaya, who wrote for the independent *Novaya Gazeta*. She traveled to Chechnya thirty-nine times between 1999 and 2001. In one of her dispatches from near Grozny in November 1999, Politkovskaya wrote:

> Our losses are immeasurable as we let the army get out of hand and degenerate into anarchy. By allowing such a war to be fought in our own country, without any rules, not against terrorists but against those who hate their own bandits perhaps even more strongly than we do, we are the losers and the loss is irreversible.[63]

Politkovskaya made many powerful enemies. In Chechnya, senior Russian officers repeatedly threatened her with rape. She survived numerous death threats and an attempted poisoning in 2004. Then, in October 2006, she was murdered in her Moscow apartment building. Experts suspect it was a contract killing.

In 2007, Putin declared the war to be over, but a secret partisan war was still underway that could last for years. Conservative estimates are that two hundred thousand Chechens have been killed in the fighting since 1994. Officially, Moscow has admitted that ten thousand federal troops were killed in combat in Chechnya, which is certainly an underestimate. Of the approximately one million Russian troops who survived, many of the veterans became alcoholics, unemployable, and anti-social, suffering from what has been termed "the Chechen syndrome."[64]

By mid-2007, the Russians were using their Chechen loyalist proxies, some of whom had been bought, while others claimed to have been disenchanted with the small number of foreign Islamic extremists who had infiltrated and dominated the separatist forces. Many utterly war-weary Chechens hoped that Putin's strong-arm tactics, allied to recon- struction, would allow Ramzan Kadyrov, Moscow's man and certainly no bleeding-heart liberal, to bring peace of sorts. Better one warlord in con- trol, they said, than several competing bandit or jihadist leaders.[65]

Chechnya was only one of many largely hidden wars, places where most media couldn't reach. Tibet was still closed to foreign correspon- dents, as was Burma, where the Karen people were exterminated. The Maoist insurgency in Nepal too was little reported.[66] The list of conflicts ignored in Africa was long. Sometimes the sheer inaccessibility of the fighting and the restrictions of authoritarian regimes deterred reporters. More often, though, it was a straightforward question of Western news values. To quote the intrepid Welsh correspondent, Jeremy Bowen, "A tra- ditional British newsroom follows a terrible arithmetic. Generally speak- ing, the further away from London, and the poorer the people, the more deaths it takes to qualify as a big story."[67]

The wars in the Balkans were extensively covered, partly because of the advent of lightweight cameras deployed by journalists as well as by ordinary citizens. This was a portent of the twentieth-first-century phe- nomenon of citizen journalists armed with cameras in their mobile phones. Wars suddenly became more difficult to hide. The wars of Islamic extrem- ism, from phone footage of the 7/7 attacks on the London Underground to the unofficial recording of Saddam Hussein's hanging, resulted in an ex- plosion of images. These reports by amateurs were increasingly absorbed into mainstream news. They may have dramatized the stories, but they may also have undermined the professionals' anxious search for context in this bewildering new world disorder.

# 6

# THE MIDDLE EAST AND AFGHANISTAN

As American writer P. J. O'Rourke once quipped, "The press stands accused of holding the Israelis to higher moral standards than it holds the other peoples of the Middle East. That's not our fault. Moses started that."[1] Numerous volumes allege press bias on both sides of the Arab–Israeli conflict.[2] In fact, the Arab–Israeli conflict is probably the most difficult of the Middle Eastern conflicts in terms of media objectivity. The Western media have been consistently accused of systematically failing to cover the Islamic world impartially. This charge is analyzed in Palestinian American literary theorist Edward Said's influential work *Covering Islam*, published in 1981.[3] Said argued that Western reporting of events in Islamic countries has been superficial and cliché-ridden, tainted by cultural bias, and at times dangerously xenophobic. American political scientist Samuel P. Huntington's later work on the alleged clash of civilizations added fuel to the fire.[4] The events of 9/11 suggested that both Said's and Huntington's warnings were becoming tragically self-fulfilling.

Said's critique contended that Western media coverage of the Middle East was conditioned by strategic and economic interests—primarily oil supplies—and that events in the region were traditionally reported from the angle of threats to the production, distribution, and pricing of oil. The early 1970s witnessed the rise of oil power in the form of the Organization of Petroleum Exporting Countries (OPEC); the period also marked the rise of Arab terrorist groups. Although it is too simple to ascribe Western interests in the Middle East as being only, or mainly, about oil, it is equally simplistic to suggest that Middle Eastern terrorism is only related to Israel and that the United States became the target of the 9/11 attacks because of its support for Zionism. The arrival of continuous global satellite broadcasting in the late 1980s and 1990s might have framed the Arab–Israeli clash in such terms, leading one to conclude that television in particular is event driven and perhaps even incapable of complex issue-based coverage. It may also be argued, though, that Said's critique has been challenged by the televised coverage of the recent major conflicts in Israel, Iran, Iraq, and Afghanistan.

## ISRAEL VERSUS THE PALESTINIANS

As in Africa, the news in the Middle East was generally negative—wars, coups, terrorism, and underdevelopment—throughout much of the late twentieth century. While Israel was not the cause of Arab underdevelopment, it became the symbol of the Arab world's failure to redress its many deficiencies. With the founding of Israel in 1948, much of the world favored the infant state. After the Holocaust, many Western correspondents believed that Israel deserved to succeed, though why the Muslim Palestinians should pay for the Christian West's guilt about Jews' treatment during WWII was never fully established. The Palestinian-Israeli dispute was a head-on collision between Western and Middle Eastern values, a dispute over borders and historical rights compounded by highly distorted images of the adversary, and a chronic regional arms race allied to superpower intrigue.

After the surprise military victory in what Israelis call the War of Independence in 1947–8, the Jewish state earned the reputation as a military underdog. This underdog image was reinforced by the victory in the 1956 war, although the support of France and Britain tempered it. It was fully restored, however, in the blitzkrieg of 1967's Six-Day War, when Israel defeated the combined armies of its Arab neighbors, Egypt, Jordan, and Syria.[5] This defeat led to the occupation of Syrian, Palestinian/Jordanian, and Egyptian territory, and also prompted Israeli hubris and a reluctance to rapidly trade land for peace. As one of Israel's most distinguished political scientists, Yehoshafat Harkabi, said, though, "Israel's problem is that with the best will in the world it cannot meet the Arabs' demand, because it is unlimited and cannot be satisfied as long as Israel exists."[6] Western statesmen and most correspondents did not agree with this bleak conclusion and spent the next forty years exploring ways to reconcile Palestinians and Israelis.

Israel also benefited from the so-called Jewish lobby, especially in America, which became the military protector of the Middle East's sole democracy. Added to this idea that Jews hold influence in politics and government, among other arenas, was Christendom's fascination with the Holy Land and a Jerusalem now united under Israeli rule. This fascination played into a powerful Armageddon complex in the American Christian right, which has been satirized as "doomsday chic."[7] Israel's victories were ascribed to the biblical prophecies that would soon bring about Christ's return. Americans were also alarmed by the rise of terrorism and concerned about Israelis' well-being, especially after live terrorist television was born at the Munich Olympics in September 1972, when Palestinian guerrillas massacred eleven Israeli athletes.

Israel's much-vaunted intelligence services were fixated on terrorism, which was why the conventional attack by Egypt and Syria on the Yom Kippur holiday in October 1973 caught the Israel Defense Forces (IDF) off guard. Prime Minister Golda Meir gave the order to assemble Israel's nuclear weapons at Dimona in the Negev. This order soon leaked to Washington, which immediately provided the biggest airlift of military equipment the world had yet seen. Israel counterattacked effectively, and the USSR and the United States intervened to prevent another total Arab military defeat.[8]

Israel buttressed its military image in the Western media with its daring and successful rescue mission of the hostages held at Entebbe, Uganda, in July 1976. Books and movies on the mission rapidly ensued. For an American military traumatized by the recent Vietnam disaster and haunted by the searing pictures of Americans escaping in helicopters from the Saigon embassy, the IDF in Entebbe exemplified the successful use of force. According to an American cultural historian, "After Entebbe, and after Saigon, Israel became a prosthetic for Americans. The 'long arm' of Israeli vengeance extended the body of an American nation no longer sure of its own reach."[9]

## IRAN

Said's critique of Western media's role in the Islamic world was amply vindicated in the case of the 1979 fall of the Shah of Iran, Mohammed Reza Pahlevi. The British and the American press were little prepared for this major event. The pruning of foreign desks in major British newspapers had almost destroyed the old area specialists, and only one of the three hundred Western journalists who flocked to Iran could speak Persian. Western intelligence agencies were also caught unprepared. The Cold War was still in full swing and the opponents of the Shah were dubbed, interestingly, Islamic Marxists. The Shah had been considered a modernizer by his people and was popular among them, except for the handful of fanatics, beturbanned, black-robed and self-flagellating. Most correspondents, though, neglected to ask why the Shah needed a large and viciously omnipotent secret police if he had strong support. In Afghanistan, the same turbanned extremists were in the holy war against communism. Afghan fundamentalists were freedom fighters, Muslim militiamen—at worse, noble savages, and at best, plucky anti-Soviet heroes. Ironically, Osama bin Laden, organizing those same Afghan fighters, was then a pin-up boy for the CIA.[10]

The Islamic leaders who brought down the Shah were usually portrayed in the Western media as history's slow learners, anti-modern fanatics, and their militancy as forms of madness without roots.[11] One acute observer, Hamid Mowlana, argued that the reportage of Iran was related to U.S. interests in the region. He further argued that the Iranian revolution was crudely depicted as ultra-religious conservatives' reactions against a Shah determined to drag "his stubborn, backward people into the present century," rather than a mass movement, led by clergy, to rectify deep-seated economic and social inequalities.[12] Likewise, Mowlana attacked the Western media for creating the myth of liberalization under the Shah, when his regime was notorious for stifling criticism, torturing dissenters, censoring the Iranian media, and outlawing opposition parties. When the regime collapsed, the British press analyzed the impact on employment in Britain, because of contracts lost to American and British companies, and ignored the conditions of the people in Iran.[13]

In reaction to U.S. support of the fallen Shah, revolutionary students stormed the U.S. embassy in Teheran on November 4, 1979, and held four hundred personnel hostage. The U.S. military countered by launching a mission, named Operation Eagle Claw, to rescue them. It ended, though, in bloody failure at a secret landing strip in the Iranian desert when a C-130 aircraft collided with a helicopter. The world learned of the fiasco when pictures were sent from Iran of grinning ayatollahs picking through the wreckage. The pictures reinforced the failures of Jimmy Carter's presidency and was another reminder of how Israeli hostage rescues were more successful than the U.S. military's.

Washington needed proxies to do its work. A classic example was the dual containment policy for Iraq and Iran. When Iraq invaded Iran in 1980, Baghdad expected a quick victory and the easy seizure of disputed territory. Instead, it became the longest conventional war of the century, with more than one million casualties.[14] Saddam Hussein's invasion inadvertently consolidated the Islamic revolution in Iran, while the 1982 counterinvasion by Teheran similarly had the unintended consequence of consolidating the rival Ba'athist regime. Baghdad secured the key support of fellow Sunni regimes in Saudi Arabia and Kuwait. Eventually, the two superpowers, the USSR and the United States, also conspired to contain Iran as it gained battlefield advantage. Washington, in effect, opened up a second front by placing its naval forces in the Gulf to ensure the security of oil tankers. Nevertheless, many Western companies became mired in murky defense contracts with Iran. With one contract, in particular, the U.S. government became embroiled in the major scandal, Irangate. In 1986, it was revealed that the United States had been selling arms to Iran, officially branded as a terrorist state, in exchange for the release of American hostages in Lebanon. The story emerged not through the investigative reporting skills of American journalists such as Bob Woodward and Carl Bernstein of Watergate fame in the early 1970s. It emerged from Lebanon, in its magazine *Ash-Shiraa*. This unexpected source indicates the decline of American foreign correspondence after the 1970s.

After eight years of fighting and a military draw, Iran concentrated on building its revolution in one country, in a replay of the Bolshevik experience of the 1920s. Iran's revolutionary anti–American ideals had not contaminated the crucial Gulf States. Iraq, however, had become militarized and was soon to threaten U.S. interests in the region, not least by invading Kuwait. Washington's policy of playing Iraq and Iran against each other did not contain either in the long term.[15] Western television media poorly reported the war, except for the last stages, or the so-called Tanker War, not least because neither authoritarian regime provided foreign correspondents with regular access. Furthermore, evidence of Baghdad's use of chemical weapons against its own Kurdish population was slow to filter out to the West.

## AFGHANISTAN

The war that began in Afghanistan in 1979 had a profound impact on the whole Islamic world.[16] When the Soviets invaded, hatred of the USSR was grafted onto raw nationalism, local Afghan tribalism, and religious fervor. The jihad was declared before Soviet tanks rolled in on Christmas Day 1979 to support the pro-Marxist regime in Kabul. The tribal warriors disliked any government, let alone a communist one backed by what they considered foreign infidels. Previous attempts at land reform and improvements in women's conditions had incensed rural conservatives, both landlords and peasants. The Soviets, as with the British before them in the nineteenth century, soon discovered that defeating and controlling the Afghans were two entirely different feats.[17] In the early years, the Soviets' war did not resemble the United States' Vietnam War. First, the Soviets were fighting on their own doorstep. Second, despite the mounting casualties, Soviet media and public opinion were muzzled. Finally, although Afghanistan was ideal guerrilla terrain, the tribal fighters were not natural soldiers. Convinced of their innate martial qualities, they were reluctant to undergo training and spent as much time praying as working out tactics or maintaining their weapons. By sheer doggedness, though, they managed to keep the Red Army at bay. The Soviets controlled the cities and, initially, the air. The mujahedin, comprising some forty major political groups, controlled perhaps 80 percent of the country.

The mujahedin war was undermined, though, by tribal and political feuds; the "muj," as the correspondents called them, spent as much time ambushing each other as attacking the invaders. Their rigid individualism was both the guerrillas' main strength and weakness. No Tito or de Gaulle emerged to seize overall leadership, though, in the north, the renowned "Lion of the Panshir," Ahmed Shah Massud, was an effective and charismatic military commander, who was suitably lionized by the few tough correspondents who managed to reach his lair. But the persistent divisions were partly a legacy of traditional social structures in which elders reached the decisions, and fighters were hesitant to venture outside their own villages. As the inveterate traveller and photographer Nick Danziger observed, "The civil war was more about tribal and sexual apartheid than about the defeat of a foreign invader."[18] The holy warriors had to work out a fundamental dilemma: to fight a modern war they had to give up their instinctive individualism and tribal ways, which is what they were fighting communism to defend.

Many of the part-time muj, numbering approximately one hundred and fifty thousand men, regarded military operations as a highly individual ritual, performed on a whim or to save face according to their eccentric, often ferocious, code of honor. The intensity and tide of the war varied immensely. The conflict in the Tajik-inhabited highlands of the north often bore little resemblance to the fighting in the Pushtun desert regions of the south. A heavy Soviet offensive, tribal feud, or the death of a popular commander could quickly and dramatically alter local conditions, although the news could take weeks or months to trickle back to the respective guerrilla headquarters in Pakistan's Peshawar.

Afghanistan was not a media war in the same way Vietnam or Lebanon was. Few U.S. television teams reached the heart of the fighting. Covering Afghanistan was risky in the extreme, and film crews had to be prepared for days and days of long, hard marches. No press helicopters commuted to the battlefields from plush hotels or massage parlors, as in Saigon. It was not a popular war for journalists.

Phillip Knightley quotes Peter Worthington, the editor of the *Toronto Sun*, who claimed that Afghanistan was one of the worst reported wars of recent times: "The fighting there is the subject of rumour, unconfirmed reports, and widespread ignorance, and the media are the prime villains."[19] This assessment is unfair. Although it *was* poorly reported, the terrain, extreme difficulties of access, and sheer volatility of the muj made access to the fighting often nearly impossible. British journalists Sandy Gall and Nigel Ryan endured a series of mishaps and mayhem when they tried to film the early stages of the war, which included losing their cameras when escorting muj rode off with their horses during an attack.[20] Working with the muj, especially in frequent combat, and under attack from Soviet Hind gunships, could disrupt any filming schedule. Gall and Ryan, however, had broken the golden rule: never get separated from your camera. Peter Jouvenal, a British ex-soldier who often worked with the BBC's John Simpson, was the doyen of film camera crews in Afghanistan. Despite understanding the country and its people better than anyone else, he—as with most combat camera crews—was reluctant to write about his experiences. Cameraman Tim Lambon, later the deputy foreign editor of Channel Four News, was a frequent visitor to Afghanistan, and to nearly all other combat zones. Regardless of winning numerous journalism awards, he never committed his experiences to paper beyond short articles. An exception was Sebastian Rich, of ABC and then ITN, who wrote a memoir (but with the help of a journalist) titled *People I Have Shot.*[21]

A few journalists, such as Peter Jouvenal,[22] often alongside the BBC's John Simpson, had the courage and stamina to return regularly to Afghanistan, but even fewer continued to follow the story after the Soviets quit the country in 1989.[23] American filmmaker Jim Burroughs returned repeatedly to give a wider context to the Afghan tragedy via the traditional long form documentary. In terms of new coverage, though, Afghanistan fell off the map.[24] This blindness also applied, fatally, to intelligence agencies. Just a handful of Westerners chronicled the rise of the Taliban and its crucial links with Pakistan's Inter Services Intelligence agency (ISI). Even fewer tracked the rise of the one-eye mullah, Mohammed Omar, as the presiding genius, "the saint on the satellite phone," though the title mullah had as much connection with spiritual integrity as the term comrade has with solidarity.[25] An exception was British freelance journalist Michael Griffin, who wrote a detailed and elegant account of the Taliban's rise, and the hospitality extended to Osama bin Laden in 1996.[26] Griffin related the political complexities of Afghanistan to the dominant issue in the whole region:

> The conflicts in Nagorno-Karabakh, Abkhazia, Turkish Kurdistan and Chechnya in the 1990s were all linked by a single golden theme: each represented a distinct, tactical move, crucial at the time, in determining which power would ultimately became master of the pipelines which . . . will transport the oil and gas from the Caspian Basin to an energy-starved world. Global demand, like

global population, will double in the next 25 years and Azerbaijan, Kazakhstan and Turkmenistan sit on the largest known reserves of unexploited fuel on the planet. These resources offer the West a unique opportunity to break free of its dependence on the Gulf, which still furnishes 40 percent of U.S. demand. . . .[27]

Although the oil issue is again the principal focus for much journalistic analysis, it is difficult to argue against oil security being an important factor in the biggest multi-national war the region had yet witnessed.

## THE GULF WAR

The Iraqi invasion of Kuwait in August 1990 posed the first major challenge to the post–Cold War era. The significance of the event is clear in hindsight. It brought Western infidel troops, including female soldiers, to the holy land of Mecca and prompted fears of a new era of crusades in the minds of some devoted Muslims who were prepared to turn to extremism. At the time, though, the senior President Bush talked more optimistically in terms of a new world order to replace the bipolar world that had disappeared. As evidence of this new world order, he pointed to the formation of a remarkable thirty-five-nation coalition prepared to oppose militarily the Iraqi invasion under UN resolutions—and under U.S. leadership. Crucially, this coalition consisted of Arab as well as Western nations, while Israel was persuaded to stay out. Shortly after the initial invasion, stories began to emerge from Kuwait of Iraqi atrocities, such as how babies were being plucked from their incubators and thrown on the floor. The propaganda war soon geared up to full speed, and the media inevitably was caught up in the crossfire. Subsequently, the incubators story was revealed to have been the creation of a public relations firm, Hill & Knowlton, working for the Kuwaiti government-in-exile.[28] Six and a half months later, in January 1991, this "coalition of the willing" launched Operation Desert Storm to liberate Kuwait. Saddam Hussein called for the "Mother of All Battles" against the "Devil in the White House," who responded by calling the Iraqi dictator a "new Hitler." War's first casualty, however, was dead long before the actual fighting began.

In this second Gulf War, with the first being the Iran-Iraq War, the most striking element of the reporting was how much the coverage was alike in form and content.[29] There was remarkably little official censorship, despite complete books being subsequently devoted to that subject, and numerically, there were more field reporters from more news organizations than in any previous conflict. Whether this event merited so much attention at the time is open to speculation, especially since the break-up of the Soviet Empire was still in progress. The news organizations, however, reduced their staffs in Moscow and Eastern Europe and instead swarmed to the Middle East. September 11th was eventually to show they were right to do so, although the extent to which the magnifying glass of continuous global television coverage in 1991 actually helped to spark the flames of the "war on terror" must remain open to debate.

The arrangements for the release of war information to the correspondents were perhaps the most sophisticated to date. A Joint Information Bureau (JIB) staffed by scores of public affairs officers trained in the art of media relations, nicknamed "Jiblets" by the media, was established in Dhahran, Saudi Arabia. Colin Powell later admitted that all military spokesmen were auditioned: "In the twenty-four hour coverage of the TV world, we could no longer put just anyone, no matter how well informed, in front of the cameras."[30] And Operation Desert Storm, or "Granby" to the British, also witnessed the full implementation of the pool system instituted by Gen. Winant Sidle in the 1989 Panama operation. With around fifteen hundred journalists in Dhahran and Riyadh, the so-called hotel warriors were dependent on information supplied at daily JIB press conferences. With more than three hundred in pools with troops in the field, combined with the countless hundreds reporting from news nodes such as London and Washington, one might have expected diverse coverage. What emerged, however, was monopoly disguised as diversity. As one commentator quipped, "Never in the field of recent conflict has so little been disclosed to so many by so few."[31]

In contrast to earlier conflicts, though, authorities were releasing a remarkable amount of information. This realization prompted Pentagon spokesman Pete Williams to comment that the Gulf War witnessed "the best coverage we've ever had."[32] Although he did not mean that the media had uncritically reproduced themes desired by the Pentagon, this was what resulted. One exception is what might be termed the Baghdad loophole. For the first time, reporters were in the enemy capital throughout the conflict while their own countries' air forces attacked it. Historically, the equivalent would have been reporters from Nazi Germany being present during the London Blitz or Soviet reporters covering the fall of Berlin from German lines. In the past, reporters would have been regarded as "eyes and ears of the enemy," as spies for the other side. This new situation, though, reflected the internationalization of news organizations that was taking place by the early 1990s. More specifically, the reason for the reporters' presence in Baghdad was due to Saddam Hussein's conviction about the so-called Vietnam Syndrome. Saddam recognized that although he might not be able to win the war militarily against the American-led coalition, he could undermine popular support for the war in coalition countries by permitting the Western media to transmit explicit images of mutilated bodies of women and children. Such a strategy is a testimony to the exaggerated belief in the power of television to change policy, which will later be discussed in the section on the CNN effect. For the moment, however, note that Desert Storm signaled the start of a process that effectively mobilized the media from enemy countries as an asymmetrical weapon against those countries. For example, the North Vietnamese entreated Western celebrities such as Jane Fonda to visit Hanoi. Saddam's ploy of allowing Western reporters to stay for as long as the war lasted meant that the they could no longer argue that they were simple observers of war. They had become, wittingly or unwittingly, active participants.

It has become something of a myth that the only Western news organization present in Baghdad during the Gulf War was CNN. The BBC and NHK were also present, while a newspaper reporter from the Spanish *El Mundo* had his pieces translated for the *Guardian.* While many people recall viewing the war break out live on television on January 16, 1991, the images they were watching were not moving or live; CNN's live audio reports were transmitted over a still map of Baghdad montaged with the faces of three reporters who described the assault they were seeing from their hotel window. It was more similar to the radio reports of American correspondents in the London of 1940 than the live reports via videophones from the embedded reporters in Iraq in 2003. Several days passed before CNN could get the videotape out of Iraq via Jordan and before viewers witnessed the memorable green-tinted night skies of Baghdad peppered with tracer fire and explosions. At the end of January, CNN finally broadcasted both words and pictures in real time from the Iraqi capital.

An estimated one hundred million people worldwide with access to CNN, in addition to the millions of others who watched as their local stations switched to the CNN commentary, may have been mesmerized by this footage. It was, however, more drama than news since the journalists were uninformed during this opening nighttime bombing raid. Clearly caught up in the excitement on that first night, CNN reporters Peter Arnett, Bernard Shaw, and John Holliman were later criticized for their commentary. For example, Shaw said to Arnett, "It looks like a fireworks finale on the fourth of July display. . . . Peter, you're chuckling, but that to me is not an exaggeration." "I'm chuckling with nervousness, Bernie, not with derision," Arnett replied. Arnett was a veteran field war correspondent whereas Shaw, an anchor, was only in Baghdad to interview Saddam Hussein. Nonetheless, this dramatic commentary ended at nearly 10:00 P.M. (EST) when Shaw announced, "We've got to run. Somebody's knocking on the door. John and I are going to hide," followed by, "This is Peter Arnett signing off for a minute, and I'll see what the action is outside." A new age of real-time reporting had begun, though. CNN, dubbed "Chicken Noodle News" by its rivals when founded in 1980, had changed the nature of war reporting. Now we had witnesses to history—live on television.

No matter the accuracy of the correspondents' reports, the U.S. military was conscious of the potential for violation of their operational security. Baghdad was not carpet-bombed; it was targeted with a new generation of precision-guided weaponry that proved remarkably accurate in hitting its intended target. With this "command and control warfare," the principal targets were Iraqi air defense systems and communications systems that enabled the Iraqi command to direct its forces in the field. At daybreak on January 17, only military installations and other strategic targets in Baghdad had been hit. Elsewhere in Iraq, especially in the south where around half a million Iraqi troops were stationed, it was a different story, though. There were no Western journalists covering the carpet bombing of that region from thirty thousand feet by Vietnam-era B-52s. It emerged after the war that only 8 percent of the ordnance used to bomb Iraq was electronically guided, or "smart," which meant 92 percent was indiscriminate, or "dumb." From the outset, the real war was absent from the media war.

The media war had placed the world's microscope on the Baghdad air raids at the expense of showing where the real war was being fought. There was dispute, however, over whether the media was serving as a tool for Iraqi propaganda. When the Iraqis escorted Peter Arnett to the bombed site of what they claimed was a baby milk plant (clearly marked as such in fresh paint in English), he was accused back home of being a traitor. The coalition countered the rising Iraqi accusations of its barbarism by claiming the baby milk plant site was really an installation for the development of chemical weapons. Although arguments over the true function of the plant still persist, perhaps the best evidence is circumstantial. Since the Iraqis had never escorted Western journalists to the sites of bombed military installations, why would they begin to? These Iraqi-led tours would give too much away from an intelligence point of view. One coalition pilot did say, "It certainly was interesting for us to come back and land and watch the [CNN] replays. . . . We could actually pick out who some of the bombs belonged to. . . . There was some good in having good old Peter Arnett on the ground."[33] If the factory was really a baby milk plant—and several journalists visited there after the war and lightened their coffee with its white power—then it was an intelligence mistake. Any further targeting mistakes or other collateral damage were made quickly accessible to Western journalists, forcing the coalition to be on the defensive.

The speed of media reporting was making this into a propaganda issue. The initials BDA, a military acronym for bomb damage assessment, could have easily stood for broadcasting damage assessment. The coalition did not deliberately target Iraqi civilians, but Saddam's totalitarian infrastructure was based on the old Soviet-style system of dual or multi-purpose installations and of rotating their functions. Minders from the Iraqi Ministry of Information carefully monitored the reporters in Baghdad, instructing the reporters on what they could and could not say and taking them to bomb sites that could serve Iraqi propaganda rather than coalition intelligence. Arnett and his colleagues were only too aware of these manipulations; some were conscious of the dilemma between their patriotism and their duty to report what they observed. Arnett even claimed that his reports were coded in a language that was designed to fool his minders. On February 13, 1991, came the critical moment around which these debates came into sharp focus.

When two laser-guided bombs smashed through the roof of the Al Firdos installation in Baghdad's Amiriyah suburb, the Stealth bomber pilots who launched them believed they were targeting a command and control installation. However, more than four hundred people—mainly women, children, and the elderly—were using it as an air-raid shelter. When reporters staying at the Al-Rashid Hotel were awoken by their Iraqi minders in a hurry to escort them to the scene of massive devastation, they were given free reign to report without fear of censorship. The reporters witnessed and filmed chaotic scenes of horribly charred remains of those inside being brought out to ambulances. The correspondents then visited the Yarmuk Hospital where, outside, Iraqi nurses were drawing back the blankets covering the dead to show the world what coalition air power was doing to the ordinary people of Iraq. Angry relatives screamed and wailed in grief at the cameras—a defining moment of the war.

Most Western news organizations chose to edit out the most graphic of these images on grounds of taste and decency. Even so, what was broadcast was still shocking. The day following the airing in Britain, the *Daily Mail* accused the BBC of being the Baghdad Broadcasting Corporation, which, in effect, was shooting the messenger. Coalition spokespeople went into overdrive and claimed that they didn't understand why civilians would take refuge in a command bunker since the coalition targeted only military installations. Unlike in the baby milk plant episode of several weeks earlier, many people had been killed, which made the coalition air strikes look less precise than its spokespeople had been suggesting. As with the baby milk plant, however, the function of the Al Firdos installation had most likely been changed, in this case from a command bunker to a civilian air raid shelter. The intelligence on its use was old, and coalition bombing targets had slipped down the timescale of the air tasking order (ATO) due to the region's worst weather in living memory. By the time Al Firdos came to the top of the list, its function had changed.

Saddam's belief in the Vietnam Syndrome was now put to the test. Although evidence suggests that the coalition modified its targeting policy on Baghdad as a result of these images, there is no evidence that the Al Firdos footage tipped Western public opinion on the war. The tabloids suggested that Saddam had deliberately sacrificed his own people as a propaganda ploy, to undermine Western public support for the war. The public, though, was not falling for his scheme.

The war consisted of a five-week aerial bombing campaign followed by a rapid ground assault into Kuwait and southern Iraq that was over in one hundred hours. Both aspects of the war—the aerial and the ground— were intrinsically problematic for the media coverage. First, journalists were not allowed to go on carpet bombing missions, and, even if they had been allowed, they would have seen only distant puffs of smoke thirty thousand feet below. They would have heard nothing except the roar of the plane's engines. Aerial warfare is war fought at a distance, and the early retreat of the Iraqi air force to Iran ensured coalition air superiority. Second, the ground war was fought largely at night, as most modern battles are, and the media was equipped with few up-to-date night vision cameras. Besides, coalition forces moved so rapidly that the pool reporters could hardly stop the advance and ask soldiers to take their copy from their media reporting teams (MRT—the official name of the pools) to the forward transmission units (FTU) behind the advance. As a result, the public saw neither the devastation of the Iraqi army by the carpet bombing nor the ferocity of the rapid assault into Kuwait until the end—even then the footage showed images of the war's aftermath, such as burning oil wells and bombed-out convoys.

Some journalists, out of frustration, broke away from the pool system and reported independently. Indeed, they managed to enter Kuwait City before the military and film the liberation as if it were Paris in 1944. These journalists joined a small band of brothers known as the "unilaterals," or "mavericks," a term describing reporters who would not conform to the coalition's media management systems either in the pools or in Riyadh and Dhahran. Their presence in Kuwait City was a dangerous business; roaming around the battlefield without military protection subjected them to arrest or even assault. Following the Iraqis' arrest of a CBS unilateral crew on the Kuwaiti border early in the campaign, it was unlikely that the unilaterals could cover the war from outside of Baghdad. Only a year earlier, the Iraqis had hanged London *Observer* journalist, Farzad Barzoft, for roaming through the country unescorted and without permission. Indeed, following the first land battle of the war in the Saudi seaside resort of Khafji, which the Iraqis had seized at the end of January as a propaganda coup, pool reporters screamed at one unilateral covering the coalition's counter-offensive, "You asshole. You'll prevent us from working. You're not allowed here. Get out. Go back to Dhahran!"[34]

While the pool system may have given reporters a chance to witness the military action, most reporters disliked it, because it undermined the traditional competitiveness of the media. Journalists do not like sharing their material. They are looking for a scoop, and anything that gives them an advantage over their fellow reporters. The pool reporters, however, had to consent to the security review agreements drawn up by the military. From a military point of view, these agreements were largely designed to prevent valuable information, such as troop sizes and locations, from reaching the enemy. Reporters either had to agree to the arrangements, and in the process allow prior military scrutiny of reports and possible censorship, or have no access at all.

The press corps was therefore dependent on military sources for information about what was happening. The primary concern of the military, especially now that there was a real-time media environment, was operational security (OPSEC). As with many journalists in the Kuwaiti area of operations, however, security was a daunting and increasingly difficult task. For example, the arrival into the commercial sector of the Inmarsat satellite telephone, which was then the size of a large brick, created a potential nuisance for the military minders. The BBC's most prominent female correspondent, Kate Adie, believed that the satellite phones were "clearly engineered for hotel balconies rather than desert trenches." Those reporters who were equipped with the Inmarsat satellite phones were instructed not to use them because "they could radiate signals to the Iraqis."[35] Whether the Iraqis possessed such tracing technology at that time was doubtful, but, in case this rule was violated, the coalition kept a watchful eye on their use. One British television crew was even arrested after an airborne warning and control system (AWACS) aircraft monitored an allegedly illegal call to its London base. Whether such efforts to control the theater information environment were disproportionate to the risks involved, the military's thirst for control and power was also evident in the pools: journalists were not allowed to transmit live using their satellite equipment. However, evidence suggests that the Iraqis attacked Khafji, because they had viewed from television pictures, filmed by unilaterals, that the town was empty.

Back at the JIB, however, the military found use in the live daily-televised press conferences. Many reporters there were not military or defense specialists and were unversed in military jargon. When they asked for clarification or asked questions that could not be answered on OPSEC grounds, they looked ignorant to a live global television audience. In fact, military representatives bypassed the traditional mediating role of journalists and directly addressed viewers. Polls indicated that Americans would trust the military far more than the media and were content to suspend knowledge of the truth until after the war, if it saved lives in the process.

The military was also fortunate to have Vietnam veteran Gen. Norman Schwarzkopf, nicknamed "The Bear." A larger-than-life character, General Schwarzkopf knew how to play to an audience, and he regularly gave live press conferences. He charmed the press, an indication of how much journalists like to be briefed by the organ grinder rather than his monkeys, terms frequently used by correspondents. Access to the overall field commander gave the briefings enormous credibility, and Schwarzkopf's use of language was florid and well measured; for example, he famously used "bovine scatology" as a response to an Iraqi claim. In the early days of the war, with very few pool reports coming back from the front, because of little ground activity, the reporters, dubbed the hotel warriors, were growing restless. Their reports of the war were largely based on what military spokespeople communicated to them, and apart from the Baghdad loophole, the message essentially was, "We are winning, and we will go on winning."

In an attempt to placate an increasingly restless press corps, the military began to release videos of missile strikes against Iraqi targets. The smart weaponry carried cameras, and their videos conveyed through cross hairs strikes of remarkable accuracy. Incidentally, no videos were initially released of the few missiles that missed their targets, and none taken by the high-level bomber crews were released either. At one press conference, Schwarzkopf even showed a video of a bridge being attacked with an Iraqi truck passing through the cross hairs before the explosion. His commentary ran, "And now in his rear-view mirror—the luckiest man in Iraq!" The journalists present laughed. Anchors back at base were clearly siding with the military and speaking the same language. CBS's Charles Osgood described the initial bombing of Iraq as "a marvel" following two days of what the same network's Jim Stewart described as "picture-perfect assaults." Journalists copied the disingenuous phrase "collateral damage" to draw a veil over the death and injury to civilians. Media analyst

Norman Solomon described it as "linguicide" while a British commentator wrote, "Rarely has it been so obvious that language is volatile stuff, that it succumbs easily to manipulation, to the sedulous distortions of propagandists and censors . . . words have been used to salve the conscience, to cordon off the truth, rather than to communicate it."[36]

Then the media was provided the chance to report on events for itself. The Iraqis started firing Scud missiles at Saudi Arabia and at Israel. Journalists scrambled to the building roofs to see the nighttime light shows as coalition air defenses launched Patriot missiles to repel "dumb" weapons. Anchors in New York and Atlanta pleaded live on air for their reporters to seek the sanctuary of air raid shelters rather than risk their lives to cover the attacks. NBC's Arthur Kent was perhaps the most famous, with millions watching him go live as follows:

> Get us up on audio. Please get us up. Hello, New York? This is Saudi Arabia. This is not a drill. Hello, New York? [Holding up gas mask]. This is Saudi Arabia. This is not a drill. New York? OK, let's go. We're firing Patriots. We've got flares and we've got sirens. Let's go—focus! [Explosions in distance. Kent ducks.] There goes a Patriot, let's go!

Kent's heroics earned him two nicknames among an admiring audience: "the Satellite Dish" and the "Scud Stud." The reporter as star had arrived, although Kent was deeply disturbed at this development and was concerned that it might become the future's norm. He was right.

In Israel, Scud attacks were reported live, including one supposedly on Jerusalem's Old City, though it actually was never attacked since it is a Muslim holy city as well. Television reporters donned gas masks in fear of chemical weapons strikes, which also never happened. Live television was failing its audiences, despite certainly exciting them. One psychologist dubbed the viewing of live reports of Iraqi attacks as "Scudavision." Live coverage was becoming more about excitement than about reality, what Nik Gowing later called "the tyranny of real time." The cynic might say that real-time reportage was about excitement over non-events, or media-manufactured events, for the "infotainment" of the audience that accordingly could feel part of history as it happens—or as it wasn't happening. A collective fantasy had developed, in which war had become entertainment, a video game in which the horrors of real war—the death, the brutality, and the destruction—were absent.

All this might suggest a poor media performance during the Gulf War. Such judgments, though, rest on viewer's expectations of the media

in wartime. If audiences expect the media to report the truth, then reporters and editors need time to verify the information they are given by different sources before going public with their reports. Live television had
changed the rules of the game. The media had conveyed an accurate impression of the events, really a one-sided war, and because they were
dependent on coalition sources, they had reproduced the coalition line.
After all, coalition sources were presumed to be more credible than Iraqi
sources, and even the Western journalists' presence in Baghdad had to be
tempered with on-screen warnings that their reports "were subject to
Iraqi censorship." The media, however, also gave the impression that the
coalition's war was being fought by hi-tech coalition weaponry, which
was a distortion of the reality. Since only the Americans, British, French,
and Saudis were allowed to hold press conferences in Saudi Arabia, the
media and the public were dependent on those sources.

The devastation being wreaked on the Iraqi military, and their very
high rate of combat deaths, was absent from the coalition sources and,
consequently, the media. Despite the omission of these images in Western
media outlets, combat camera crews had taken footage; it was, however,
not released until several years after the war was over. Would those who
had complained about the "video-game war"—who were also largely part
of the antiwar factions—view the actual war on television? Was this not
essentially a propagandist stance, similar to the Vietnam Syndrome, where
if audiences watched such horrors, they would agitate to stop the war?
This line of thinking resurfaced during the Balkan wars after the BBC's
Martin Bell called for a "journalism of attachment." Again, it is linked to
the issue of the alleged CNN effect and whether television images possess
the power to change policy.

As for the military, especially the post–Vietnam U.S. military, it now
had a template with which to handle the hundreds of journalists from
worldwide media flocking to areas of combat operations. The U.S. military
had vastly improved since the post–World War II invasion of Grenada. The
media dutifully represented the U.S. military's desired image of war, and
despite the unilaterals and the Baghdad loophole, that image largely benefited the coalition. How different, though, was this media management
from the propaganda of the Saddam regime?

A controversial point of friction in the military-media relationship
was whether the media had been deliberately used as part of the military
deception plan in the buildup to the ground war. The plan involved sending messages to the Iraqis that the impending coalition assault on Kuwait
would take place from the sea rather than the now famous, but misnamed,
"Hail Mary play." Why American journalists didn't question Schwarzkopf's

terminology is curious as the attack was not out of last-minute desperation. The operation would see coalition ground forces swing up to the west of Kuwait in a lightning advance and cut off the retreating Iraqi forces before they could reach home. Codenamed Operation Desert Sabre, this deception plan called for the feint of amphibious operations, the seizure of the Qurah and Faylakah islands in the Persian Gulf, and the movement of seventeen thousand U.S. Marines northwards up the coast. Meanwhile, the British Rhino Force played recordings from previous training exercises, tank movements, and communications traffic as it kicked up clouds of dust, or "coat trailing," moving west along the Kuwaiti/Saudi border. The plan worked. When coalition forces reached Kuwait City, the Iraqi guns were pointed out to sea, ready to repel the supposed seaborne assault.

There was a question over whether the media was used to underpin this activity. Many journalists believed they had been exploited, because it was well known that the Iraqis were watching CNN, as in the case of Khafji. Certainly reporters noticed that they were now being given access to training exercises of the Marines going ashore and indeed to more and more naval-related stories. Reporters in the British pool, however, were briefed on the entire battle a week before the actual assault began. As Colin Wills of the *Mirror* recognized, this briefing was an astute move by Gen. Rupert Smith:

> We knew the entire battle plan a week before the land war started. On a professional level, needless to say, it was very frustrating. To be in the know and not be able to file a word was like being given the secret of alchemy and at that same instant being struck dumb.[37]

The degree to which the British pool reporters, but not the Americans, were entrusted with such gold dust and then trusted not to publish it may have been a legacy from the Falklands War and the bonding that took place between journalists and soldiers then. The Americans still had Vietnam on their minds.

When interviewed, several of the military minders involved with the journalists at sea suggested that they were not at fault if the journalists assumed that a naval assault would take place. They maintained that they never actually said this assault would happen. Because the reporters were reliant on the military for their information, their assumptions on the breadth and validity of the knowledge given by the military may be naïve. This line of argument, however, throws emphasis back onto media performance. And again, the problem arises of generalizing about the media, which, in fact, is a heterogeneous body of people with varying degrees of experience, understanding, and insight. After all, it is often forgotten that *Newsweek* published a highly accurate map of the likely land assault on February 11, 1991, almost two weeks before the invasion was launched. Several days prior, the *Guardian* published a fairly accurate map of the likely main attacks. All of this precise reportage was forgotten in acrimonious debates after the war, with some reporters furious with the military's manipulation of the media, and most military representatives content to adopt a stance that, if lives of coalition soldiers were saved thanks to the deception plan, then it was fully justified. One wonders whether the public would side with the military or the media on this one.

Perhaps the issue revolves around not only how much the public sees but also how much it chooses to see when armies go to war in the information age. Add to this issue the military fear that, if the public sees too much, it would be repulsed and shift to an antiwar stance. Although little evidence suggests that this reaction would happen, the military nonetheless worried that television images of the ground war's aftermath, especially of the burned-out convoy of fleeing Iraqi vehicles on the highway running north out of Kuwait City, would jeopardize its mission. Indeed, although images of the "highway of death" surfaced three days after the battle, which suggests a military embargo, warnings from Kuwait to the White House about their potential impact may have had an influence on Washington's decision to end the coalition advance after a mere one hundred hours. As Colin Powell wrote in *A Soldier's Way*, "The television coverage . . . was starting to look as if we were engaged in slaughter for slaughter's sake."[38]

How much influence these images actually had must be balanced against other factors that prompted not a ceasefire but "a cessation of hostilities." The UN mandates authorizing the war only did so to expel Iraq from Kuwait. In the months and years that followed, debate—prompted initially by David Frost's interview with Schwarzkopf—over whether the coalition forces should have entered Baghdad and removed Saddam persisted. Regime change at that time, though, was not the official policy, and had the coalition pursued the Iraqi army farther into Iraq, its Arab members would have undoubtedly split away, causing more diplomatic problems than the war had solved militarily.

Removing Saddam may not have been the official policy in 1991, but evidence suggests that covert operations attempted to dismantle his regime by nonmilitary means. This involved several "black" propaganda radio stations broadcasting incitements at the end of the war to the Kurds in the north and the Shi'as in the south to rise up and overthrow the dictator.

Instead of receiving military assistance from the coalition, those active in the uprisings were brutally suppressed by Iraqi forces. Furious, several Iraqis who had participated in these broadcasts, broke their silence and went on CNN to claim that they had been working for the CIA. The only assistance the rebels received was humanitarian drops of food relief for the Kurds in the north. British Prime Minister John Major said he urged the Americans to initiate this relief effort, Operation Provide Comfort, after watching the plight of the Kurds on television news reports. The Shi'a uprising, however, was not televised, which meant that there was no pressure to send any relief to those rebels.

When British forces entered the Shi'a areas of Iraq in 2003, they were surprised at the locals' unenthusiastic reaction. The 15 UK Psychological Operations Group quickly realized why and published a leaflet that simply said, "This time we won't let you down." Skeptical Iraqis remembering the 1991 "betrayal" failed to reach for their rose petals to greet their supposed liberators.

## THE INTIFADAS

The Gulf War resonated throughout the myriad conflicts in the region, not least in Lebanon. In June 1982, the IDF had struck at Palestinian resistance/terrorist groups in Lebanon. Israeli armor reached Beirut in a mere six days, but a prolonged siege ensued. Constant pictures of Israeli artillery pounding Palestinian camps began turning world opinion, except generally in the United States, away from the Jewish state and more toward the Arab cause. Worse, the Israelis gave the Lebanese militias control over the Palestinian camps, which resulted in bloodshed at Sabra and Shatila. Robert Fisk, a British journalist with an international reputation for covering injustices in the Arab world, penned famous dispatches of the massacres.[39] The Israelis withdrew, though they maintained a security belt in the south, and an international peacekeeping force, drawn from the United States, France, Italy, and Britain, entered Beirut. The forces did not stay long. In October 1983, Hezbollah bombed U.S. Marine barracks. Although the French were attacked at the same time, it was photographs of the American disaster that seized world attention.[40] The media continued to focus on Lebanese anarchy and particularly the taking of Western hostages, which included journalists.

Because of their complexity, the origins of the Lebanese wars defy classification. Internal religious rivalries, such as Muslim versus Christian, and Shi'a versus Sunni, allied with ideological and class hostilities and tribal feuds had been exploited by the outside powers. In this international battlefield, Syria, the Palestine Liberation Organization (PLO), and

Iran had been major contenders. America, Saudi Arabia, Russia, France, and Iraq also stirred the pot. The Syrian army had helped the Lebanese army recapture much of the country, although the southern region was still a hodgepodge of UN troops, militias, Palestinian insurgents, and Israeli-backed Lebanese proxies. For years, a sign hung in the office of Timur Göksel, the official who dealt with the press in the UN zone. It read, "If you think you understand Lebanon, you've not been properly briefed."[41] The Israeli invasion displaced the PLO leaders, notably Yasser Arafat, from the country. In 1991, the Palestinian cause was further damaged in the West by the PLO's support for Saddam Hussein. This was a poor publicity move by Arafat who, as the Israelis always said, "never missed an opportunity to miss an opportunity." As radical Islamic groups began to win over more and more adherents, the relationship between the PLO and the Palestinian people began to sour.

A series of uprisings that were collectively known as the intifada, which literally means "a shaking off," accelerated the fall out between the PLO and the Palestinian people. The first Palestinian uprising began in 1987 and lasted six years. Both the first and the more aggressive second intifada, which began in 2000, were born out of deep-seated and bitter frustration with both the Israeli occupation and the ineffectual Arab leadership.[42]

The Gulf War's Scud missiles had undermined the old Israeli military argument about strategic depth—the need for land to buy time in case of another Arab invasion. This thinking was based upon previous wars, of armored ground attacks threatening to slice up the Jewish state. This argument was seriously flawed in the new missile age in the region. While Israel could rely on unconditional support from Washington, American public opinion was changing. The media image of the tiny democratic state of Holocaust survivors had been tarnished by the military occupation of the West Bank and Gaza. With the collapse of the Soviet Union, Israel was no longer seen as the only necessary and reliable ally in the region. Instead, it was becoming a strategic liability, costing American taxpayers $3 billion a year in military aid.

The Gulf War had improved Israel's conventional military position. Its enemy Syria had lost its Soviet patron, and Iraq had been humbled. America had become the linchpin of the Middle East. The Arabs, cowed by American weapon wizardry in the Gulf, had lost interest in fighting Israel. In one sense, though, Saddam had won an accidental victory: he had placed the Palestinian uprising back at the center of the world stage. By 1993, after a series of conferences and accords, most notably in Oslo, the Palestinian Authority was established in parts of the occupied territories.

Yasser Arafat, however, seemed unable to contain the endemic corruption or the rise of Islamic fundamentalist groups such as Hamas. The Israelis withdrew from southern Lebanon, yet found no peace. The IDF reacted with reprisals raids, as the zealots sent suicide bombers into Jewish areas.

Funded in part by Saudi Arabia and Kuwait, Hamas garnered enough money to provide a basic welfare system for the Palestinian poor. Hamas leaders enjoyed a reputation of austerity, while Arafat's Palestinian Authority wallowed in corruption and nepotism. Contrary to most Western opinion, Palestinians came to support Hamas not because of its violence or Islamism, but "because it is kind."[43] The impact of television reporting of the uprisings, especially by Al-Jazeera, the new Arab television station founded in Qatar in 1995, was likened to the alleged effect of Vietnam War coverage. The dramatic pictures from the occupied territories created a sense of immediacy and support in the "Arab street." Israel could no longer claim to be using reasonable force to contain the Palestinians when Al-Jazeera showed otherwise, daily and hourly. This coverage of the second intifada meant that the formidable Israeli media faced real Arab competition for the first time. Nachman Shai was the head of an Israeli special media team set up to counter this threat. Predictably, he blamed television for inciting the intifada: "This war is a television war. This is completely different from the Gulf War. It has become a daily struggle over which side will have the most air time; which side will have won the latest propaganda war."[44]

Israel and Jewish lobbies worldwide, realizing the media-savvy Palestinians and Al-Jazeera had outflanked them, fought back. They accused Al-Jazeera of bias, although it had been the first Arab channel to regularly feature interviews with Israelis. Israel also criticized the Associated Press, Reuters, and Agence France-Presse news services, which collectively supply 80 percent of the world still and television news images. Israel's Government Press Office (GPO), and even the lumbering IDF, also improved their media act. They claimed that the pictures did not report the real story. There was, however, little evidence of an anti-Israeli media conspiracy. This reporting did create a pattern to the reality programming of television news on the conflict. The complex crisis was reduced, as the American columnist Douglas Davis articulated, "to a monochromatic, single-dimensional comic cutout, whose well-worn script featured a relentlessly brutal demonically evil Ariel Sharon and a plucky, bumbling, misunderstood Yasser Arafat, the benign father of Palestine, in need of a little TLC (plus $50 million a month) from the West."[45]

In the summer of 2007, however, the Palestinians fought a civil war among themselves. Hamas gunmen conquered Gaza, while pro-Fatah forces held on to the tattered Palestinian Authority in the West Bank. Israel stood back as its enemies attacked one another. The media now proclaimed the "two-state solution": Gaza ruled by Islamists, who refused to recognize Israel, and in the West Bank the more secular Fatah, who were prepared to handle the Jewish state.

Hundreds of news bureaus and journalists on permanent postings have been based in Jerusalem, as well as numerous visiting freelancers and staff members who sifted the ancient overworked soil for new scoops. About nine hundred articles on events in Israel, the West Bank, and Gaza were published each day in the English language alone, seventy-five more times than any other area of comparable population.[46] Israelis question why they are at the center of media attention, to which there are several answers. Jerusalem is the home of three great world religions—Christianity, Judaism, and Islam. It is also a fulcrum of the long-running Middle East crisis, perhaps even one of Huntington's tectonic plates in the clash of civilizations. American journalist Stephanie Gutmann, in her indictment of media bias against Israel, suggests that the hostile image-making has declined; presumably bin Laden had an inadvertent part in that. For over a decade, she continued, only one Web-based voice, the Committee for Accurate Middle East Reporting in America (CAMERA), called for more accurate reporting of Israel. Since then, groups of online media monitors have sprung up, some of which are specifically dedicated to measuring the output of individual major news organs. The *Los Angeles Times*, the *Washington Post*, and *Le Monde* are analyzed daily for anti-Israeli bias. She also commended the "democratic, irreverent spirit" of the blogosphere. Gutmann, a journalist herself, is, however, wrong to claim that there is "a natural tendency for journalists and terrorists to collude." She cited examples in Iraq, echoing U.S. military complaints, where camera crews from Associated Press and Reuters, "by amazing coincidence" repeatedly found themselves where insurgents achieved some of their greatest carjacking and kidnapping successes. To Gutmann, journalists are not "priests of neutrality." They do stray from professional standards and sometimes exhibit "petty vendettas, craven desires to be with the cool kids, secret shames, blind spots—and sometimes even diligence and brilliance."[47]

## MEDIA INFLUENCE

Until the late 1980s, Edward Said's critique of Western coverage's weaknesses was persuasive. Israel's publicity machine was also effective, at least in the United States. The fall of the Shah was both an intelligence and media failure. The Iran-Iraq War was poorly interpreted and covered, though the authoritarian regimes had mostly restricted independent media access. Afghanistan was also inadequately reported, but mainly because of its terrain and the anarchy of the mujahedin. Despite brave and repeated forays by journalists such as Peter Jouvenal, John Simpson, and Ed Girardet of the *Christian Science Monitor*, little of the strategic direction of Afghanistan's ten-year war was revealed. The Soviets may have been equally unaware of the war's developments along with muj groups themselves, who were locked in their own internecine feuds. Lebanon was intensely covered, although the constant abductions, not least of Western journalists, rendered continuous media surveillance difficult and often nearly impossible.

When the first intifada broke out, Israel initially outmaneuvered the Palestinians in the media war. Soon, though, the insurgents began playing effectively to the international gallery. The Western media did have an impact on portraying the resistance in the West Bank and Gaza as a result of Israeli injustice. The Israeli attempts at official control were unsuccessful. The correspondents' need for official information was low, and the international media had sufficient resources to cover the region consistently. Compared with the vast desert land of the Gulf War, this conflict's small area of terrain was conducive to rapid and comprehensive reporting. Duration is important too; whereas the Gulf War was short and sharp, the intifadas were long-running sagas. Jerusalem, moreover, was already a media capital, containing a well-established press corps with numerous contacts. There were no sophisticated weapons technologies to learn, no sweeping strategic plans to decipher, and no major cultural barriers to surmount as the action, like in Saigon, was on the doorstep of comfortable hotels with well-stocked bars. Unlike the Gulf War, "journalists could cover the intifada without ever having attended a single class in 'Army 101.'"[48]

As in South Africa, previously a state under siege, the cause and effect impact of the cameras was intensely discussed in Israel. The Palestinians reacted to the news media's presence during confrontations by becoming more militant. Similarly, the presence of the foreign press usually, but not always, tempered the use of excessive force by Israeli security forces. After 1995, the arrival of Al-Jazeera meant that not only Arabs outside the territories, but Palestinians as well, became fixated with live coverage. While Al-Jazeera has never denied that its footage rallied support for the Palestinian cause, it has maintained that this was a natural, yet unintended, consequence of the events being shown rather than a deliberate attempt at propaganda.[49] Nevertheless, the twenty-four-hour Arabic-language station played a major role in altering the media and political balance of power in favor of the Palestinians.

In the Gulf War, the role of the news gatherer was far more passive, "that of a faithful servant dutifully providing services to their Allied masters."[50] The military's power over the news media was a question of supply and demand. Only the military could fill the tremendous news holes that existed. This dominance was reinforced by the journalists' lack of knowledge and access. The U.S. military, often staffed by public affairs officers who had graduate degrees in journalism, understood how to influence the journalists more than the journalists understood how to obtain and, crucially, process information about the military.[51] Indeed, the private military view was that journalists in theater "couldn't distinguish a tank from a turd." The media then became another weapon in the Allies' massive arsenal to defeat Saddam Hussein. *Guardian* correspondent Maggie O'Kane described it thus, "A tale of how to tell lies and win wars, and how we, the media, were harnessed like 2,000 beach donkeys and led through the sand to see what the British and U.S. military wanted us to see in this nice clean war."[52] The British Sunday newspaper the *Observer* was the only paper to publish at the time the most famous photograph of the war— the burnt corpse of a soldier on the Basra Road. It was not shown in the United States. The photographer behind the image, Kenneth Jarecke, "believe[d] it was worth risking your life for the truth. The problem was we couldn't get near it."[53]

# 7

# THE LONG WAR

Famous combat photographer James Nachtwey lived by the World Trade Center. On September 11, he grabbed his camera, like all good journalists, and headed in the direction from which everyone was fleeing. "I made my way through the smoke to photograph the skyscraper where it lay in ruins in the street. . . . Then I heard what sounded like a huge waterfall in the sky. I looked up and saw the second tower falling straight down at me." Nachtwey realized that he had no time to take a picture. He ran to safety, and survived. War correspondent Bill Biggart was also shooting pictures, and he remained to take what he thought would be the shots of a lifetime. His camera, undamaged, was found near his body. In the final frame was an image of the second tower as it began to implode.[1] The media fight-back started straight away. "Buildings collapsed. Democracy stands," ran the leader of the *Los Angeles Times*, a few hours after the attack.[2] Nevertheless, except for Pearl Harbor, the American war of independence, and the self-inflicted wounds of the Civil War, 9/11 was the first time Americans had suffered major military harm on their own soil.

The 9/11 abomination changed the world dramatically, as have the events that flowed from it: the declaration of the "war on terror," the invasions of Afghanistan and Iraq, the development of a U.S. strategy of preemptive war, and the introduction of new legislation in the Western democracies that threatens traditional civil liberties. Historian John Lewis Gaddis observed, "It's as if we were all irradiated, on that morning of 11 September 2001, in such as way as to shift our psychological make-up—the DNA in our minds—with consequences that will not become clear for years to come."[3]

And yet, 9/11 may have crystallized long-existing currents in world politics.[4] The optimism of the post–Cold War new order had already faded. Jihadism had long been a real threat, as evidenced in a previous attack on the same World Trade Center in 1993. The 2001 onslaughts were a serious intelligence failure in the same way that Pearl Harbor was; in both cases, the writing was already on the wall.[5] The attacks also provided an opportunity for the Bush administration to implement pre-existing ideas, especially the removal of Saddam Hussein, as part of a neoconservative vision to transform the regimes of the oil-rich Middle East into a system—in theory, a democracy—favorable to Western interests. Instead, the use of U.S. military power, especially in Iraq, alienated NATO allies and potential ones in the Middle East.

In the Cold War, the West eventually won the battle of ideas. In the long war that followed 9/11 the West increasingly lost the media war and the moral high ground. In the field in Palestine, Iraq, and Afghanistan, the Western coalition's military use of the media was outflanked by the insurgents' propaganda. By 2008 it was by no means clear who was going to triumph in the self-fulfilling clash of civilizations.

## AFGHANISTAN

Though the war in Afghanistan was militarily successful for the West, the media were thwarted at every stage, from the difficulty of crossing over into Afghanistan, to the danger of covering the war once inside, to imposed restrictions by the U.S. forces. The onset, though, held promise for the military and even the media. The Islamic world displayed some sympathy, or at least toleration, for Washington's rapid invasion of Taliban-ruled Afghanistan, the sanctuary for al-Qaeda. The jihadist training camps were viewed by Western intelligence as a tempting target, though in retrospect it might have been easier to have accepted the Taliban's offer to try Osama bin Laden under Sharia law. In October 2001, special forces from the United States, UK, and Australia arrived in Afghanistan to support the Northern Alliance, a coalition of clans, tribes, and warlords who had long fought the Taliban. The Northern Alliance was in mourning for its charismatic leader, Ahmed Shah Massud, who had been assassinated by al-Qaeda two days before 9/11. The media mobilized its mass formations too, both in Pakistan and northern Afghanistan. CNN field producer Kieran Baker described the mayhem of fifteen hundred journalists who descended on Islamabad and the Marriott Hotel in particular. Baker wrote, "The growing demands of expectations of TV news reminds me increasingly of how the film industry operated: by the end of this operation we had ten drivers, a fleet of four-wheeled vehicles, five fixers and translators, and over 50 staff."[6]

Embedded journalists were in this war as well. According to Bryan Whitman, deputy assistant secretary of defense for public affairs, the Pentagon had a significant number of reporters aboard the ships at sea on the

**176**

first day of the war, when the Tomahawk cruise missile shooters engaged targets.[7] Journalists attempting to access the war on the ground had a much tougher time, especially dealing with the bureaucracy in Tajikistan. Others sought to cross into Afghanistan from Pakistan. BBC's John Simpson, despite his 6' 4" frame, managed a famous crossing in a burqa. When *Sunday Express* journalist Yvonne Ridley tried this tactic, she was caught by the Taliban.[8]

Even when correspondents wheedled into the enclave held by the Northern Alliance, it was hard going. While the international press viewed Afghanistan as a great story, the Afghans viewed the journalists as an easy means to the only currency that held any actual value for them—the U.S. dollar—and would use persuasion or force without pause to obtain it. Australian Paul McGeough delivered one of the best accounts of being cooped up in this perilous enclave. He described how domestic journalism is a competitive and ugly business, but, in war zones, even the most hardened loners look out for one another with a camaraderie based on a simple truism: on the road, you need to find strangers whom you can trust, especially when the bullets start flying. "There are only three boxes," wrote McGeough, "and you have to tick them off quickly as you assess prospective candidates: do they share your security worries, do they have a broad view of the story that is likely to keep you together on the road, and will they drive you mad?"[9] McGeough wasn't exaggerating the dangers. Three journalists with him were killed by a Taliban counterattack on November 11, 2001. He barely survived himself. A week later, four journalists, two men from Reuters and correspondents for *El Mundo* and *Corriere della Sera*, were shot by armed men on their way from Jalabad to Kabul.

From an "economy of force" Western perspective, the war in Afghanistan was a successful and rapid war. Special forces, the use of proxy armies, and that old war-horse, the B-52 bomber, soon forced the Taliban out of Kabul. Another old war-horse, John Simpson, was the first journalist to "liberate" the Afghan capital for the BBC. The BBC, though, did not have a good war. It had been scooped by Al-Jazeera, which had a bureau in Kabul and had a monopoly of the coverage from the Taliban side. An original experiment in impartial twenty-four-hour news reporting in a region long characterized by state-controlled media, Al-Jazeera broke the Anglo-American "media imperialism" in the Arab and Muslim world. CNN was said to film the launch of cruise missiles, but Al-Jazeera recorded what happened when they landed. As the historian of the news station articulated, "It was ironic that the puritanical Taliban tolerated Al-Jazeera, but the United States would not."[10] Al-Jazeera's portrayal of the war in Afghanistan prompted Washington to realize its absence in the Arab and

Muslim media. U.S. forces reacted by laying waste to the station's HQ in Kabul, although no one was killed. Journalists began to feel that they were being targeted by both sides, a suspicion intensified by the wars that followed.

Though President Bush had vowed to capture or kill bin Laden, he ultimately failed. The Saudi arch-terrorist and his commanders escaped from Afghanistan into the Pakistan tribal areas, despite major U.S. engagements at Tora Bora in December 2001, and in Operation Anaconda in March 2002. Both engagements were set in the forbidding Afghan highlands, where guerrillas had traditionally fared better than conventional armies. Although much has been written about these U.S. failures, the simplest explanation initially offered was that bin Laden bribed key warlords to help him escape.[11] Yet, with a multimillion-dollar bounty on bin Laden's head, a more plausible explanation was the shared affinity of religious and political support, allied to a visceral hatred of the infidel Americans.

Apart from the failure to capture bin Laden, the war in Afghanistan was a victory for the American military, especially over the media. The coalition relied on air power, which is impossible for the media to cover, and special forces' operations, which are always off-limits to journalists. A few pools were arranged, yet they were soon abandoned, unilaterally in the case of CNN's Christiane Amanpour. If the Western control of the media was relatively ad hoc in Afghanistan, the U.S. military was simultaneously devising a very detailed system of manipulation in the forthcoming onslaught on Iraq.

## "WITH US OR AGAINST US"

Although bin Laden escaped and the Taliban administration collapsed, both regrouped in Pakistan paradoxically. Pakistan's president, Gen. Pervez Musharraf, responded to George Bush's challenge: "You are either with us or against us." Musharraf accepted the economic and military inducements and sided publicly with Washington. At the same time, however, he could not alienate his own Islamic parties and intelligence services by abandoning the Taliban completely—particularly since India had supported the Northern Alliance. Moreover, fiercely independent tribal areas had always ignored Islamabad's writ. Thus, Bush's Manichean imperative was never going to be fully followed in the Islamic world, even by moderate pro-Western governments.

Many Islamic rulers viewed the build-up to war in Iraq with grave suspicion, despite the personal dislike many felt for Saddam Hussein. Nearly all regarded the Anglo-American policy with even more suspicion: that its preemptive strategies based on dubious dossiers and poor intelligence about weapons of mass destruction were part of a crusade against Islam, not jihadist terrorists. Many sensed that Americans agreed with the old Washington jest, "What is all of *our* oil doing under *their* sand?" Correspondents would later prove that these doubts about the war were well grounded. After the war, investigations, particularly one by Mick Smith, later the defense correspondent of the London *Sunday Times*, revealed the "Downing Street Memos." These memos showcased deliberate attempts by U.S. officials to dupe the government into war by manipulating the UN weapons inspection process, as well as strong-arming Saddam Hussein into war by launching an escalation of operations over the southern no-fly zone, which was effectively the beginning of the air war in May 2002. They also disclosed Blair's commitment to war as early as April of that same year. Although the content of the memos was sensational, U.S. media were hesitant to cover the story because of questions over their veracity, or because some American newspapers were portrayed as being supportive of the received wisdom in Washington.

Above all, it was the one-sided backing of Israel, with Washington's blind eye to UN resolutions critical of the Jewish state, that continued to rankle in the Arab street. The security barrier that Israel was building to keep out suicide bombers appeared as de facto borders in the West Bank. The Israeli Defense Forces (IDF) also reoccupied towns, most notoriously Jenin on April 3, 2002. For eight days, Merkava tanks, armored personnel carriers, and Cobra helicopters firing wire-guided missiles waged war on Hamas and Islamic jihad insurgents in the town. Twenty-three IDF troops were killed. Giant armored bulldozers, the size of double-decker buses, were brought in to flatten the centers of resistance. About 25 percent of the cinder-block houses were destroyed. Palestinian propaganda claimed that five hundred civilians were massacred; the IDF put the initial figure of civilian deaths at one hundred. The final figure was fifty-two Palestinians killed.[12] Al-Jazeera's reporting of the siege of Jenin galvanized Arab opinion throughout the Middle East, though its reporting of the casualties was fair and contradicted the Palestinians' exaggerated claims of deliberate wholesale massacres. A history of the Arab television station noted, "Al-Jazeera has helped to quench the culture of conspiracy among the Palestinians; occasionally, as in Jenin, this has even been of advantage to the Israelis."[13]

The town of Jenin, however, has become almost synonymous with the word massacre. The Israelis refused to take any journalists with them on the Jenin operation, which created an information vacuum that was filled with speculation and disinformation by adversaries. The Palestinians, in particular, proved skillful in communicating their point of view across the Internet during the "Electronic Intafada." The lessons of Jenin were twofold. First, Israelis learned that ignoring the media meant enemies could easily sabotage their political agenda and image during war. Second, the media learned that other forms of information dissemination would form if they were shut out. As a result, the media no longer held a monopoly in the global information space.

Despite the media flak, Britain's Tony Blair, in public, continued to side with George Bush's stance on the Arab-Israeli conflict, though in private the prime minister urged his American counterpart to accelerate a settlement. An element of the Anglo-American closeness was Blair's belief that the U.S. president would do his utmost to resolve the Arab-Israeli conflict by creating, rather than merely promising, a two-state solution. In turn, Bush praised the British premier in public often: "We have a no more valuable friend. . . . As we say in Texas, he's a standup kinda guy."[14] He relegated, though, Britain's prime minister to the role of junior partner, especially regarding Israel. Soon, this alliance would be tested by Bush's resolve to declare war on Iraq.

Though neoconservatives in Washington needed little persuasion to go to war against Iraq, the House of Commons did. The case depended on a series of propositions about the nature of the Saddam regime; its secret obsession with weapons of mass destruction; its ability to deceive UN weapons inspectors; its cooperation with jihadists and other terrorists and its willingness to hand over WMDs to them; the fragility of Saddam's popularity; and his removal's consequences for the whole region. While these propositions drew on intelligence information, they would not be refuted by the mainstream media until they faced the actual audit of war.[15] Although preemptive war strategies must be founded on good intelligence, the Western intelligence was misled on the above propositions. Intelligence agencies corrupt their purpose if they fall into line with political demands and fail to voice uncertainties over their evidence, especially if it is used publicly in the media as a casus belli. Blair and Bush stood accused of hoodwinking both national and international opinion.

In the United States, the CIA was humbled. It had been designed to be the dominant force in the U.S. intelligence community and independent of the military to protect it from becoming the tool of the general staff. The CIA was pushed aside, as Secretary of Defense Donald Rumsfeld inflated the role of his department's own Defense Intelligence Agency (DIA). Semi-covert organizations like the Office of Strategic Influence (OSI) and the Office of Special Plans (OSP) were created to sell the case for war against Iraq. In the age of the Internet, however, it was difficult, if not impossible, to keep secrets—at least not for long. Knowledge of both organizations soon seeped out to the media. Nevertheless, the civilian politicians were still calling all the shots. Equally, you could argue that the *civilians* in the Pentagon, Rumsfeld, Feith et al., were stove-piping intelligence from the DOD's Office of Special Plans directly to the White House.

But the end result was that caution advocated by many British and American generals was ignored. Their after-the-event indignation did not surface in the press for another two to three years.

Before the Iraq War, the deliberate and constant drip-feeding of anti-Saddam propositions by intelligence leaks to the media, especially to major American papers such as the *New York Times*, created a vicious circle. Journalists stood accused of "mainlining uncut propaganda" and reporting "faith-based intelligence" in a "mawkish, cheapskate attempt to push Americans into war."[16] In the long term, bearing in mind the importance of open-source information, the numerous pro-war stories had an insidious effect on intelligence estimates. The combination of hyped newspapers stories and the selective use of intelligence data by politicians powerfully impacted the public and policy. According to a senior U.S. intelligence official, "As they embellished what the intelligence community was prepared to say, and as the press reported that information, it began to acquire its own sense of truth and reality."[17] Washington and London were about to face reality in what Winston Churchill once called "the thankless deserts of Mesopotamia." Or, as Jon Stewart of America's tongue-in-cheek newscast *The Daily Show* would dub it, "Mess-o-potamia."

## THE IRAQ WAR

It is a striking testimony to both the power and the ignorance of the Western media that they instilled in the public the perception that the Iraqi war of 2003 should be labeled the Second Gulf War. In historical fact, it is the third. Although this might seem semantic nitpicking, the distinction is important in the Middle East where the Iran-Iraq War of the 1980s is regarded as the first Gulf War. Moreover, the region's people view the mislabeling as further evidence of Western ignorance of Middle Eastern culture and history. This perception has had serious consequences in the years after the combat phase of the war, as coalition forces attempted to "win the hearts and minds" of the Iraqi people as what was supposed to be a "liberation" of Iraq from the Saddam regime turned into an insurgency against the "coalition occupiers." In fact, new soldiers being deployed to the region were briefed not to refer to the war as the Second Gulf War.

The attack on Iraq in 2003 was, for the United States, very much part of the "Global War on Terror." Militarily, however, the "coalition of the willing" that was assembled to fight it consisted of only four nations: the United States, Britain, Australia, and Poland. Secretary of State Colin Powell said, however, that the coalition comprised thirty nations, with another fifteen preferring to remain anonymous. Veteran reporter Martin Bell was tart: "To call them a coalition was a supine use of language."[18] Significantly, although U.S. bases in Arab states were used, there were no formal Arab military contributions, unlike in 1991, and no absolutely clear-cut UN resolutions authorizing the invasion. The war was perhaps the most controversial conflict of modern times—at least outside of the United States where the controversy really only began after the combat phase of operations. The media reflected the national positions of their respective governments: in the United States, the media were largely pro-war; in France and Germany, the media were antiwar; in Britain, the media were deeply divided. Interestingly, in Spain and Italy, the media reflected more the position of public opinion than the pro-war governments. The Spanish government, though, was to pay the price for their stance when Madrid was subjected to terrorist bomb attacks on the eve of the March 2004 general election. The pro-war government was shortly voted out of office in an eleventh-hour surge by its main Socialist opponents.

From the point of view of the military-media relationship, the two most striking controversies of the 2003 war in Iraq were the process of "embedding" journalists with coalition forces and the coalition's alleged attack on Baghdad's Palestine Hotel—where many unembedded journalists were staying—as U.S. forces liberated the city. On April 8, Reuters's Taras Protsyuk and Spanish cameraman José Couso were both killed by American tank fire at the Palestine Hotel. The media later attacked the U.S. Army for its contradictory claim that it had been taking fire from the hotel before it struck. A third debate of major significance that emerged in Britain after the war related to journalists' role in covering controversial events leading up to the invasion, namely the Hutton Enquiry into the death of WMD expert Dr. David Kelly. (A parliamentary enquiry preceded the Hutton report, the Butler Enquiry followed it.) Kelly spoke to reporters, particularly the BBC's Andrew Gilligan who went on to say that the government had "sexed up" intelligence dossiers. Gilligan and both the BBC's director-general and chairman were forced to resign, despite the fact that Gilligan's assertions were generally accurate. Kelly, who was authorized by the Ministry of Defence to brief reporters on technical matters, was scapegoated by the MoD, and committed suicide, according to the official enquiry into his death. Some investigators, however, have questioned the official verdict.

For Britain, Operation Telic, the UK's designation of what the United States labeled Operation Iraqi Freedom, was perhaps the most controversial foreign military intervention since the 1956 Suez Crisis. Public and media opinion at home was deeply divided, two senior Cabinet ministers resigned, and eventually the editor of one of Britain's major tabloid newspapers was forced to quit over publishing faked photographs of British soldiers' mistreating Iraqi prisoners. In the United States, the war became more controversial after the event, or rather after President Bush declared an end to the war's combat phase aboard the USS *Abraham Lincoln* on May 1, 2003, with a banner touting "Mission Accomplished" behind him. As some observers noted, it was Bush's "Top Gun moment," as the stage-managed event aboard the aircraft carrier was beamed around the world.

Though Baghdad may have fallen, Saddam Hussein remained at large until December 2003, when his capture became another global media event framed by a memorable sound-bite, this time by coalition civilian administrator L. Paul Bremer: "Ladies and gentleman, we got him." Saddam's supporters had killed more American troops by this point than during the combat phase of operations, and parts of Iraq seemed to be undergoing full-scale insurrection. Back in the United States, debates began to rage about whether the country was embroiled in "another Vietnam," and questions about the justification for the war emerged as no WMDs were found. The *New York Times* even apologized to its readers for its uncritical acceptance of White House assertions, not least about the spurious connection between Saddam Hussein and 9/11. In a 2002 poll, an astonishing 70 percent of Americans said that there was such a connection. Bush and Blair survived subsequent elections, a testimony to their resolve, or to the shortcomings of their political opponents.

## EMBEDS AND FEMBEDS

"Embedding" was a new label on an old bottle. Back in 1942, war correspondent Ernie Pyle would have seen himself as embedded, as would the twenty-nine British journalists who accompanied the task force to the South Atlantic in 1982. Now it sparked more controversy as thousands of journalists clamored for accreditation. For the American-led coalition forces, accreditation was designed to provide the media with "minimally restrictive access" to the frontline with little censorship (within the confines of OPSEC).[19] That this approach was related to wider strategic information operations was evident from the Pentagon's embedding agreement with the media, issued six weeks before the start of the Iraqi war:

Media coverage of any future operation will, to a large extent, shape public perception of the National Security Environment now and in the years ahead. This holds true for the U.S. public, the public in Allied countries whose opinion can affect the durability of our coalition, and publics in countries where we conduct operations, whose perceptions of us can affect the cost and duration of our involvement. Our ultimate strategic success in bringing peace and security to this region will come in our long-term commitment to supporting our democratic ideals. We need to tell the factual story—good and bad—before others seed the media with disinformation and distortions, as they most certainly will continue to do. Our people in the field need to tell our story.[20]

This directive can be read in a number of ways. If the journalists in the field were embedded with the troops, then they could surely see the story for themselves and report it to the wider world beyond the battlefield. Did this then mean that soldiers were to report their stories to the wider world via the embeds? This would shape the media as more of a conduit for the official version of events and thus more open to charges of propaganda. Or was the directive a method for ensuring journalists interpreted what they were seeing in a manner that was conducive to, or coincided with, the soldiers' stories? Again, this would then lay the media open to charges of vigorously supporting the military. Many members of the military had long been frustrated by the press corps' apparent lack of knowledge and understanding of soldiering, especially since the press corps had little practical experience of military life since the end of the draft in the United States and national service in Britain. Such journalists may not have fully comprehended war events unless soldiers explained them. It was a nice twist from "seeing is believing" to "believing is seeing."

Before looking at how this relationship worked during combat operations, other notable aspects of the Pentagon's February 2003 embedding agreement require examination. Apart from accompanying air, sea, and ground forces "to ensure a full understanding of all operations," the media would also be "given access to operational combat missions, including mission preparation and debriefing, whenever possible."[21] Dropping in on units in the tradition of "parachute journalism" was not to be allowed; embedded journalists were expected to stay for weeks and even months, sharing the billeting, transportation, and other facilities afforded to the soldiers they were accompanying. While they were not allowed their own transportation, they did have to bring their own equipment, which they would load, maintain, and use themselves. The importance of speedy reporting within a real-time environment was fully appreciated. The agreement purported to enable reporters "to tell [their] story in a timely manner" and also stated that "no communications equipment for use by media in the conduct of their duties will be specifically prohibited."[22] As a contingency, "in the event of commercial communications difficulties, media are authorized to file stories via expeditious military signal/communications capabilities."[23] As for the philosophy behind any possible delay or prevention of copy, "the standard for release of information should be to ask 'why not release' vice 'why release.' Decisions should be made ASAP, preferably in minutes, and not hours."[24]

The news organizations rather than the military allocated which reporters should become embedded. Freelancers would also have to be nominated by a recognized news outlet. This system resulted in bizarre appointments, such as Iran-Contra scandal figure Lt. Col. Oliver North and talk show host Geraldo Rivera for Fox News. Embedded reporters were to sign a release indemnifying the military from any lawsuit should something happen to them, although "the personal safety of correspondents is not a reason to exclude them from combat areas."[25] The unit commander had the right to exclude a reporter who was not deemed physically fit to undergo the "rigorous conditions required to operate with the forward deployed forces. . . . Gender will not be an excluding factor under any circumstance."[26] Incidentally, female reporters became known as the "fembeds." The reporters would have to adhere to a mutually agreed set of ground rules and were reassured that these rules would "recognize the right of the media to cover military operations and are in no way intended to prevent release of derogatory, embarrassing, negative or uncomplimentary information."[27] All interviews with service personnel were to be on the record, the embeds could not carry firearms, and their reports had to be generic rather than specific on such matters as troops sizes, positions, and equipment.

At the end of the list was an amusingly worded item: "Use of lipstick and helmet-mounted cameras on combat sorties is approved and encouraged to the greatest extent possible."[28] The inadvertent humor that stemmed from the mention of the tiny lipstick cameras was tied into media commentary on the fembeds. Over the previous decade, amidst charges of "dumbing down" the news for purposes of "infotainment," the competition for declining audiences had resulted in what one veteran British female correspondent had described as the "babe factor." Female war correspondents had achieved fame because of their journalism skills in the past, but now many women were being ostensibly employed more for their appearance than their ability.[29] Moreover, female correspondents' youth, and hence their inexperience, meant that they were dependent on military spokespeople to explain the current happenings. This dependency was implicitly understood in the U.S. Public Affairs guidelines, although no reference was made to the cultural difficulties that Western female reporters might experience when reporting from Islamic societies. The British equivalent of the Pentagon's guidance was the *Green Book*, produced by the Ministry of Defence and updated in the early 1990s. The British were apparently caught by surprise by the American embedded system, as there is no reference to it in this document. Instead, there is mention of accredited correspondents who would be limited in number and still deployed in pools. In stark contrast to the Pentagon, which accepted any journalist dispatched, in the UK's arrangements the Ministry of Defence granted reporters ultimate accreditation, thereby giving it a theoretical power to veto any reporter. The main concerns of the *Green Book* related to operational security, reporting of casualties, and filming prisoners of war.

Once the fighting began, the experience of the embedded reporters varied, naturally, according to the experience of the units to which they were attached. Around 660 journalists were embedded with U.S. forces and 150 with the British, but only 10 percent of the total number of correspondents were involved in frontline combat. Nonetheless, those reporting live from the battlefield provided some of the most spectacular television footage ever seen. "It was like watching through 600 straws," said one senior American news executive, although arguably 540 of those straws showed nothing, such being the nature of combat. Viewers were seeing for the first time what ordinary soldiers had already discovered about the reality of war: there were moments of incredible brutality punctuated by long periods of boredom.

The sheer scale of the media presence was staggering. The BBC sent two hundred of its people to the region, its largest foreign assignment ever. CNN fielded the same presence, while the three major American networks of ABC, NBC, and CBS sent some five hundred staff members to Kuwait. The *New York Times* deployed thirty employees to the region. There were also the new regional Arab media players, the most significant of which were Al-Arabiya, Abu Dhabi TV, and Al-Jazeera.

Talk of that tired axiom, the "fog of war," pervaded the first week of fighting. Multitudes of reporters, especially those fueling the relentless appetites of the twenty-four-hour live broadcasting services (radio and television), were transmitting to viewers countless pieces of information; for reporters to stand back, take a deep breath, and form a considered opinion was close to impossible. "This media war has swiftly become a fiendishly complex campaign, long on assertion and painfully short on delivery. Too many hearts, too many different minds," one senior British journalist concluded.[30] The resultant confusion was more akin, however, to a snowstorm of information than to a fog generated by the military authorities, mainly because the media management arrangements were far less intrusive than they had been in 1991. Gen. Tommy Franks was much less of a star performer than "Stormin' Norman" Schwarzkopf; Franks imposed his personality and policies on the media far less effectively than Schwarzkopf did. Aside from Franks, the main reason the media arrangements were less intrusive was that the Gulf War had first been conducted by an air war lasting a month, followed by a 100-hour ground war that was fought at night. In 1991, a news blackout initially was imposed, although this ban was quickly lifted as the progress of the forces grew. That progress, however, was so swift that some pool reporters found that they were unable to get their copy back to the forward transmission units for timely use. As a result, viewers did not see that part of the conflict until it was over.

In 2003, the ground war began simultaneously with the air war. There were no pools this time; the journalists were embedded with the forces. Moreover, technology had considerably improved since 1991, and the embeds were able to broadcast live from the battlefront—within the usual constraints of operational security. This advance in technology was foreshadowed in Afghanistan when John Simpson broadcasted from the front line via his videophone. Though his pictures were not the usual broadcast standard, they provided an unprecedented window into the battlefield. As Operation Iraqi Freedom began with a rapid push towards Baghdad, journalists gave running commentaries of the columns' progress in real time.

One of the embedded journalists, Brian Appleyard of the London *Sunday Times*, wrote, "At first this device seemed like a propaganda triumph. The early shots of the U.S. Cavalry blazing across the desert with CNN's Walter Rogers bouncing alongside excitedly in his Humvee said exactly what the Pentagon wanted to hear—'there is no opposition, and it's breakfast in Baghdad.'"[31] He continued:

> But then we woke from the dream of a quick, clean war and cheering Iraqis. Sandstorms, militia and fedayeen got in the way. Saddam—or one of his doubles—was alive and, more to the point, he was on television. Within a few days it was clear that the Iraqis were actually winning the propaganda war.
>
> They are winning because, in stark contrast to the coalition, they keep it simple. They broadcast the message: we're still here

and we will win. Furthermore, they let reporters in Baghdad say more or less what they liked, censoring them invisibly to the viewer by restricting their movements.

And so we drink thirstily from the Baghdad trickle and then turn round to be drowned from the coalition flood. The key problem is the embeds. They are all over southern Iraq . . . and they're all babbling excitedly, reacting, understandably, to every shot that's fired and every rumour that flashes around the battlefield. . . .

The embeds are certainly tightly controlled, but the effect of their reports has been a massive loss of control for the military. The sheer volume of their reportage has swamped the media and wrong-footed the generals. Whether they like it or not, the mood now is that there has been a psychological and military miscalculation of enormous proportions and that has spread a damaging and depressed uncertainty amongst the British and American electorates.

As for [William Howard] Russell's question—"Am I to tell these things or hold my tongue"—well, there is no answer, there is only context. The context today is that of an enervated audience brought face to face with life on a battlefield they are not equipped to understand. The first casualty of war is the truth and the wound is fatal.[32]

Of this snowstorm, Brian Appleyard likened the phenomenon to the Hollywood movie *Groundhog Day*:

The 24-hour news channels have become televisual hypertext. A banner headline beneath the picture tells us the story currently being covered, but, beneath, a news ticker keeps telling us other stories. What is true? What is important? Press the red interactive button and it gets worse—screens and menus proliferate. Ironically, the screen I found most restful was the still, commentary-free shot of the Baghdad skyline on BBCi [the BBC's interactive TV services]. Only there, it seemed, was life going on as normal.[33]

This rampant media coverage caused some tension with the politicians, not least because the Iraqi town of Umm Qasr was reported to have been taken on nine separate occasions before it actually fell. CNN stated that the town had been overtaken at the same time Al-Jazeera reported only heavy fighting. The UK Ministry of Defence announced three times over three days that it was secure, before it fell. Geoff Hoon, the UK secretary of state for defence, blamed imprecise language. The coalition had not clearly differentiated the port and the town itself, which shared the same name. "Umm Qasr is a town similar to Southampton," he communicated to the House of Commons, meaning that the port and town were in separate places. "He's either never been to Southampton, or he's never been to Umm Qasr," said one British soldier on patrol in Umm Qasr. "There's no beer, no prostitutes, and people are shooting at us. It's more like Portsmouth."[34] The media also had a field day with conflicting claims about the widely reported but fictitious Shi'a uprising in Basra. "Don't look now, but the Shiites have hit the fan," according to Fox News anchor Neil Cavuto.[35] As Foreign Secretary Jack Straw noted: "Twenty-four hour news actually changes the reality of warfare. The media is changing the nature of warfare, it is not just reporting on it."[36]

P. J. O'Rourke's comment on embedding was typically succinct: "One of the few benefits of being a journalist is that you're not in the army. The whole idea of putting you in the army and not giving you a gun—gee, no thanks."[37] Chris Ayres, who quoted O'Rourke's comment in his book *War Reporting for Cowards*, was by his own admission not cut out to be a military correspondent. He had been covering the celebrity circuit in Los Angeles for the London *Times* before being embedded. Prepared for the "worst camping trip of his life," Ayres confessed that the first casualty was not so much truth but personal hygiene.[38] He admitted that he was more interested in staying alive than staying objective. "It was then I realized the true genius of the embedding scheme. *It had turned me into a Marine.* I was thinking like a fighter, not a reporter. And yet I wasn't a fighter. I was an idiot in a blue flak jacket."[39] In this context, only four embedded journalists were fatalities in the first phase of the war, one of whom died of natural causes. Unilaterals suffered a more deadly toll: nine were killed. Incidentally, in the thirteen years of the U.S. involvement in Vietnam, the death toll was sixty-five Western reporters. Journalists were statistically ten times more likely to die than Western soldiers during the actual invasion.[40] About twenty-four correspondents were disembedded out of seven hundred and fifty for a variety of offenses or because of exhaustion or illness.

What was the overall assessment of embedding? Martin Bell said that it meant that journalists were not being accredited but rather recruited.[41] Phillip Knightley's verdict was even gloomier:

A radical American plan for managing wartime media perpetuated an illusion that the Iraq war was a triumph for modern media and its technology. In reality it was an overwhelming victory for the military and its propagandists. . . . Given the increased danger; greater degree of manipulation and control by government; and the new emphasis on seeing the war through the eyes of soldiers, the age of the war correspondent as hero appears to be over.[42]

Don McCullin, the renowned war photographer, was also scathing in his assessment:

> If you're "embedded" with the army, you don't have the real freedom to be among the population. You're basically a dog on a leash, and who wants to be like that? It's so different now. When I was in Vietnam with the American army during the Tet offensive, I could do what I wanted. I was sleeping under tables, yards from dead Vietnamese bodies. I photographed dying and terribly injured American soldiers. I am sure the Americans wouldn't stand for that now.[43]

It was a short one-sided campaign; a veteran reporter argued that one of Saddam's statues put up more of a fight than Saddam had himself.[44] Yet the war produced excellent writing. John Lee Anderson's *The Fall of Baghdad*, for example, has been compared with John Reed's *Ten Days that Shook the World* and George Orwell's *Homage to Catalonia*.[45] Anthony Shadid of the *Washington Post* is an Arab-American of Lebanese descent; he provided a fine perspective from the Iraqis' point of view in *Night Draws Near: Iraq's People in the Shadow of America's War*.[46] Thus, Knightley's verdict might be premature. Moreover, many heroic reports by journalists in Iraq came out after the initial invasion. Then coalition forces were not in a position to protect themselves properly, much less the media.

## ATROCITY STORIES

Even before the war started, tales of the brutality of Saddam's regime were deeply rooted in Western minds. Indeed, on the eve of hostilities, Leader of the Opposition Iain Duncan Smith informed Parliament on how

> his [Saddam's] main victims have been his own people. The tale of his rule of lawlessness is a litany of horror. Dissident women are raped, children are tortured and prisoners are trapped in steel boxes until they confess or die. As we have heard, chemical weapons have been used against the Kurds, and Shi'a villages razed to the ground.[47]

Such statements were confidently based on evidence gathered for years by human rights organizations such as Amnesty International, including reports of tongue amputations and rapes of female family members by the fedayeen for slander against Saddam Hussein.[48]

On March 27, President Bush and Prime Minister Blair held their first wartime summit. They did not miss the opportunity to reinforce their message about the brutality of the regime the coalition was fighting. Their purpose for the summit was to counter the most recent media skepticism about military and civilian casualties, reports of brutal fighting, and doubts about the length of the war. President Bush commented on images of two British soldiers slain execution style that Al-Jazeera had aired (the pictures were not shown by British broadcasters): "If anyone needed any further evidence of the depravity of Saddam's regime, this atrocity provides it."[49] This statement caused a minor storm in the UK, especially when the families of the two fallen soldiers, Sapper Luke Allsopp and Staff Sgt. Simon Cullingworth, were given extensive media coverage about how distressed they were at President Bush's remark; the Ministry of Defence had led them to believe that their sons had been killed in action. A few days later Gen. Mike Jackson was said, by one colleague, to have been "as close as I have ever known to a senior military officer calling his prime minister a liar."[50]

At their joint press conference, President Bush also emphasized the moral stand of a democracy fighting a brutal dictatorship, citing reports that Iraqis were murdering citizens to blame the coalition for their deaths and were considering the use of chemical weapons. Bush said one Iraqi dissident had his tongue cut out and then bled to death after being tied to a stake in the town square, adding, "That's how Saddam Hussein retains power." He continued, "If he uses weapons of mass destruction, it will just prove our case. And we will deal with it. We've got one objective in mind. That's victory, and we'll achieve victory."[51]

In his radio address to the nation on Saturday, March 29, President Bush reiterated the atrocities he maintained the Iraqi enemy in the previous week had committed:

> In the last week the world has seen firsthand the cruel nature of a dying regime. In areas still under its control, the regime continues its rule by terror. Prisoners of war have been brutalized and executed. Iraqis who refuse to fight for the regime are being murdered. An Iraqi woman was hanged for waving at coalition troops. Some in the Iraqi military have pretended to surrender, then opened fire on coalition forces that showed them mercy.

Given the nature of this regime, we expect such war crimes, but we will not excuse them. War criminals will be hunted relentlessly and judged severely.[52]

Later that day, the Iraqi information minister, Mohammed Saeed al-Sahaf, accused the coalition of killing 140 civilians over the previous twenty-four hours and denied allegations that Iraqi soldiers were disguising themselves as civilians.[53] Coalition sources, however, confirmed that an apparent suicide bomber had killed four American soldiers from the 1st Brigade of the 3rd Infantry Division when a taxi stopped at a checkpoint outside Najef, the first of many such incidents to be reported in the war.[54] Iraqi television said President Saddam Hussein had awarded the bomber, a junior army officer, Ali Jaafar al-Noamani, two posthumous medals.[55] More bombers would follow, threatened the Iraqis.[56] Fox News, however, reported that the suicide bomber was a Saudi citizen linked to al-Qaeda.[57]

The emotive association of suicide bombers with the Iraqis' irregular warfare tactics helped bring the war on terrorism back into focus. This correlation was further augmented by simultaneous reports from the northern front that U.S. special operations units entered into combat operations for the first time with Kurdish Peshmerga troops against the Ansar-al-Islam, a terrorist group of around seven hundred members that had been linked with al-Qaeda.[58] Ironically, two members of U.S. special units were reported killed in an ambush in Afghanistan on that day.

## SHAPING THE INFORMATION SPACE

British viewers awoke on Tuesday, March 25, to reports that coalition aircraft had bombed a market in the al-Shaab district of Baghdad, with the loss of at least fourteen civilian lives. The Iraqis maintained it was a deliberate attack on civilians. In response to a reporter's question at a United States Central Command (CENTCOM) briefing later that day, Deputy Director of Operations Brig. Gen. Vince Brooks said:

We did have an air mission that attacked some targets, not in that area but in a different area, and during that period of time, they encountered surface-to-air missile fire . . . we've seen uncontrolled surface-to-air missile fire. And what I mean by that is, normally they are controlled by radar, but there's a hazard to turning on a radar against one of our aircraft, a very certain hazard, and so the firing crews have decided not to turn on the radar, and fire the missiles ballistically. They're also using very old stocks, we've discovered, and those stocks are not reliable, and missiles are going up and coming down. So we think it's entirely possible that this may have been, in fact, an Iraqi missile that either went up and came down, or given the behaviors of the regime lately, it may have been a deliberate attack inside of town.[59]

Worse was to come. On Friday, March 28, another marketplace was bombed, this time killing fifty-two people in a working-class suburb of Baghdad.[60] Iraq blamed the coalition. Echoing the baby milk plant story, each side was jostling to dominate the media agenda about who were the good guys and who were the innocents. The media were ill-equipped to evaluate the complexities of bomb damage assessment. The military was trying to master the art of broadcasting damage assessment. What was lost—at least within the short span of the 24/7 news cycle—was the truth.

"Shock and awe," the term used by the media for Operation Iraqi Freedom, was part of a command and control doctrine that integrated a psychological element into the military campaign. Brian Appleyard, who said the Gulf War was a "lockdown and a turkey shoot" in which "operational imperatives came first, truth a poor second," was among the few to recognize the new role of the media in information operations. He wrote:

> Twenty-four-hour live on-the-spot television news with all its accompanying technology put an end to any hopes of a Falklands style shutdown when GW2 came round. So, instead, the plan was to weaponize the media as an aspect of "psy-ops"—psychological warfare. They would be part of the "new kind of war" dreamt up by Donald Rumsfeld's Pentagon think-tankers. In this war technology would win quickly and cleanly and the grateful Iraqis would flood, cheering onto the streets, to welcome liberal democracy. So why not let us watch?[61]

After the first few days, however, especially after the failure of the opening decapitation strike, the coalition appeared as though it were fighting with one hand tied behind its back. Self-imposed limits on the deployment of firepower to minimize civilian casualties were part of the overall strategy to persuade the Iraqis that the war was about the removal of Saddam Hussein and not against them. The Iraqi propaganda machine was projecting the liberation of Iraq as an invasion by foreign mercenaries, and resistance surprised observers. As Rumsfeld explained:

> The outcome of this conflict is not in doubt. The regime will be removed. But, for our coalition of free people, we believe it is

important not just to win, but to win justly. The power of our coalition derives not simply from the vast overwhelming force at our disposal, but from the manner in which we employ that force. The Iraqi people will see how we employ our force and know that we are coming not to occupy their country, not to oppress them, but to liberate their country.[62]

Nonetheless, the failure to witness any further mass desertions was disappointing from the coalition's point of view. In the aftermath of the previous Gulf War, when rebellions had occurred in the north and the south, the southern Shi'a uprising had received very little media attention—and no coalition assistance other than the establishment of the no-fly zone. Memories of that failure undoubtedly played a part in the reluctance of the civilian population to rise up again, at least until they could be reassured that the Saddam regime's grip in the region had been destroyed. Often this involved attacks on the symbolism of the regime, as when British forces entered Basra, on Saturday, March 29, and destroyed two murals of Saddam.[63] But to reinforce the psychological-military force nexus, the British also destroyed a building in which two hundred loyalist fanatics were meeting. None were reported to have exited the building. As a direct refutation of the coalition's posture as liberators, the Iraqis responded by charging that the British were attacking civilian installations, food depots, and other attacks on the civilian population itself. As Michael Clarke wrote:

> The U.S. has got all the means to get messages across but has far too little effort into understanding which messages are likely to work and which to insult the intelligence of a proud people. The British outside Basra feel they have a better approach—from the wording to use on leaflets, to the "message by action" in al-Zubayr [on 23 March] when they identified the house of the much-feared local Ba'ath party leader and drove a Warrior light tank through his bedroom wall to snatch him straight from bed into custody. The Iraqis rather respect that. But the British approach to psyops is getting short shrift from their American commanders.[64]

The Iraqi Ministry of Information was bombed on the night of March 28 and in the early morning of March 29, a day after the main communications center, including the telephone exchange, was hit. Also, on March 29, BBC Monitoring reported that Baghdad's radio frequencies had been taken over by the coalition and was now broadcasting anti-Saddam statements.[65] Despite reports of several strikes against Iraqi television and radio, the regime's propaganda was still broadcasting throughout the first week. Saddam named the heroes defending the Iraq motherland, including a farmer who was said to have shot down an Apache helicopter. Antiwar demonstrations from around the world featured prominently in news bulletins. From the annual Academy Awards ceremony in Hollywood, Michael Moore—author of *Stupid White Men*—was shown denouncing President Bush and the war. After ten days, London's *Sunday Times* pointed out that "the coalition should be winning the propaganda battle convincingly with Saddam's rotten regime. As things stand it is, at best, a draw."[66]

In Rumsfeld's March 28 briefing at the Pentagon, one journalist asked him if there was any deliberate attempt to disguise the number of dead and wounded. He replied indignantly:

> Oh, my goodness! Now, you know that wouldn't be the case. There's no . . . no one in this government, here or on the ground, is going to underreport what's happening. That's just terrible to think that. Even to suggest it is outrageous. Most certainly not! The facts are reported. [Pounds fist.] When people are killed, they're killed and we face it. When people are wounded, we say so. When people are missing and we know they're missing, we say so. And when we're wrong and they wander back into camp, as several have recently, having been lost or with other units, we say so. Absolutely not![67]

When, on Saturday, March 29, the media spent most of the day reporting that the coalition had ordered a pause of four to six days in the advance of Baghdad to regroup—later denied by CENTCOM spokesmen—the Iraqi information minister called the reports a coalition deception and said Iraq would "cut the snake [of coalition convoys] in half." Iraqi satellite television, meanwhile, showed pictures of three damaged American tanks and another vehicle abandoned near Najaf. The presenter said the crews had fled after a confrontation with Iraqis. Al-Jazeera television quoted an Iraqi military spokesman as saying Iraq had shot down a total of five coalition fighter planes, six drones, four helicopters, and one hundred and thirty cruise missiles, as well as having destroyed over one hundred tanks and other armored vehicles.[68] Iraqi spokespeople made ludicrous claims, including the famous comment by the Iraq minister of information, Mohammed Saeed al-Sahaf, dubbed "Comical Ali" by the British media and "Baghdad Bob" by the Americans. He had declared live on air that no American tanks were in Baghdad, only to have those nonexistent tanks shown clearly in the background.

Coalition reports were far more credible, though the former editor of the liberal *Guardian* could still opine, "If, for reporters and their readers, there is one thing worse than the fog of war, it is the queasy perception that those in charge of the shooting match haven't the foggiest idea what is going on."[69] And not the foggiest idea about an exit strategy. The American-staged toppling of the Saddam statue in Baghdad's Paradise Square on April 9 gave the media a sense of closure. That scene was their exit strategy. The embeds nearly all drifted away, and the media's money and resources quickly dwindled. If the embeds were a critical part of shaping the information space, both within Iraq and the strategic environment beyond it, then they could not be relied on to fall into line with future public affairs or information operations strategies. The Pentagon was subsequently to contract out work to PR firms. And, as the insurgency worsened, debates about winning Iraqi hearts and minds through information operations (or "smile ops" as some skeptics labeled it) became subsumed by worldwide outrage about media revelations in Abu Ghraib and elsewhere. It should not be forgotten, however, that the notorious photographs of the mistreatment of Iraqi prisoners in Abu Ghraib were not taken by reporters, but by the soldiers themselves.

## THE OCCUPATION FIASCO

The occupation fiasco was not inevitable. The disaster was created by the intellectual acrobatics of simultaneously "worst-casing" the original Iraqi threat while "best-casing" the subsequent costs of occupation.[70] One of the best accounts of the endless blunders during the occupation was by Thomas E. Ricks, the *Washington Post*'s senior Pentagon correspondent, in his bestselling book *Fiasco: The American Adventure in Iraq*.[71] In the book, Ricks quotes Pamela Hess, a seasoned reporter for the United Press International (UPI). "Abominable" was the term she used to describe the media operations of the Coalition Provisional Authority (CPA), the American administration in Baghdad. In Hess's view, the CPA's relationship soured with the press because of its insistence that all was well and the reporters' consequent determination to disprove that contention. "Had they been more willing to admit that things were bad instead of putting lipstick on the pig, I think reporters would have been kinder," she said.[72] The CPA acted more as a monitor of the media than a provider of information. Paul Bremer, the American viceroy, seemed strangely detached in the "Emerald City," the Green Zone of seven square miles protected by 17-foot-high blast walls.[73]

The first nine months were marked by disaster—from the security vacuum that led to a locust-storm of looting to the army's insane de-

Ba'athification that sent tens of thousands of armed, angry, unemployed young men into the streets. The initial military impetus and latent Iraqi gratitude, which caused the fall of Saddam, was lost, as was the core of the hearts and minds campaign. The capture of Saddam in December 2003 made little difference. Later, his bungled execution was a publicity disaster for the West and the Baghdad government. Pictures taken illicitly on a mobile phone by someone present at the hanging were yet another reminder that everyone carrying cameras was now a potential journalist. This phenomenon has been dubbed by some as "citizen journalism." Many professional reporters, however, resent this phrase, preferring "electronic witnesses" as a more appropriate description of people who record historical events on portable digital equipment and are supposedly incapable of interpreting the events as professional journalists would.

The transfer of power to an interim Iraqi government in June 2004 did not appear to improve matters either. In the previous April, the U.S. military was fighting a major battle in Fallujah. In November, a second major offensive was launched in the same town, "a modern-day Stalingrad with dust for snow."[74] A British television team from Channel 4 News, Lindsey Hilsum and cameraman and producer Tim Lambon, was at the heart of the fighting. Their reports won a series of major journalism awards.[75] The *Economist*, often the voice of the British establishment, editorialized, "The very fact that Americans are having to fight so fiercely inside a major city, 18 months after liberating Iraq from Saddam Hussein, is a sign of how close Mr. Bush's Iraq policy is teetering towards failure."[76] The conservative *Daily Telegraph* in London pointed out, however, that "a snobbish tendency among the British," who believed that American forces were "trigger-happy and unwilling to engage the enemy at close quarters," had been dispelled.[77]

In October and November 2005, Tim Lambon and Lindsey Hilsum were working in the south of Iraq; "I think the Brits have lost control of Basra and the south," Lambon wrote in his personal log. He continued:

> They are now bit players with little influence, guarding their own patch and moving in great danger between their bases. In terms of the insurgency, from my experience of these things [Lambon had been a frontline soldier in the Rhodesian war, as well as covered numerous wars as a cameraman/producer], they have lost the war and it is irrecoverable despite what Tony Blah [sic] and his compadres might keep spouting. . . . And what of the Yanks further north? Same thing. . . . Iraq is not a country moving

inexorably towards democracy and freedom; it's a deeply divided
ex-state on the verge of a civil war. . . ."[78]

In the United States, the media were beginning to reappraise
their previously uncritical support of the war.[79] An initial casualty was
Judith Miller of the *New York Times*. During a special prosecutor's investigation into the leaking of a CIA agent's identity, it was alleged that her
ties with the wily Ahmad Chalabi, the favored Pentagon Iraqi exile before
the war, had led to false front-page scoops that became fodder for White
House propaganda.[80] In November 2005, she resigned her post at the
*Times*, which had earlier delivered a harsh assessment of its own performance. Daniel Okrent, the newspaper's ombudsman, said that a few stories "pushed Pentagon assertions so aggressively you could almost sense
epaulets on the shoulders of editors."[81] In the *New York Review of Books*,
Michael Massing's verdict was that many major newspapers had erred,
but that the *New York Times* stood out in particular: "Compared to other
major papers, the *Times* placed more credence in defectors, expressed
less confidence in inspectors, and paid less attention to dissenters."[82]

Many op-ed columns also recanted their opinion of Iraq. *Newsweek*
columnist Fareed Zakaria, once a respected hawk on Iraq, wrote that the
president's "strange combination of arrogance and incompetence" had
proved "poisonous" for American foreign policy. "On almost every issue
involving postwar Iraq—troop strength, international support, the credibility of exiles, de-Baathification, handling Ayatollah Ali Sistani—Washington's
assumptions and policies have been wrong," he charged.[83] Even the saintly
*Washington Post* began a critical self-examination of its stories leading up
to the war, though it did include a defensive caveat to its self-flagellation:
"Whether a tougher approach by the *Post* and other news organizations
would have slowed the rush to war is, at best, a matter of conjecture." That
comment prompted a flood of angry letters from readers saying that citizens of a modern democracy did need to know the full facts.

An avalanche of books by journalists critical of the Bush war policy
swept the American capital.[84] Perhaps the most influential was the trilogy
by the doyen of Washington journalists, Bob Woodward. In his third volume, *State of Denial*, he crafted a poignant vignette on Donald Rumsfeld's
return, in his seventies, to the office of secretary of defense, a post that he
had held twenty-five years before: "He resembled John Le Carré's fictional Cold War British intelligence chief, George Smiley, a man who 'had
been given, in late age, a chance to return to the rained-out contests of
his life and play them after all.'"[85] Rumsfeld resigned not long after these
words were published. Another architect of the war, Paul Wolfowitz, had

already stepped down from his post at the Pentagon. As with Robert McNamara after the Vietnam debacle, Wolfowitz set off to head the World Bank, yet more as a self-vindication presumably, unlike McNamara's act of atonement.[86] Wolfowitz was later forced to resign after a media frenzy over his relationship with Shaha Riza, an employee of the World Bank. After a promotion and significant pay raise negotiated by Wolfowitz, Riza was transferred out of the bank. Documentaries also joined the assault on Bush. A film castigating the bias of Fox News titled *Outfoxed: Rupert Murdoch's War on Journalism* was a polemical satire in the same vein as Michael Moore's *Fahrenheit 9/11,* which grossed more than $100 million in the United States alone. Most of the books and films appealed to liberal sensibilities or, as the Washington joke ran, to neo-conservatives who had been mugged by reality. Comedian Al Franken's book, *Lies and the Lying Liars Who Tell Them,* set out to debunk the myth of liberal control over the media.[87] Though the Bush-friendly Fox News remained the most popular news channel in the United States, the Washington media scandals continued. The alleged leak of CIA agent Valerie Plame's identity resulted in the ill-fated *New York Times* journalist Judith Miller's eighty-five-day imprisonment in July 2005 for refusal to reveal sources. This sentence reinforced the media self-flagellation described earlier. In the end, Lewis "Scooter" Libby, the vice president's chief of staff, took the rap for the leak from the White House—not his superior, Dick Cheney—becoming the highest-ranking White House official to be convicted in a government scandal in years (though President Bush commuted Libby's jail sentence). Ten of the eighteen witnesses at Libby's trial were journalists. Ugly truths emerged about reporters who subscribe to the tenet of protecting sources first and informing the public second. Nevertheless, other prosecutors will seek testimony from the press, forcing more and more journalists to betray their sources, and the public interest will suffer. At the same time, Reporters Without Borders published a press-freedom index: America ranked 53 out of 168, trailing behind Bosnia and the Dominican Republic.[88]

In further criticism, regarding Iraq, CNN's Christiane Amanpour aired her belief that the U.S. government had muzzled the press. In early 2007, she said, "Journalism had gone soft. The right questions weren't asked in the lead-up to the Iraq war, and now the whole world is paying the price. Two years ago everybody got their spine back."[89]

Journalists, especially in the United States, began to question what the administration was withholding from the media. The Abu Ghraib disclosures set a precedent for subsequent scandals—for example, those concerning wire taps and secret rendition to overseas prisons. But the willingness of journalists to stall publication, whether for alleged national security reasons, for the convenience of politicians, or to protect sources, raised the question again: What else are they not disclosing?[90]

Two cases in particular raised American concern about military veracity. On April 22, 2004, Cpl. Pat Tillman, of the 2nd Ranger Battalion, was shot in Afghanistan. He was the first professional football player to be killed in combat since the Vietnam War. His decision to serve in Iraq and later Afghanistan had been the subject of extensive media attention, much of it welcomed by the Army because of its potential to boost recruitment. He was killed in action in Afghanistan and was posthumously promoted and awarded the Silver Star and Purple Heart medals for heroism during the firefight. Initially, the Army refused to release the full details of Tillman's death to the media or to his family. However, the *Washington Post*, among other newspapers, investigated the story.[91] It turned out that the firefight had been between members of Tillman's unit; he had been killed by friendly fire. The Army very soon initiated a series of effective enquiries into Tillman's death, which led to a criminal investigation. At a 2007 congressional hearing, Tillman's brother Kevin, also a Ranger and sports star, criticized the Pentagon for using them both as props in a Pentagon public relations exercise.

In the same hearing, Pfc. Jessica Lynch testified about battlefield misinformation. In March 2003, Lynch's convoy was ambushed near Nasiriyah, in southern Iraq. Her time as a prisoner of war and subsequent rescue by American forces initiated numerous media stories, a book, and an NBC television movie, transforming her into a "Rambo from West Virginia." The Pentagon's first official report, however, said that she had not appeared to have defended herself against the Iraqis. Lynch had never fired a shot and had indeed been protected in captivity by Iraqi medical staff. In this case, the media (and local politicians in West Virginia) were to blame for the initial hype, not the military, though they did little to counter the flag-waving around the saving of Private Lynch.

Iraq inflicted another high-profile American military casualty in June 2007. Gen. Peter Pace, chairman of the joint chiefs of staff, was not reappointed, even though he was widely expected to stay on. Vice Chairman Adm. Edmund Giambastiani, also retired. The official version of the reasons behind these reappointment proceedings was that they would have been a "divisive ordeal" for the military. The effective sacking of the two most senior American military officers was scheduled for Friday, June 8, an opportune time for two reasons. First, the weekend television news shows were considered much "softer," because bad news was much easier to bury in the summer. Second, since the news would be breaking on Friday, the story would probably be stale by the following Monday. Instead, on June 8, the America media provided saturation coverage of the tearful return to prison of heiress Paris Hilton. The departure of the officers received minor airtime on the major talk shows. Cynical news managers in the Pentagon seemed to have assessed the media correctly.

Meanwhile, conditions in Iraq grew worse. By the end of 2006, U.S. military combat deaths had reached 3,000. Bush deployed 21,500 more troops in a surge in January 2007, augmented by 7,200 troops in March. By January 2008 the troop surge had achieved some tactical success in reducing the violence. Nevertheless, the Iraq Body Count, a private British volunteer organization, estimated the total of Iraqi civilians killed as 60,000, although the distinguished British medical journal the *Lancet* in October 2004 estimated that 100,000 Iraqis had been killed since the start of the war.[92]

Bad news doesn't get better with age.[93] In Iraq, as the country's communities collapsed in an ethno-sectarian civil war of savage proportions, the news worsened. In truth, it was not one war, but a patchwork of acute civil wars. Unless the limited tactical surge success became a strategic triumph throughout Iraq, President Bush had few valid options remaining, except withdrawal. His public rationale rested on two premises, one tragic and the other inaccurate. First, in defense of his last-ditch surge policy, the president appeared to be partly arguing that more soldiers needed to fall to honor the memory of those who had already fallen. Second, he requested time for the Iraqi army "to step up to the plate" to defend the Baghdad government. But there was no Iraqi army. "It was more accurate to describe them as forces on secondment from the Badr Army, or the peshmerga, benefiting from coalition training and advice to be used, not to stabilise a unified Iraq, but to promote their particular ethno-sectarian interests," according to one view published in a journal of Britain's Royal Institute of International Affairs.[94] Managing the exit strategy and politely asking Iraq's neighbors to avoid a wider regional war were President Bush's last resorts.

A revived Washington press corps, anxious to atone for its previous docility, was still met by a Bush administration frozen in *omerta*, as evident in the indictment of Scooter Libby. To quote David Halberstam's famous phrase, "the best and the brightest" had failed over Vietnam. The less stellar policymakers in Bush's administration remained loyal, even when they slipped out of the government or were indicted. In the British view, American governments are chronically handicapped by the lack of a civil service hierarchy independent of politicians that could give impartial advice. Whitehall, beholden to a more belligerent local media, however, probably would have behaved similarly, despite the mandarins' angst about

U.S. occupation policies. London agreed to every policy decision in the two-war strategy. Tony Blair gambled, in the pretense that the UK, politically, was an equal partner. In Bob Woodward's third volume of his trilogy, the only references to Blair are how much, or how little, he should be informed.[95] It was Britain's disgrace, too.

## THE OTHER OCCUPATION

"There are 11 million mines in this country—almost one for each person living here." The sergeant's voice booms in the briefing tent at Kabul airport. It is 2:30 in the morning and freezing cold. He also warns of the endemic diseases including anthrax and cholera. "Afghanistan has eleven types of venomous snakes and there are scorpions everywhere." He goes into some detail about a scorpion hiding in an Italian officer's trousers. The sergeant also notes, "The driving here is terrible. And, by the way, prostitutes are available, but it's illegal. And remember the police are heavily armed. They use RPGs [rocket-propelled grenades] for traffic control."[96]

This guide to the dangers and peoples of Afghanistan was a military briefing in May 2002 to tired journalists and fresh troops. A British general was commanding five thousand troops from nineteen nations in the International Security Assistance Force (ISAF). ISAF, later a NATO force, was distinct from the U.S. troops fighting in the east of the country still chasing bin Laden and Taliban remnants. As in Iraq, the Western troops were charged with bringing democracy, reconstruction, and peace, particularly via training a new national army and police force. The recently installed president, Hamid Karzai, controlled about 10 percent of the country; journalists dubbed him the "mayor of Kabul." His government had to negotiate with the rest, which meant using force or bribes. British troops were quite effective in stabilizing the capital. Many schools, even for girls, were opened. Kabul's Western-backed government—whose mantra was "disarmament, demobilization, and reconstruction"—needed money, and quickly, if it were to survive.

The promised reconstruction money didn't arrive in time or in sufficient quantities. Banditry, warlordism, and drug-running were rampant, the anarchy enabling the Taliban to regroup and take over much of the Pashtun south. Production of opium held the Afghan system together. If disbanding Saddam's army was the prime mistake in Iraq, threatening to destroy the opium crop was the disaster in Afghanistan. Ninety percent of the heroin on European streets allegedly came from Afghanistan. According to former EU Commissioner Chris Patten, "we created a particularly malign version of the Common Agricultural Policy. Demand exploded and no serious effort was made to control supply."[97] Instead of banning or controlling the heroin supply, some experts viewed legalization as the only rational route, especially considering the worldwide shortage of morphine-related medical drugs. Instead, occasional attempts were made to destroy a few opium fields in the south. Then, the Americans threatened to indulge in mass spraying, which was considered manna from heaven for Taliban propagandists. Meanwhile, production and profits exploded. "For Afghanistan's drugs lords, business was very good under the United States Central Command," according to a distinguished American journalist.[98] Some correspondents, however, supported the war on drugs in Afghanistan. "Name your crisis in Afghanistan—insurgency, corruption, porous borders, weak government control—and at its source you'll find the raw, sticky gum of opium," wrote Washington-based writer Sam Dealey.[99]

The five-thousand-plus British troops in the south, especially in Helmand Province, bore the brunt of the fighting as Taliban commanders ordered their own surge in 2005 and 2006. At home, the UK suffered its worst-ever terrorist attack when four British-born or British-resident suicide bombers hit the London transport infrastructure on July 7, 2005. By this stage, the British had privately agreed with Washington to withdraw from Iraq to strengthen their operations in Afghanistan. A two-front war was threatening to break the British army. As ever, the British complained about heavy-handed U.S. tactics in Afghanistan. The anger thus generated spread into the lawless tribal areas that snaked 1,700 miles between Pakistan and Afghanistan. As Iraq descended into the sectarian hell of Shi'a versus Sunni, the internal conflict in Afghanistan raged within the largest Sunni ethnic group, the Pashtuns, who were divided between the anti-Western fundamentalists, many of whom lived in Pakistan or the adjoining tribal areas, and the pro-Western, less fundamentalist Pashtuns who dominated the government and the security forces in Kabul. Though the Afghan army had performed better than its equivalent in Iraq, President Karzai's grip on the country was loosening by 2007. As with Iraq, Afghanistan's fate would be dictated by its citizens and its neighboring states, not an army of occupiers. The return of a chastened Taliban to Kabul, probably by negotiation this time, threatened defeat for the war-devastated people of Afghanistan, for the reputation of NATO, and for the West in general. The Taliban's presence in Kabul's government was better, though, than an actual major Western military reversal on the ground in the Afghan plains.[100]

Afghan government policy forced British troops to defend isolated positions, known as "platoon houses," in Helmand Province. The Taliban came close to capturing a number of them. In mid-summer 2006, a British journalist was nearly killed while on patrol with members of the Parachute Regiment. Because of the danger involved, the Ministry of Defence stopped mounting media visits to the platoon houses, assuming that Western journalists could not access the region on their own. The Taliban, however, continued to publicize its own successes. The Ministry eventually backed down and allowed journalists access, including Mick Smith of the London *Sunday Times*. In his view, "despite the Terry Lloyd incident [when a British non-embedded journalist was killed by American friendly fire in Iraq], U.S. forces are generally much more receptive to a media presence—there was a *New York Post* journalist embedded with the U.S. Marines who killed Lloyd."[101]

Chris Hughes, of the mass-circulation British tabloid the *Daily Mirror*, summarized in March 2007 his experiences in southern Afghanistan:

In November 2006 I was part of a team that reported from Nowzad in Helmand province, southern Afghanistan, and wrote several spreads detailing how British troops were (and at the time of writing still are) under fire daily and nightly from rebel forces and what it is like to be with them when that happens. We detailed what "reconstruction" means—in the sense that, after RPG [rocket-propelled grenade] attacks, thousands of machine-gun rounds and cannon sorties from British Harrier jets, they would leave several Taliban dead and a town in ruins. Afterwards the Brits would—under air cover from NATO jets—fill in a hole in the street, just to show the Taliban they were not going to let the war stop them from trying to help the local community. Filling in that hole in the street took two jets, a troop of Royal Marines and a dozen engineers, and we debated the futility of this. More than 50 Brits have been killed in Afghanistan since 2001 and I would like to think reports like the one we filed from Nowzad may have helped people back home decide whether it is worth it. Every death of a British soldier we report in our paper has a political impact because the Secretary of State, each time, sees fit to deliver a statement on the death. So I believe strongly that if we keep writing about what is happening out there we will keep making politicians uncomfortable about the decisions they are making. I don't necessarily believe that they are wrong, I just think we should keep hammering away at them to keep on their toes. It's their job to be questioned constantly and that's what we are doing.[102]

As the British death toll mounted in both countries during 2006, the "bring-the-troops-home" mood expanded and threatened to undermine the lame-duck premiership of Tony Blair. When the chief of the general staff, Gen. Sir Richard Dannatt, criticized policy in Iraq and said occupation troops were sometimes exacerbating the crisis, the British media switched into overdrive. Never before had Britain's most senior serving soldier challenged government policy openly. Dannatt's soldiers and the majority of the public praised his courage, though it threatened a constitutional crisis in addition to feeding the media frenzy.[103]

## TROUBLES ELSEWHERE

### DARFUR

When the United States launched its invasion of Iraq, a rebellion erupted in Darfur, Sudan's western region, which is the same size as Texas. Later, bin Laden welcomed this revolt as a new front. Although Sudan had long been at the top of the U.S. agenda, after 9/11 Sudan's government in Khartoum had conjured up a massive charm offensive to woo Washington away from sending more cruise missiles.[104] In 1998 President Clinton attacked Khartoum with cruise missiles; thereafter the Islamist regime tried to appease Washington. In a rare foreign policy success for the United States in 2005, American diplomats played an important role in ending the fifty-year war between Sudan's north and south. Strangely, neither the Bush administration nor the American media covered much of the story. The new war in Sudan's west territories, however, drew major media coverage. Hundreds of thousands were killed in the fighting and millions turned refugees, prompting accusations of genocide from the State Department. This mass extermination, however, was not ethnic cleansing on the Bosnian model. The combatants were all Muslims—indeed ardent Muslims—who had fought over land and grazing rights for decades; many Darfurians blamed the imperial land allocation system when the British conquered the area in 1916. Though the African Union (AU) sent in a small, inadequate force to monitor, it could not stop the extensive atrocities committed by both the insurgents and the Khartoum government. When a UN force was mooted, the Sudanese regime interpreted this discussion as Western intervention. In late 2007, a joint UN-AU hybrid force was sent. Direct Western military intervention, unlikely because of overstretch in

Iraq and Afghanistan, perhaps could have united Darfur's many factions in a joint war against infidel outsiders.[105]

Though inaccessible, Darfur became an emotive, if intermittent, story for television. The regime in Khartoum was always blamed, yet not always fairly. In fact, the complexities of this war were rarely explored adequately in the media.[106] Analyst Alex de Waal and the *Guardian*'s Jonathan Steele were notable exceptions in the UK, while Sam Dealey and Scott Anderson covered the war effectively for American publications.[107] U.S. troops on the ground, presuming any could be spared, were highly unlikely in Darfur. Instead NATO and UN advisers augmented the AU troops in a hybrid peacekeeping force, which was still ineffective. There was no military solution to the problem. None of the insurgents could win in Darfur, nor could peacekeepers impose peace where there was none. The extensive Western political pressure that had ended the main north-south civil war was required. The Pentagon was aware of the growth of al-Qaeda-style groups in the region. Inadvertently stoking the fire in Darfur could have galvanized jihadism throughout northern Africa, making it a source of Islamic extremist pressure on Western Europe.

The big story was not being articulated properly, not even the tragedy in Darfur that had prompted such international attention. If the AU forces could not organize their own pay corps, then they would never assemble an efficient public affairs system. The insurgents were too distracted by in-fighting to handle media management, while Khartoum's clumsy attempts at media-military relations were usually counterproductive. Furthermore, with the famine-like conditions and the intimidating tribal complexities, it is no wonder that so few journalists spent long enough in the country to get a handle on the story.

## LEBANON

Lebanon was complicated as well, but much more accessible and comfortable than Darfur for the journalists. The thirty-four-day conflict in Lebanon in the summer of 2006 crystallized many of the simmering issues in the Middle East, as the West lay exposed in Iraq, Afghanistan, and North Africa. The war was begun by accident. Hezbollah had not expected that its seizure of two Israeli soldiers would prompt such a massive response by Israel. Hezbollah's highly potent kind of warfare could have profound strategic impact throughout the Middle East. Previously Israel could capture Beirut in a week, but in 2006, it struggled for more than a month to control small villages on its own border.

The Arab media lambasted the British and the Americans for not backing a UN ceasefire early in the conflict, interpreting this delay as a desire to allow Israel the time to defeat Hezbollah. They may have been accurate in this assumption. The Arab television stations, notably Al-Jazeera, broadcast nonstop coverage of the insurgents' resistance to Israel's weaponry, which failed to shock and awe. The BBC coverage was also impressive.[108] The *Independent*'s Robert Fisk, long a resident of Lebanon, was well placed to augment his fine reputation for outspoken commentary on the region.

A novel hybrid, Hezbollah blended the sophistication and weaponry of a formal army with the near-invisibility of a hit-and-run insurgency. Fighting as tenaciously as the Viet Cong, Hezbollah dramatically modernized classic guerrilla tactics. Traditional armies are large, often cumbersome, and organized in a disciplined hierarchy. Networks such as Hezbollah had numerous, widely dispersed, agile, and able soldiers who could improvise quickly, not least in their use of high-tech communications for broadcasting propaganda around the Arab world.

White flags were not in evidence. Arab media highlighted Hezbollah's decision to face the Israeli military, unlike Arab forces in earlier wars. Morale, organization, hi-tech weaponry, and the cult of martyrdom generated effective resistance. Insurgents were adapting and rapidly learning from one another. After 2006, lessons on elaborate air-conditioned bunker systems were undoubtedly being Power-Pointed around the jihadist world. Previously Israel had managed to wipe out conventional armies in days—even when caught by surprise, such as in the 1973 war. In contrast, the IDF was ground down in 2006 and suffered major casualties at home because of rocket attacks. Israel's military and political media machine not only struggled to persuade the outside world of any successes, but also caused its own Jewish population to question the capacity of the generals and politicians who led the war. Israel's lively and often irrepressible press would soon attack the country's military performance. And, unlike the *mechdalim* (the mistakes) of 1973, there could be no excuse of a surprise attack.

Hezbollah performed better than the conventional forces of every Arab state that had fought Israel since 1948. It won a stunning propaganda victory and shattered Israel's deterrence posture. Hezbollah leader Hassan Nasrallah achieved what Osama bin Laden could never do: he had united Shi'as and Sunnis, especially the young, throughout the region to believe that the Muslim renaissance could only come into being through force. If Iraq had demonstrated the limits of U.S. power, the war in Lebanon displayed Israel's weaknesses. Radical Islam was the victor. The IDF experience gave the United States pause before seriously considering an attack on Iran to prevent its nuclear program.[109] The Iranians might fight as effectively as their students in Hezbollah.[110]

Arabs were not used to military victories. Hezbollah's success galvanized jihadists worldwide. Its mentor, Iran, displayed a long reach, ranging from attacks in Latin America to likely command of sleeper cells in the United States. The supine political response of the Sunni Arab leaders, who privately loathed Shi'a success, played badly in the Arab street.[111] Militant Islam threatened to displace secular despotisms including Syria, a supporter of Hezbollah, which acted as Iran's expeditionary force in Lebanon.

The media, of course, encamped in droves in Beirut and along the Israeli border with Lebanon. Understandably most of their reportage was of the bang-bang variety, although some later placed the war in context.[112] This summer war, however, along with chaos in Iraq and the resurgence of the Taliban in Afghanistan, was a major watershed in the long war against jihadism.

## HEARTS AND MINDS IN THE LONG HAUL

The United States conducted an abysmal propaganda war in the first five years of the war on terror. The Pentagon then altered the original meaning of the war on terror and fashioned it as more of an enemy of an ideology, not a method of fighting. Donald Rumsfeld opted instead for "a global struggle against violent extremism."[113] President Bush was also wisely advised to stop his use of "crusade." It made little difference, though, on the ground in Afghanistan and Iraq. In November 2001, U.S. planes "accidentally" hit the Al-Jazeera office in Kabul; two years later the accident was repeated when the station's Tareq Ayoub was killed in Baghdad. As one of Al-Jazeera's former reporters concluded, "So long as Al-Jazeera continues to challenge this [U.S.-dominated] media order, its journalists and bureaux will remain in American sights."[114] Strategically, the United States failed, according to Rumsfeld, because "our federal government is really only beginning to adapt our [media] operations to the twenty-first century. For the most part, the U.S. government still functions as a five-and-dime store in an eBay world."[115] The Secretary of Defense quoted Ayman al-Zawahiri, bin Laden's chief lieutenant: "More than half of this battle is taking place in the battlefield of the media. We are in a media battle in a race for the hearts and minds of Muslims."[116]

In Iraq, much more than a "five and a dime" were spent on buying hearts and minds. Over three years, several hundred million dollars were spent on an assortment of media projects designed to sell "good news" stories about the occupation. Perhaps the most notorious involved an American company, the Lincoln Group—contracted to pay for positive news stories written by U.S. military personnel and placed in Iraqi publications—which was accused of being "an unethical weapon of mass deception."[117] Some senior officers in the Pentagon and Democrats in Congress argued that it was hypocritical for the country to promote democratic principles of freedom of speech and political transparency in Iraq while the military was paying to disseminate propaganda there. Alvin Snyder, formerly in the U.S. Information Agency, said that this was "psy-ops journalism . . . a new breed of journalists are following the money trail to the Pentagon."[118] Though Rumsfeld argued that nontraditional means of getting the message across were required, he criticized the practice of buying space in Iraqi papers. A military enquiry, however, found no evidence of wrongdoing, except for minor contractual issues.[119] The *Washington Post* editorialized that, whether or not it violated regulations, it was still a questionable idea. Insiders in the Pentagon suggested that the buying of good news subsequently carried on as before.[120]

Ginger Cruz, the director of strategic communications in the Green Zone's U.S. embassy in Baghdad, commented in a draft report in late 2006 that "without popular support from the U.S. population, there is a risk that troops will be pulled back. . . . Thus there is a vital need to save popular support via message." Most of the sixteen domestic messages for the American public could be boiled down to the obvious: "There are no quick and easy answers." The secret draft then had a section for Iraqi messages. Underneath the heading was written "TBD"—to be determined. The rest of the document could be summarized thus: The United States has clearly lost the battle for Iraqi public opinion.[121]

The insurgents, especially in the Sunni heartland, were becoming media-savvy. Most large-scale attacks on U.S. forces were being filmed with high-resolution cameras, often from multiple camera angles, and then expertly edited before being set to inspiring religious soundtracks. In a few cases, the attacks were launched primarily to generate fresh footage. Compilation DVDs were sold in Baghdad markets for as little as 50 cents. As the rapid dissemination of the film of Saddam's hanging proved, new cell-phone technology made jihadist videos easy to download and circulate. Such films, allied to the graphic images shown on popular Arab television satellite channels, all gave the impression that coalition forces were on the run. Particularly popular, and not only in Iraq, were the slickly produced adventures of "Juba the sniper." In the fifteen-minute video, the camera follows an American soldier from a distance as he stands near his vehicle and chats with a fellow soldier. Then the sound of rifle fire is heard. The soldier is seen falling to the ground, as his panicked comrades swarm around him.[122] Such videos discouraged cooperation with U.S. troops and inspired donations and recruits for the jihadists. "One of these videos is worth a division of tanks to those people [insurgents]," said Robert Steele, a former U.S. Marine Corps intelligence officer.[123] Along with its planted material in Iraqi newspapers (viewed with utter skepticism by Iraqis), the U.S. propaganda effort was bureaucratic and unwieldy, compared with the small and nimble insurgent propaganda systems that relied on the Web and cell-phones for rapid results.

A British expert on counterinsurgency, Dr. John Mackinlay, commented on the coalition's failure thus: "In crude terms our inability to engage the Muslim audience arose from a collision between the government-controlled information machinery of the West, outraged Muslim sensibilities and a 'free' press characterized by its under-regulated lust for sensationalism." Few journalists would agree with him, especially about the under-regulation, though they might concur with his argument that "after the 1991 war the Americans demonized the Arab as the new villain. In a series of sand, oil, and special-forces films, Hollywood directors, seldom acclaimed for their subtlety, portrayed the Arab black-hat stereotype as 'inferior, chaotic, corrupt and violent.'"[124]

News stations such as Al-Jazeera gave Arabs an alternative that reaffirmed rather than denigrated their self-image:

> In Afghanistan Al-Jazeera had been popular because it was the only network there. During the invasion of Iraq Al-Jazeera was watched through choice. It had broken the hegemony of the Western networks and, for the first time in hundreds of years, reversed the flow of information, historically from West to East.[125]

But it would be wrong to blame the media for the fall of the West in the Middle East. It was Western policy and its implementation, not the messenger. Martin Bell summarized the recent adventures: "The United States and Britain didn't make a coalition, but a gang of two, a latter-day Don Quixote and Sancho Panza, armed and dangerous and tilting at oilfields."[126] Neoconservative dreams of reforming the Middle East died in places such as Fallujah, Ramadi, and Tal Afar. Chris Hughes, the defense correspondent of the *Daily Mirror*, offered his obituary on the American occupation:

> There are plenty of Americans in Iraq, military and otherwise, who are decent men and women doing their best to help the Iraqis rebuild their country. But for all George Bush's talk of winning "hearts and minds" a significant number of U.S. soldiers on

the ground seem little more than gum-chewing grunts with nothing but scorn for the people they have conquered.

The major incidents have made headlines around the world— the massacres in Falluja and Haditha, the Abu Ghraib disgrace, the rape of a young girl and the murder of her family in the summer of 2006. But dreadful as these (we hope) isolated happenings are, it's the humdrummery, the banal, everyday abuse and the casual contempt that too many American soldiers show the Iraqi population that is truly unforgivable.[127]

Iraq had failed the reality test; the state possessed no WMDs and no link with al-Qaeda. Doing away with Saddam may have benefited Iraqis, but it was also a major diversion in the fight against al-Qaeda. Instead, it has been a propaganda gift to the jihadists. As the grand old man of American columnists, George F. Will, observed in March 2006: "All three components of the 'axis of evil'—Iraq, Iran, and North Korea—are more dangerous than they were when that phrase was coined in 2002."[128] The ranks of Islamic extremists have been massively boosted, while exhausting American resources to confront the expanded threat. "Worse still," he continued, "President Bush has lost the war of ideas that, in the end, was the most potent American weapon for battling the nihilism of radical Islam."[129]

Many experts who did their time in Iraq, both military officers and war correspondents, reached the same conclusion: Iraq threatened a military defeat or at the very least a serious diplomatic defeat for the Americans and the British. Many wanted Washington to relearn the lessons of the Cold War: the need for alliances, not least in Europe; economic and cultural engagement; and subtle diplomacy, especially with Iran and Syria, keys to a semblance of an orderly withdrawal from Iraq.[130]

# 8

# THE MECHANICS OF REPORTING WAR AND PEACE

The Western media tend to report on big wars involving their own troops. Smaller wars, and even genocides, get less air time. And peace-keeping secures very little attention indeed. Veteran journalist Mort Rosenblum once asked in a book title, *Who Stole the News?* is it the fault of media manipulation by Western governments, or are the media to blame? Once the media—with the much-vaunted CNN Effect—were considered all-powerful, but the twenty-first century, so far, has witnessed an apparent reduction in the influence of the Fourth Estate.

## REPORTING PEACE

An inescapable characteristic of what was once easily called peace-keeping is that it rarely makes the news headlines, except perhaps when things go wrong. From the plethora of stories, evidence indicates that the media are extremely interested in warfare, although admittedly news organizations do not cover every rising conflict that takes place on the planet at any given time. As a consequence, wars appear to burst from nowhere into breaking news and, once finished, the countries in which they took place return to relative media obscurity.

The 1990s decade is replete with examples of this, from Somalia to Kosovo, from Bosnia to East Timor, and from Rwanda to Haiti. Waging peace, in other words, is far less likely to attract journalistic attention than waging war. This phenomenon could be explained as the result of media interest only in bad news and that, because peacemaking is usually a success story over time, it lacks the characteristics of a "good story." This undoubtedly plays a role, in light of the fact that media are interested in the deployment of armed forces to dangerous environments—especially when their home nations are involved. "Our" wars attract intense media coverage; "their" wars far less so—unless they too become our wars through international military intervention. But when the war is over, our media find that the cost of retaining a presence, with teams of reporters staying in upmarket hotels and using up expensive satellite time, is disproportionate to the returns gained in good copy or pictures, and so they move on. This "parachute journalism" is extremely frustrating for peacekeepers and means that wars are treated as short paragraphs in the first draft of world history. Peace is treated as if it were merely a punctuation mark.

Parachute work tends to be derivate, ethnocentric, superficial, and susceptible to propaganda. Yet so-called peacekeeping can also be a dangerous business, as the aftermath of Operation Iraqi Freedom illustrated. But even the Anglo-American war in Afghanistan after 9/11 virtually disappeared for a couple of years from the media spotlight once Kabul was secured from the Taliban, with the remaining serious crisis reappearing only sporadically when soldiers were killed or after an assassination attempt on the new leadership. When the International Security Assistance Force became a NATO operation, it did attract more media attention in Europe and especially in Britain, which took command of the renewed war in 2006 against the Taliban in southern Afghanistan. The relative media inattention from 2002 to 2006 could be crudely explained away by the media being more interested in events than in issues, and this would also belie the claims of some officials about the power of media coverage in prompting military interventions in the first place. "The media got us in, and the media got us out" [of Somalia], claimed one, while another described the lack of media interest in Sudan as "Somalia without CNN."[1]

To a great extent, the recent debate about media coverage of foreign interventions has its origins in the Vietnam War, when what had been a historically cooperative military-media relationship broke down. Especially after 1968, the American public could watch the horrors of this "uncensored war"[2] on their color television sets. Instead of analyzing the lessons learned from military inadequacies or political failures of will, the media was targeted as a scapegoat as the United States suffered its first public defeat in its military history. But this was a modern equivalent of the "stab-in-the-back" theory. Few who believe that the United States lost the war in the living rooms of middle America seem to question how a democracy could wage war for another five years—longer than U.S. involvement in World War II—with such alleged hostile media coverage. Nonetheless, the myth of "the Vietnam syndrome" has informed debates about the relationship between war and the media ever since.

A good deal has now been written about these developments. The literature on peacekeeping and the media, however, is still quite small. Diplomacy is a complex business, often conducted quietly away from the prying gaze of the media, and in any case hardly makes for exciting television. Hence dramatic foreign news stories, such as Libya's renunciation of weapons of mass destruction in December 2003, seem to intensify and ignite quickly when in fact they are the result of months of quiet negotiations. By extension, images of soldiers patrolling foreign streets garner limited attention, especially if no one is firing at them. How much media attention is today afforded to the UN's longest peacekeeping operation, in Cyprus? What happened to Sierra Leone in the British media? Where did Panama, Grenada, or Haiti go from American media coverage?

These questions are not without significance in the relationship between government, media, and public opinion. As one scholar has written:

> As conflicts in distant countries have little bearing on the everyday lives of citizens, whether or not they are aware of the magnitude of a crisis, and whether or not they are concerned, is entirely dependent on the level of media coverage. Where the public is at a level of awareness sufficient to incite widespread concern, approval ratings of the government will be affected as the public focuses on their government's response to the conflict, raising the price of inaction from the point of view of the government. Likewise, where there is a media blackout of a major humanitarian crisis, the price of inaction will be insignificant, and approval ratings unaffected. In this way, the media has the power to control the price of inaction by governments in humanitarian crises, regardless of the actual humanitarian price of inaction.[3]

The inability of the media to sustain their interest in peacemaking became even more profound with the end of the Cold War in 1991, although there are more deployments of peacekeeping forces now than during that period. The sheer variety and complexity of international crises since then, from collapsing states unhooked from superpower patronage to civil wars and their resultant humanitarian crises, has not been well served by television, a medium incapable of compressing such complexity into three-minute news reports.[4] The emotive nature of images from such crises, however, prompted Kofi Annan, when he was UN undersecretary for peacekeeping operations, to suggest that

> from Ethiopia onward, the role of the media took an entirely new tack. The target of reporting shifted from objectivity to sympathy, from sustaining intellectual commitment to engaging emotional involvement. . . . It sometimes seemed that the media was no longer reporting on the agenda, but setting it.[5]

It is certainly true that the media tend to report on complex emergencies through the front window of human interest stories. Virgil Hawkins noted:

> Attracting viewers and readers means grabbing and keeping their interest, and this requires keeping stories simple, sensational, and easy to understand. This has resulted in the emergence of the coverage of conflict as an oversimplified "morality play," in which one side in a conflict is portrayed as evil, and the other as a victim, with a formula that puts pressure on the international community to intervene and rescue the victim.[6]

Images of lines of fleeing refugees (Kosovo), traumatic images of starving children (Ethiopia, Somalia), and victims of genocide (Rwanda, Bosnia) can appeal to human compassion, but they do not in themselves prompt international interventions. Indeed, the Rwanda Steering Committee report even claimed that "inadequate and inaccurate reporting by international media on the genocide itself contributed to international indifference and inaction."[7] The decision to intervene may or may not be prompted by dramatic images, as many politicians have testified, but the decision itself is still a political one.

## THE DECLINE OF FOREIGN NEWS REPORTING

The transition over the last two decades from traditional peacekeeping operations to what may now be called humanitarian interventions or perhaps nation-building has taken place against significant shifts in the way global news organizations report world events. In that period international journalism developed the technological capacity to bring news instantaneously from almost anywhere while, paradoxically, media organizations have tended to reduce their commitment to foreign news reporting. This was particularly pronounced in the United States prior to 9/11. In 1998, for example, only 2 percent of total American newspaper coverage was claimed to be devoted to international news, compared to 10 percent in 1983.[8] Network television coverage similarly dropped from 45 percent of total broadcast output in the 1970s to 13.5 percent in 1995.[9] No *Time* magazine cover in 1997 featured a foreign affairs story (as compared with eleven in 1987), while that magazine's international news coverage followed *Newsweek* in a reduction to almost 10 percent.[10] Specialized foreign and defense correspondents all but disappeared in Britain and the United States, and those who survived found it increasingly difficult to secure a place for their stories.[11] Moreover, owing to the end of national military service in the UK and of the draft in the United States, current front-line war report-ers, like the politicians, have little or no experience of soldiering.[12]

Such reality is hard to reconcile with the widespread popular belief in the so-called CNN Effect—that real-time television services drive the foreign policy decision-making process.[13] CNN's domestic American ser-vice follows the pattern of the other networks, although greater coverage of foreign events is more evident on CNN International, as befitting its global audience. In normal times, however, even on such rival networks as BBC World and Sky News, it is not so much a question of twenty-four-hour rolling news but the same or similar news bulletins being repeated on the hour, twenty-four times a day. Where these news organizations come into their own is during an event like the attack on the World Trade Center or the opening of the Iraq War. But it is hard not to conclude that live television follows events rather than drives them, and serious re-search has demonstrated that when a government's policy is firm, televi-sion images can be and are resisted; it is only when the policy is weak or embryonic that an impact is possible.[14] It was, for example, American non-intervention policy in Rwanda—and even in Bosnia down to 1995—that made the Clinton administration actively resist the most traumatic reports of genocide in those countries. And the dramatic images from Somalia several years earlier in fact followed rather than preceded the decision to intervene. As one researcher pointed out: "In all of 1991, Somalia got three minutes of attention on the three evening network news shows. From January to June 1992, Somalia got 11 minutes."[15] The CNN Effect is, in short, largely a myth.

It would, however, be difficult to deny that the very process of ob-servation can change the nature or the course of an event. People behave differently when a camera is pointed at them, and if they are doing some-thing wrong they rarely welcome observers. And when the observers come under fire, then they become part of the story, especially when journalists are killed.[16] Nobody is more interested in the media than the media them-selves. When Radio Television Serbia was briefly knocked off the air by a NATO air strike during the 1999 Kosovo conflict, a worldwide media out-rage ensued.[17] Interestingly, no corresponding concern rose when Anglo–U.S. targeting of Iraqi radio and television occurred in 2003, although when an American tank fired a shell into the Palestine Hotel in Baghdad, killing two journalists among the press corps housed there, speculation arose that the media was viewed by the military as having become part of the problem rather than the solution.[18]

In peacekeeping operations, the military has experienced frustra-tion at the lack of media interest.[19] For example, around eight hundred journalists were embedded with Anglo–American forces during Operation Iraqi Freedom. Once the war fighting phase was declared over on May 1, 2003, however, most news organizations demobilized their reporters, and the military found great difficulty in filling available embedding slots in the months that followed.[20] This was despite the fact that more soldiers lost their lives in that period than during the invasion itself.[21] The embedded system had provided viewers with probably the most spectacular combat footage ever seen from the front line of a war. But the urban warfare that followed in the consolidation of victory did not easily fit into traditional definitions of war fighting or peacekeeping. So frustrated did some Americans become at the constant flow of bad news stories about Iraqi resistance attacks on coalition "invaders" that they felt compelled to launch a public relations campaign to counter the media impression that postwar Iraqi reconstruction was a complete disaster.[22] Not until the capture of Saddam Hussein in December 2003 did this situation begin to reverse, at least temporarily.[23]

Peacekeepers had traditionally been portrayed in the media as the "good guys" versus the "bad guys," peace being good and war being bad. This image was dealt a blow with the fall of the UN-protected "safe area" of Srebrenica on July 11, 1995. The complexity of the Balkans conflicts of the 1990s was not well served by Western news media coverage that was confusing and biased against the Serbs, when in fact atrocities were committed by all parties. The United Nations Protection Force (UNPROFOR) was portrayed as noble in its missions to create demilitarized zones and support humanitarian relief but was ineffective in deterring military action in the safe areas until the fall of the safe havens sealed its fate.

NATO had been unable to secure any UN mandate for its Kosovo campaign. In fact, Article 2.7 of the UN Charter expressly forbade intervention in the internal affairs of sovereign states. But endless television news footage of suffering civilians—especially "innocent" women and children—appeared to place the morality of intervention above international law.[24] The Labour government's policy of non-intervention in the Balkans between 1991 and 1995 effectively made the Kosovo conflict of 1999 the West's war of contrition caused by its earlier hesitance to intercede.

The BBC's documentary series *The Death of Yugoslavia* in 1996 explained the full context to the public, while another documentary in the same year, *No Place to Hide,* was the first real attempt to rescue peacekeeping's tarnished image. The BBC drama series released in 1999, the ironically named *Warriors,* portrayed the British peacekeeping role in Bosnia through the eyes of a group of young soldiers from the Cheshire Regiment. The four main characters begin the tour with little to complain about except the cold, but when they see women and children being murdered as their houses are destroyed, while they are powerless to do anything but watch, they become confused and frustrated. Upon their return to Britain six months later, they faced a difficult readjustment to normal life, and their trauma spills over into their relationships with each other and with their loved ones. *Warriors* was broadcast several months after the NATO "humanitarian intervention" in Kosovo. Many Brits took away the message that none of their military personnel should be sent into such situations only to be restricted by obstacles such as a UN mandate.

This implicit motivation was explored more explicitly in such movies as *Savior* (1998), based on a real-life story from Bosnia in 1993. Directed by a former prisoner of war, the Serb director Peter Antonijevic, and starring American Dennis Quaid, the film tracks the redemption of a man (Quaid) who has lost his wife and child to an Islamic terrorist attack, which motivates him to become a mercenary for the Serbs. The film depicts the brutal atrocities committed by Serb forces and Quaid's salvation and conversion back to the cause of peace through his protection of an innocent woman, who had been raped by a Muslim, and her child.

*Welcome to Sarajevo* was another exercise in redemption from guilt. The central theme is whether reporters should risk death to get a story in an environment in which objective reporting is extremely difficult. This situation boils over when the British journalist realizes that a local orphanage is under steady bombardment from Bosnian Serb artillery. Determined to turn the crisis around, he reports from the orphanage as often as possible, hoping this will spark outrage—and action—in the world community. When this fails to materialize, he abandons any last semblance of objectivity and decides to take action himself by smuggling a small girl from the orphanage out of the country and back to Britain. The use of original television news coverage of the conflict adds to the film's authenticity, but the film stands out because of the theme of whether reporters should use their medium as an agent for provoking international intervention in other people's wars.

Another British reporter, the BBC's Martin Bell, also addressed this issue. As earlier discussed, Bell was so disturbed by the international community's failure to intervene in Bosnia, a mere three-hour flight from London, that he called for a "journalism of attachment." Objective reporting, he argued, was largely a myth, and he increasingly reported on stories about the victims of war rather than the mechanics of waging a war. Because he saw television news reports as a propagandistic medium, capable of provoking international intervention and the peacekeeping required subsequently to maintain the peace, he played a role from the decision to bomb the Serbs to the negotiations that resulted in the Dayton Peace Agreement.[25] However, when Bell became disillusioned with journalism's change of the late 1990s to "infotainment," he watched as Britain imported the American obsession with ratings driven by commercial imperatives and the fall of hard news.[26]

Similar ideas have prompted some scholars to call for "information intervention" in order to prevent crises from developing into bloodbaths. The phrase was first coined by Jamie F. Metzl, an American authority on humanitarian intervention, out of frustration at the failure of the international community to intervene in time to prevent the Rwandan genocide.[27] At the core of the idea was the belief that

> a country gives up an element of its sovereignty when it severely violates the human rights of its citizens. In that situation, the international community is justified in being more aggressive, including by using information tactics, than would otherwise be the case. Information intervention is the use of information in that aggressive manner when this is justified on strong human rights grounds.[28]

Effectively an argument for propaganda to prevent the development of ethnic hatred, this idea ran contrary to long-held views about both propaganda and international law. It saw propaganda (or what Metzl called "counter-information") as a positive force and international law as outdated. Metzl continued: "We need to explore what can be done between the impossible everything and the unacceptable nothing. The political cost of doing everything is usually prohibitive. The moral cost of doing nothing is astronomical."[29] Although Western democracies had developed mechanisms for dealing with hate speech domestically, there was no international equivalent for dealing with the kind of incitements to genocide perpetuated by Radio Mille Collines in Rwanda. Just as the Bush Doctrine supported preemptive war against "rogue" states that support terrorists or might one day provide them with weapons of mass destruction, information intervention was an argument for preemptive propaganda to prevent collapsing states from degenerating into internal chaos and violence.

## THE MEDIA IN POST-CONFLICT INTERVENTIONS

Until the international community accepts or develops the kind of mechanisms needed to activate what might be called preemptive peacekeeping, it remains the case that when the pressure to "do something" reaches the point that something has to be done, it invariably takes the form of military action. The United States in particular has demonstrated its military capacity to enforce what the Bush Doctrine calls "regime change." Yet what follows the combat phase is more of an indicator for deciding whether the military intervention was justified in the long term (as distinct from whether it was "just" under international law, outdated or otherwise). Indigenous media reconstruction is regarded as part of the process of nation-building following armed interventions. In such societies as Bosnia, Kosovo, and Iraq, where no tradition of a free media existed because they were part of the state propaganda machine, introducing democratic and independent media systems is essential to the eventual exit strategy by military combatants. A striking disparity prevails here between democratic governmental suspicion of the power of the media in forcing interventions in the first place, frustration at the sudden loss of international media interest once the military intervention is completed, and the enormous efforts expended subsequently on introducing new indigenous media systems that will foster democratic values.

In military circles, the conviction has emerged that "victory is no longer determined on the ground, but in media reporting."[30] As one observer pointed out, "this is even more true in peace support operations where the goal is not to conquer territory or defeat an enemy but to persuade parties in conflict (as well as local populations) into a favored course of action."[31] This was the real significance of Operations Joint Endeavour and Joint Guard, the NATO-led multinational force designed to implement the Dayton Agreement. The 1995–1999 experience of SFOR and IFOR in Bosnia of "shaping the information space" in support of the mission was to have considerable impact on developing "information warfare" concepts emerging out of the Gulf War experience and the doctrine of "information operations" that was to supersede it in the second half of the 1990s.

Indigenous media reform was one strand of the process meant to create a climate of peace and reconciliation in Bosnia, although journalists felt this to be the responsibility of non-military and non-governmental organizations.[32] But as long as a NATO presence persisted, SFOR needed to communicate not only with local media (however hostile they remained) but also directly with the local populations, as well as with the international media presence in the region. Centered on Sarajevo, the Coalition Information and Press Centre operated along by now well-established NATO Public Information principles, namely a proactive campaign designed to tell reporters as much of the truth as could be told (within constraints of operational security and force protection), as accurately and as timely as possible. Daily press conferences, regular press releases, and the arrangement of interviews with commanders became its routine work, while the overriding message in the early days was that SFOR was not an invading force and that it was well led, well equipped, and ready to respond through the use of force if necessary.

By 1998, an independent media commission was established in Bosnia and Herzegovina as an interim system for the post-conflict environment. This model was later borrowed by the UN Mission in Kosovo with the creation of a temporary media commission pending return to domestic rule. Traditionally, international peacekeeping forces had been invited into a country to help keep warring factions apart, usually with a UN mandate. While the semblance of neutrality was maintained, this made hearts-and-minds activities a little easier both within country itself and within the international community. But the emerging Bush Doctrine, which had as one of its key components the policy of regime change coupled with the preemptive war and the promotion of democratic values in the succession stage, made this look more like "nation building" or even "democracy building," or, worse still, neo-imperialism.[33] With Saddam deposed, scores of new newspapers appeared in Iraq, although some of them, lacking a democratic journalistic tradition, failed to even attempt objective reporting. Those that were regarded as inciting attacks against the occupying forces were closed down. This made military sense, but ham-fisted planting of stories in the Iraq media usually did not. This damaged the cause of building a "beacon of democracy" in Iraq and exposed the United States to charges of censorship and hypocrisy. While Washington was in theory promoting freedom of speech for the post-Saddam media as part of the cultivation of Iraqi democracy, some critics pointed to the decline of press freedom at home because of the compliance of the America media in supporting the war uncritically.

The transformation of the media from their traditional watchdog role to one in which they appear to be mere lapdogs of government justifications contradicts the notion of the free media being an essential ingredient of exporting democracy. But when the media choose to support a democratically elected government rather than are forced to support an un-elected one, this would seem to be infinitely preferable to a totalitarian model. The real irony is that the effects are virtually the same.[34] Instead of dissent, the drive to "go live" creates an illusion of audiences participating in history as it happens, while this kind of participatory viewing appears to rewrite the media's traditional role as mediator between events and the public.

## THE MEDIA OPERATORS: HIDDEN PERSUADERS?

Despite popular myths and ingrained military suspicion of journalists, veteran correspondents and fighting soldiers in Western armies usually get on very well in war zones. After all, they share a passion for different branches of the same profession: understanding warfare. As Martin Bell aptly summarized the relationship with British forces, "the army and media are partners in the same enterprise."[35] Often they are similar in temperament, though rarely in physical fitness. When setting up the embeds in 2003, the UK Ministry of Defence allowed units to specify numbers of correspondents and any special operational requirements. The Parachute Regiment and the Royal Marines chose not to include female correspondents, on the grounds that these units operate rapidly on foot. "That was something of a broad assumption given the fitness levels of journalists, regardless of gender," according to one academic report on the war.[36] Even if veteran journalists have not had formal military training, which many have or at least used to, then their long years under fire often make them more combat-savvy than many young professional soldiers. It has to be said, however, that the demise of the specialist defense correspondent from all but the largest media outlets has had an impact on the military. When a big event happens, the military is presented with media from a wide background. One experienced officer, for example, had to contend with a children's TV journalist in the 2003 war. And as the military gets more technical, not least with its sophisticated equipment, fewer and fewer journalists can understand not just the kit, but the overall campaign.[37] Nevertheless, freed of the alphabet soup of military jargon and acronyms, veteran correspondents nearly always make a better fist of explaining what war really is about. The further removed from military headquarters and the closer to the front line, the better the military-media relationship tends to be. Tactically, nearly always, and operationally frequently, the interface between correspondent and warrior works. At the strategic level it becomes more a political issue, often a matter of spin rather than hard facts.

The British military refer to relations with correspondents, particularly in the field, as "media operations." It has always been a part of military doctrine that media ops should be distinct from propaganda operations (including psychological operations: PSYOPS), public information operations (P Info), and Information Warfare (IW). Propaganda has always been an element in warfare: to influence the home front, allies, enemies, and neutrals. Propaganda has been defined by some scholars as biased or misleading information used to promote a political cause. P Info is primarily about keeping a public informed, thereby gaining their understanding and support. Both PSYOPS and P Info can overlap—what is information to one person is propaganda to another. The spectrum of so-called black, gray, and white operations runs all the way from unvarnished truth to downright lies. Traditionally, the British army has been wary of PSYOPS, which some see as a "black art." It has been suspicious of media ops too, but it became an axiom of media training in the army: "Don't lie to journalists. Don't tell them everything or even much, but just don't lie." That at least was the simple bedrock message of modern British media operations; above all, keep media ops (the supposed straightforward honest truth) separate from psychological operations that are usually directed at enemy target audiences. An adjunct was "keep the press informed and busy, otherwise they'll go looking for perhaps unfavorable news elsewhere."

Since the Crimean War, the British military has been exercised by issues of press restrictions. The main bone of contention was always the catchall of "operational security"—giving away useful information to the enemy, particularly if it threatened soldiers' lives. Often it was used as an excuse to exclude the media. The nature and quality of "minders" ("escorts" in the U.S. military) was a longstanding bugbear for correspondents. Security review was a pivotal issue in the Falklands: journalists' copy was checked by minders with the fleet and bureaucrats back in Whitehall. Communication technology was restricted in the Falklands, another irritant for hacks. The pool system has caused endless friction between military and the media; John Pilger famously called it "ruling by pooling." And privileged access and briefing to some war correspondents (usually the most experienced, influential, or politically favored) inevitably niggled the pack mentality of many correspondents. After decades of wrangling about these issues with the military, most journalists missed the big story: how the Pentagon was planning a coup to capture their own hearts and minds in 2003.

Despite many debates and much arcane military jargon in doctrine manuals, the various "tools of influence" became merged in both the United States and United Kingdom, especially after 9/11.[38] The American concept of "full-spectrum dominance" implied control not just in space, on land, at sea, and in the air, but in the realms of information too. Information dominance became a vital element of combat power.[39] New military thinking, under the rubric of network-centric warfare, aimed to combine the interoperability of all military systems, from the computers in headquarters in the United States, to individuals in tanks and fighter aircraft. The technical advances that permitted such integration were applied to the softer sciences of information dominance. Now military and foreign policy would include media management, PSYOPS, and overt relations with the press. Mix it all in with liberal doses of smart PR and advertising techniques and—presto!—you achieve information dominance. Such, at least, was the theory.[40]

The next step was to try to match up this American system with allies, especially Britain. Alastair Campbell, Tony Blair's main media adviser, had already shaken up the turgid bureaucracy of NATO's media machine during the Kosovo war. He was instrumental in establishing the Coalition Information Centres (CICs) in London, Washington, and Islamabad during the 2001 war in Afghanistan. These centers helped to bridge the gap among the different times zones in the twenty-four-hour news cycle. In Washington, the CIC morphed into the Office of Global Communications, or OGC. This was supposed to explain the USA's strategic goals in the war on terrorism. (The Pentagon created the short-lived Office of Strategic Influence (OSI), set up by Donald Rumsfeld, who in March 2002 was forced to close it down overnight because of intense press criticism and concerns among White House media advisers and senior military public affairs specialists. "Strategic influence" soon became dubbed "strategic lying" by media critics.) The OGC included not just senior diplomats and military personnel but also public relations experts, especially Victoria Clarke. Before "Tori" Clarke had joined the Pentagon, she had run the Washington office of a big PR firm, Hill & Knowlton, of the "babies-torn-from-incubators" scam in the lead-up to the 1991 war against Saddam. There is some evidence that news of the existence of the OSI was actually leaked to the press from Clarke's office, revealing the considerable tensions even within the Pentagon itself about fusing psyops and deception techniques into media operations under the umbrella of what was now being called information operations.

The OGC coordinated with Campbell's group in Downing Street (though the formal location was the Foreign Office Information Directorate, geographically just around the corner from the prime minister's residence). From this matrix sprang the dodgy dossiers and false intelligence on WMD, which provided the British "justification" for the 2003 war, even though we learned subsequently that the American president had not insisted upon Britain's participation.[41] Indeed, Bush had been so worried about the prime minister's domestic political situation, that he even suggested noninvolvement by Britain. Tony Blair disregarded this option, seemingly in the belief that joining with the Americans would provide Britain with greater influence in Washington's decision making. In this, he was to be proved wrong.

The wartime Washington and London command-and-control propaganda groups were linked to U.S. Central Command (CENTCOM) in Qatar, the Forward Press Information Center in Kuwait, and then, at the bottom of the food chain, the minders on the ground—the U.S. public affairs officers and British media ops personnel. The system was much more complicated than this, of course. Even the process within the British Ministry of Defence would require a large handbook to explain the various internal groups, let alone how the various bits of other ministries fitted into the jigsaw. Through a Cross-Government Implementation Group as an integration mechanism, the Foreign and Commonwealth Office, the Department for Trade and Industry, and the Department for International Development all had an input, as well the Ministry of Defence. The News Release Group was another pan-government body that produced themes and strategic messages, which were then distributed to the various ministries.

All the media manipulators attempted to avoid conflicting news releases and announcements. A mild-mannered Welsh civil servant, David Howard, headed the Ministry of Defence's Communications Planning Unit (CPU), which was tasked with smoothing internal frictions and then coordinating MoD's themes and messages before working with the other departments. This unit helped to produce a supposedly "joined-up" information campaign that guided the daily "prayer meetings" of ad-hoc media experts in the Ministry of Defence. The members would meet at around 8:45 to 9:00 AM in Whitehall's MoD HQ, after speed-reading the thick pile of overnight news clippings. Already the overnight planning team (the Iraqi theater of operations was three hours ahead of London) would have produced a planning grid for the briefing of the "O Group"—the Chief of the Defence Staff and other top brass.[42] The Prime Minister would be briefed about the same time as the Ministry of Defence prayer meeting was in session. The usually brisk and efficient meetings would last typically an hour or so and there would be an open discussion, with rapid decisions being made on what would be that day's "lines to take"—the key messages. Facts were supposed to be the currency, not spin.[43] If the British system was complex enough, the connections with Washington and HQs in theater made it even more so. Even the Defence Select Committee of the House of Commons struggled to work it all out.[44]

If no spin was tolerated at the operational level, at least in the British Ministry of Defence, nor was there to be any fodder for conspiracy theorists. The research by Cardiff University's School for Journalism, Media, and Cultural Studies was a rare example of academics outside the loop identifying an important element in Ministry of Defence operational thinking: "there is no institutional memory."[45] Military officers had a turnover of a maximum of three years, while senior civil servants in the Directorate of Corporate Communications (renamed the Directorate General of Media and Communications in 2004) could be there for much shorter periods.[46] The civilian directors of this section usually stayed for far less than three years; two moved on to promotion in the Defence Intelligence Staff.

Middle-ranking civil servants had a much longer track record; they knew the ropes, but were too junior to influence any strategic level of institutional memory. Moreover, policy was never "militarized": civilians were rarely intimidated by even the most robust of senior officers. This was part of the Ministry of Defence, and indeed British civil service, style. Meanwhile, in the field, Intelligence Corps officers, for example, frequently complained of poor handover of information when previous officers had left the theater. Hence the passion in the Ministry of Defence for "lessons learned exercises." It was a case of constantly re-inventing the wheel because of poor methods of recording institutional memory and previous experiences, all part of the traditional British military ethos of the talented amateur.

Nowhere did this apply more than to media operations. Public relations officers once held the "equivalent status of mess wines members or children's party organiser."[47] Officers used to describe PR and media ops as "career stoppers" and as outside "the magic G3 [Plans and Operations] circle."[48] Army officers are trained to risk their lives, not their careers. The amateurishness was exposed by the press reactions to the Falklands War. The Ministry of Defence struggled to improve its performance by using reservists. The Navy's media ops reserve team had previously been staffed by former regulars, while the army brought in civilian journalists with a taste for occasional military service. A few were regional BBC journalists, which might suggest an obvious conflict of interest, while at the same time accepting that the army needed professional input. Some of these army reservists did excellent jobs. A good example was Lt. Col. Robert Partridge, who was the deputy director of the Press Information Centre in Kuwait during the 2003 war. "My speciality," he said, "is making guns go bang in the film industry."[49] Ironically this small army of journalists in uniform rarely wrote about their experiences; one of the reasons was the Ministry of Defence's strict rules of media disclosure, reinforced by the stringent Official Secrets Act.[50] The rules, though, were sometimes breached. Witness, for example, generals' memoirs, bestseller *Bravo Two Zero* by ex-SAS trooper "Andy McNab," the special exception given to Victoria Cross winner Johnson Beharry, and in April 2007 the eccentric Ministry of Defence decision to allow some, but not all, of the fifteen service personnel held hostage by the Iranians to sell—not freely give—their stories to the media. This decision caused a moral furor in the British media (even from the newspapers who hypocritically were bidding for the story), forcing Defence Secretary Des Browne to stop all further interviews by the former captives. A return to normality followed with reintroducing the rule that no serving soldiers should sell their stories to the media.

The 1991 Gulf conflict and the Balkan wars had impelled the Ministry of Defence to upgrade its media ops policy. As the BBC's Nik Gowing noted in 1997: "No longer is there an under-funded, second rate information strategy staffed by under-experienced reservists. Instead high calibre, fast stream offices have been given responsibility for running a well-resourced, proactive operation."[51] British correspondents had played a part in this transformation, not least in helping in joint exercises and lecturing at military colleges. At one such event, held at the Royal Military Academy, Sandhurst, in 1995, one of the correspondents most popular with the army, the BBC's Kate Adie, said:

> The armed forces need their personalities. . . . If the fears of timorous civil servants about a "cult of personality" had been allowed to prevail, not one of the heroes of British military history would ever have emerged. . . . The military are nothing if not plain spoken; they should be allowed to speak up a little more.[52]

The Balkans made media stars out of a handful of British colonels. No longer was media work a career-stopper. The 2003 war also made U.S. and UK military spokespeople household names. In the Gulf, a senior Ministry of Defence civil servant, Simon Wren, enforced a tough-minded, well-organized strategy. Unlike the more reclusive and formal American media advisers, he was exceptionally accessible to correspondents, especially with his regular "background briefings." In Whitehall, he had the backing of regular officers such as Lt. Col. Paul Brook and Squadron Leader Tom Rounds, who had the unenviable task of allocating embeds to military units.

After the war, the Ministry of Defence again reorganized its media apparatus. The media and communication directorate had been renamed and restructured. Angered by some alleged leaks and perceived over-friendliness with selected correspondents, the secretary of state ordered a fusion of the separate media units for the three services. They had indeed played one off against the other in old-fashioned inter-service rivalry, but the main intention of the new reforms was to reinforce political control. The media directors of the three services could no longer speak fully to journalists either on or off the record, and this undermined the relationship. An outsider, journalist James Clark, was made director of news. In the Ministry of Defence Main Building, the usual mix of military and civilian press officers staffed a round-the-clock office; alongside were an array of civilian planners. The new factor was the Defence Media Operations Centre (DMOC). This was a tri-service organization "capable of delivering a rapidly deployable media operations capability and cutting-edge train-ing."[53] Though the Ministry of Defence had used its own mobile film and photographic combat crews before, it had been fairly ad hoc. The new organization included two Joint Media Operations Teams (JMOTs), self-sufficient units with all the latest hi-tech equipment. In ten years, the British military had moved from the cult of the amateur to an emulation of the American professional model. And yet it had not taken the much-debated final step of setting up a distinct media corps as the Americans and Australians had done long before.

While at the strategic level, U.S. and UK media management (or manipulation) had tended to coalesce, there were still important differ-ences. In the 2003 war, for example, the Pentagon saw the embedding program as part of an overall "perception management" strategy, while the Ministry of Defence tried hard to keep media operations quite separate from psychological operations and propaganda. Officials were less focused on the wider strategic influence of media coverage. But strategy in the United States was also flawed since the Pentagon was concerned more with the domestic audience. Despite the fact that they allowed an Al-Jazeera reporter to embed with U.S. forces, the Pentagon assumed that the mostly American embedded journalists would be broadly sympathetic to their mission, while the Ministry of Defence was accustomed to and ready for much more difficulty from its own reporters. The Ministry of Defence's media bible, the *Green Book*, last revised in 1992, was not spe-cifically updated for the Iraq War, while the U.S. Public Affairs Guidance document was created especially for the information war in Iraq. The Pentagon's focus on PR aspects of warfare was reflected in the name it gave its 2003 war operation: "Operation Iraqi Freedom," while the Minis-try of Defence deployed a computer to provide the anodyne title of "Operation Telic."

Besides the traditional British military disdain of PR, another reason for the different style was political. The Pentagon had long been planning for war. Britain had to pretend that it was going through the motions of negotiating a peaceful solution. No inevitable conflict could be assumed, especially in dealing with a media that would influence a House of Com-mons deeply divided on fighting Saddam.[54] This led not only to numerous last-minute ad hoc problems with media ops, it also caused serious and fatal shortcomings in British procurement and deployment to the Gulf.

The longer-term determination of U.S. strategy made planning for the information war much bolder. And the style was more Hill & Knowlton than Clausewitz. A survey by media specialists at Cardiff University noted:

The distinctions in the military between information operations, psychological operations, public diplomacy and public affairs may indeed be blurring, but the evidence is that the development of the embeds policy and its American implementation was largely driven by a public relations agenda.[55]

The invasion of Iraq was a perfect PR news story. It was short, and broadcasters could devote massive resources to it. The Pentagon and the MoD provided correspondents with front-row seats. The media could hardly resist. What would be televised was the actual progress of the war, not *why* it was being fought in the first place. Dramatic twenty-four-hour coverage was bound to swing Anglo-American public opinion over to supporting their troops, glossing over why they were there and what would be the consequences for Iraq. Saddam had been demonized by the PR machine; the killing of Iraqi civilians rarely appeared on Western screens. In their eagerness for unprecedented *access,* the media generally lost the *substance* of what they were doing. They inadvertently became part of the PR strategy. They had been captured by their sources.

It took several years of an increasingly bloody Iraqi insurrection for the American media to start asking really awkward questions of the Bush administration. This would suggest before then a considerable PR success story—at least on the home front where it was considered unpatriotic to question the government's motives over Iraq. Abroad, it was quite a different matter. Anti-American sentiment had never been so vociferous, even among traditional NATO allies such as France and Germany. In the Islamic world, it was a catastrophe. This prompted a re-invigorated debate about the merits of public diplomacy—planned governmental "informational" activities, including broadcasting, to win overseas hearts and minds. The loss of credibility over such events as the toppling of the Saddam statue in Baghdad, or even the spin surrounding Pvt. Jessica Lynch's rescue from Iraqi captivity, would be hard to regain. In the aftermath of the combat phase of the Iraqi conflict in 2003, two American writers had warned:

> In the wake of this conflict, we should ask ourselves whether we have made the mistake of believing our own propaganda, and whether we have been fighting the war on terror against the wrong enemies, in the wrong places, with the wrong weapons.[56]

By 2006, the message had finally been received and attempts were under way to revamp the official U.S. propaganda machine under the umbrella term "Strategic Communications." For it was at this strategic level that the real information war against al-Qaeda needed to be addressed. Sun Tzu advocated that you should not only know your enemy, but you should also know yourself.

Coordinating government departments, intelligence agencies, and the military in a commitment to effective strategic communications made sense, provided the strategy didn't undermine its goals by being caught out in a web of deceit and lies. In 2008 Nick Davies's controversial book, *Flat Earth News*, launched a devastating attack on how U.S. strategic communications had corrupted the truth-telling which is the essence of effective journalism. He listed numerous examples of experienced journalists swallowing propaganda. Davies summarized his argument thus:

> The pattern is clear. From Zarqawi to Saddam, from Afghanistan to Iraq, from Washington DC to Tashkent: there is a steady flow of fabrication. The storyline about Zarqawi is part of a larger storyline about Al-Qaeda which is part of a larger storyline about terrorism which, in turn, is part of a global storyline about US foreign policy and its opponents. The notorious misinformation about the weapons of mass destruction is simply one element in this pattern.[57]

Under U.S. law the CIA is not allowed to plant false stories in the domestic media, but Davies cites numerous examples of how foreign stories blew back into the USA. In Britain the common practice of the intelligence agencies feeding favored correspondents is not illegal. Though the military and the State Department and the UK FCO generally inject their material into the media more or less overtly, through their PR arms, Davies said that the intelligence agencies, with huge budgets, were working by subterfuge. It bears repeating: coordinating a counter-strategy to Islamic extremism is vital to Western success, but subversion of the media in the democracies smacks of short-term and counter-productive thinking. From the perspective of good journalism practice, the strategic communications behemoth had been hobbled by its numerous internal disputes. NATO, Washington, and London had trouble with even the nomenclature of the system. And turf wars proliferated: the CIA had harbored a decades-long suspicion of Department of Defense covert action, for example. The State Department and the DoD had been frequently at loggerheads; this was replicated in Whitehall. And the French, of course, displayed highly individualistic tendencies, often opposed to Anglo-American policies.

Davies, an award-winning journalist himself, quoted author and former MI6 officer John Le Carré who said that MI6 had "controlled large parts of the press" in the UK. That may have been partly true during the Cold War, though *Flat Earth News* does provide chilling examples of government influence rather than control in the post 9/11 era. Davies noted that the PR industry, which creates pseudo events masquerading as domestic news and the new machinery of international propaganda, was far more influential than the traditional bête noirs, domineering proprietors and ad-spend. But Davies also praised the *Washington Post's* military correspondent Tom Ricks, who painstakingly revealed that much of Zarqawi's reputation as an alleged al-Qaeda mastermind in Iraq was the work of U.S. strategic communications. Though many hard-bitten foreign correspondents had been duped by American and British propaganda, Ricks was a shining example of hard work and skepticism of official sources.

A tiny percentage of journalists become foreign correspondents and even fewer become regular commuters to what their nineteenth century forebears called the "seat of war." Davies's critique may be true of many domestic reporters, who are too overworked, lazy, or brow-beaten to disdain the avalanche of PR stories. It is far less true of the special breed of war hacks. So what is it that makes them different?

## WHAT MAKES WAR CORRESPONDENTS TICK?

This branch of the trade is seen as glamorous but also very dangerous, particularly in Iraq. Andrew Marr, one of Britain's highest profile political reporters, described foreign correspondents—a broader category that embraces the war hacks—as the "aristocracy" of the media. "Travel, excitement—and *meaning* as well; a certain sense of moral superiority, along with expense accounts." He continued:

> Robert Fisk emphasizes the loneliness of being a good foreign correspondent and the consequent need to construct an imagined community of fellow tradesmen. More than any other group of journalists, foreign correspondents have a family tree of heroes and heroines, and a sense that they are a tribe, albeit a scattered and dysfunctional one. They are rarely admirers of head office.[58]

Marr was not a war correspondent. Anthony Lloyd, of the *Times* and a former army officer, was. So Lloyd had free license to describe his fellow war reporters as:

> . . . an affable clan of damaged children, a concentration of black sheep taking their chances in the casino of war . . . they could fight and fuck one another with the abandon of delinquents in

care, but they also looked after one another, linked by altruistic camaraderie common to any pariah group. I fitted in just fine.[59]

Lloyd was eccentric, daring and, *inter alia,* a self-confessed heroin addict. He literally came under the category of "war junky," addicted to the dangers of the trade. After returning from the Balkans, he observed, "I was delighted with most of what the war offered me: chicks, kicks, cash and chaos; teenage punk dreams turned real and wreathed in gun smoke."[60]

It was never just a male addiction. Emma Daly, of the *Independent,* recalled her time in Sarajevo: "You grow accustomed to distant gunfire, a lullaby soothing you for another night. Sometimes you thrill to the thunder of artillery, adding an edge to sex, arousing in the way of a violent storm raging against the windows back home." She added: "War brings out the best and worst—as some sink to the lowest depths of depravity and cruelty, so others rise to display a generosity of spirit, a courage that is overwhelming, and that, for me at least, outweighs the evil."[61]

Journalists are rated alongside second-hand car salesmen in public esteem, but war correspondents tend to be an exception, especially if they secure a lot of "face-time" on TV. Some high-profile stars, however, have entered "the land of the inauthentic," according to Martin Bell (who has described himself as a "war zone thug"):

> It is possible these days to enjoy a successful career as a virtual foreign correspondent, without actually travelling very far or doing very much or taking any risks. All that is required of you is to look sincere, apply your make-up, throw no tantrums, take your turn to be dish monkey, write fast and stay close to your communications.[62]

Moreover, some well-known journalists, especially in the United States, have become too expensive to risk in real combat zones; some foreign correspondents now completely avoid "bang bang."

This book, however, has been about journalists, both staffers and freelances, who have spent much if not most of their time in harm's way. What makes a good war correspondent? It was Nicholas Tomalin of the *Sunday Times,* killed in the Golan Heights in 1973, who famously remarked that all it takes is a certain way with words, a plausible manner, and rat-like cunning. If only it were that easy. Nevertheless, young journalists nearly all say they want to do the job. They have a choice. They can laboriously climb up the ladder of their news organizations or they can learn a language or two and go out to headline combat zones in places such as Iraq and hope to become a "stringer" for those big news organizations that are short of volunteers from their regular full-time staff. A handful will make it via these routes, and half of those who do could die, go mad—or go sane and come home. Newcomers face many obstacles:

> It is expensive to watch a war—you need cameras and/or computers, access to satellite phones and flak jackets, insurance and someone to pay for the $50,000 medical evacuation plane (just in case), black market-food and fuel, translators or language lessons. Then you need to persuade someone to show you the ropes, tell you the safe routes in and out, the tricks of survival.[63]

Given such difficulties, why do war correspondents do it? It is a mixture of adrenaline, curiosity, professional pride, maybe the lure of a Pulitzer or perhaps a belief that they can have some effect in a disordered world. They probably don't do it for the money: there is no danger money paid by the British media. The risk of death or wounding is too high for mere financial inducement, even for the top TV staffers. Freelance war correspondents often risk all for very little money indeed. The correspondents themselves usually don't know what motivates them, though they will reluctantly offer one-liners in their memoirs or to fellow journalists. Rory Peck, an utterly fearless freelance cameraman, who was killed in action during the 1991 coup in Russia, was asked shortly before his death why he did what he did: "You get paid to travel to the most interesting places at the most interesting times. What do you lose? Each time you lose a little bit of your heart."[64]

The risk of death is high. Iraq has already taken more war journalists' lives than World War II (68), Vietnam (66), the Balkans (36), and Korea (17). Different organizations use different criteria to classify reporters, but the average conservative estimate by spring 2007 was more than 70 killed in Iraq.[65] One Paris-based organization estimated that 64 journalists were killed in Iraq in a single year—2006, although this figure included drivers, translators, and technicians, 90 percent of whom were Iraqis. Other organizations include only full-time journalists and cameramen in their roll of honor. The Brussels-based International Federation of Journalists said that 2006 was "a year of tragedy" with at least 155 murders, assassinations, and unexplained deaths. Reporters without Borders said that at least 81 journalists were killed on duty in 21 countries, the highest total since 1994. Iraq continued to be the most dangerous.[66]

Of course, not all the worldwide media killings were of war correspondents. That does not negate the point that Iraq proved continuously fatal for the war reporter's craft. The formal BBC guidance is that "no story is worth a life," but the BBC and the other media still sent its (increasingly reluctant) journalists to the country. Was it worth the risk? In 2007 Iraq was the biggest story in the world and journalists had to try—despite the numerous limitations—to provide an impartial account. The U.S. and British military were acting in the name of their citizens. Someone had to monitor their behavior. The contrary argument was that it was reckless to send correspondents who did not have a military background. They were holed up in the Green Zone or severely restricted even when they lived outside. More persuasive was the argument that, by giving an impression they were reporting freely, the journalists had been co-opted by the occupying forces who wanted to demonstrate that things were improving or would improve, one fine day.[67]

Yet they still went: perhaps out of duty, or to protect or promote their careers, or because they felt the suffering of the Iraqi people should be told, especially in the West. Some journalists become deeply attached to the cultures and countries they cover. The veteran of veterans, Peter Jouvenal, developed a deep affection for Afghanistan, including marrying an Afghan woman. War correspondents such as Jouvenal became specialists, harking back to the days of in-depth reporters who learned the language and culture. Modern "parachutists," however, are generalists, experienced in crises, not countries. And the multiskilling required of today's reporters can mean that next week's war correspondent was last week's food reporter.

Some self-deception is usually involved in constantly returning to wars. As one Balkan veteran noted, ". . . no journalist or photographer believes that he will be the next casualty. Death or injury is something that happens to the other chap. In the firing line we all believe we are immortal."[68] The last point, however, may well apply only to younger correspondents. Peter Jouvenal drew on statistics about Spitfire pilots in World War II when he noted, "Although their life expectancy was short, the longer they flew the safer they became."[69] Many who defy death as often as Jouvenal become deeply superstitious, carry talisman, or perform little rituals. Others busy themselves with the mundane. "You spend about 90 percent of your time involved with logistics; food, shelter and safety," said Kate Adie. "You spend your time that way to avoid being shot or blown up or blown away."[70]

Black humor is frequently the only way to sustain sanity in war zones, especially humor at other correspondents' expense. In Afghanistan, one inexperienced correspondent moaned to his cameraman, an ex-soldier, about being pinned down in a trench by attacking Russian

**235**

gunships. He replied brusquely, "If you don't have a sense of humour, you shouldn't be in Afghanistan . . . Besides, if it was easy, everybody would be doing it."[71] Thomas E. Ricks provides another example. Jackie Spinner, a *Washington Post* reporter was working near the Abu Ghraib prison when two men tried to shove the small, reserved Spinner into a car. Confusing her beginner's Arabic phrase, she tried to yell that she was a journalist, but instead shouted, "I'm a vegetarian"—which happened to be true, but irrelevant. Luckily, she was rescued by two passing Marines.[72]

All war correspondents have to face death occasionally and fear much of the time. They learn to deal with it in different ways. BBC's Jeremy Bowen explained:

> In all the wars I have ever seen I have had moments of abject terror. But they were just moments, or a few minutes at least. You cannot be frightened the whole time, even if the place you are in is dangerous all the time, because, if you were, you would not be able to function. Human beings are adaptable. You can learn to absorb and ignore a lot of what is going on around you.[73]

Jeremy Bowen knew when to call it a day, though he still carried on reporting. Like him, the birth of their own children persuades some correspondents to quit frontline combat reporting. Others burn out and stop, sometimes quoting the old adage, "The monkeys all were starting to look alike. Only the cages were different."

But what of war correspondents who are psychologically damaged, but who still continue? War can be a potent narcotic. Like any narcotic, it is highly addictive; it can and does kill. Journalists will write about post-traumatic stress disorder (PTSD) in soldiers, but will rarely admit that they are suffering from it themselves.[74] They will confess sometimes, particularly the war junkies, that they enjoy the adrenaline rush which soldiers call a "combat high." To survive, war correspondents have to indulge in some self-deception to blank out the conditions they work in. Just as journalists often believe that they are peculiarly immune from subjectivity, so too they believe they can confront war with impunity. This may be a precondition of being able to survive in war zones, but that does not lessen the psychological damage, especially when they return home to their spouses (if they still have one). Editors, in the comfort of their offices, often play along with the self-deception of their people in the field. This immunity is part of the myth of the war correspondent as hero, someone who can record endless suffering without suffering himself or, increasingly, herself.

Some do suffer serious psychological symptoms, though this is not new. After a decade of war photography, Robert Capa started to exhibit many of the symptoms of PTSD: restlessness, heavy drinking, irritability, depression, survivor's guilt, lack of direction, and barely concealed nihilism. He said his dreams were haunted by death, which he admitted to his then-girlfriend, the actress Ingrid Bergman.[75] Recent research has suggested that a substantial minority of today's war correspondents also develop psychological problems such as PTSD.[76]

> The more remarkable observation, perhaps, is that most emerge relatively unscathed. Through a complex interplay of factors that determine motivation, a self-selection process is at work ensuring that most journalists who choose conflict as their area enjoy what they do, are very good at it, and keep the life-threatening hazards from undermining their psychological health.[77]

But those who did develop psychological symptoms rarely received treatment in the past. This was perhaps because of the wider macho culture that enveloped the profession. Many news organizations tended to join in this conspiracy of silence—even though the BBC and CNN in more recent years pioneered counseling for their correspondents. But the journalists themselves tended to shun any form of therapy, perhaps because of embarrassment, ignorance and, above all, that their future careers would suffer if news of their treatment reached the ears of their bosses. But Iraq and the murder of the *Wall Street Journal* reporter Daniel Pearl forced some veterans to think again. Many hacks had been killed accidentally by stray bullets or artillery, or deliberately because they were mistaken for combatants, or because a warlord wanted to suppress some nasty atrocity or two. Pearl was a cautious man who looked out for his safety and acted like any other journalist would. He was decapitated because of his Jewish religion, as well as his nationality. "In the post-September 11 world seething with religious and ethnic hatred, nationality has joined religion as the new risk factor for journalists."[78]

It has been suggested that reportage is the natural successor to religion, at least in the Western world.[79] A few decades ago most of the planet's population would exhibit no day-to-day knowledge or curiosity about how most of the other inhabitants of the globe were faring. Today an ordinary person's mental space may be filled (and may have to be refilled daily or hourly if there is an important breaking story) with accurate reports about the activities of complete strangers. This constitutes a revolution in mental activity. In previous ages in the West religion was a permanent backdrop, as it still is in the Muslim world. Today the "news" provides modern humans with a release from their humdrum routines, and the daily illusion of communication—perhaps even communion—with a reality greater than themselves as individuals. Like religion, modern reporting is obsessed with death. War reporters gravitate naturally to massacres and military mayhem. Religion had been mankind's answer to death; the Christian belief in personal immortality is an obvious example. Modern reporting endlessly feeds the audience with accounts of the deaths of other people, and so places the viewer continually in a position of being a survivor. "In this way reportage, like religion, gives the individual a comforting sense of his own immortality."[80]

This argument may seem rather far-fetched, though a columnist in the *Guardian* made a parallel point during the Balkan wars: ". . . today's foreign correspondents are really impotent priests, the sounders of moral clarions to the world, bringing home despatches from horror spots for which, they cry, something must be done."[81]

As with the military, war correspondents probably contain a similar number of saints and sinners, with a minor sprinkling of barking eccentrics and the very occasional psychopath. War correspondents may be as brave as the soldiers they write about, though the military would say correspondents were less disciplined, while correspondents would perhaps prefer the term more independent. Historically, most soldiers have been "convinced that the sole and single purpose of every journalist is to destroy their careers."[82] But the military soon learned how to use the media for their own ends. In the Balkans, Lt. Col. Bob Stewart described the media's role in peacekeeping operations as a "very useful adjunct of our armoury—and there are no Rules of Engagement we have to comply with before using them."[83] After the military dominance in the 2003 campaign against Iraq, war correspondents felt they were on the back foot.

Nevertheless, still they followed the sound of gunfire. They went, in the words of *Life* magazine's famous combat photographer, Larry Burrows, "to show the interested people and to shock the uninterested."[84] Burrows was killed when the helicopter he was traveling in with three other photojournalists was shot down by the Viet Cong over Laos in 1971.

# 9

# NO MORE HEROES?

$B$efore 9/11, policymakers sometimes talked despairingly about the new media power, and some television news personnel were often eager to agree. But, as British television journalist Nik Gowing noted: "TV's unquestioned ability to provide a contemporaneous, piecemeal, video–ticker-tape service—a tip sheet of raw real-time images virtually instantly—must not be confused, as it usually is, with a power to drive policymaking."[1] Despite former UN Secretary-General Boutros Boutros-Ghali's claim that CNN had become a "sixteenth member of the Security Council," television has never driven foreign policy, although occasionally it might have some impact. Television journalists are far less influential than they sometimes think.[2] If any hacks believed in the myth of media power, as presumably some did, they may have been inspired to topple dictators or uncover unjust wars in the name of Pulitzer prizes, pride, professionalism, or even personal gain. In reality, while investigative journalism might have greater impact domestically, proving cause and effect of foreign reporting is far more nebulous.

## WITNESSES TO HISTORY

It does not matter if journalists rarely have the political impact some of them think they possess. They can still be witnesses, recording the first draft of history with all its flaws. Even if no political impact resulted at all from their work, Channel Four correspondent Lindsey Hilsum's words are worth remembering: "It is important that we as journalists tell the truth for its own sake, not because it's likely to change government policy."[3] So also does CBS journalist Allen Pizzey's comment that "If we do our jobs properly, we negate the age-old excuse, 'we didn't know,' as a way to justify inaction or indifference in the face of brutality, suffering and injustice. 'You did, because we told you.'"[4] Both Pizzey's and Hilsum's views constitute the highest ideals of the profession. The BBC's Alan Little was more pessimistic on the role of journalist as moral witness: "A lot of us, especially in Bosnia, thought that the effect of our being there and bearing witness would have a beneficial effect, would in fact change things. In fact, it didn't change anything."[5] Little is a very fine journalist, but he is too pessimistic on this point. Journalists were there to record what happened in some places some of the time. Some of the horrors were recorded. Until the last days of World War II, no foreign journalist recorded Auschwitz for the outside world. At least the concentration camps in Bosnia were filmed early in the Balkan wars. No one could say, "We didn't know." That is the prime directive of the craft.

Taking a long view, there will always be friction in wartime between the media and the military. It is in every democratic citizen's interest that this is so. Sadly, in this post-9/11 "long war," increasingly and regrettably portrayed not just as a struggle for the survival of a nation but for a whole civilization, war correspondents can expect more of what they received in the 2003 Iraqi war.

Yet this study has shown that correspondents do not need military officers to censor them or bend them to their will. In nearly all wars journalists will tend to take sides, despite their vocation's mission and their training. In wars of national survival, they will instinctively veer toward patriotism. In wars of choice, if they are embedded, often they will subconsciously bond with their hosts. If they are freewheeling in conflicts such as Bosnia or Rwanda or Darfur, they may well consciously indulge in advocacy. War correspondents may swear to be watchdogs rather than lapdogs, but they are also human when confronted by massacre, mutilation, and the murder of their colleagues. Nevertheless, their individual bravery and intellectual acumen may often be of heroic proportions.

In most wars for most of the time most of the war correspondents were on-side—by volition, not compulsion. The fall of the Berlin Wall and the dissolution of communism spawned a new world disorder, however, with a mosaic of long-suppressed conflicts that did not challenge the very existence of Britain or America. This was a little like revisiting the golden age of the nineteenth century. Correspondents could roam across the Balkans, not free from danger, but at least unleashed from military minders and government censors. By Phillip Knightley's definition, war correspondents could once again become heroes.

And yet soon Knightley would write the profession's obituary because of the media's performance in the 2003 war. The media were again effectively corralled as they had been in the 1991 Gulf War. Then one U.S. Marine officer observed: "We didn't view the news media as a group of

people we were supposed to schmooze. We regarded them as an environmental feature of the battlefield, kind of like the rain. If it rains, you get
wet."[6] The media are today accepted by the military as a natural part of
military strategy. They are sometimes seen as a threat, but there is a modern recognition that they can be "managed" or controlled as part of the
wider information war.

The descendants of William Howard Russell and his specials in the
nineteenth century and of the war correspondents in the twentieth century
will resist the new doctrine of strategic communications. In the looming
future wars of the twenty-first century, despite all the hi-tech media management of the military and political spin-doctors, the same "luckless tribe"
will try to speak truth to power, despite all the odds stacked against them.

Throughout history, wars have usually been chronicled in favor of
the victors. The Crimean War was a bloody success for the British, though
William Howard Russell's reports helped bring down the government in
London. His reputation, however, as the father of modern war reporting
was earned not as a result of the political repercussions of his writing but
because he pioneered accurate frontline journalism. For the next fifty years,
journalists moved relatively unimpeded across numerous imperial battlefields. Most of these conflicts were small wars. But the two World Wars
were struggles for national survival, and journalists were sometimes compelled (but usually they eagerly volunteered) to become patriots with pens.
Later, the Cold War demanded a general conformity from the press. Images of nuclear mushroom clouds encouraged self-censorship. True, exceptions existed from 1914 to 1989, where individual bravery, determined
investigation, or political conviction went against the tide of conformity.
Occasionally, major stories such as My Lai were uncovered.

## THE CNN EFFECT?

From this sense of intermittent freedom allied to new technology
emerged the myth of the "CNN Effect." The mantra was chanted: television can make and unmake American presidents and drive diplomacy,
particularly in the democracies. George H. W. Bush commented: "I learn
more from CNN than I do from the CIA."[7]

For the last 100 years, after every major media innovation, near-
apocalyptic warnings about the perils of communications and media technology abounded. Foreign ministries magnified the potential effects of the
invention of the telegraph in the mid-nineteenth century. Then came tele-
phones, radio, television, satellites, and the Internet. Now we are in the
era of the "citizen journalist" when ordinary people equipped with mobile

phone cameras can transmit images to global audiences instantaneously. Journalists and diplomats alike have no time for mature reflection given the twenty-four-hour news cycle that prompts hasty reactions and the overdramatization of each "crisis." Each generation tends to become mesmerized by the latest high-tech communication device and swears that it will usurp its predecessor. Yet radio did not replace newspapers, nor did television completely displace radio. The Internet is capable of streaming both—and much more.

CNN News was soon to be one of many real-time news services and was challenged and perhaps superseded by BBC World and the Rupert Murdoch-owned Sky and Fox News. A thoughtful senior BBC World journalist, Nik Gowing, contributed a series of groundbreaking papers demolishing the CNN-effect argument.[8] Then in 1996 the Qatar-based television station Al-Jazeera arrived to rival Western domination of news for the Middle East and broadcast information and opinions not found elsewhere. The myth of CNN media power was founded on the false doctrine that television lost the war for the Americans in Vietnam. As this book has indicated, the North Vietnamese army and Viet Cong won the war; CBS or ABC did not lose it. Journalists do not lose wars, even though PR-influenced information strategies may be a vital ingredient in winning them. But if governments are losing a war or have lost one, journalists—blinkered as they may be sometimes—will eventually notice. Television did not cause the (then) greatest defeat in American military history, although many U.S. decision-makers, especially in the military, believed it did, and for a very long time. Even today some senior U.S. military officers will display knee-jerk symptoms of the Vietnam-era television syndrome. They blame the messenger, as we frequently see in Western reactions to Al-Jazeera. While television provides a lens, however, political leadership should provide the focus—a clear strategic goal. "Pictures drive diplomacy . . . only when there is a vacuum of political leadership," argued Johanna Neuman, the foreign editor of *USA Today* in an influential book published in 1996.[9] Neuman was taunted in America because she was a foreign editor with no foreign correspondents. Despite the expansion of media outlets (and office managers), the numbers of foreign correspondents throughout the media were slashed in the 1990s. "War tourists" and parachute journalists increasingly replaced the old hands who had set the standards for their successors to follow but who were now operating within a completely different global news environment.

The British military took on board the Vietnam myth and developed its own antidote but this time about a victory, not a defeat. In the Falklands, the Royal Navy ruled the seas and shaped the story. That war disclosed extensive government intimidation and manipulation of the media, and occasionally the willing connivance of the press in the patriotic interests of deceiving both the enemy *and* the British public. The U.S. government tried to apply the Falklands lessons in both Panama and Grenada. But it was in the 1991 war against Saddam Hussein in Iraq that the Falklands model was applied most effectively; the coalition secured ground control over the media before it won air superiority over the Iraqis. The allegedly negative power of television had been tamed—despite the Baghdad "loop-hole" wherein three CNN television journalists were already entrenched in the Al-Rashid Hotel. Peter Arnett, John Holliman, and Bernard Shaw reported the action live as the world watched American bombs light up the Baghdad sky. While in Saudi Arabia, never before had so many journalists been forced to cover a war stone-cold sober. At last the Pentagon had avenged its loss of control from the Vietnam era.

The Gulf conflict was billed as the first real-time, live satellite-television war. Actually viewers saw little of the war and not much of that was live or informative. But it was fast. While the press conferences on television gave the impression of bored, rude, dumb, and unpatriotic questions from scruffy journalists, immaculately dressed military briefers appeared professional, patient, and wise. Paradoxically, despite the chained media in the Gulf, the idea that media drove diplomacy was again trumpeted, yet the U.S. government used the media for its own purposes to spread disinformation about an amphibious landing that would change the course of the war, for example, and to warn Iraqi commanders not to use chemical weapons.

Events are reported faster today—Nik Gowing's "tyranny of real time"—which can cause errors by hacks as well as diplomats. And so governments have to respond faster. Television can confirm data gathered from other sources, but it can also beat traditional sources of information-gathering, especially in a rapidly moving international crisis. Diplomats, like all civil servants, prefer to work slowly and systematically. TV images can, therefore, be a nuisance factor. Jamie Shea, in the spotlight as the NATO spokesman during the Kosovo war, said:

> The ability of the media to dramatise events and create a global audience for conflict puts policymakers under pressure to take decisions faster and with less time for reflection than in any other time in previous history. This increases the chances of those decisions being the wrong ones.[10]

The political effects: the media may sometimes prioritize the political agenda, but it does not dictate responses. Graphic pictures—"stick action" or gore—can sometimes influence the *process* much more than the policy itself.[11] Dramatic coverage of wars may create a political resonance if it happens to hit a critical, usually unpredictable, void in the news cycle. And it would have to coincide with a moment of policy panic, when governments have no clear strategies.[12] Daniel Hallin, in his classic account of the Vietnam media warfare, argued that the impact of the media on policy was proportional to the level of consensus in a society about the aims of the war. So to create any effect on government, the stories should also resonate with the popular will.[13]

In Iraq in 1991 the Shias rose up in the aftermath of Saddam's defeat, but no Western cameramen were present as witnesses. The rebellion was brutally suppressed by Saddam in an information void. In the north, Western cameras provided heart-wrenching pictures of Kurds fleeing into the snow-covered mountains.[14] British Prime Minister John Major sketched a novel plan, literally on the back of an envelope, to create a safe haven protected by a no-fly zone. Washington and London had been caught unaware by the drama over Kurdish refugees. This was an example of pictures having an effect as a result of a policy vacuum and decision-makers being caught off guard.[15]

The media was unchained completely in the Balkans. Bosnia could claim to be the first true television war—or the nearest any medium could get to "real war." Lightweight cameras proliferated among soldiers, victims, voyeurs, and reporters. The general mayhem invited explosive pictures of bombed babies in marketplaces, mass rape, concentration camps, refugees, and even UN hostages. It was a constant drumbeat by journalists who wanted Western governments to do something—anything. Martin Bell admitted later that he was a founding member of the "Do Something Club." In the policy and moral vacuum that was Bosnia, the media seemed to be providing not a policy but a slogan: intervention, intervention, intervention. The media, however, were highlighting dilemmas but did not suggest ways of resolving them. Quite simply, American and European governments did not want to send large ground forces into the Balkan quagmire. So some cosmetic concessions were offered to public opinion—"pseudo-action" such as the deployment of peacekeepers who could by definition not enforce peace, and short-term diplomatic solutions, such as safe havens that were not safe.

Bosnia's bloodstained television coverage could nudge governments a little by raising the emotional temperature, but if presidents and foreign ministers did not want to act, then they would choose to ride out the media storm. This is what happened over the Rwanda genocide, to the eternal shame of the UN. Media can move governments occasionally and grudgingly, usually when decision-makers are caught off-guard. The converse holds that if governments are committed to a policy, they will expend time, money, and, crucially, political capital in winning over public opinion and the media. This explains the apparent contradictory example of Somalia. Television pictures of starving children were said to have sucked in U.S. troops, and TV images (particularly the dead U.S. soldiers dragged through the streets of Mogadishu) forced them out ten months later. President Bill Clinton, however, was not prepared to expend political capital by shoring up a disagreeable policy on Somalia that had been a last-minute humanitarian flourish by his predecessor. Powerful pictures in Somalia there may have been for both presidents, but it was politics, not media coverage, that decided which way the policy would bend.

War correspondents regularly risk their lives and thus like to believe that their reports do make a difference. They usually do not set out to change governments or their policies, but it is only human nature for journalists to admire the effects of their own work, especially if it includes the aura of humanitarian relief. In Bosnia, daily reports over an extended period might have struck a chord with the general public, but they were unlikely to speed a change in policy unless diplomacy was already moving in that direction—in this case the 1995 air strikes against the Serbs. Diplomacy could have prevented the Balkan wars; once they had broken out, the major powers offered alibis for a policy of inaction. As long as the belligerents were determined to fight on, the West could do little militarily on the ground—short of a replay of Desert Storm—except to wait until the contestants reached what Clausewitz called the culminating point: the imminent collapse of the Bosnian Serbs.

Even the most cynical journalists sometimes feel that they can do some good and effect some change for the better. In reality, a foreign or war correspondent is lucky if he or she makes a big difference more than once in their careers. A classic example is BBC's Michael Buerk's moving film on the Ethiopian famine in 1984. The drama of a truly exceptional report and its timing may prompt extra charity or pieties at the UN. But rarely do political realities improve on the ground, however. Even in the extreme case of Rwanda, daily doses of televised misery may speed messages but not implement change. Moral outrage and international aid are often disguises for diplomatic inaction. And, crucially, it depends on what governments see as their national interest, and what can be done cheaply. British intervention in Sierra Leone, a former colony, was considered "doable," but Sudan, also formerly under British rule, was not. Douglas Hurd, a former UK foreign secretary, famously used the term "virtuous intervention," but what he really meant was significant humanitarian results at a small cost, although only if it was entirely in British interests.[16]

Politicians as well as journalists can deceive themselves about media clout. Philippines President Ferdinand Marcos controlled nearly all the media and the guns. The majority of his army, however, refused to use their weapons to reverse electoral defeat. The Chinese Communist Party—despite the initial presence of cameras—took a different course in Tiananmen Square. After allowing cameras to record Mikhail Gorbachev's high-profile visit, when the crowd turned into "pro-democracy" protesters, the plugs were pulled—literally, as CNN was broadcasting live on air—before the consequent slaughter took place. As such, the media was almost irrelevant in both cases. In crises, state monopoly of military power and the will to use it are often impervious to media challenges, although the collapse of communism in the USSR perhaps obviated this general rule in Eastern Europe, although not in Putin-era Russia, which has largely crushed domestic media opposition and kept independent journalists out of Chechnya. And Burma provides a more recent example in Asia of guns trumping the media. Governments adapt and react, as they did to the telegraph, radio, television, and the Internet. Television, even at the height of CNN influence and the alleged CNN effect in the 1990s, could never replace politics and diplomacy, although it might force it to become more discreet. For example, the Oslo peace talks on the Middle East carefully avoided the media. Skilled politicians and diplomats are very rarely victims of media attention. The successful are usually its masters.

## HACKS VERSUS THE "BEAN COUNTERS"

If correspondents could look back on perhaps two golden ages of freewheeling opportunities to report wars—1856 to 1914 and the Balkans in the 1990s—then 9/11 ushered in a return to wars of perceived national survival in a manner reminiscent of the World Wars of the last century. The so-called war on terror has often been considered a convenient replacement for the Cold War. The Anglo-American information strategies in the lead up to, and the conduct of, the invasion of Iraq emasculated the Western media, though not Al-Jazeera. Ironically, the neoconservative agenda had indeed created democracy in the Middle East, but it was highly localized in a Qatar-based news station, and it was to work mightily against the Bush administration's policies. In 2003, so humbled were the Western media, and especially its war correspondents, that the principal chronicler of the profession, Phillip Knightley, declared: "The age of war correspondent as hero appears to be over."[17] He should have tried saying that to correspondents in Fallujah in Iraq or Helmand Province in Afghanistan during the failed occupations that followed the Iraq War.

A series of popular feature films—*Salvador, Under Fire, The Killing Fields* and *The Year of Living Dangerously*—have represented the war correspondent as courageous rebels usually committed to truth. And some of the hacks' memoirs confirm this heroic image. This may be partly self-aggrandizement but also the journalists' instinct to make a livelier narrative out of what can be a life of hard work and bureaucratic tedium punctuated by bouts of terror and dysentery.[18] Nevertheless, most war correspondents, even the bravest, rarely mention what others would call heroics. During small dinner parties with their peers in Washington or London, in conversations almost unfathomable to outsiders, they might air their hopes and fears. In public, if asked about their profession, they would always simply say, "I'm a journalist," never "I'm a war correspondent." Much of the "bang bang" had been done by freelance cameraman, for example, by the pioneering Frontline TV News. Two of the four founders were killed in action. The company closed because even the best action footage rarely paid the rent, let alone a mortgage.[19] Rarely do combat journalists—freelancers or staffers—achieve fame. Most of the best film work, especially from freelancers, is often voiced over in the studio by stay-at-home staff journalists. And the office-bound often get the credit. The John Simpsons and Christiane Amanpours tend to be the exceptions. Many of the other senior war correspondents mentioned in this book are not household names.

The claims about TV power are usually made by politicians or sit-tight journalists, rarely by the war correspondents. Television journalists are far less important than their big salaries and sometimes bigger egos might suggest. Working journalists in the field are more concerned with other issues, not the political impact of their material nor often the lack of context when the program is aired alongside other "packages" in the newsrooms at home. TV provides action, not process, pictures rather than ideas, and stereotypes rather than complexity. "New York wants John Wayne movies, not talking heads," said one correspondent during the Vietnam War.[20] Not much has changed in that respect.

This is what TV pundits call "dumbing down." A former SAS officer who worked as an ITN correspondent in Bosnia had spent years setting up a report on the resistance movement in Iran. Just as he was about to risk a dangerous trip to film illegally inside Iran, his news editor told him to drop it all for a story on the finances of the Spice Girls. "This is what the viewers would rather see," the editor told him.[21]

This is redolent of Martin Bell's comment from Bosnia: "I have even wondered, occasionally, whether it isn't easier to deal with the warlords than the editors."[22] All correspondents in the field have problems with editors at home, not least because few of them have ever got their boots dirty in foreign wars. They constitute the well-springs of "received wisdom" or what Bell called "departments of preconceived notions." Few had risked more than a breakdown on the New York subway or London's Underground. Courtesy is required, however, because correspondents need to have their expenses signed off by these same office-bound editors.

Dumbing down is also the fault of the viewers and readers. The couch potatoes, for whom the hacks risk their lives, have increasingly short attention spans. Except for big wars, when "our boys" go into battle, most TV stations prefer domestic celebrity stories. In the summer of 2006, Iraq fell off the UK media agenda while all lights focused on the 24/7 real-time saga to rescue a whale that had swum up the River Thames. Here, we admittedly do need to caution about over-generalization: the "media" is a truly heterogeneous body about which it is difficult to generalize—just like the military. But many newspapers are even worse than we have depicted. Public radio and television in the United States and the BBC, especially its Radio Four, as well as the UK's Channel Four News, remain often lonely flag-bearers of serious commentary. As media scholar Jean Seaton observed: "There is more news in the world, but it is produced by less specialized, more general reporters. They know less, they cost less, but they produce news that is disseminated more powerfully than ever before."[23]

De-contextualized, dumbed-down war reporting has also been sanitized. The reality of war has been "good-tasted" away. War has been prettified, and perhaps after 9/11 this makes it more acceptable, not least to viewers and voters. Images of the falling victims of the World Trade Center attacks disappeared almost immediately from news reports. It may suit the military and certainly the government not to see too much gore, both of the victims on the other side and the injuries and deaths of Western troops. The media may also fear alienating their customers if the unvarnished truth were told. Slaughter has to be rationalized, but it also has to be rationed.[24] On the other hand, despite the high costs of sending teams loaded with equipment half way around the world, wars can be good business for TV stations. They boost ratings and thereby income from advertisers, provided there is not too much blood on the lens. Jim Burroughs, an independent filmmaker who covered the Afghan wars had this to say on the role of the "bean-counters," the accountants:

> Their interest is only in what they call "the bottom line." Perhaps this is not the worst thing in the world of business, but for journalism it is catastrophic. Because journalism, like medicine, is

meant to be more than a business, and to be governed by more than the rules of business.[25]

Another concern is the role of spooks. Journalists are increasingly subjected to manipulation by the intelligence agencies although, as this book has outlined, this is not a new problem. There are many examples of correspondents being recruited as secret agents. Equally dangerous to the profession is the practice of agents going undercover as hacks. And since 9/11, the planting of fabricated stories on reporters, as part of a strategic communications programme, has played into black propaganda campaigns to justify wars.[26] Potentially less fatal is the professional concern about the erosion between commentary and news reportage—"comm-portage." This is more of an issue in newspapers, but opinions on air, in the middle of factual reporting, can be disguised by skillful broadcasters with an agenda of their own.[27] So journalists get it wrong, perhaps because they have been duped by intelligence or because of their own failings or personal political agendas. When the media make mistakes, they can run a correction. When the military cock up, people often die. When the intelligence agencies get it wrong, unnecessary wars can result. When they all interact and get it wrong together, you can get a long war that is going disastrously wrong. All share a responsibility for turning the base metal of Islamic extremist violence into the golden currency of terror. Religious nationalism dressed up as holy war is not new. Nor is the result: committing human flesh to hard steel and explosives on behalf of an idea. What has changed dramatically in this new century is the aftershock. As a well-known British columnist observed:

> Terrorism is 10% bang and 90% an echo effect composed of media hysteria, political overkill and kneejerk executive action, usually retribution against some wider group treated as collectively responsible. This response has become 24-hour, seven-day-a-week amplification by the new politico-media complex, especially shrill where the dead are white people.[28]

Correspondents can be both perpetrators and victims. Perhaps what Knightley really meant was that the days of the heroic impact of war reporting were over because of the current military/government strangulation. Knightley's *The First Casualty* redounds with epic accounts of John Reed's (partisan) portrayal of the Russian revolution and Wilfred Burchett's description of Hiroshima in 1945. In this regard, Knightley's obituary for the war correspondent may well be partly correct. And yet, despite all the technological change and government spin, journalists today can still be found who would qualify for Knightley's pantheon. This book started with a comment by BBC's Jeremy Paxman, and, since he always likes to have the last word, let us include his words among our last: "Essentially journalism is a matter of instinct, the expression of primitive curiosity and an instinctive urge to cause trouble, to be difficult, coupled with an atavistic distrust of anyone in authority."[29] Many of today's war correspondents possess these qualities in spades.

A few brave "soldiers of the press" who make up the "little army of historians who are writing history from the canon's mouth", to quote from Alfred Hitchcock's *Foreign Correspondent*, still maintain William Howard Russell's legacy. War reporting is necessary, not just as a witness to history in the killing fields, but "to monitor the centres of power" in authoritarian states and in Western democracies, where government spin and propaganda can dupe apathetic voters and hard-bitten correspondents alike.[30] In the final analysis war reporting is not as glamorous as many Hollywood movies suggest. It is not about victory or defeat, but death. It represents the total failure of the human spirit, and also the total failure of politics to provide alternative solutions. This book suggests that war reporters have far less impact than is often assumed. That is perhaps the real tragedy: showing the reality of conflict could help eventually to outlaw war on our crowded planet. Sadly, politicians will continue to keep war correspondents busy.

# NOTES

## CHAPTER 1: THE ORIGINS OF WAR REPORTING

1. For a useful summary of this epic, see Robert Giddings, *Echoes of War: Portraits of War from the Fall of Troy to the Gulf War* (London: Bloomsbury, 1992), viii–x.
2. Thucydides, *The History of the Peloponnesian War*, trans. Richard Livingstone (New York: Oxford University Press, 1960).
3. See Xenophon, *The Persian Expedition*, trans. Rex Warner (Harmondsworth: Penguin, 1949).
4. It stands a comparison, for example, with Antony Beevor's *Stalingrad* (London: Viking, 1998).
5. Julius Caesar, *The Conquest of Gaul*, trans. S. A. Handford (Harmondsworth: Penguin, 1951) cited in John Carey, ed. *The Faber Book of Reportage* (London: Faber and Faber, 1987), 12. For a useful summary of classical military history, see J. E. Lendon, *Soldiers and Ghosts: A History of Battle in Classical Antiquity* (New Haven, CT: Yale University Press, 2005).
6. Josephus, *The Jewish War*, in *Works*, Loeb Classical Library, 1926, in Carey, ibid., 14.
7. See R. R. Davies, *The Revolt of Owain Glyn Dŵr* (Oxford: Oxford University Press, 1995).
8. Samuel Daniel, *The Civil Wars Between the Two Houses of York and Lancaster*, cited in Trevor Royle, *War Report: The War Correspondent's View of Battle from the Crimea to the Falklands* (Edinburgh: Mainstream, 1987), 13.
9. Ibid., 15.
10. Robert Wilkinson-Latham, *From Our Special Correspondent: Victorian War Correspondents and Their Campaigns* (London: Hodder and Stoughton, 1979), 16–17.
11. Quoted in Johanna Neuman, *Lights, Camera, War: Is Media Technology Driving International Politics?* (New York: St Martin's Press, 1996), 27.
12. Wilkinson-Latham, *From Our Special Correspondent*, 21.

13. Sir Daniel Lysons, *The Crimean War from First to Last* (1895) quoted in Robert Giddings, *Imperial Echoes: Eye-Witness Accounts of Victoria's Little Wars* (London: Leo Cooper, 1996), 100.

14. Caroline Chapman, *Russell of The Times: War Despatches and Diaries* (London: Bell and Hyman, 1984), 41–2.

15. Quoted in Royle, *War Report*, 24.

16. Cited in Chapman, *Russell of The Times*, 32.

17. Cited in Wilkinson-Latham, *From Our Special Correspondent*, 57.

18. Giddings, *Imperial Echoes*, 118.

19. Cited in Wilkinson-Latham, *From Our Special Correspondent*, 58.

20. Ibid.

21. Cited in Miles Hudson and John Stanier, *War and the Media* (Stroud: Sutton, 1997), 17.

22. Phillip Knightley, *The First Casualty: The War Correspondent as Hero, Propagandist and Myth Maker* (London: Quartet, 1982), 16.

23. Quoted in Royle, *War Report*, 26.

24. Cited in Chapman, *Russell of The Times*, 186.

25. For a revisionist account of the Crimean war, especially the Baltic campaigns, see Andrew Lambert and Stephen Badsey, *The War Correspondents: The Crimean War* (Stroud: Sutton, 1994).

26. Philip M. Taylor, *Munitions of the Mind: A History of Propaganda from the Ancient World to the Present Day* (Manchester: Manchester University Press, 3rd ed., 2003), 165. For a useful recent survey of war photography, see Duncan Anderson, *Glass Warriors: The Camera at War* (London: Collins, 2005).

27. Knightley, *The First Casualty*, 17.

28. Nathaniel Lande, *Dispatches from the Front: A History of the American War Correspondent* (Oxford: Oxford University Press, 1996), xi.

29. For a sympathetic portrayal of Raglan, see Christopher Hibbert, *The Destruction of Lord Raglan* (London: Longman, 1961).

30. Lande, *Dispatches from the Front*, 6.

31. Ibid., 49–52.

32. Introduction by John Keegan in Phillip Knightley, *The Eye of War: Words and Photographs from the Front Line* (Washington, DC: Smithsonian, n.d.), 6.

33. Neuman, *Lights, Camera, War*, 32–33.

34. Ibid., 33.

35. J. Cutler Andrews, *The North Reports the Civil War* (Pittsburgh: University of Pittsburgh, 1950), 202.

36. Knightley, *The First Casualty*, 38.

37. Henry Villard, "Army Correspondence," *Nation*, July 27, 1865, cited in Knightley, *The First Casualty*, 21.

38. Knightley, *The First Casualty*, 31, 33.

39. John F. Marzalek, *Sherman's Other War: The General and the Civil War Press* (Memphis: Memphis State University, 1981), 34.
40. Richard Lacayo and George Russell, *Eyewitness: 150 Years of Photojournalism,* (New York: Time, 1995), 14.
41. *New York Daily Tribune,* March 8, 1865, cited in J. Cutler Andrews, *The North Reports,* 6.
42. See Neuman, *Lights, Camera, War,* 35.
43. John Black Atkins, *The Life of Sir William Howard Russell,* vol. 2, 1911, 373, cited in Roger T. Stearn, "War Correspondents and Colonial Wars c. 1870–1900," in John M. Mackenzie, ed. *Popular Imperialism and the Military, 1850–1950* (Manchester: Manchester University Press, 1992), 139.
44. John M. Mackenzie, "Popular Imperialism and the Military" in Mackenzie, *Popular Imperialism,* 16.
45. Stearn, "War Correspondents and Colonial Wars," 144.
46. Wilkinson-Latham, *From Our Special Correspondent,* 190.
47. Giddings, *Echoes of War,* 199.
48. For an elaboration of this theme, see J. Morris, *Heaven's Command* (Harmondsworth: Penguin, 1986), 431–8.
49. Victorian England was aghast that "natives" armed largely with spears could defeat a modern army. For a useful summary of the reasons for the debacle, see Saul David, *Military Blunders: The How and Why of Military Failure* (London: Robinson, 1997), 251–67.
50. Cited in Morris, *Heaven's Command,* 438.
51. Knightley, *The First Casualty,* 52.
52. Royle, *War Report,* 38.
53. Giddings, *Echoes of War,* 204.
54. Ibid., 203.
55. For a useful military summary of the Sudan wars, see Philip J. Haythornthwaite, *The Colonial Wars Sourcebook* (London: Arms and Armour Press, 1995), 216–25. For a general background, see two excellent books by a well-known war correspondent of the Second World War: Alan Moorhead's *The White Nile* and *The Blue Nile* (various editions).
56. Lande, *Dispatches from the Front,* 127.
57. Ibid.
58. Knightley, *The First Casualty,* 56.
59. Ibid., 59.
60. Peter Young and Peter Jesser, *The Media and the Military: From the Crimea to Desert Strike* (London: Macmillan, 1977), 29.
61. Thomas Pakenham, *The Boer War* (Johannesburg: Ball, 1982).
62. For details of Steevens's death, see Royle, *War Report,* 62-3
63. Ibid., 574. For a general background on the conflict in South Africa, see Paul Moorcraft, *African Nemesis: War and Revolution in Southern Africa, 1945–2010,* (London: Brassey's Ltd., 1994), 7–21. Some historians have

argued that much of the suffering in the camps was caused by the Boers themselves, especially their reluctance to accept modern medical practices. For a useful summary, see Andrew Roberts, "They brought it on themselves," *The Spectator,* October 2, 1999, 21.

64. Hudson and Stanier, *War and the Media,* 33. See also Stephen Badsey, "The Boer War as a Media War," http://www.defence.gov.au/Army/ahu/books_articles/ConferencePapers/The_Boer_War_Badsey.htm.

65. Wilkinson-Latham, *From Our Special Correspondent,* 204.

66. Ibid., 31.

67. Royle, *War Report,* 69–70.

68. See Bennett Burleigh's *The Natal Campaign,* originally published in 1900; various editions.

69. T. Davenport, *South Africa: A Modern History* (Johannesburg: Macmillan,1987), 221. For a sympathetic appraisal of Boer sentiments in this period, see J. Meintjes, *De La Rey: Lion of the West* (Johannesburg: Keartland, 1966).

70. Raymond Sibbald, *The War Correspondents: The Boer War* (Stroud: Sutton, 1993), 232.

71. Knightley, *The First Casualty,* 59–61.

72. Ibid., 61–2.

73. Young and Jesser, *The Media and the Military,* 30–31.

74. Ibid.

75. Knightley, *The First Casualty,* 62.

76. Ibid.

77. *The New World,* December 12, 1894, quoted in Knightley, *The First Casualty,* 58.

78. Stearn, "War Correspondents and colonial wars," 145.

79. Knightley, *The First Casualty,* 51.

80. Ronald Hyam, *Empire and Sexuality: The British Experience* (Manchester: Manchester University Press, 1991), 33.

81. Ibid., 34.

82. Cited in Wilkinson-Latham, *From Our Special Correspondent,* 101.

83. T. H. S. Escott, *Masters of English Journalism,* 355–6, cited in Stearn, "War Correspondents and Colonial Wars," 155.

## CHAPTER 2: THE WORLD WARS

1. Arthur Ponsonby, *Falsehood in Wartime* (London: Allen and Unwin, 1928), 57.

2. Lucy Masterman, *C.F.C. Masterman: A Biography* (London: Cassell, 1929), 296.

3. Walter Raleigh, *The War and the Press* (Oxford: Oxford University Press, 1918), 12.

4. Niall Ferguson, *The Pity of War* (London: Allen Lane, 1998), 220. "Anastasie" was the name given to wartime censorship of soldiers'

letters. See Martha Hanna, "A Republic of Letters: The Epistolary Tradition in France during World War I," *American History* Review, vol. 108, no. 5 (December 2003) 1338–61. In Britain, besides formal means of media control, various secret propaganda units were established in 1914. One of the most effective was based in Wellington House, London. From this base, Charles Masterman, a Liberal MP, covertly arranged the publication of a wide range of anti-German literature. Unlike the self-aggrandizing press barons, Masterman achieved a great deal and said very little. See M. L. Sanders and Philip M. Taylor, *British Propaganda during the First World* War (Basingstoke: Macmillan, 1982) and Andrew Steed, "British Propaganda and the First World War" in Ian Stewart and Susan L Carruthers, eds. *War, Culture and the Media: Representations of the Military in 20th Century Britain* (Trowbridge: Flick Books, 1996).

5. Hansard, 5th series (Commons) vol. 65, col. 2155.

6. Colin Lovelace, "British Press Censorship during the First World War" in R. Boyce, J. Curran and P. Wingate, eds. *Newspaper History from the Seventeenth Century to the Present Day* (London: Constable, 1978), 310.

7. Peter Young and Peter Jesser, *Media and the Military: The Crimea to Desert Strike* (Basingstoke: Macmillan, 1997), 34.

8. Ferguson, *The Pity of War*, 230.

9. R. Pound and G. Harmsworth, *Northcliffe* (London: Cassell, 1959), 469.

10. Trevor Royle, *War Report: The War Correspondent's View of Battle from the Crimea to the Falklands* (Edinburgh: Mainstream, 1987), 96.

11. Lord Burnham's phrase, cited in Sir Edward Cook, *The Press in War-Time: With Some Account of the Official Press Bureau* (London: Macmillan, 1920), 178.

12. Ferguson, *The Pity of War*, 213.

13. See Gary S. Messinger, *British Propaganda and the State in the First World War* (Manchester: Manchester University Press, 1992), 249–56. See also Peter Buitenhuis, *The Great War of Words: Literature as Propaganda 1914-18 and After* (London: Batsford, 1989), and Martin Stephen, *Poetry, History and Myth in the Great War* (Leo Cooper, 1996). For the story of how the British were forced to re-enter the propaganda field in the years that followed, see Philip M. Taylor, *The Projection of Britain: British Overseas Publicity and Propaganda, 1919–39* (Cambridge: Cambridge University Press, 1981).

14. See Philip M. Taylor, *British Propaganda in the Twentieth Century: Selling Democracy* (Edinburgh: Edinburgh University Press, 1999), 59. See also J. Lee Thompson, *Northcliffe: Press Baron in Politics, 1865–1922* (London: J. Murray, 2000).

15. Sanders and Taylor, *British Propaganda during the First World War*, 263.

16. Paul Fussell, *The Great War and Modern Memory* (Oxford: Oxford University Press, 1977), 12. Lloyd George confided in his memoirs about the catastrophic errors in the three great battles of Verdun, Somme, and

Passchendaele: "It is the story of the million who would rather die than own themselves cowards—even to themselves—and also of the two or three individuals who rather the million perish than they as leaders should own—even to themselves—that they were blunderers." *War Memoirs,* 1938, cited in Robert Giddings, *Echoes of War: Portraits of War from the Fall of Troy to the Gulf War* (London: Bloomsbury, 1992), 253.

17. Robert B. Asprey, *The German High Command At War: Hindenberg and Ludendorff and The First World War* (London: Warner, 1994), 52.
18. Nathan A. Haverstock, *Fifty Years at the Front: The Life of War Correspondent Frederick Palmer* (Washington, DC: Brassey's, Inc. 1996), 167.
19. Ibid., 191.
20. Phillip Knightley, *The First Casualty: The War Correspondent as Hero, Propagandist and Myth Maker* (London: Quartet, 1982), 113.
21. Royle, *War Report,* 104. (Also, A. J. A. Morris, *The Letters of Lieutenant-Colonel Charles à Court Repington: Military Correspondent of The Times, 1903–1918* (Stroud: Sutton, 1999).)
22. Ibid., 107.
23. Cited in Cate Haste, *Keep the Home Fires Burning* (London: Allen Lane, 1977), 33.
24. Knightley, *The First Casualty,* 79. An American poem called "News from the Front" satirized the official censors thus:

> The Allies at Germans lunged
> And won a fight at name—expunged.
> But the French's army was defeated,
> Upon the field of place—deleted
> From Town-Blue-Pencilled, lovely spot,
> The unions galloped, fierce and hot,
> But hundreds bit the dust and grass,
> In the place-Press-Bureau-Would-Not-Pass.
> The hottest work in the field,
> Burst around locality—concealed.

First published in the *Sphere,* November 7, 1914, cited in Martin J. Farrar, *News from the Front: War Correspondents, 1914–1918* (Stroud: Sutton, 1998), ix.
25. Ferguson, *The Pity of War,* 221.
26. Ibid., 247.
27. Ibid., 230.
28. Cited in James Curran and Jean Seaton, *Power Without Responsibility: The Press and Broadcasting in Britain* (London: Routledge, 1990), 46.
29. Ferguson, *The Pity of War,* 230.
30. *Evening Standard,* October 23, 1969, cited in Knightley, *The First Casualty,* 88.
31. Quoted in Knightley, *The First Casualty,* 109. For a discussion of what people wanted to know, especially regarding the Somme film and how

much was faked, see "Silent Suffering," *Sunday Times* magazine, October 8, 2006.

32. Siegfried Sassoon, *Memoirs of an Infantry Officer* (London: Faber and Faber, 1930), 176. For a general background, see J. G. Fuller, *Troop Morale and Popular Culture in the British and Dominion Armies, 1914–1918* (Oxford: Oxford University Press, 1990).

33. Ferguson, *The Pity of War*, 239.

34. Philip Gibbs, *Adventures in Journalism* (London: Heinemann, 1923), 231.

35. Royle, *War Report*, 106.

36. See G. D. Sheffield, "Oh! What a Futile War: Representations of the Western Front in Modern British Media and Popular Culture," in Stewart and Carruthers, *War, Culture and the Media*. Sheffield is critical of the exaggerated historical legacy of the war poets: "At bottom, the media obsession with a handful of unrepresentative soldiers reflects the fact that British perceptions of the First World War too often stem from literary rather than historical sources." (65). See also, Dan Todman, *The Great War: Myth and Memory* (London: Hambledon and London, 2005). See also Samuel Hynes, *The Soldiers' Tale: Bearing Witness to Modern War* (London: Pimlico, 1998).

37. Alan Clark, *The Donkeys* (London: Hutchinson, 1961); the title refers, of course, to the view that British troops were lions led by donkeys. A. J. P. Taylor, *The First World War: An Illustrated History* (London: Hamish Hamilton, 1963).

38. See, for example, John Terraine, *The First World War, 1914–1918* (Basingstoke: Papermac, 1984). In particular, Terraine has helped to restore the reputation of Field Marshal Haig.

39. Lloyd Clark, "Civilians entrenched: the British home front and attitudes to the First World War, 1914–18," in Stewart and Carruthers, *War, Culture and the Media*, 48. Social advances during the war have been questioned. See, for example, John Bourne, "Total War 1: The Great War," in Charles Townshend, ed. *The Oxford History of Modern War* (Oxford: Oxford University Press, 2005), 136–7; Anthony Livesey, *The Atlas of World War One* (London: Viking, 1994), 181–2.

40. Hugh Cecil, "Why the press hid the truth," *Sunday Times,* April 12, 1998.

41. For an elaboration of this argument, see Martin J. Farrar, *News from the Front,* 219–24.

42. Cecil, "Why the Press Hid the Truth."

43. Sheffield, "Oh! What a Futile War," 59, 64.

44. See Hew Strachan, *The First World War* (London: Simon and Schuster, 2003), 227, 249. Also, Brock Millman, *Pessimism and British War Policy 1916–1918* (London: Frank Cass, 2001).

45. Fussell, *The Great War and Modern Memory,* 316. Fussell has been criticized extensively for his historical errors, but his main themes about cultural impact remain valid.

46. Neville Lytton, *The Press and the General Staff* (London: Collins, 1921), vii.

47. John Keegan, *The First World War* (London: Hutchinson, 1998), 8.

48. Maj. Gen. John Fuller, "Gallipoli" in Ernest Hemingway, ed. *Men at War* (New York: Crown, 1955), 641.

49. James Morris, *Farewell the Trumpets: An Imperial Retreat* (Harmondsworth: Penguin, 1987), 195.

50. Martin Gilbert, introduction to Max Arthur, *Forgotten Voices of the Great War* (London: Ebury, 2003), 2.

51. Ibid.

52. Douglas Porch, "Total War 1," 122.

53. Morris, *Farewell the Trumpets*, 200.

54. Strachan, *The First World War*, 331.

55. Phrase coined by Great War correspondent Gregory Mason, cited in Haverstock, *Fifty Years at the Front*, 164.

56. Duncan Anderson, *Glass Warriors: The Camera at War* (London: Collins, 2005), 110.

57. Sir Hugh Cudlipp, *The Prerogative of the Harlot: Press Barons and Power* (London: Bodley Head, 1980), 265.

58. Benny Morris, *The Roots of Appeasement* (London: Frank Cass, 1992). His study analyzed, inter alia, the *Economist*, the *New Statesman*, the *Spectator*, *Sunday Times* (London), and *Observer*.

59. John Keegan, *A History of Warfare* (London: Hutchinson, 1993), 372. See also T. Taylor, *The Breaking Wave: The German Defeat in the Summer of 1940* (London: Weidenfeld and Nicholson, 1967). The Italian interest in air power went back to 1911–12. During the war against the Turks in Libya, the Italians had used aircraft for military purposes for the first time in history.

60. Cited in Knightley, *The First Casualty*, 128.

61. Ibid., 153. For Lawrence's response, see Desmond Stewart, *T. E. Lawrence* (London: Paladin, 1979) 175–6.

62. Anderson, *Glass Warriors*, 112.

63. Knightley, *The First Casualty*, 156. See also Herbert Mathews, *Eyewitness in Abyssinia* (London: Secker and Warburg, 1937).

64. Cited in Nicholas Rankin, *Telegram from Guernica* (London: Faber and Faber, 2003), 35.

65. Cited in Anderson, *The Glass Warriors*, 121.

66. Knightley, *The First Casualty*, 170.

67. Anderson, *Glass Warriors*, 122.

68. Hugh Thomas, *The Spanish Civil War* (London: Pelican, 1986), 346–8.

69. Anderson, *Glass Warriors*, 124. See also Richard Whelan, *Robert Capa* (Lincoln: University of Nebraska Press, 1994) 97; Robert Giles, Robert W. Snyder and Lisa DeLisle, *Profiles in Journalistic Courage* (Edison,

NJ: Transaction, 2001) 40; John Taylor, *Body Horror: Photojournalism, Catastrophe and War* (Manchester: Manchester University Press, 1998), 58; David Thomson "An Image Greater than Its Truth," September 27, 2003: http://www.smh.com.au/articles/2003/09/26/1064083175 656.html?from=storyrhs.

70. Royle, *War Report*, 127.

71. Knightley, *The First Casualty*, 181.

72. George Orwell, *Looking Back on the Spanish Civil War* (New York: Mercury, 1961), 211. For a useful summary, see "Fascism and the English," in Fred Inglis, *People's Witness: The Journalist in Modern Politics* (New Haven, CT: Yale University, 2002), 125–47.

73. Cited in Royle, *War Report*, 139.

74. For a useful summary of the debate, see Knightley, *The First Casualty*, 187–93. See also Thomas, *The Spanish Civil War*, 626–7. An excellent update of the debate can be found in Rankin, *Telegram from Guernica*, 114-47.

75. John Hooper, *The Spaniards* (Harmondsworth, UK: Penguin, 1987), 22.

76. Knightley, *The First Casualty*, 200

77. Royle, *War Report*, 140.

78. Norman Stone, "Too Keen on Saving Private Ryan," *Sunday Times* (London), News Review, August 2, 1998.

79. A. J. P. Taylor, *The Origins of the Second World War* (Harmondsworth, UK: Penguin, 1964); see also John Keegan's analysis, *The Second World War* (London: Hutchinson, 1989), 10–30.

80. Richard Overy, "Total War II" in Townshend, *The Oxford History of Modern War*, 144.

81. Ibid., 148.

82. *Young and Jesser, The Media and the Military,* section titled "World War II: More of the Same," 37–42.

83. Angus Calder, *The People's War: Britain 1939–45* (London: Panther, 1971), 584.

84. Ibid., 586. Colonel M. R. N. Bray, "The Relationship between the Government and the Media in Time of War," (M. Phil thesis, Downing College, Cambridge, 1984), 43. Bray quotes Brendan Bracken in the House of Common on censors: "The reasons they are like mules is that they have no pride in their ancestry and they have no hope of posterity."

85. Cited in Richard Havers, *Here is the News: The BBC and the Second World War* (Stroud: Sutton, 2007), ix.

86. Cited in Lande, *Dispatches from the Front,* 225–7.

87. Nicholas John Cull, *Selling War: The British Propaganda Campaign Against American "Neutrality" in World War II* (Oxford: Oxford University Press, 1995), 3. See also Paul Moorcraft, review of *Selling War, Journal of Strategic Studies*, June 1998, vol. 21, no. 2, 108–10.

88. Robert L. McLaughlin and Sally E. Parry, *We'll Always Have the Movies:*

*American Cinema During World War II* (Lexington: University Press of Kentucky, 2005).

89. S. P. MacKenzie, *British War Films, 1939–45* (London: Hambledon and London, 2001).
90. See Tom Pocock's autobiography, *Alan Moorehead* (London: Pimlico, 1990).
91. Royle, *War Report*, 148.
92. Richard Collier, *The Warcos: The War Correspondents of World War II* (London: Weidenfeld and Nicholson, 1989), 47.
93. Cited in Royle, *War Report*, 148.
94. Ibid., 150. Wilmot traveled with a sound recordist. And transport was needed for bulky equipment weighing five hundred pounds; by 1944, the BBC was using lightweight recording machines which weighed under fifty pounds.
95. Cited in Collier, *The Warcos*, 86.
96. John Hughes-Wilson, *Military Intelligence Blunders and Cover-Ups* (London: Robinson, 2004), 60.
97. Fletcher Pratt, quoted in Knightley, *The First Casualty*, 260.
98. Clare Boothe, cited in Collier, *The Warcos*, 110.
99. Pocock, *Alan Moorehead,* 183.
100. Collier, *The Warcos*, 158.
101. Ibid., 163.
102. Ibid., 173.
103. Ibid., 179.
104. The phrase is war artist John Groth's, cited in ibid., 187.
105. BBC, *War Report: From D-Day to VE Day* (London: BBC, 1994), 34.
106. See Vasily Grossman, *A Writer at War: Vasily Grossman with the Red Army 1941-1945*, edited and translated by Antony Beevor and Luba Vinogradova, (London: Pimlico, 2006).
107. Khaldei took perhaps the best-known picture from the Russian side of the war. For a while he was a Soviet favorite, taking portraits of the party elite. But in 1948 he lost his job—either because he was Jewish or because he had expressed favorable opinions about Tito; either was an offense that could lead to firing in the time of severe Stalinist paranoia.
108. Anderson, *Glass Warriors*, 145–8.
109. Morris, *Farewell the Trumpets*, 453.
110. Knightley, *The First Casualty*, 317.
111. Young and Jesser, *The Media and the Military*, 44.

## CHAPTER 3: THE COLD WAR (OF WORDS)

1. Cited in Trevor Royle, *War Report: The War Correspondent's View of Battle from the Crimea to the Falklands* (Edinburgh: Mainstream, 1987), 171.
2. Martin Walker, *The Cold War* (London: Vintage, 1994), 5. Walker was the American bureau chief for the *Guardian* when he wrote this book.

3. Or the "anti-fascist protection barrier," as its humorless architects dubbed it. Nikita Khruschev, the Soviet leader, liked to boast that the city was "the testicles of the West: every time I want to make the West scream, I squeeze on Berlin." President John Kennedy conceded, however, that "a wall is a hell of a lot better than a war." See Frederick Taylor, *The Berlin Wall: 13 August 1961–9 November 1989* (London: Bloomsbury, 2006).

4. Duncan Anderson, *Glass Warriors: The Camera at War* (London: Collins, 2005), 151.

5. Cited in Royle, *War Report*, 177.

6. Anderson, *Glass Warriors*, 152–3.

7. Royle, *War Report*, 187.

8. Ibid., 189–96; Tom Hopkinson, *Of This Our Time* (London: Hutchinson, 1984). When Hopkinson edited *Drum*, he secured exclusive eyewitness accounts and photographs of the 1960 Sharpeville massacre in South Africa. Active in journalism training in Africa and the UK in particular, he helped to set up the pioneering Centre for Journalism Studies at Cardiff University.

9. I. F. Stone, *The Hidden History of the Korean War 1950–1951* (New York: Monthly Review Press, 1952).

10. Colonel Lewis B. "Chesty" Puller to reporter Keyes Beech in "This Was No Retreat," *Chicago Daily News*, December 11, 1950, in Nathaniel Lande, *Dispatches from the Front: A History of the American War Correspondent* (Oxford: Oxford University Press, 1966), 277.

11. Samuel Hynes, *The Soldier's Tale: Bearing Witness to Modern War* (London: Pimlico, 1997), xiii–iv.

12. Richard Crockatt, *The Fifty Years War: The United States and the Soviet Union in World Politics, 1941–1991* (London: Routledge, 1995), 106.

13. Max Hastings, *The Korean War* (London: Michael Joseph, 1988), 409.

14. Henry Kissinger, *Diplomacy* (New York: Touchstone, 1994), 491.

15. See Michael Hickey for a very readable account of the British perspective: *The Korean War: The West Confronts Communism 1950–1953* (London: Murray, 1999).

16. Anderson, *Glass Warriors*, 158.

17. Brian Lapping, *End of Empire* (London: Paladin, 1989), 335.

18. Robert Harris, *Sunday Times*, August 12, 1990, cited in W. Scott Lucas, *Divided We Stand: Britain, the US and the Suez Crisis* (London: Hodder and Stoughton, 1991), ix.

19. Lucas, *Divided We Stand*, 157. For a classic example of straightforward but effective reporting of the initial landing, see report by Donald Edgar of the London *Daily Express*, "The Suez Invasion" in Jon E. Lewis, ed. *The Mammoth Book of War Correspondents* (London: Robinson, 2001), 450–54.

20. See Barry Turner, *Suez* (London: Hodder, 2006); William Roger Louis Jr.,

*Ends of Imperialism: The Scramble for Empire, Suez and Decolonization* (London: Tauris, 2006); Martin Woollacott, *After Suez* (London: Tauris, 2006).

21. David Rennie, "The Hungarian Who Could Have Started World War III," The *Spectator*, October 21, 2006, 16.

22. See Philip M. Taylor, "Desert Storm Blowback: Psychological Operations in Operation Iraqi Freedom" in Lars Nicander and Magnus Ranstorp, eds., *Terrorism in the Information Age—New Frontiers?* (Swedish National Defence College, Forsvarchogskolan, Stockholm, 2004), 108–28.

23. Anderson, *Glass Warriors*, 163.

24. Cited in Fred Inglis, *People's Witness: The Journalist in Modern Politics* (New Haven, CT: Yale University Press, 2002), 226.

25. Quoted in Alistair Horne, *A Savage War of Peace: Algeria 1954–1962* (Harmondsworth: Penguin, 1985), 60.

26. The French collectively tried to blank out the humiliation, and the historical truths, of the occupation. The impression created was not of a small minority, but almost the whole country resisting the Nazis. A 1969 film, a four-and-a-half-hour epic called, in English, "The Sorrow and the Pity," powerfully challenged the self-deceiving myth.

27. Peter Young and Peter Jesser, *The Media and the Military: From the Crimea to Desert Strike* (Basingstoke: Macmillan, 1997), 56–60.

28. Lou di Marco, "Losing the Moral Compass: Torture and Guerre Révolutionnaire in the Algerian War," *Parameters*, Summer 2006.

29. Lapping, *End of Empire*, 220.

30. Royle, *War Report*, 202.

31. Anderson, *Glass Warriors*, 161.

32. Charles Allen, *The Savage Wars of Peace: Soldiers' Voices 1945–1989* (London: Future, 1991), 120.

33. Lapping, *End of Empire*, 498.

34. Cited in Bernard Porter, "How Did They Get Away with It?" *London Review of Books*, vol. 27, no. 5, March 3, 2005.

35. David Anderson, *Histories of the Hanged: Britain's Dirty War in Kenya and the End of Empire* (London: Weidenfeld, 2004); Caroline Elkins, *Britain's Gulag: The Brutal End of Empire in Kenya* (New York: Henry Holt, 2004).

36. Porter, "How Did They Get Away with It?"

37. Allen, *The Savage Wars*, 167.

38. Lapping, *End of Empire*, 370.

39. Robert Taber, *War of the Flea* (Washington, DC: Potomac Books, 2002).

40. Cited by Charles Townshend, "People's War" in Townshend, *The Oxford History of Modern War*, 194.

41. Gary Webb, *Dark Alliance: The CIA, the Contras and the Crack Cocaine Explosion* (New York: Seven Stories Press, 1999).

42. The phrase is General Bernard E. Trainor's.
43. (Lt. Col.) John Hughes-Wilson, *Military Intelligence Blunders and Cover-ups* (London: Robinson, 2004), 206.
44. A U.S. POW cited in Lande, *Despatches from the Front*, 309.
45. London *Daily Mirror* reporter Donald Wise, quoted in Tim Bowden, *One Crowded Hour, Neil Davis, Combat Cameraman, 1934–85* (North Ryde, N.S.W.: Imprint, 1990), 175.
46. Cited in Inglis, *People's Witness*, 96.
47. John Pilger, *Heroes* (London: Pan, 1987), 190.
48. Richard Beeston, *Looking for Trouble: The Life and Times of a Foreign Correspondent* (London: Brassey's, 1997), 104.
49. McNamara's first apologia was his *In Retrospect: The Tragedy and Lessons of Vietnam* (New York: Vintage Books, 1996); see also his *Argument Without End: In Search of Answers to the Vietnam Tragedy* (New York: Public Affairs, 1999). It was interesting to speculate whether a similar tome would emerge from the secretary of defense during the 2003 Iraq invasion.
50. Frederik Logevall, *Choosing War: The Lost Chance for Peace and the Escalation of War in Vietnam* (Berkeley: University of California Press, 2001); Michael Lind, *Vietnam The Necessary War: A Re-interpretation of America's Most Disastrous Military Conflict* (New York: Touchstone, 2002); Lewis Sorley, *A Better War: The Unexamined Victories and the Final Tragedy of America's Last Years in Vietnam* (New York: Harcourt Brace, 1999).
51. Michael Herr, *Dispatches* (London: Picador, 1979), 54.
52. Peter Arnett, *Live from the Battlefield* (London: Corgi, 1994), 91.
53. Ibid., 113.
54. Max Hastings, *Going to the Wars* (Basingstoke: Macmillan, 2000), 83.
55. Cited in Inglis, *People's Witness*, 244.
56. See, for example, Kevin Williams, "The Light at the End of the Tunnel: Mass Media, Public Opinion and the Vietnam War" in John Eldridge, ed. *Getting the Message* (London: Routledge, 1993).
57. For a summary of Griffiths's work, see Russell Miller, *Magnum* (London: Secker and Warburg, 1997).
58. Gloria Emerson, "Remembering Women War Correspondents" in Tad Bartimus et al., *War Torn: Stories of War from the Women Reporters Who Covered Vietnam* (New York: Random House, 2002), xx.
59. Knightley, *The First Casualty: The War Correspondent as Hero, Propagandist and Myth Maker* (London: Quartet, 1982), 349–50.
60. Arnett, *Live from the Battlefield*, 257.
61. David Halberstam, *The Best and Brightest* (New York: Ballantine Books, 1972).
62. Susan L. Carruthers, *The Media at War* (Basingstoke: Macmillan, 2000), 151.
63. Young and Jesser, *The Media and the Military*, 80.

64. The phrase is *Time* magazine Jonathan Larsen's, cited in Knightley, *The First Casualty*, 388.
65. Daniel C. Hallin, *The "Uncensored War": Vietnam and the Media* (Oxford: Oxford University Press, 1986), 213.
66. "The Media, the War in Vietnam and Political Support: A Critique of the Thesis of an Oppositional Media" in Daniel C. Hallin, *We Keep America on Top of the World—Television Journalism and the Public Sphere* (London: Routledge, 1993).
67. William M. Hammond, *Reporting Vietnam: Media and Military at War* (University Press of Kansas, 2000), 290–6.
68. John Keegan, "Bush is Wrong: Iraq is Not Vietnam," *Daily Telegraph*, October 20, 2006.
69. Robert Fox, *Eye Witness Falklands* (London: Methuen, 1982), 9.
70. House of Commons Defence Committee (hereafter HCDC), 1982, 1.
71. Robert Harris, *Gotcha: The Media, the Government and the Falklands Crisis* (London: Faber and Faber, 1983), 20.
72. D. Morrison and H. Tumber, *Journalists at War: The Dynamics of News Reporting During the Falklands Conflict* (London: Sage, 1988), 1–5.
73. Ibid., 5.
74. Brian Hanrahan and Robert Fox, *"I Counted Them All Out and I Counted Them All Back": The Battle for the Falklands* (BBC, 1982), 19.
75. See the *Sunday Times* Insight Team, *The Falklands War: The Full Story* (London: Sphere, 1982), 144-5.
76. HCDC, 1982, 43. In fact there were some still photographs taken of the surrender by a soldier who was present.
77. Harris, *Gotcha*, 57.
78. Morrison and Tumber, *Journalists at War*, 99.
79. Fox, *Eye Witness Falklands*, 75.
80. Martin Howard, "Managing Media: The MoD View after September 11," 2002 Rolls Royce lecture, Cardiff University.
81. Hansard (Commons), April 4, 1982.
82. The *Sun*, April 8, 1982.
83. HCDC, 1982.
84. Hughes-Wilson, *Military Intelligence Blunders and Cover-ups*, 260–307.
85. For a poignant naval view of the media, and the war in general, see David Tinker, *A Message from the Falklands* (Harmondsworth, UK: Penguin, 1983). Lieutenant Tinker, RN, died three days before the end of the war. The *Observer* called Tinker "the nearest we are likely to get to a Falklands Wilfred Owen."
86. For a useful study of how opposing voices were stilled, see Glasgow University Media Group, *War and Peace News* (Maidenhead: Open University, 1985). Also, D. Mercer, G. Mungham, and K. Williams, *The Fog of War: The Media on the Battlefield* (London: Heinemann, 1987). For a very different perspective, see the views of the Falklanders portrayed

vividly in Graham Bound, *Falkland Islanders at War* (Barnsley: Pen and Sword, 2002).

87. See, for example, Peter Jenkins, "Patriotism Has Worked Its Old Magic," *The Guardian*, June 16, 1982.

88. Knightley, *The First Casualty* (2004 edition), 478.

89. Ibid., 481.

90. Max Hastings, *Going to the Wars*, 384.

91. Young and Jesser, *The Media and the Military*, 130.

92. *Washington Post*, October 29, 1983, cited in Young and Jesser, *The Media and the Military*, 131.

93. Greg McLaughlin, *The War Correspondent* (London: Pluto, 2002), 85.

94. Jane E. Kirtley, "The Eye of the Sandstorm: The Erosion of First Amendment Principles in Wartime," *Government Information Quarterly*, vol. 9, no. 4, 473–90.

95. W. Lowther, "Counting the Hidden Cost: Media Distortions in the Panama Invasion 1989," *McLeans*, January 22, 1990.

96. See Richard Keeble, *Secret State, Silent Press: New Militarism, the Gulf and Modern Images of Warfare* (Eastleigh: John Libbey, 1997), 42–54.

97. William Boot, "Wading Around in the Panama Pool," *Columbia Journalism Review*, March/April 1990. William Boot was the pseudonym of Christopher Hanson of the *Seattle Post-Intelligence*.

98. Young and Jesser, *The Media and the Military*, 153.

99. Colin Powell, *A Soldier's Way* (London: Hutchinson, 1995), 413, cited in Young and Jesser, *The Media and the Military*, 155.

100. Young and Jesser, *The Media and the Military*, 157.

101. Mark Hertsgaard, *On Bended Knee: The Press and the Reagan Presidency* (New York: Farrar, Straus, Giroux, 1988).

102. Jonathan Mermin, *Debating War and Peace: Media Coverage of U.S. Intervention in the Post-Vietnam Era* (Princeton, NJ: Princeton University Press, 1999), 36–65.

103. For a lively account of the invasion, see Bob Shacochis, *The Immaculate Invasion* (London: Bloomsbury, 1999).

104. See Frances Stonor Saunders, *Who Paid the Piper? The CIA and the Cultural Cold War* (London: Granta, 1999).

105. Townshend, *The Oxford Modern History of War*, 175–6.

106. Walker, *The Cold War*, 347.

107. Ibid., 351.

108. David Pryce-Jones, *The War That Never Was: The Fall of the Soviet Empire, 1985–1991* (London: Phoenix, 1995), 437.

109. Robert Skidelsky, *The World After Communism* (Basingstoke: Macmillan, 1995), 195.

110. Kissinger, *Diplomacy*, 835–6.

111. Michael Burleigh, *Sacred Causes: Religion and Politics from the European Dictators to Al Qaeda* (London: HarperPress, 2006).

## CHAPTER 4: AFRICAN "SIDESHOWS "?

1. Susan D. Moeller, *Compassion Fatigue: How the Media Sell Disease, Famine, War and Death* (New York: Routledge, 1999), 312.
2. Michael Ignatieff, *The Warrior's Honor: Ethnic War and the Modern Conscience*, (London: Chatto and Windus, 1988), 25.
3. Graham Handcock, *Lords of Poverty: The Power, Prestige and Corruption of the International Aid Business*, (New York: Atlantic Monthly Press, 1992).
4. The London *Times* leader "Playing at Peace," July 17, 1992.
5. Jonathan Benthall, *Disasters, Relief and the Media* (London: Tauris, 1993), 219.
6. Mort Rosenblum, "Lack of Information or Lack of Will?" in Ed Giradet, ed. *Somalia, Rwanda and Beyond: The Role of the International Media in Wars and Humanitarian Crises* (Dublin: Crosslines Global Report, 1995), 79. See also his *Who Stole the News? Why Can't We Keep Up with What Happens in the World and What Can We Do About It?* (New York: John Wiley, 1993). Rosenblum had worked for Associated Press for thirty years.
7. Frank Barton, *The Press of Africa: Persecution and Perseverance* (New York: Africana, 1979), ix.
8. L. J. Martin, "Africa" in J. C. Merrill, *Global Journalism* (London: Longman, 1983).
9. Al J. Venter, "Why Portugal Lost Its African Wars" in Al J. Venter, ed., *Challenge* (Gibraltar: Ashanti, 1990).
10. Coverage of these events led to the title of Edward Behr's famous book, *Anyone Here Been Raped and Speaks English?* (London: New English Library, 1982), 136. "Teddy" Behr ascribed the infelicity to a BBC reporter in the Congo.
11. Anthony Clayton, *Frontiersmen: Warfare in Africa Since 1950* (London: University College of London, 1990), 96.
12. Ibid., 98.
13. Frederick Forsyth, *The Biafra Story: The Making of an African Legend* (Harmondsworth, UK: Penguin, 1969). This book marked Forsyth's transition from journalist to author. See also Martin Meredith, "Nigeria's Civil War" in his *The First Dance of Freedom: Black Africa in the Postwar Era* (London: Abacus, 1985). And for a useful snapshot of TV coverage, see Sandy Gall, *Don't Worry About the Money Now* (London: New English Library, 1988), 290–307.
14. See Christopher Hope, *White Boy Running* (London: Secker and Warburg, 1988), 281, and Anthony Sampson, *Black and Gold* (London: Hodder and Stoughton), 15. Also, Paul Moorcraft, *Guns and Poses: Travels with An Occasional War Correspondent* (Guildford: Millstream, 2001), 9. Moorcraft was vice-chairman of the press club (The Quill Club) which was the watering hole for Western correspondents in Salisbury (Harare).

See also his *A Short Thousand Years: The End of Rhodesia's Rebellion* (Salisbury: Galaxie, 1979); and, with Peter McLaughlin, *The Rhodesian War: A Military History* (Barnsley, UK: Pen and Sword, 2008), and "Rhodesia" in Paul Moorcraft, *African Nemesis: War and Revolution in Southern Africa, 1945–2010* (London: Brassey's, Ltd, 1990). A useful summary of the war can be found in Paul Moorcraft, "Rhodesia's War of Independence," *History Today*, vol. 40, September 1990.

15. Coauthor Moorcraft interviews, 1979–81, with Ken Flower, head of the Rhodesian Central Intelligence Organisation. Flower said that a British Marine brass band and a company of paratroopers would have done the trick—the few South African hotheads in the Rhodesian Light Infantry would have been sorted out by loyalists. White Rhodesians were generally intensely loyal to the Crown but they despised the Labour government. For a detailed account of intelligence issues, see Paul Moorcraft, "The Fall of the Republic: The Collapse of White Power in Rhodesia, 1976–1980" (unpublished doctoral thesis, Pretoria, University of South Africa, 1988).

16. For a comment on Cecil's death, see Ed Harriman, *Hack: Home Truths About Foreign News* (London: Zed, 1987), 124–5. Richard Cecil was a colleague and squash partner of coauthor Paul Moorcraft, who interviewed witnesses of the incident. Cecil sometimes carried a gun, as did many of the correspondents, even when working for liberal British newspapers. Despite much discussion of the issue and the refusal of some journalists to bear arms (Moorcraft worked inter alia for *Time* magazine, which did not allow the carrying of weapons), many felt it necessary to be armed outside the towns. The guerrillas rarely asked for press cards before opening fire on whites.

17. Unlike South Africa, blacks could vote on a restricted franchise and had limited seats in parliament. In 1979 universal franchise was introduced. The separate roll for whites was removed after two general elections, as per the Lancaster House agreement.

18. For a perceptive if rather languid account of the mood of whites at the end of the war, see Denis Hills, *The Last Days of White Rhodesia* (London: Chatto and Windus, 1981). For a brilliantly written but also highly personalized bestseller of this period, see Alexandra Fuller, *Don't Let's Go to the Dogs Tonight: An African Childhood* (New York: Random House, 2001).

19. For a lively account of foreign correspondents in Rhodesia, see Chris Munnion, "Secrets of the Sergeants' Mess" in his *Banana Sunday: Datelines from Africa* (Rivonia: William Waterman, 1993). Munnion, who worked for the London *Daily Telegraph*, was rightly considered the doyen of foreign hacks in this period.

20. Coauthor Moorcraft interview, Salisbury, 1979.

21. Coauthor Moorcraft interview, Johannesburg, 1981.

22. Jeremy Brickhill, "Zimbabwe's Poisoned Legacy: Secret War in Southern Africa," *Covert Action Quarterly* 43 (Winter 1992–93), 58–60.

23. Coauthor Moorcraft interview, Salisbury, 1979.

24. Various discussions with coauthor Moorcraft, 2001–5.

25. David Martin and Phyllis Johnson, *The Struggle for Zimbabwe* (London: Faber and Faber, 1981).

26. Martin Meredith, *The Past Is Another Country*, (London: André Deutsch, 1979). David Caute produced a more literary account in his *Under the Skin: The Death of White Rhodesia* (London: Lane, 1983). A comprehensive summary of white attitudes is in Peter Godwin and Ian Hancock, *Rhodesians Never Die: The Impact of War and Political Change on White Rhodesia c. 1970–1980* (Oxford: Oxford University Press, 1993). Godwin was a Rhodesian-born journalist who wrote for the London *Sunday Times* and later worked for the BBC. He also wrote a minor classic on his childhood in the country: *Mukiwa* (London: Picador, 1996).

27. Phillip Knightley, *The First Casualty: The War Correspondent as Hero and Myth-Maker from the Crimea to Iraq* (Baltimore: The John Hopkins University Press, 2004), 471.

28. See Elaine Windrich, *The Mass Media in the Struggle for Zimbabwe* (Gwelo: Mambo, 1981); and Julie Frederikse, *None But Ourselves: Masses vs. Media in the Making of Zimbabwe* (London: Currey, 1982).

29. Sadly, and ironically, Ian Mills died the day coauthor Moorcraft wrote this sentence; he had intended to send the veteran journalist this section for his comments.

30. See Richard West's *Diamonds and a Necklace* (London: Hodder and Stoughton, 1989).

31. Robert Blake, *A History of Rhodesia* (London: Methuen, 1977), 390.

32. For details, see Mervyn Rees and Chris Day, *Muldergate: The Story of the Info Scandal* (Johannesburg: Macmillan, 1980).

33. The phrase is South African journalist Rian Malan's in his "Not All the News Is Fit to Print," *Frontline*, December 1989, 9.

34. Quoted in ibid.

35. According to Elaine Potter's thesis, the Afrikaans-language newspapers acted as a sort of a mild internal opposition as well as a mobilizer for Afrikaner nationalism (Elaine Potter, *The Press as Opposition* [London: Chatto and Windus, 1975]). Hachten and Gifford argued later that Pretoria had launched a "total onslaught" on the media (W. A. Hachten and C. A. Giffard, *The Press and Apartheid* [Madison: University of Wisconsin, 1984]). Radical writers such as Ruth and Keyan Tomaselli maintained that all white-owned media, as tools essentially of capitalist mining houses, offered only cosmetic opposition to apartheid: R. Tomaselli, K. Tomaselli and J. Muller, *The Press in South Africa* [London: Currey, 1987]).

36. See in particular his *South African Dispatches* (Harmondsworth, UK: Penguin, 1986), especially 166–8.

37. For a recent South African perspective on military influence, see Hilton Hamann's *Days of the Generals*, (Cape Town: Zebra 2001). Hamann was the military correspondent of the Johannesburg *Sunday Times*.

38. For a comprehensive summary of all these wars, see Moorcraft, *African Nemesis*. Moorcraft made a number of TV documentaries while traveling in territory controlled by Renamo, the main anti-Marxist rebel movement in Mozambique. The best surveys of the destabilization wars were Joseph Hanlon, *Apartheid's Second Front* (Harmondsworth, UK: Penguin, 1986) and *Beggar Your Neighbours* (London: Catholic Institute for International Relations, 1986). See also Phyllis Johnson and David Martin, eds. *Destructive Engagement* (Harare: Zimbabwe Publishing, 1986) and their *Apartheid Terrorism: The Destabilization Report* (London: Commonwealth/Currey, 1989).

39. Fred Bridgland, *The War for Africa: 12 Months That Transformed a Continent* (Gibraltar: Ashanti, 1990); Helmoed Römer-Heitman, *War in Angola: The Final South African Phase* (Gibraltar: Ashanti, 1990). For an overall assessment of the main battle at Cuito Cuanavale (1987–88), see Greg Mills and David Williams, *Seven Battles That Shaped South Africa*, (Cape Town: Tafelberg, 2006), 167–88.

40. See his obituary in the London *Telegraph*, November 2, 2006.

41. Quoted in the South African *Financial Mail*, November 8, 1985.

42. Joseph Lelyveld, *Move Your Shadow* (London: Abacus, 1987). Rian Malan, *My Traitor's Heart: Blood and Bad Dreams: A South African Explores the Madness in His Country, His Tribe and Himself* (London: Bodley Head, 1990). Malan and coauthor Moorcraft were part of a small coterie of writers who contributed to *Frontline*, an eccentrically antigovernment magazine edited by the equally eccentric, though charming, Denis Beckett. Beckett was a compulsive fiddler with others' prose, spoke in a strange mix of Afrikaans, English, and street-*taal* (language) and often forgot to pay his writers. Another excellent book was by Allister Sparks, *The Mind of South Africa: The Story of the Rise and Fall of Apartheid* (London: Mandarin, 1991). Sparks was the former editor of the *Rand Daily Mail*.

43. Max du Preez and Jacques Pauw, "Exposing Apartheid's Death Squads, 1988–94" in John Pilger, ed., *Tell Me No Lies: Investigative Journalism and its Triumphs* (London: Vintage, 2005), 191–213.

44. *The Bang Bang Club: Snapshots from a Hidden War* (London: Arrow, 2001).

45. Ibid., 261.

46. For a full account of this incident, see Tom Carver, "End of the Right" in *The Best of "From Our Own Correspondent"* (London: Tauris, 1994), 12–14.

47. One of the best accounts of this period is Patti Waldmeir's *Anatomy of a Miracle* (Harmondsworth: Penguin, 1997); see also John Simpson's *Dispatches from the Barricades* (London: Hutchinson, 1994), 256–87.

For a black journalist's perspective, see Rich Mkhondo, *Reporting South Africa* (London: Currey, 1993). For an academic survey, see Gordon S. Jackson, *Breaking Story: The South African Press* (Boulder, CO: Westview, 1993).

48. Conversation with coauthor Moorcraft, Johannesburg, 1994.

49. http://www.guardian.co.uk/rwanda/story/0,14451,1183896,00.html. Lindsey Hilsum went on to become the multiple-award-winning international editor for Channel 4 News in London. See also Lindsey Hilsum, "Where is Kigali?" *Granta,* 1995, vol. 51, 145–79.

50. Donatella Lorch, "Genocide versus Heartstrings" in Giradet, *Somalia, Rwanda and Beyond,* 104.

51. http://news.bbc.co.uk/1/hi/programmes/panorama/3577575.stm. Steve Bradshaw produced a BBC Panorama program, *When Good Men Do Nothing,* to commemorate the tenth anniversary of the genocide. (The 2005 film, *Hotel Rwanda,* based on a true story, added to the Western guilt complex.)

52. Ibid.

53. Ibid.

54. Fergal Keane, *Season of Blood: A Rwandan Journey* (Harmondsworth, UK: Penguin, 1996), 186.

55. Moeller, *Compassion Fatigue,* 143.

56. Peter Young and Peter Jesser, *The Media and the Military: From the Crimea to Desert Strike* (Basingstoke, UK: Macmillan, 1997), 213.

57. S. Livingston and T. Eachus, "Humanitarian Crises and U.S. Foreign Policy: Somalia and the CNN effect reconsidered," *Political Communication,* 1995, vol. 12, 413–29.

58. Susan L. Carruthers, *The Media at War* (Basingstoke, UK: Macmillan, 2000), 220.

59. Moeller, *Compassion Fatigue,* 142.

60. Young and Jesser, *The Media and the Military,* 221–2.

61. Cited in Moeller, *Compassion Fatigue,* 146.

62. Carruthers, *The Media at War,* 223.

63. Johanna Neuman, *Lights, Camera, War* (New York: St. Martin's, 2006), 21.

64. See Andrew Natsios, "Illusions of Influence: The CNN Effect in Complex Emergencies" in R. Rotberg and T. Weiss, eds. *From Massacres to Genocide: The Media, Public Policy and Humanitarian Crises* (Washington, DC: Brookings Institution, 1996), 163. See also Nik Gowing, "Real-time Television Coverage of Armed Conflicts and Diplomatic Crises: Does It Pressure or Distort Foreign Policy Decisions?" (Harvard, Joan Shorenstein Barone Center, Working Paper 94, 1.)

65. Greg McLaughlin, *The War Correspondent* (London: Pluto, 2002), 147–8; C. Jensen, *Censored: The News That Didn't Make the News and Why* (New York: Four Walls, 1994), 234–8.

66. Neuman, *Lights, Camera, War,* 229. L. Minear, C. Scott and T. Weiss, *The*

*News Media, Civil War and Humanitarian Action* (Boulder, CO: Lynne Reinner, 1996), 55.

67. Moeller, *Compassion Fatigue,* 154.

68. Paul Moorcraft, http://www.guardian.co.uk/sudan/story/0,,1747924,00.html. Jonathan Steele, "A Brutal Civil War But Not Genocide," *Guardian,* Sept 18, 2006. http://commentisfree.guardian.co.uk/jonathan_steele/2006/09/sorry_george_clooney_but_the_1.html.

69. Sam Kiley, "My Agony and Some Ecstasy in Reporting Africa," *Times* (London), September 26, 1998.

## CHAPTER 5: EUROPE'S INTRA-STATE CONFLICTS

1. Duncan Anderson, *Glass Warriors: The Camera at War* (London: Collins, 2005), 187. See also photojournalist Paul Harris, *Somebody Else's War: Reports from the Balkan Frontline* (Stevenage: Spa, 1992).

2. Gen. Lewis MacKenzie, the Canadian commander of UNPROFOR, put it slightly differently: "Dealing with Bosnia is a little like dealing with three serial killers. One has killed 15. One has killed 10. One has killed five. Do we help the one who has only killed five?" Testimony before the U.S. House Armed Services Committee, May 25, 1993, 41.

3. Misha Glenny, *The Fall of Yugoslavia* (Harmondsworth: Penguin, 1992), 31. The Serbs were guilty of intentionally killing a large number of journalists. Anthony Loyd of the London *Times,* worried about being captured and killed by Serb forces, said: "The Serbs hated what the foreign press did almost as much as the foreign press hated what the Serbs did." Anthony Loyd, *My War Gone By, I Miss It So* (New York: Penguin, 2001), 308.

4. Mark Thompson, *A Paper House: The Ending of Yugoslavia* (London: Vintage, 1992), 198. The simplistic critique of Serb's culpability was analyzed, consciously from the left, by Diana Johnstone in *Fool's Crusade: Yugoslavia, NATO and Western Delusions* (London: Pluto, 2002).

5. Anderson, *Glass Warriors,* 188.

6. Mark Urban, *UK Eyes Alpha: The Inside Story of British Intelligence* (London: Faber and Faber, 1996), 213.

7. The coauthor includes himself in the pusillanimous category of those who did not stay for the whole siege. See Paul Moorcraft, *Guns and Poses: Travels with an Occasional War Correspondent* (Guildford: Millstream, 2001), 321–27. See also Paul Moorcraft "The Wars of Wishful Thinking: an Interim Report on NATO's Balkan Campaigns," *New Zealand International Review,* July/August 1999, 18–22.

8. Janine di Giovanni, *The Quick and the Dead* (London: Phoenix, 1995), 7. Another excellent journalist's account is by Roger Cohen of the *New York Times: Hearts Grown Brutal: Sagas of Sarajevo* (New York: Random House, 1998).

9. Frequently made comments by locals to coauthor Moorcraft during his time in the Balkans.

10. Ed Vulliamy, *Seasons in Hell: Understanding Bosnia's War* (New York: St Martin's Press, 1994), 5. Perhaps the most accessible historical context for the Bosnian war can be found in Noel Malcolm, *Bosnia: A Short History* (London: Macmillan, 1994). Malcolm worked for the *Spectator* and later the *Daily Telegraph*.

11. A useful survey can be found in Mark Thompson, *Forging War: The Media in Serbia, Croatia, Bosnia and Hercegovina* (Luton: University of Luton, 1999).

12. See Tom Gjelten, *Sarajevo Daily: A City and Its Newspaper under Siege* (New York: HarperCollins, 1995).

13. For example, Roy Gutman of *Newsday*, whose dispatches were published as *Witness to Genocide* (Basingstoke: Macmillan, 1993).

14. Miles Hudson and John Stanier, *War and the Media* (Stroud: Sutton, 1997), 288.

15. Michael Nicholson, *Natasha's Story* (London: Macmillan, 1994).

16. John Swain, "The Army Hasn't Captured Us War Reporters Yet," *Sunday Times* (London), March 26, 2000.

17. See David Rohde, *Endgame: The Betrayal and Fall of Srebrenica, Europe's Worst Massacre Since World War II* (New York: Farrar, Straus, Giroux, 1997).

18. For a development of this theme, see Charles William Maynes, "Squandering Triumph: The West Botched the Post-Cold War World," *Foreign Affairs*, January–February 1999, 16–22. Maynes is a former editor of the journal.

19. Gen. Sir Michael Rose, *Fighting for Peace* (London: Harvill, 1998), 75. For another soldier's perspective, see Milos Stankovic, *Trusted Mole* (London: HarperCollins, 2000). Stankovic was one of the three fluent Serbo-Croat speakers in the British army. He acted as Rose's translator. Besides saving many Bosnian lives, he was awarded medals for gallantry, and then accused, unjustly, under the Official Secrets Act, of being a Serb spy. He was arrested while starting his course at the Joint Services Command and Staff College on October 16, 1997. The JSCSC had just opened for the first time and his arrest by the Ministry of Defence police caused quite a stir in the college and the army. Coauthor Moorcraft was teaching in the next seminar room at the time of the arrest. Stankovic was acquitted. See also Colonel Bob Stewart, *Broken Lives: A Personal View of the Bosnian Conflict* (London: HarperCollins, 1994). Stewart was the British commander in central Bosnia between October 1992 and May 1993.

20. Martin Bell, *In Harm's Way* (Harmondsworth: Penguin, 1996), 29.

21. James Gow, Richard Paterson, and Alison Preston, eds. *Bosnia by Television* (London: British Film Institute, 1996), 84.

22. For further details of Bell's thoughts see his "TV News: How Far Should We Go?" *British Journalism Review*, vol. 8, no. 1, 1997, 7–16.
23. Cited in Bell. *In Harm's Way*, 141.
24. Cited in Susan L. Carruthers, *The Media at War* (Basingstoke: Macmillan, 2000), 240; Bell, *In Harm's Way*; and "TV News: How Far Should We Go?" 7–16.
25. Gow et al., *Bosnia by Television*, 113.
26. See John Burns, "The Media as Impartial Observers or Protagonists: Conflict Reporting or Conflict Encouragement in Former Yugoslavia," in Gow et al., *Bosnia by Television*, 92–100.
27. Eliot Cohen, "The Mystique of U.S. Air Power," *Foreign Affairs*, vol. 73, no. 1, January–February 1994, 109.
28. For an interesting view of NATO's squabbling generals, see Richard Norton-Taylor, "Robertson's Plum Job in a Warring NATO," the *Guardian*, August 3, 1999.
29. Peter Dunn, *All Aboard the Atrocity Bus* (London: The Journalist's Handbook, Carrack Media, 1999), 4, cited in Knightley, *The First Casualty*, 504. Coauthor Moorcraft worked briefly in the UK Ministry of Defence media ops team in Pristina at the beginning of NATO involvement. His perception was of a very hard-working and open attempt by the military to "feed the reptiles," as the army jargon went. See Paul Moorcraft, "After Milosevic: The Implications of NATO's Intervention in Kosovo," *New Zealand International Review*, September/October 1999, 2–5.
30. The *Guardian*, Media, June 21, 1999, 2–3, cited in Knightley, *The First Casualty*, 513–14.
31. Alistair Horne, "Serbs, Lies and Videotape," *Spectator*, July 3, 1999, 13.
32. See Alastair Campbell, "Media and the War in Kosovo," *RUSI Journal*, August 1999, 32.
33. For a incisive comment on the manipulation of the media by NATO, see Jon Swain, "Lost in the Kosovo Numbers Game," *Sunday Times* (London), October 31, 1999, 25.
34. Knightley, *The First Casualty*, 519.
35. Ibid., 525.
36. Editorial. "Too Many Truths" *British Journalism Review*, vol. 10, no. 2, 1999, 3.
37. Michael Ignatieff, *Virtual War: Kosovo and Beyond* (London: Chatto and Windus, 2000).
38. Editorial. "Too Many Truths" *British Journalism Review*, vol. 10, no. 2, 1999, 5.
39. Johnstone, *Fool's Crusade*, 2.
40. Diana Johnstone, "Seeing Yugoslavia through a Dark Glass: The Ideological Uniformity of the Media," in Lenora Forstel, ed. *War, Lies and Videotape: How Media Monopoly Stifles Truth* (New York: International Action Center, 2000), 156–157.

41. See Philip Hammond and Edward S. Hermann, "First Casualty and Beyond," in Philip Hammond and Edward S. Hermann, eds. *Degraded Capability: The Media and the Kosovo Crisis* (London: Pluto, 2000), 208.

42. Ibid., 201.

43. For an analysis of their electronic war, see Philip M. Taylor, "Propaganda and the Web War," *The World Today,* June 1999, 10–12.

44. Thomas Harding, "Bosnians Still Face Decades of Danger," *Daily Telegraph,* March 26, 2007.

45. James Pettigrew, "Kosovo: Nation in Waiting," *World Today,* vol. 61, no. 2, February 2005, 18–20; Colum Lynch, "UN Mediator Calls for Kosovo Independence," *Washington Post,* March 21, 2007.

46. P. J. O'Rourke, *Holidays In Hell* (London: Picador, 1988), 283.

47. Ibid.

48. Desmond Hamil, *Pig in the Middle: The Army in Northern Ireland, 1969–1984* (London: Methuen, 1985), 171.

49. Peter Taylor, "The Military, the Media and the IRA," in Stephen Badsey, ed. *The Media and International Security* (London: Cass, 2000), 36.

50. *Guardian,* Oct 18, 1993, cited in Carruthers, *The Media at War,* 187.

51. Philip Schlesinger, *Putting "Reality" Together: BBC News* (London: Methuen, 1987). For a wide-ranging account, see Liz Curtis, *Ireland, The Propaganda War: The British Media and the "Battle for Hearts and Minds"* (London: Pluto, 1984).

52. Coauthor Moorcraft was on patrol in 1999 in Pristina with soldiers from Ulster. One tough sergeant was boasting of his long experience in house-to-house searches "back home": "Learned all I know from there," he said. In the next breath, he shouted at a group of Kosovo Albanians who had illegally taken over a Serb house, "Open up or I'll kick down the door." "They must have different doors in Belfast," the coauthor said quietly to him. "That one is reinforced steel." Without a comment, or hesitation, the sergeant sent his squad around the back to enter via the windows.

53. See, Patrick Bishop and Eamonn Mallie, *The Provisional IRA* (London: Corgi, 1988), 387–410.

54. Peter Young and Peter Jesser, *The Media and the Military: From the Crimea to Desert Strike* (Basingstoke: Macmillan, 1997), 77.

55. David Miller, *Don't Mention the War: Northern Ireland, Propaganda and the Media* (London: Pluto, 1994).

56. Carruthers, *The Media at War,* 190.

57. O'Rourke, *Holidays in Hell,* 280.

58. This refers to the title chosen by David Millar for his book on the media coverage of Northern Ireland.

59. David Loyn, *Frontline: The True Story of the British Mavericks Who Changed the Face of War Reporting* (London: Penguin, 2005), 267. Anthony Loyd of the London *Times* made a similar comparison: "It was an

act of mass murder. In Bosnia I had seen men guilty of attempting to take innocent life; in Chechnya I found the Russians as cold-bloodedly culpable in their complete disregard for innocent life. Basically, they just blew the place to pieces." Loyd, *My War Gone By*, 243. For an academic study of comparative media coverage of Bosnia and Chechnya, see B. A. Taleb, *The Bewildered Herd: Media Coverage of International Conflicts and Public Opinion* (Lincoln, NE: iUniverse, Inc., 2004).

60. Quoted in Loyn, *Frontline*, 269.

61. John Pilger, ed. *Tell Me No Lies: Investigative Journalism and Its Triumphs* (London: Vintage, 2005), 410.

62. Jeremy Bowen, *War Stories* (London: Simon and Schuster, 2006), 200–15.

63. Anna Politkovskaya, "Chechnya: Dirty War" in Pilger, *Tell Me No Lies*, 409–32. See also Arkady Babchenko, *One Soldier's War in Chechnya*, (London: Portobello, 2007). Like Politkovskaya, Babchencko worked for *Novaya Gazeta*.

64. "The Warlord and the Spook," Russia and Chechnya Briefing, *The Economist*, June 2, 2007.

65. For a recent account by a Western journalist, from the London *Daily Telegraph*, see Adrian Blomfield, "In the Front Line of Putin's Secret War," *Daily Telegraph*, March 27, 2007.

66. See, for example, Paul Moorcraft, "Revolution in Nepal: Can the Nepalese Army Prevent a Maoist Victory?" *RUSI Journal*, October 2006, vol. 151, no. 5, 44–50.

67. Bowen, *War Stories*, 218.

## CHAPTER 6: THE MIDDLE EAST AND AFGHANISTAN

1. P. J. O'Rourke, *Holidays in Hell* (London: Picador, 1988), 254.

2. The classic text on media bias in favor of Israel is Christopher Mayhew and Michael Adams, *Publish It Not: The Middle East Cover-Up*. First published in 1975, the 2006 edition has an informative introduction by a former BBC Middle East correspondent, Tim Llewellyn (Oxford: Signal, 2006). See also, Greg Philo and Mike Berry of the Glasgow University Media Group, *Bad News from Israel* (London: Pluto, 2004). A powerful response, claiming concerted bias against Israel, can be found in Stephanie Gutmann, *The Other War: Israelis, Palestinians and the Struggle for Media Supremacy* (San Francisco: Encounter, 2005). A thorough and balanced analysis of the alleged bias can be found in Hugh Miles, *Al-Jazeera: How Arab TV News Changed the World* (London: Abacus, 2006).

3. Edward W. Said, *Covering Islam: How the Media and the Experts Determine How We See the Rest of the World* (London: Vintage, 1997).

4. Samuel P. Huntington, *The Clash of Civilizations and the Remaking of the World Order* (London: Touchstone, 1998).

5. For a useful recent account of the war, see BBC Middle East correspondent Jeremy Bowen's *Six Days: How the 1967 War Shaped the Middle East* (London: Simon and Schuster, 2003).

6. For a development of this point, see Paul Moorcraft, *Guns and Poses: Travels with an Occasional War Correspondent* (Guildford: Millstream, 2001), 253–4.

7. Melani McAlister, *Epic Encounters: Culture, Media and US Interests in the Middle East Since 1945* (Berkeley: University of California, 2005), 172.

8. For a short summary of the military and psychological responses in Israel to the 1973 war, see Paul Moorcraft, *Israel Since the Yom Kippur War* (London: Anglo-Israel Association, 1976).

9. McAlister, *Epic Encounters,* 187.

10. The CIA funded the Afghan resistance, and this later included bin Laden, but too much has been made of the direct financial linkage. Bin Laden used his own, not the CIA's, money. For one side of the argument, see Richard Miniter, *Disinformation: 22 Media Myths that Undermine the War on Terror* (Washington, DC: Regnery, 2005), 11–22. The funding issue was popularized in *Charlie Wilson's War,* a 2007 film about Democratic Texas Congressman Charlie Wilson, who conspired with zealous CIA agents to fund the Afghan fighters. Tom Hanks, who starred, captured Wilson's charm, but not his macho recklessness.

11. For a good summary of the debate in the early 1990s, see Leon T. Hadar, "What Green Peril?" *Foreign Affairs*, Spring 1993, vol. 93, 27–42.

12. Hamid Mowlana, "The Role of the Media in the US-Iranian Conflict" in A. Arno and W. Dissanyake, eds. *The News Media in National and International Conflict* (Boulder, CO: Westview, 1984), 87. See also W. A. Dorman and E. Omeed, "Reporting Iran the Shah's Way," *Columbia Journalism Review*, vol. 17, no. 5, January–February 1979, 27–33.

13. Anthony Smith, *The Geopolitics of Information: How Western Culture Dominates the World* (London: Faber and Faber, 1980), 99–100.

14. The longest conventional war between two states. Vietnam was a civil war; China and Japan's conflict over Manchuria never reached the point where one state declared war on the other.

15. For a clearly written and balanced account of the war, see Dilip Hiro, *The Longest War: The Iran-Iraq Conflict* (London: Paladin, 1990). Also Efraim Karsh, *The Iran-Iraq War: A Military Analysis*, Adelphi Paper 220, Spring 1987.

16. For a perceptive overall analysis of the war, see Mohammad Yousaf and Mark Adkin, *The Battle for Afghanistan: The Soviets versus the Muhahideen during the 1980s* (Barnsley, UK: Pen and Sword, 2007).

17. For a very readable short account of the three imperial British wars in Afghanistan, see T. A. Heathcote, *The Afghan Wars* (London: Osprey, 1980).

18. Cited in Moorcraft, *Guns and Poses,* 159.

19. Phillip Knightley, *The First Casualty: The War Correspondent as Hero and Myth-Maker from the Crimea to Iraq* (Baltimore: John Hopkins University, 2004), 477.
20. Sandy Gall, *Behind Russian Lines: An Afghan Journal* (London: Sidgwick and Jackson, 1983). His companion, Nigel Ryan, takes a slightly different view in his often amusing, *A Hitch or Two in Afghanistan* (London: Weidenfeld and Nicholson, 1983).
21. Sebastian Rich, *People I Have Shot* (London: Gollancz, 1990). Another memoir by a daredevil cameraman is Jon Steele, *War Junkie: One Man's Addiction to the Worst Places on Earth* (London: Corgi, 2003).
22. For an insight into the enigmatic Jouvenal, see David Loyn, *Frontline: The True Story of the British Mavericks Who Changed the Face of War Reporting* (London: Penguin, 2005) *passim.* Coauthor Moorcraft worked with him briefly in the early days of the anti-Soviet war in Afghanistan. He seemed to be cast from the same heroic mold as such adventurers as Wilfred Thesiger.
23. See, for example, John Simpson, *Strange Places, Questionable People* (Basingstoke, UK: Macmillan, 1998), 476–512.
24. See Jim Burroughs, *Blood on the Lens: A Filmmaker's Quest for Truth in Afghanistan* (Washington, DC: Potomac Books, 2007).
25. The phrase is Michael Griffin's in *Reaping the Whirlwind: Afghanistan, Al Qa'ida and the Holy War* (London: Pluto, 2003), 48, 57.
26. Ibid.
27. Ibid., 93.
28. John R. MacArthur, *Second Front: Censorship and Propaganda in the Gulf War* (Berkeley: University of California Press, 1992).
29. See Philip M. Taylor, *War and the Media: Propaganda and Persuasion in the Gulf War* (Manchester: Manchester University Press, 1992, 1997).
30. Colin Powell, *A Soldier's War* (London: Hutchinson, 1995), 529.
31. BBC TV, *Newsnight*, February 6, 1991.
32. Cited by William Boot, "The Pool," *Columbia Journalism Review*, May–June 1991, 24–7.
33. Cited in Taylor, *War and the Media*, 275–6.
34. *The Independent*, February 6, 1991.
35. "Reporting the war: a collection of experiences and reflections on the Gulf," a discussion paper published by the British Executive of the International Press Institute, May 1991, 2.
36. Taylor, *War and the Media*, 45–6.
37. Ibid., 233.
38. Powell, *A Soldier's War*, 520.
39. See, for example, "It Was the Christians: The Massacre at Chatila," in John Carey, ed. *The Faber Book of Reportage* (London: Faber and Faber, 1987), 679–82.

40. Duncan Anderson, *Glass Warriors: The Camera at War* (London: Collins, 2005), 176.

41. For coauthor Moorcraft's personal experience of working in southern Lebanon, see *Guns and Poses,* 259–64.

42. Miles, *Al-Jazeera,* 72.

43. Ibid., 72.

44. Ibid., 81.

45. Cited in Gutmann, *The Other War,* 3.

46. Ibid., 5–6.

47. Ibid., 271.

48. Gadi Wolfsfeld, *Media and Political Conflict: News from the Middle East* (Cambridge: Cambridge University Press, 1997), 204.

49. Miles, *Al-Jazeera,* 96.

50. Wolfsfeld, *Media and Political Conflict,* 197.

51. Ibid., 200.

52. Cited in Paul Gallagher, "The Media and the Military: An Uneasy Alliance," the *Cormorant,* 9, 2007, 19. The *Cormorant* is the annual UK publication for military officers who have endured joint staff college training.

53. Ibid.

## CHAPTER 7: THE LONG WAR

1. Duncan Anderson, *Glass Warriors: The Camera at War* (London: Collins, 2005), 196.

2. Cited in Fred Inglis, *People's Witness: The Journalist in Modern Politics* (London: Yale, 2002), 370.

3. John Lewis Gaddis, *Surprise, Security and the American Experience* (New Haven, CT: Yale University, 2004), 5.

4. For a good summary of this debate, see Caroline Kennedy-Pipe and Nicholas Rengger, "Apocalypse Now? Continuities or Disjunctions in World Politics after 9/11" in *International Affairs,* vol. 82, no. 3, May 2006, 539–52. For a history of how the CIA had been tracking bin Laden, see Steve Coll, *Ghost Wars: The Secret History of the CIA, Afghanistan and bin Laden: from the Soviet Invasion to September 10, 2001* (New York: Penguin, 2004). Coll is a *Washington Post* editor who won a Pulitzer in 1990.

5. For a partisan but informative perspective, see David N. Bossie, *Intelligence Failure: How Clinton's National Security Policy Set the Stage for 9/11* (Medford, OR: WND, 2004), and Bill Gertz, *Breakdown: How America's Intelligence Failures Led to September 11* (Washington, DC: Regnery, 2002).

6. Kieran Baker, "Conflict and Control: The War in Afghanistan and the 24-Hour News Cycle," in Daya Kishan Thussu and Des Freedman, *War and the Media* (London: Sage, 2003), 244.

7. Bryan Whitman in Judith Sylvester and Suzanne Huffman, *Reporting*

from the Front: The Media and the Military (Lanham, MD: Rowman and Littlefield, 2005), 45.

8. See Yvonne Ridley, In the Hands of the Taliban (London: Robson, 2001).

9. Paul McGeough, Manhattan to Baghdad (Sydney: Allen and Unwin, 2003), 86. Coauthor Moorcraft was on the receiving end of such an assessment in 1984 under similar circumstance in Afghanistan. He failed the test. Tim Lambon, ex-special forces and now with Channel Four News, kept a devastating private diary of the coauthor's leadership of a film crew, albeit under daily attacks. They remain close friends, however.

10. Hugh Miles, Al-Jazeera: How Arab TV News Challenged the World (London: Abacus, 2005), 124.

11. Gary Bernsten and Ralph Pezzullo, Jawbreaker: The Attack on bin Laden and Al-Qaeda (New York: Three Rivers, 2005), 306. See also Philip Smucker, Al Qaeda's Great Escape: The Military and the Media on Terror's Trail (Washington, DC: Brassey's, Inc., 2004).

12. Coauthor Moorcraft was in Jenin in the immediate aftermath. See his "The West Bank: Can There Ever Be Peace?" in Paul Moorcraft, Gwyn Winfield and John Chisholm, eds, The New Wars of the West: Anglo-American Voices on the War on Terror (Havertown, PA: Casemate, 2005), 226–41.

13. Miles, Al-Jazeera, 378.

14. Cited in Con Coughlin, American Ally: Tony Blair and the War on Terror (London: HarperCollins, 2006), 351.

15. For a good summary of this debate, see Lawrence Freedman, "War in Iraq: Selling the Threat," Survival, vol. 46, no. 2, Summer 2004, 7–50.

16. The quotes, in order, were cited in: Mark Thomas, foreword, in David Miller, ed. Tell Me Lies: Propaganda and Media Distortion in the Attack on Iraq (London: Pluto, 2004), x; Michael Massing, Now They Tell Us: The American Press and Iraq (New York: New York Review of Books, 2004), 25; Robert Fisk, The Great War for Civilisation: The Conquest of the Middle East (London: Harper Perennial, 2006), 139.

17. Rand Beers, who served on the staff of the National Security Council during the run-up to the war. Cited in Thomas E. Ricks, Fiasco: The American Military Adventure in Iraq (London: Penguin, 2006), 56.

18. Martin Bell, Through the Gates of Fire: A Journey into World Disorder (London: Weidenfeld and Nicholson, 2003), 199.

19. Public Affairs Guidance on Embedding Media during possible future operations in the US Central Command's Area of Responsibility, February 2003. Available online at http://www.defenselink.mil/news/Feb 2003/d20030228pag.pdf; OPSEC, military abbreviation for operational security.

20. PA Guidance.

21. Ibid.

22. Ibid.

23. Ibid.
24. Ibid.
25. Ibid.
26. Ibid.
27. Ibid.
28. Ibid.
29. For an interesting discussion of the role of women (or the lack of a role) in the war on terrorism, particularly the imagery of 9/11, see Jayne Rodgers, "Icons and Invisibility: Gender, Myth, 9/11" in Tussu and Freedman, *War and the Media,* 200–12.
30. Peter Preston, "Here Is the News: Too Much Heat . . . Too Little Light," *Observer,* March 30, 2003.
31. Brian Appleyard, "Lost in the Media Blitz," *Sunday Times* (London), March 30, 2003.
32. Ibid.
33. Ibid.
34. This amusing anecdote was widely quoted. Cited here by Miles, *Al-Jazeera,* 245.
35. Ibid., 247.
36. Kamal Ahmed and Gaby Hinsliff, "Downing Street in BBC 'Bias' Row," *Observer,* March 30, 2003.
37. Cited in Chris Ayres, *War Reporting for Cowards* (New York: Grove, 2005), 153.
38. Ibid., 175, 178.
39. Ibid., 231.
40. Bill Katovsky and Timothy Carlson, *Embedded: The Media at War in Iraq* (Guilford, CT: Lyons, 2003), xi. For details of journalists killed in the war, see The International News Safety Institute, *Dying to Tell the Story: The Iraq War and the Media, a Tribute.* (Brussels: International News Safety Institute, 2003).
41. Bell, *Through Gates of Fire,* 186.
42. Phillip Knightley, *The First Casualty* (Baltimore: The John Hopkins University Press, 2004), 529, 548.
43. Cited in Alison Roberts, "A Chronicler of War" in *London Evening Standard,* January 31, 2007.
44. Bell, *Through Gates of Fire,* 197.
45. John Lee Anderson, *The Fall of Baghdad* (New York: Penguin, 2004). Anderson was a staff writer for the *New Yorker.*
46. Anthony Shadid, *Night Draws Near: Iraq's People in the Shadow of America's War* (New York: Holt, 2005).
47. Hansard, March 18, 2003, col. 775.
48. *Amnesty International Annual Report,* 2001.
49. David Jackson, "Troops Will Stay in Iraq 'However Long it Takes,' Bush

Says," *Philadelphia Enquirer*, March 27, 2003. http://www.philly.com/mld/philly/news/politics/5498384.htm.

50. "Iraqi Suicide Bomber Kills Four as Saddam Threatens War in the UK," *Sunday Times* (London), March 30, 2003.

51. Jackson, "Troops Will Stay in Iraq," *Philadelphia Enquirer*, 27 March 2003. http://www.philly.com/mld/philly/news/politics/5498384.htm.

52. Radio address to the nation by the President, March 29, 2003. www.whitehouse.gov/news/releases/2003/03/20030329.html.

53. BBC website, March 29, 2003. http://news.bbc.co.uk/1/hi/world/middle_east/2897699.stm.

54. BBC website, March 29, 2003. http://news.bbc.co.uk/1/hi/world/middle_east/2898173.stm.

55. "Iraqi Suicide Bomber Kills Four," *Sunday Times* (London), March 30, 2003; Hassan Hafidh, "Iraq Hails Suicide Bomber, Air Strikes Hit Baghdad," March 29, 2003. http://www.reuters.com/newsArticle.jhtml;jsessionid=R5ZN25FINPYI2CRBAEKSFFA?type=topNews&storyID=2471294.

56. Brian Hanrahan, BBC 1 Evening News, March 29, 2003.

57. Fox News, March 29, 2003, 4:45 pm GMT.

58. Jim Ure's report aired on BBC World, March 29, 2003, 6:35 pm.

59. CENTCOM briefing, March 27, 2003. www.centcom.mil/CENTCOM News/Transcripts/20030329.htm. For a different take on this, see Paul Moorcraft, "The Missiles That Miss," *New Statesman*, April 7, 2003, 20–22.

60. Suzanne Goldenberg, "52 Die in Baghdad Market Blast," *Guardian*, March 29, 2003.

61. Brian Appleyard, "Lost in the Media Blitz," *Sunday Times* (London), March 30, 2003.

62. DoD News briefing, Friday, March 28, 2003, www.defenselink.mil/news/Mar2003/t03282003_t0328sd.html.

63. BBC World, March 29, 2003.

64. Michael Clarke, "Request Backup," *Sunday Times* (London), March 30, 2003.

65. BBC Radio Five Live, March 29, 2003.

66. "Tell It Straight," *Sunday Times* (London), March 30, 2003.

67. DoD News briefing, Friday, March 28, 2003, www.defenselink.mil/news/Mar2003/t03282003_t0328sd.html.

68. http://news.bbc.co.uk/1/hi/world/middle_east/2897711.stm.

69. Peter Preston, "Here Is the News: Too Much Heat," *Observer*, March 30, 2003.

70. Ricks, *Fiasco*, 4.

71. Ibid., *passim*.

72. Cited in Ricks, *Fiasco*, 209.

73. See Rajiv Chandrasekaran, *Imperial Life in the Emerald City: Inside Iraq's Green Zone* (New York: Knopf, 2006).

74. The phrase is that of the *Daily Mirror's* defense correspondent, Chris

Hughes, *Road Trip to Hell: Tabloid Tales of Saddam, Iraq and a Bloody War* (London: Monday, 2006), 250.

75. They received in a short time two Emmy awards, a BAFTA, a Headliner Award, a New York TV Award, and an Amnesty award.

76. Cited in Paul Moorcraft, "Exit from Baghdad" in *Armed Forces Journal* (Washington), March 2005, 51.

77. Idem.

78. Email to coauthor Moorcraft, October 22, 2005.

79. Before the war, the American media were dubbed "the President's men." See, for example, Matthew Engel, "Bushwhacked," *Guardian* (Media) January 13, 2003.

80. See Michael Isikoff and David Corn, *Hubris: The Inside Story of Spin, Scandal and the Selling of the Iraq War* (New York: Crown, 2006), 390–6. Isikoff worked for *Newsweek* and Corn for *The Nation*.

81. Cited in David Teather, "The War on Bias," *Guardian* (Media), August 23, 2004.

82. Cited in Ricks, *Fiasco*, 384. See Massing, *Now They Tell Us*, for a full analysis of Ricks's quote.

83. *Newsweek*, May 17, 2004, cited in Ricks, *Fiasco*, 380. The coauthor, Paul Moorcraft, must also own up here: he became a repentant hawk, too. He supported the war but grew rapidly disenchanted with the U.S. military's failure to listen to its own State Department's and the UK's advice on the occupation.

84. Some of the most controversial were Isikoff and Corn, *Hubris*, Ron Susskind, *The One Percent Doctrine: Deep Inside America's Pursuit of its Enemies since 9/11* (New York: Simon and Schuster, 2006); and Frank Rich, *The Greatest Story Ever Sold? The Decline and Fall of Truth* (New York: Penguin, 2006).

85. Bob Woodward, *State of Denial: Bush at War, Part III* (New York: Simon and Schuster, 2006), xiv.

86. George Packer, *The Assassin's Gate: America in Iraq* (New York: Farrar, Straus, and Giroux, 2005), 447.

87. Al Franken, *Lies and the Lying Liars Who Tell Them* (E. P. Dutton, 2003).

88. Norman Pearlstine, "How Libby's Trial Hurt the Press," *Time*, June 11, 2007.

89. *Guardian's* Quote of the Week (Media), January 22, 2007.

90. See Kristian Williams, "Keeping the State's Secrets" in *World Today*, February 2006, 16–17. Williams was the author of *American Methods: Torture and the Logic of Domination* (Cambridge, MA: South End, 2006).

91. Steve Coll, "Army Spun Tale Around Ill-Fated Mission," *Washington Post*, December 6, 2004, for a useful summary of the case.

92. See figures in "Four Years of War," *Washington Post*, March 19, 2007. Also Moorcraft et al., *The New Wars of the West*, 304–5.

93. Gen. Norman Schwarzkopf cited this phrase he attributed to Gen.

Creighton Abrams in his Gulf War memoir, *It Doesn't Take a Hero* (London: Bantam, 1993), 344.

94. Gareth Stansfield, "Beyond the Point of No Return" in *World Today*, vol. 63, no. 1, January 2007, 6.

95. Bob Woodward, *State of Denial.*

96. Paul Moorcraft, "Afghanistan: A Personal Perspective" in Moorcraft et al., *The New Wars of the West,* 169–72.

97. Chris Patten, *Not Quite the Diplomat: Home Truths about World Affairs* (London: Allen Lane, 2005), 100.

98. James Risen, *State of War: The Secret History of the CIA under the Bush Administration* (New York: Free Press, 2006), 162. Risen won a Pulitzer in 2006.

99. Email communication to coauthor Moorcraft, April 2007. See also Sam Dealey, "At War in the Fields of the Drug Lords," *GQ,* October 2006.

100. See Paul Moorcraft, "Is Afghanistan to Be Another Iraq?" *Business Day* (Johannesburg) July 31, 2006.

101. Email correspondence between Smith and coauthor Moorcraft, March 2007. For details of Terry Lloyd's death see International News Safety Institute, *Dying to the Tell the Story*, 21-31. The specific targeting of hacks in Iraq was something new, according to some writers (though they had also been deliberately killed in Bosnia as well): see Phillip Knightley, "History or Bunkum" in Miller, ed. *Tell Me Lies*, 100-107. See also Herbert N. Foerstel, *Killing the Messenger: Journalists at Risk in Modern Warfare* (Westport, CT: Praeger, 2006).

102. Email correspondence between Hughes and coauthor Moorcraft, March 2007.

103. For a summary of the crisis, see Paul Moorcraft, *"No End in Sight,"* Washington Times, October 16, 2006.

104. For the background on U.S.-Sudanese relations, see Paul Moorcraft "Sudan: The bin Laden Connection" in Moorcraft et al. *The New Wars of the West,* 215–25.

105. For a summary of the dangers of UN intervention, see Paul Moorcraft, "A Replay of Iraq Beckons in Darfur, if We Send in Troops," *Guardian*, April 6, 2006.

106. David Hoile, *Darfur: The Road to Peace* (London: ESPAC, 2008). Despite being partisan, this is still a useful analysis of the media's coverage. See also Nick Davies, *Flat Earth News* (London: Chatto and Windus, 2008), 151. Darfur, according to Davies, broke too many rules of journalism: " . . . expensive and difficult to cover, too complicated (just who are the good guys out there?), slow-burning, boring, depressing and no Americans."

107. See, for example, Scott Anderson "How Did Darfur Happen?" *New York Times Magazine*, October 17, 2004; see also Richard Miniter, "The New Afghanistan and the Next Battlefield?" in his *Shadow War: The Untold*

*Story of How Bush Is Winning the War on Terror* (Washington, DC: Regnery, 2004).

108. For a summation of the casualties, on its impressive website, see http://news.bbc.co.uk/1/hi/world/middle_east/5257128.stm.

109. The South African veteran war correspondent mentioned earlier in the book, Al J. Venter, had turned his attention to the Middle East. See his *Iran's Nuclear Option: Tehran's Quest for the Atom Bomb* (Havertown, PA: Casemate, 2005).

110. See Paul Moorcraft, "Hezbollah rising," *Washington Times,* Aug 15, 2006.

111. One of the main unintended consequences of the Iraq war was the rise of Shi'a triumphalism throughout the Middle East. For an instructive essay on this, see Channel Four's Lindsey Hilsum, "A War of Unintended Consequences" in Moorcraft et al., *The New Wars of the West,* 195–200.

112. See, for example, Jeremy Bowen, *War Stories* (London: Simon and Schuster, 2006), 282–96.

113. Eric Schmitt and T. Shanker, "Washington Recasts Terror War as 'Struggle,'" *New York Times,* July 27, 2005.

114. Faisal Bodi, "Target practice," *Journalist,* (UK) January–February 2006, 10. The publication is the organ of the UK National Union of Journalists. See also debate cited in footnote 101.

115. "New Realities in the Media Age: A Conversation with Donald Rumsfeld," Council on Foreign Relations, New York, February 17, 2006, transcript, 2.

116. Ibid.

117. See Sheldon Rampton and John Stauber, *The Best War Ever: Lies, Damned Lies and the Mess in Iraq* (New York: Tarcher/Penguin, 2006).

118. http://freddevan.com/wordpress/2006/11/16/lincoln-group-unethical-weapon-of-mass-deception/.

119. Mark Mazzetti, "Propaganda Effort in Iraq a Mistake, Rumsfeld Says" *Los Angeles Times*, February 18, 2006; Pauline Jelinek, "Propaganda Program in Iraq Legal," Associated Press, October 19, 2006.

120. "Planted Propaganda," editorial, *Washington Post*, October 23, 2006. For a very succinct, and damning, list of stories which had been planted in the Western media in general as part of the strategic information campaign, see Davies, *Flat Earth News*, 218–9.

121. Scott Johnson, "We are Losing the Infowar," *Newsweek,* January 15, 2007, 10–13.

122. Declan Walsh, "Their Business is Jihad," *Guardian,* March 20, 2007.

123. Cited in Johnson, "We are Losing the Infowar," 13. For a British perspective on the hearts and minds campaign, see Steve Tatham, *Losing Arab Hearts and Minds* (London: Hurst, 2006).

124. John Mackinlay, "Losing Arab Hearts and Minds," review essay, *RUSI Journal,* vol. 151, no. 4, August 2006, 86.

125. Miles, *Al-Jazeera,* 279. See also Silvia Gaiani, "Al Jazeera and the Information Warfare," *Islamica,* Issue 20, 2007.

126. Bell, *Through Gates of Fire,* 190.

127. Hughes, *The Road to Hell,* 256.

128. George F. Will, "Rhetoric of Unreality: Where Is Iraq after Nearly 3 Years of War?" *Washington Post,* March 2, 2006.

129. Rich, *The Greatest Story Ever Sold?,* 223.

130. See Paul Moorcraft, "Why the West Must Exit Now," *Sunday Express,* Sept 17, 2006.

## CHAPTER 8: THE MECHANICS OF REPORTING WAR AND PEACE

1. Cited in Nik Gowing, "Real Time Television Coverage of Armed Conflicts and Diplomatic Crises: Does It Pressure or Distort Foreign Policy Decisions?" JFK School of Government discussion paper 94-1, Harvard University, June 1994, 64.

2. See Daniel Hallin, *The "Uncensored War": The Media and Vietnam* (Oxford: Oxford University Press, 1986).

3. Susan D. Moeller, "Locating Accountability: The Media and Peacekeeping," *Journal of International Affairs,* Spring 2002, vol. 55, no. 2, 369–90.

4. Jonathan Randal, "The Decline, but Not Yet Total Fall, of Foreign News in the U.S. Media," Joan Shorenstein Center on the Press, Politics and Public Policy, Harvard University working paper, 2000, no. 2000-2.

5. Kofi Annan, "Peace-keeping in Situations of Civil War," *New York University Journal of International Law and Politics,* vol. 26, 1994, 624.

6. Virgil Hawkins, "The Price of Inaction: The Media and Humanitarian Intervention," *The Journal of Humanitarian Assistance,* 2001. www.jha.ac/articles/a066.htm. See also John C. Hammock and Joel R. Charny, "Emergency Response as Morality Play: The Media, the Relief Agencies, and the Need for Capacity Building," in *From Massacres to Genocide: The Media, Public Policy, and Humanitarian Crises,* Rotberg and Weiss, eds. (Cambridge, MA: World Peace Foundation, 1996), 115–16.

7. *The International Response to Conflict and Genocide: Lessons from the Rwanda Experience,* by the Steering Committee for Joint Evaluation of Emergency Assistance to Rwanda. Published by the Danish Foreign Ministry, 1996, vol. E, 66.

8. David Shaw, "Foreign News Shrinks in Era of Globalization," *Los Angeles Times,* September 27, 2001.

9. C. Moisey, "The Foreign News Flow in the Information Age," Joan Shorenstein Center on the Press, Politics and Public Policy. Harvard University discussion paper D-23, November 1996.

10. For further details, see J. Hoge, "Foreign News: Who Gives a Damn?" *Columbia Journalism Review,* vol. 36, November–December 1997, 48–52;

G. Utley, "The Shrinking of Foreign News: From Broadcast to Narrowcast," *Foreign Affairs*, vol. 76, no. 2, 1997, 2–10; Jonathan Randal, "The Decline, but Not Yet Total Fall, of Foreign News in the U.S. Media."

11. David Shaw, "Foreign News Shrinks in Era of Globalization," *Los Angeles Times*, September 27, 2001.

12. Martin Bell, *Through the Gates of Fire* (London, Weidenfeld and Nicholson, 2003), 43.

13. Moeller, "Locating Accountability."

14. Piers Robinson, *The CNN Effect: The Myth of News Media, Foreign Policy and Intervention* (London, Routledge, 2002).

15. Jim Naureckas, "Media on the Somalia Intervention: Tragedy Made Simple," March 1993, http://www.fair.org/extra/9303/somalia.html.

16. Adeel Hassan, "To Die For: Why Journalists Risk All," http://www.cjr.org/archives.asp?url=/02/5/clarke.asp.

17. Joel Simon, "Propaganda War in Serbia," http://www.cpj.org/dangerous/spring99/Serbia05May99.html.

18. Phillip Knightley, "Turning the Tanks on the Reporters," *Observer,* June 15, 2003. See also Nik Gowing, "Into the Firing Line," http://www.britishcouncil.org.co/english/governance/article.htm.

19. Lt. Col. Gerald S. Venanzi, "Democracy and Protracted War: The Impact of Television," http://www.airpower.maxwell.af.mil/airchronicles/aureview/1983/Jan-Feb/venanzi.html.

20. *The Media Report,* May 15, 2003: "What Happened to the War?" http://www.abc.net.au/rn/talks/8.30/mediarpt/stories/s853513.htm.

21. B. Arnoldy, "In the Vanguard of 'Peaceful Occupation,'" *Christian Science Monitor*, April 8, 2003.

22. Charles J. Hanley, "U.S. Starts Iraqi 'Good News' Offensive," *Washington Post*, October 17, 2003.

23. "Good News Is . . . No News," *Mother Jones* website, November–December 2003 issue, http://www.motherjones.com/news/dailymojo/2003/12/12_525.html.

24. Adam Roberts, "NATO's 'Humanitarian War' Over Kosovo," *Survival,* vol. 41, no. 3, October 1, 1999.

25. Robinson, *The CNN Effect.*

26. Bell, *Through the Gates of Fire.*

27. J. Metzl, "Information Intervention: When Switching Channels Isn't Enough," *Foreign Affairs*, vol. 76, no. 6, November–December 1997, 15–20.

28. M. Thompson, "Defining Information Intervention: An Interview with Jamie Metzl," in M. E. Price and M. Thompson, *Forging Peace: Intervention, Human Rights and the Management of Media Space* (Edinburgh: Edinburgh University Press, 2002), 41.

29. Ibid.
30. P. Combelles Siegal, *Target Bosnia: Information Activities in Peace Support Operations*, http://newmedia.leeds.ac.uk/papers/pmt/exhibits/695/combelle.pdf.
31. Ibid.
32. Monroe E. Price, ed., "Restructuring the Media in Post-Conflict Societies: 4 Perspectives—The Experience of Intergovernmental and Non-Governmental Organizations." May 2000, http://newmedia.leeds.ac.uk/papers/pmt/exhibits/1004/price2.pdf.
33. M. Ottaway, "Nation Building (Think Again)," *Foreign Policy*, September–October 2002, http://www.ceip.org/files/Publications/2002-10-15-ottaway-FP.asp?from=pubauthor.
34. Paul McMasters, "The War on Journalism," September 22, 2001, http://www.freedomforum.org/templates/document.asp?documentID=15211&printerfriendly=1.
35. Lecture to the Higher Command and Staff Course, February 2,1995, cited in A. M. A. Duncan, "Mixing with the Media" in Stephen Badsey, ed. *The Media and International Security* (London: Cass, 2000), 118.
36. Justin Lewis et al., *Shoot First and Ask Questions Later: Media Coverage of the 2003 Iraq War* (New York: Peter Lang, 2006), 63.
37. Private conversation with coauthor Taylor, 2003.
38. Robin Brown, "Spinning the War: Political Communications, Information Operations and Public Diplomacy in the War on Terrorism" in Daya Kishan Thussu and Des Freedman, eds., *War and the Media: Reporting Conflict 24/7* (London: Sage, 2003), 87–100.
39. See David Miller, "Information Dominance: The Philosophy of Total Propaganda Control?" in Yahya R. Kamalipour and Nancy Snow, eds., *War, Media and Propaganda: A Global Perspective* (Oxford: Rowman and Littlefield, 2004).
40. A very useful summary of this process in both the UK and U.S. can be found in Justin Lewis et al., *Shoot First and Ask Questions Later,* 15–36.
41. Miller, "Information Dominance."
42. Steve Tatham, *Losing Arab Hearts and Minds: The Coalition, Al Jazeera and Muslim Public Opinion* (London: Hurst, 2006) 100–2.
43. Lewis, *Shoot First.* Coauthor Moorcraft sporadically attended these prayer meetings in 2001 and 2003, when he served in the MoD Main Building in Whitehall.
44. Select Committee on Defence, House of Commons, Third Report, March 3, 2004.
45. Lewis, *Shoot First,* 35.
46. See "Media Leaks Prompt MOD Comms Revamp," *PR Week*, September

17, 2004, 7. Coauthor Moorcraft, who worked in the department, always considered the term "corporate" very odd.

47. Lt. Cdr. D. J. Pickup, "The Media and the Minder: The Royal Navy's Perspective" in Badsey, *The Media and International Security,* 146.

48. Specialities/military roles are defined in the British army by numbers G 1–7. The U.S military uses "J," not "G."

49. Robert Partridge, "Absurdity of War" in Bill Katovsky and Timothy Carlson, eds., *Embedded: The Media at War in Iraq* (Guilford, CT: Lyons, 2003), 253. Partridge, a very companionable officer, had a good way with hacks. Coauthor Moorcraft, who worked with him in Pristina, was wearing standard UK army camouflage uniform (he was serving in the MoD at the time) but rigged out with a journalist-style camera jacket with lots of pockets. Partridge joked: "Are you ready for fishing or fighting?" The military sometimes used to call hacks "fishermen" because of their multi-pocketed jackets. In civilian life, Partridge owned a company making special effects for movies, especially the use of guns and explosives. Being a ballistics expert as well as working in the film industry were useful complements to his military role.

50. An informative exception was Steve Tatham's *Losing Arab Hearts and Minds.* Lieutenant Commander Tatham, however, was a serving *regular* officer who was the Royal Navy's spokesman in theater during the 2003 war.

51. Nik Gowing, "Conflict, the Military and the Media—A New Optimism?" the *Officer,* May–June 1997, 1.

52. Kate Adie, "The Media Portrayal of the Military" in *Badsey, The Media and International Security,* 58, 61, 63. Coauthor Taylor was also a keynote speaker at this conference.

53. Andrea Webb, "Media Manoeuvres" in *Focus,* February 2006, 10. *Focus,* now *Defence Focus,* was the in-house MoD magazine. Coauthor Moorcraft was the editor of this organ for two brief periods.

54. See *Too Close for Comfort? The Role of Embedded Reporting During the 2003 Iraq War,* Summary report, Cardiff University School of Journalism, Media and Cultural Studies, undated, 16–17.

55. Lewis, *Shoot First,* 191.

56. Sheldon Rampton and John Stauber, *Weapons of Mass Deception* (New York: Center for Media and Democracy, 2003).

57. Nick Davies, *Flat Earth News* (London: Chatto and Windus, 2008), 213.

58. Andrew Marr, *My Trade: A Short History of British Journalism* (London: Pan, 2004), 327.

59. Cited in Phillip Knightley, *The First Casualty* (Baltimore: John Hopkins University Press, 2004), 507. (Lloyd was also the author of a minor masterpiece, *My War Gone By, I Miss It So* (London: Penguin, 1999)).

60. Idem.

61. Emma Daly, "Reporting from the Front Line," in Stephen Glover, ed. *Secrets of the Press: Journalists on Journalism* (London: Allen Lane, 1999), 275.

62. Martin Bell, *Through Gates of Fire: A Journey into World Disorder* (London: Weidenfeld and Nicholson, 2003), 182. The war zone thug description is in the subtitle of his book, *In Harm's Way* (London: Penguin, 1996).

63. Daly, "Reporting from the Front Line," 276.

64. Interviewed by David Loyn, *Frontline: The True Story of the British Mavericks who Changed the Face of War Reporting* (London: Michael Joseph, 2005), 257.

65. Based on State Department figures (January 12, 2007), plus figures from Reporters Without Borders, Committee to Protect Journalists, and the International Federation of Journalists.

66. Ibid.

67. Leonard Doyle, "The Big Question: Should Western Journalists Be in Iraq, and Can Their Reports Be Trusted?" the *Independent,* May 31, 2006.

68. Paul Harris, *Somebody Else's War: Frontline Reports from the Balkan Wars* (Stevenage, UK: Spa, 1992), 44.

69. David Loyn, *Frontline,* 320.

70. Kate Adie, "Dispatches from the Front: Reporting War," *Reporters and the Reported: The 1988 Vauxhall Lectures* (Centre for Journalism Studies, Cardiff University, 1988), 53.

71. Near Kabul, June 1984. Chris Everson's comments to coauthor Moorcraft.

72. Thomas E. Ricks, *Fiasco: The American Military Adventure in Iraq* (London: Allen, Lane, 2006), 425.

73. Jeremy Bowen, *War Stories* (London: Simon & Schuster, 2006), 202–3.

74. See Howard Tumber and Frank Webster, *The Media at War: The Iraq Crisis* (London: Saga, 2004).

75. Alex Kershaw, "The End of the Affair," the *Sunday Times* magazine, April 14, 2004, 26. See also Alex Kershaw, *Blood and Champagne: The Life and Times of Robert Capa* (New York: St. Martin's Press, 2003).

76. Anthony Feinstein, *Journalists under Fire: The Psychological Hazards of Covering* War (Baltimore: John Hopkins University Press, 2006).

77. Ibid., 182.

78. Ibid., 183.

79. John Carey, *The Faber Book of Reportage* (London: Faber, 1987), xxxiv–xxxv.

80. Ibid.

81. Linda Grant, "Can We Hack the Truth?" the *Guardian,* August 11, 1998.

82. Lieutenant Colonel R. C. L. Clifford and Colonel T. J. Wilton, "Media Operations and the ARRC," in Badsey, 23.

83. Bob Stewart, *Broken Lives—A Personal View of the Bosnia Conflict* (London: HarperCollins, 1993), 180.

84. Cited in the International News Safety Institute, *Dying to Tell the Story: The Iraq War and the Media, A Tribute* (Brussels: International News Safety Institute, 2003), iii.

## CHAPTER 9: NO MORE HEROES?

1. Nik Gowing, "Real-time TV Coverage from War: Does It Make or Break Government Policy?" in James Gow, et al., eds. *Bosnia by Television* (London: British Film Institute, 1996), 81–91. See also Paul Moorcraft, "CNN: The New Emperor of International Politics?" *New Zealand International Review*, November–December 1997, 22–5.
2. Dominic Pkalya, "Is Global Media Setting the Agenda for UN Peace Keeping Operations: Revisiting the UNOSOM Debacle," http://www.monitor.upeace.org/archive.cfm?id_article=397; www.una-uk.org/Ban.
3. Email correspondence with coauthor Moorcraft, March 2007.
4. Ibid.
5. Cited in Phil Chamberlain, "At the Centre of the Maelstrom," the *Journalist,* July 2005, 15.
6. Quoted in Johanna Neuman, *Lights, Camera, War: Is Media Technology Driving International Politics?* (New York: St. Martin's Press, 1996), 10–11.
7. L. Friedland, *Covering the World: International Television News Services* (London: 20th Century Fund Press, 1992), 7–8, cited in Philip M. Taylor, "The Military and the Media: Past, Present and Future," in Stephen Badsey, ed. *The Media and International Security* (London: Cass, 2000), 199.
8. Nik Gowing, "Real-Time Television Coverage of Armed Conflicts and Diplomatic Crises: Does It Pressure or Distort Foreign Policy Decisions?" Joan Shorenstein Barone Center, John F. Kennedy School of Government (Cambridge, MA: Harvard University, 1994).
9. Neuman, *Lights, Camera, War.*
10. Jamie Shea, "Modern Conflicts and the Media: Dealing with the Dilemmas," in *World Defence Systems* (London: RUSI, 2000), 36–8.
11. Warren P. Strobel, *Late Breaking Foreign Policy* (Washington, DC: U.S. Institute for Peace, 1997).
12. Nik Gowing, "Media Coverage: Help or Hindrance in Conflict Prevention," in Badsey, *The Media and International Security,* 203–26.
13. Douglas Hallin, *The "Uncensored War": The Media and Vietnam* (Oxford: Oxford University, 1989).
14. Nick della Casa, a founder member of Frontline TV News, was killed in the mountains while trying to cross over from Turkey into Kurdistan. He was accompanied by his new wife and his (ex-SAS) brother-in-law. They were also murdered by Kurdish bandits. Coauthor Moorcraft had given della Casa his first journalist's job and had worked with him in Afghanistan. The young cameraman was brave to the point of recklessness.
15. Neuman, *Lights, Camera, War,* 237.

16. Interview with coauthor Moorcraft, January 2002. See "Virtuous Intervention and Good Luck," in Paul Moorcraft, et al., *The New Wars of the West: Anglo-American Voices on the War on Terror* (Havertown, PA: Casemate, 2005), 55–9.

17. Phillip Knightley, *The First Casualty* (Baltimore, MD: Johns Hopkins, 2004), 548.

18. For a perceptive analysis of the lifestyle and working practices of correspondents, albeit in the Latin American context, see Mark Pedelty, *War Stories: The Culture of Foreign Correspondents* (New York: Routledge, 1995).

19. See David Loyn, *Frontline: The True Story of the British Mavericks Who Changed the Face of War Reporting* (London: Michael Joseph, 2005).

20. Cited in Neil Hickey, "Over There," *Columbia Journalism Review*, November–December 1996, 54.

21. Conversation with coauthor Moorcraft, 1998. See also Paul Moorcraft, "Reporting Conflict: Delusions of a Luckless Tribe," in Mike Ungersma, ed. *Reporters and the Reported: The 1999 Vauxhall Lectures,* Cardiff University, 1999, 32–44.

22. Martin Bell, "TV News: How Far Should We Go?" *British Journalism Review*, vol. 8, no. 1, 1997, 14.

23. Jean Seaton, "Why Do We Think the Serbs Do It? The New 'Ethnic' Wars and the Media," *Political Quarterly,* vol. 70, no. 3, July 1999, 66. See also Tim Allen and Jean Seaton, eds. *The Media of Conflict: War Reporting and Representations of Ethnic Violence* (London: Zed, 1999).

24. Philip M. Taylor, "The Military and the Media," 182.

25. Jim Burroughs, *Blood on the Lens*: *A Filmmaker's Quest for Truth in Afghanistan* (Washington, DC: Potomac Books, 2007), 3.

26. See, for example, David Leigh, "Tinker, Tailor, Soldier, Journalist," *Guardian* (Media), June 12, 2000, 2.

27. John Lloyd, *What the Media Are Doing to Our Politics* (London: Robinson, 2004).

28. Simon Jenkins, "This Weekend's 9/11 Horror-fest Will Do Osama bin Laden's Work for Him," *Guardian*, September 8, 2006, 36.

29. Jeremy Paxman, "All Is Not What It Seems," *Guardian* (Media), May 8, 2000.

30. See Robert Fisk, *The Great War for Civilisation: The Conquest of the Middle East* (London: HarperCollins, 2006), xix, xxiii. Fisk said that the hero of *Foreign Correspondent,* Huntley Haverstock, whose words we have quoted, encouraged the young Fisk to become a journalist. Fisk also cites Amira Hass, the Israeli journalist, who said that the prime role of journalism is to monitor the centers of power.

# SELECTED BIBLIOGRAPHY

Adie, Kate, "Dispatches from the Front: Reporting War," in Mike Ungersma, ed. *Reporters and the Reported: The 1998 Vauxhall Lectures* (Cardiff: Centre for Journalism Studies, Cardiff University, 1998).

Allen, Charles, *The Savage Wars of Peace: Soldiers' Voices 1945–1989* (London: Future, 1991).

Allen, Stuart and Barbie Zelizer, *Reporting War: Journalism in Wartime* (London: Routledge, 2004).

Allen, Tim, and Jean Seaton, eds. *The Media of Conflict: War Reporting and Representations of Ethnic Violence* (London: Zed, 1999).

Anderson, Duncan, *Glass Warriors: The Camera at War* (London: Collins, 2005).

Anderson, John Lee, *The Fall of Baghdad* (New York: Penguin, 2004).

Arnett, Peter, *Live from the Battlefield* (London: Corgi, 1995).

Arthur, Max, *Forgotten Voices of the Great War* (London: Ebury, 2003).

Ayres, Chris, *War Reporting for Cowards* (New York: Grove, 2005).

Badsey, Stephen, *Modern Military Operations and the Media* (Strategic and Combat Studies Institute Paper, No. 8, 1994).

———, ed. *The Media and International Security* (London: Cass, 2000).

Bartimus, Tad, et al., *War Torn: Stories of War from the Women Reporters who Covered Vietnam* (New York: Random House, 2002).

BBC, *War Report: From D-Day to VE Day* (London: BBC, 1994).

Behr, Edward, *Anyone Here Been Raped and Speaks English?* (London: New English Library, 1982).

Bell, Martin, *In Harm's Way: Reflections of a War-Zone Thug* (London: Penguin, 1996).

———, "TV News: How Far Should We Go?" *British Journalism Review*, No. 8 (1997): 6–16.

———, *Through the Gates of Fire: A Journey into World Disorder* (London: Weidenfeld and Nicholson, 2003).

Boot, William, "The Pool," *Columbia Journalism Review* (May–June 1991): 24–7.

Bowden, Tim, *One Crowded Hour, Neil Davis, Combat Cameraman, 1934–85* (Sydney: Imprint, 1990).

Bowen, Jeremy, *War Stories* (London: Simon & Schuster, 2006).

Bridgland, Fred, *The War for Africa: 12 Months That Transformed a Continent* (Gibraltar: Ashanti, 1990).

Buitenhuis, Peter, *The Great War of Words: Literature as Propaganda 1914–18 and After* (London: Batsford, 1989).

Campbell, Alastair, "Media and the War in Kosovo," *RUSI Journal*, No. 144 (August 1999): 31–35.

Caputo, Philip, *Means of Escape* (Guilford, CT: Lyons, 2002).

Carey, John, ed. *The Faber Book of Reportage* (London: Faber and Faber, 1987).

Carruthers, Susan L., *The Media at War* (Basingstoke, UK: Macmillan, 2000).

Caute, David, *Under the Skin: The Death of White Rhodesia* (London: Allen Lane, 1983).

Chandrasekaran, Rajiv, *Imperial Life in the Emerald City: Inside Iraq's Green Zone* (New York: Knopf, 2006).

Collier, Richard, *The Warcos: The War Correspondents of World War II* (London: Weidenfeld and Nicholson, 1989).

Cull, Nicholas John, *Selling War: The British Propaganda Campaign Against American "Neutrality" in World War II* (New York: Oxford University Press, 1995).

Curran, James, and Jean Seaton, *Power Without Responsibility: The Press and Broadcasting in Britain* (London: Routledge, 1990).

Curtis, Liz, *Ireland, The Propaganda War: The British Media and the "Battle for Hearts and Minds"* (London: Pluto, 1984).

Daly, Emma, "Reporting from the Front Line," in Stephen Glover, ed. *Secrets of the Press: Journalists on Journalism* (London: Allen Lane, 1999).

di Giovanni, Janine, *The Quick and the Dead* (London: Phoenix, 1995).

du Preez, Max, and Jacques Pauw, "Exposing Apartheid's Death Squads, 1988–94" in John Pilger, ed. *Tell Me No Lies: Investigative Journalism and Its Triumphs* (London: Vintage, 2005).

Eyal, Jonathan, "The Media and the Military: Continuing the Dialogue after Kosovo," *RUSI Journal*, Vol. 145, No. 2 (April 2000).

Farrar, Martin J., *News from the Front: War Correspondents, 1914–1918* (Stroud, UK: Sutton, 1998).

Feinstein, Anthony, *Journalists under Fire: The Psychological Hazards of Covering War* (Baltimore: Johns Hopkins University Press, 2006).

Fenton, James, *All the Wrong Places: Adrift in the Politics of Southeast Asia* (London: Granta, 2005).

Ferguson, Niall, *The Pity of War* (London: Allen Lane, 1998).

Fisk, Robert, *The Great War for Civilisation: The Conquest of the Middle East* (London: Harper Perennial, 2006).

Foerstel, Herbert N., *Killing the Messenger: Journalists at Risk in Modern Warfare* (Westport, CT: Praeger, 2006).

Fox, Robert, *Eye Witness Falklands* (London: Methuen, 1982).

Frederikse, Julie, *None But Ourselves: Masses vs Media in the Making of Zimbabwe* (London: Currey, 1982).

Fussell, Paul, *The Great War and Modern Memory* (Oxford: Oxford University Press, 1977).

Gall, Sandy, *Behind Russian Lines: An Afghan Journal* (London: Sidgwick and Jackson, 1983).

———, *Don't Worry About the Money Now* (London: New English Library, 1988).

Giddings, Robert, *Echoes of War: Portraits of War from the Fall of Troy to the Gulf War* (London: Bloomsbury, 1992).

Glasgow University Media Group, *War and Peace News,* (Milton Keynes, UK: Open University Press, 1985).

Glenny, Misha, *The Fall of Yugoslavia* (Harmondsworth, UK: Penguin, 1992).

Gow, James, Richard Paterson and Alison Preston, eds. *Bosnia by Television* (London: British Film Institute, 1996).

Gowing, Nik, "Real-time Television Coverage of Armed Conflicts and Diplomatic Crises: Does It Pressure or Distort Foreign Policy Decisions?" (Harvard, Joan Shorenstein Barone Center, Working Paper 94): 1.

———, "Real-time TV Coverage from War: Does It Make or Break Government Policy?" in James Gow, *Bosnia by Television* (1996): 81–91.

———, "Conflict, the Military and the Media: A New Optimism?" The *Officer,* (May/June 1997).

Griffin, Michael, *Reaping the Whirlwind: Afghanistan, Al Qa'ida and the Holy War* (London: Pluto, 2003).

Grossman, Vasily, *A Writer at War: Vasily Grossman with the Red Army 1941–1945* (London: Pimlico, 2006).

Gutmann, Stephanie, *The Other War: Israelis, Palestinians and the Struggle for Media Supremacy* (San Francisco: Encounter, 2005).

Hachten, A., and C. A. Giffard, *The Press and Apartheid: Repression and Propaganda in South Africa* (Madison: University of Wisconsin Press, 1984).

Hallin, Daniel C., *The "Uncensored War": Vietnam and the Media* (Oxford: Oxford University Press, 1986).

Hammond, Philip and Edward S. Herman, eds. *Degraded Capability: The Media and the Kosovo Crisis* (London: Pluto, 2000).

Hammond, William M., *Reporting Vietnam: Media and Military at War* (Lawrence, KA: University of Kansas Press, 2000).

Hanlon, Joseph, *Apartheid's Second Front* (Harmondsworth: Penguin, 1986).

Hanrahan, Brian, and Robert Fox, *"I Counted Them All Out and I Counted Them All Back": The Battle for the Falklands* (London: BBC, 1982).

Harriman, Ed, *Hack: Home Truths About Foreign News* (London: Zed, 1987).

Harris, Paul, *Somebody Else's War: Reports from the Balkan Frontline* (Stevenage, UK: Spa, 1992).

Harris, Robert, *Gotcha: The Media, the Government and the Falklands Crisis* (London: Faber and Faber, 1983).

Hastings, Max, *Going to the Wars* (Basingstoke, UK: Macmillan, 2000).

Havers, Richard, *Here is the News: The BBC and the Second World War* (Stroud, UK: Sutton, 2007).

Haverstock, Nathan A., *Fifty Years at the Front: The Life of War Correspondent Frederick Palmer* (Washington: Brassey's, Inc. 1996).

Herr, Michael, *Dispatches* (London: Picador, 1979).

Hilsum, Lindsey, "Where is Kigali?" *Granta,* Vol. 51 (1995): 145–79.

———, "A War of Unintended Consequences" in Paul Moorcraft, ed. *The New Wars of the West.*

Hiro, Dilip, *The Longest War: The Iran-Iraq Conflict* (London: Paladin, 1990).

Hoge, J., "Foreign News: Who Gives a Damn?" *Columbia Journalism Review,* Vol. 36 (November–December 1997): 48–52.

Horne, Alistair, *A Savage War of Peace: Algeria 1954–1962* (Harmondsworth, UK: Penguin, 1985).

Hudson, Miles, and John Stanier, *War and the Media* (Stroud: Sutton, 1997).

Hughes, Chris, *Road Trip to Hell: Tabloid Tales of Saddam, Iraq and a Bloody War* (London: Monday, 2006).

Hughes-Wilson, John, *Military Intelligence Blunders and Cover-ups* (London: Robinson, 2004).

Huntington, Samuel P., *The Clash of Civilizations and the Remaking of the World Order* (New York: Touchstone, 1998).

Hynes, Samuel, *The Soldier's Tale: Bearing Witness to Modern War* (London: Pimlico, 1997).

Ignatieff, Michael, *The Warrior's Honor: Ethnic War and the Modern Conscience* (London: Chatto and Windus, 1988).

———, *Virtual War: Kosovo and Beyond* (London: Chatto and Windus, 2000).

Inglis, Fred, *People's Witness: The Journalist in Modern Politics* (New Haven, CT: Yale, 2002).

International News Safety Institute, *Dying to Tell the Story: The Iraq War and the Media, a Tribute* (Brussels: International News Safety Institute, 2003).

Isikoff, Michael, and David Corn, *Hubris: The Inside Story of Spin, Scandal and the Selling of the Iraq War* (New York: Crown, 2006).

Johnson, Phyllis, and David Martin, eds. *Destructive Engagement* (Harare: Zimbabwe Publishing, 1986).

Johnstone, Diana, *Fool's Crusade: Yugoslavia, NATO and Western Delusions* (London: Pluto, 2002).

———, "Seeing Yugoslavia through a Dark Glass: The Ideological Uniformity of the Media," in Lenora Forstel, ed. *War, Lies and Videotape: How Media Monopoly Stifles Truth* (New York: International Action Center, 2000).

Katovsky, Bill, and Timothy Carlson, *Embedded: The Media at War in Iraq* (Guilford, CT: Lyons, 2003).

Keane, Fergal, *Season of Blood: A Rwandan Journey* (London: Penguin, 1996).

Keegan, John, *The First World War* (London: Hutchinson, 1998).

———, *A History of Warfare* (London: Hutchinson, 1993).

———, *The Second World War* (London: Hutchinson, 1989).

Knightley, Phillip, *The First Casualty: The War Correspondent as Hero, Propagandist and Myth Maker* (Baltimore: John Hopkins University, 2004).

———, "History or Bunkum?" *British Journalism Review,* Vol. 14, No. 2 (2003): 7–14.

Lambert, Andrew, and Stephen Badsey, *The War Correspondents: The Crimean War* (Stroud: Sutton, 1994).

Lande, Nathaniel, *Dispatches from the Front: A History of the American War Correspondent* (Oxford: Oxford University Press, 1996).

Lapping, Brian, *End of Empire* (London: Paladin, 1989).

Lelyveld, Joseph, *Move Your Shadow* (London: Abacus, 1987).

Lewis, Justin, et al., *Shoot First and Ask Questions Later: Media Coverage of the 2003 Iraq War* (New York: Peter Lang, 2006).

Lloyd, Anthony, *My War Gone By, I Miss It So* (London: Penguin, 1999).

Lloyd, John, *What the Media Are Doing to Our Politics* (London: Robinson, 2004).

Loyn, David, *Frontline: The True Story of the British Mavericks who Changed the Face of War Reporting* (London: Penguin, 2005).

Lytton, Neville, *The Press and the General Staff* (London: Collins, 1921).

MacArthur, John R., *Second Front: Censorship and Propaganda in the Gulf War* (Berkeley, CA: University of California Press, 1992).

Malan, Rian, *My Traitor's Heart: Blood and Bad Dreams: A South African Explores the Madness in his Country, His Tribe and Himself* (London: Bodley Head, 1990).

Martin, David, and Phyllis Johnson, *The Struggle for Zimbabwe* (London: Faber and Faber, 1981).

Massing, Michael, *Now They Tell Us: The American Press and Iraq* (New York: New York Review of Books, 2004).

McAlister, Melani, *Epic Encounters: Culture, Media and US Interests in the Middle East Since 1945* (Berkeley, CA: University of California, 2005).

McCain, A., and Leonard Shyles, *The 1,000 Hour War* (Westport, CT: Greenwood, 1994).

McGeough, Paul, *Manhattan to Baghdad* (Sydney: Allen and Unwin, 2003).

McLaughlin, Greg, *The War Correspondent* (London: Pluto, 2002).

Mercer, Derrick, Geoff Mungham, and Kevin Williams, *The Fog of War: The Media on the Battlefield* (London: Heinemann, 1987).

Meredith, Martin, *The Past Is Another Country* (London: André Deutsch, 1979).

Mermin, Jonathan, *Debating War and Peace: Media Coverage of US Intervention in the Post-Vietnam Era* (Princeton, NJ: Princeton University Press, 1999).

Messinger, Gary S., *British Propaganda and the State in the First World War,* (Manchester: Manchester University Press, 1992).

Metzl, Jamie, "Information Intervention: When Switching Channels Isn't Enough," *Foreign Affairs*, Vol. 76, No. 6 (November–December 1997): 15–20.

Miles, Hugh, *Al-Jazeera: How Arab TV News Changed the World* (London: Abacus, 2006).

Miller, David, *Don't Mention the War: Northern Ireland, Propaganda and the Media* (London: Pluto, 1994).

Miller, David, "Information Dominance: The Philosophy of Total Propaganda Control?" in Yahya R. Kamalipour and Nancy Snow, eds. *War, Media and Propaganda: A Global Perspective* (Lanham, MD: Rowman and Littlefield, 2004).

Miller, David, ed. *Tell Me Lies: Propaganda and Media Distortion in the Attack on Iraq* (London: Pluto, 2004).

Miniter, Richard, *Disinformation: 22 Media Myths That Undermine the War on Terror* (Washington: Regnery, 2005).

Moeller, Susan D., *Compassion Fatigue: How the Media Sell Disease, Famine, War and Death* (London: Routledge, 1999).

———, "Locating Accountability: The Media and Peacekeeping," *Journal of International Affairs*, Vol. 55, No. 2 (Spring 2002): 369–390.

Moorcraft, Paul, *African Nemesis: War and Revolution in Southern Africa, 1945–2010*, (London: Brassey's, 1994).

———, "CNN: The New Emperor of International Politics?" *New Zealand International Review*, (November/December 1997): 22–25.

———, *Guns and Poses: Travels with an Occasional War Correspondent* (Guildford, UK: Millstream, 2001).

———, "Reporting Conflict: Delusions of a Luckless Tribe," in Mike Ungersma, ed. *Reporters and the Reported: The 1999 Vauxhall Lectures* (Cardiff: Centre for Journalism Studies, Cardiff University, 1999).

———, "Rhodesia's War of Independence," *History Today*, Vol. 40 (September 1990).

———, "Sudan: End of the Longest War?" *RUSI Journal*, Vol. 150, No. 1 (February 2005): 54–59.

Moorcraft, Paul, and Peter McLaughlin, *Chimurenga: The War in Rhodesia* (Marshalltown, RSA: Sygma/Collins, 1982).

Moorcraft, Paul, Gwyn Winfield, and John Chisholm, eds. *The New Wars of the West: Anglo-American Voices on the War on Terror* (Havertown, PA: Casemate, 2005).

Morris, James, *Farewell the Trumpets: An Imperial Retreat* (Harmondsworth, UK: Penguin, 1987).

Morrison, David, and Howard Tumber, *Journalists at War: The Dynamics of News Reporting During the Falklands Conflict* (London: Sage, 1988).

Mowlana, Hamid, "The Role of the Media in the US-Iranian Conflict," in A. Arno and W. Dissanyake, eds. *The News Media in National and International Conflict* (Boulder, CO: Westview, 1984).

Munnion, Chris, *Banana Sunday: Datelines from Africa* (Rivonia, RSA: William Waterman, 1993).

Natsios, Andrew, "Illusions of Influence: The CNN Effect in Complex Emergencies," in R. Rotberg and T. Weiss, eds. *From Massacres to Genocide:* (1996).

Neuman, Johanna, *Lights, Camera, War: Is Media Technology Driving International Politics?* (New York: St Martin's Press, 1996).

O'Rourke, P. J., *Give War a Chance* (London: Picador, 1992).

———, *Holidays in Hell* (London: Picador, 1988).

Packer, George, *The Assassin's Gate: America in Iraq* (New York: Farrar, Straus and Giroux, 2005).

Pedalty, Mark, *War Stories: The Culture of Foreign Correspondents* (New York: Routledge, 1995).

Philo, Greg, and Mike Berry, *Bad News from Israel* (London: Pluto, 2004).

Pilger, John, *Heroes* (London: Pan, 1987).

———, (ed.) *Tell Me No Lies: Investigative Journalism and Its Triumphs* (London: Vintage, 2005).

Pocock, Tom, *Alan Moorehead* (London: Pimlico, 1990).

Politkovskaya, Anna, "Chechnya: Dirty War," in John Pilger, ed. (2005).

Price, Monroe E., and Mark Thompson, *Forging Peace: Intervention, Human Rights and the Management of Media Space* (Edinburgh: Edinburgh University Press, 2002).

Rampton, Sheldon, and John Stauber, *The Best War Ever: Lies, Damned Lies and the Mess in Iraq* (New York: Tarcher/Penguin, 2006).

Rankin, Nicholas, *Telegram from Guernica* (London: Faber, 2003).

Rich, Frank, *The Greatest Story ever Sold? The Decline and Fall of Truth* (New York: Penguin, 2006).

Rich, Sebastian, *People I Have Shot* (London: Gollancz, 1990).

Ricks, Thomas E., *Fiasco: The American Military Adventure in Iraq* (London: Allen Lane, 2006).

Risen, James, *State of War: The Secret History of the CIA under the Bush Administration* (New York: Free Press, 2006).

Roberts, Adam, "NATO's 'Humanitarian War' Over Kosovo," *Survival,* Vol. 41, No. 3 (October 1999).

Robinson, Piers, *The CNN Effect: The Myth of News Media, Foreign Policy and Intervention* (London: Routledge, 2002).

Rose, Michael, *Fighting for Peace* (London: Harvill, 1998).

Rosenblum, Mort, *Escaping Plato's Cave: How American Blindness to the Rest of the World Threatens our Survival* (New York: St Martin's Press, 2007).

———, *Who Stole the News? Why Can't We Keep Up with What Happens in the World and What Can We Do About It?* (New York: John Wiley, 1993).

Rotberg, R., and T. Weiss, eds. *From Massacres to Genocide: the Media, Public Policy, and Humanitarian Crisis* (Washington: Brookings Institution, 1996).

Royle, Trevor, *War Report: The War Correspondent's View of Battle from the Crimea to the Falklands* (Edinburgh: Mainstream, 1987).

Ryan, Nigel, *A Hitch or Two in Afghanistan* (London: Weidenfeld and Nicholson, 1983).

Said, Edward W., *Covering Islam: How the Media and the Experts Determine How We See the Rest of the World* (London: Vintage, 1997).

Sanders, M., and Philip M. Taylor, *British Propaganda in the First World War* (London: Macmillan, 1982).

Sebba, Anne, *Battling for the News: The Rise of the Woman Reporter* (London: Hodder and Stoughton, 1994).

Seib, Philip, *Beyond the Front Lines: How the News Media Cover a World Shaped by War* (London: Palgrave Macmillan, 2006).

———, *Media and Conflict in the 21st Century* (London: Palgrave Macmillan, 2005).

Shadid, Anthony, *Night Draws Near: Iraq's People in the Shadow of America's War* (New York: Holt, 2005).

Sibbald, Raymond, *The War Correspondents: The Boer War* (Stroud, UK: Sutton, 1993).

Simpson, John, *Strange Places, Questionable People* (Basingstoke, UK: Macmillan, 1998).

Sparks, Allister, *The Mind of South Africa: The Story of the Rise and Fall of Apartheid* (London: Mandarin, 1991).

Stech, Frank, "Winning CNN Wars," *Parameters*, (Autumn 1994): 37–56.

Steele, Jon, *War Junkie: One Man's Addiction to the Worst Places on Earth* (London: Corgi, 2002).

Stephen, Martin, *Poetry, History and Myth in the Great War* (London: Leo Cooper, 1996).

Stewart, Bob, *Broken Lives: A Personal View of the Bosnian Conflict* (London: HarperCollins, 1994).

Stewart, Ian, and Susan L. Carruthers, eds. *War, Culture and the Media: Representations of the Military in Twentieth Century Britain* (Trowbridge, UK: Flick, 1996).

Strobel, Warren P., *Late Breaking Foreign Policy* (Washington, DC: US Institute for Peace, 1997).

Susskind, Ron, *The One Percent Doctrine: Deep Inside America's Pursuit of Its Enemies since 9/11* (New York: Simon and Schuster, 2006).

Sylvester, Judith, and Suzanne Huffman, *Reporting from the Front: The Media and the Military* (Lanham, MD: Rowman & Littlefield, 2005).

Taleb, B. A., *The Bewildered Herd: Media Coverage of International Conflicts and Public Opinion* (New York: iUniverse, Inc, 2004).

Tatham, Steve, *Losing Arab Hearts and Minds: The Coalition, Al-Jazeera and Muslim Public Opinion* (London: Hurst, 2006).

Taylor, Philip M., *British Propaganda in the Twentieth Century: Selling Democracy* (Edinburgh: Edinburgh University Press, 1999).

———, *Munitions of the Mind: A History of Propaganda from the Ancient World to the Present Day* (Manchester: Manchester University Press, 3rd edition, 2003).

———, *War and the Media: Propaganda and Persuasion in the Gulf War* (Manchester: Manchester University Press, 1997).

Thomas, Hugh, *The Spanish Civil War* (London: Pelican, 1986).

Thompson, Mark, *Forging War: The Media in Serbia, Croatia, Bosnia and Hercegovina* (Luton, UK: University of Luton Press, 1999).

———, *A Paper House: The Ending of Yugoslavia* (London: Vintage, 1992).

Thomson, Alex, *Smokescreen: The Media, the Censors, the Gulf War* (Tunbridge Wells, UK: Laburnham & Spellmount, 1992).

Thussu, Daya Kishan, and Des Freedman, *War and the Media* (London: Sage, 2003).

Townshend, Charles, ed. *The Oxford History of Modern War* (Oxford: Oxford University Press, 2005).

Tumber, Howard, and Jerry Palmer, *The Media at War: the Iraq Crisis* (London: Sage, 2004).

Tumber, Howard, and Frank Webster, *Journalists under Fire: Information War and Journalistic Practice* (London: Sage, 2006).

Venter, Al J., "Why Portugal Lost Its African Wars," in Al J. Venter, ed. *Challenge* (Gibraltar: Ashanti, 1990).

Vulliamy, Ed, *Seasons in Hell: Understanding Bosnia's War* (New York: Simon and Schuster, 1994).

Waldmeir, Patti, *Anatomy of a Miracle* (London: Penguin, 1997).

West, Richard, *Diamonds and a Necklace* (London: Hodder and Stoughton, 1989).

Wilkinson-Latham, Robert, *From Our Special Correspondent: Victorian War Correspondents and Their Campaigns* (London: Hodder and Stoughton, 1979).

Williams, Kevin, "The Light at the End of the Tunnel: Mass Media, Public Opinion and the Vietnam War," in John Eldridge, ed. *Getting the Message* (London: Routledge, 1993).

Windrich, Elaine, *The Mass Media in the Struggle for Zimbabwe* (Gwelo, Zimbabwe: Mambo, 1981).

Wolfsfeld, Gadi, *Media and Political Conflict: News from the Middle East* (Cambridge: Cambridge University Press, 1997).

Woods, Donald, *South African Dispatches* (London: Penguin, 1986).

Woodward, Bob, *State of Denial: Bush at War, Part III* (New York: Simon and Schuster, 2006).

Wright, Evan, *Generation Kill: Living Dangerously on the Road to Baghdad with the Ultraviolent Marines of Bravo Company* (London: Bantam, 2004).

Young, Peter, and Peter Jesser, *The Media and the Military: From the Crimea to Desert Strike* (Basingstoke, UK: Macmillan, 1997).

# INDEX

# THE AUTHORS

**Paul L. Moorcraft** is the director of the Centre for Foreign Policy Analysis, London, an independent think tank dedicated to conflict resolution. He also works as a crisis management consultant to international companies as well as serving as a visiting professor at Cardiff University's School of Journalism, Media, and Cultural Studies.

Professor Moorcraft has been a freelance TV producer/war correspondent in over thirty war zones in Africa, the Middle East, Asia, and the Balkans. He has also been a correspondent for numerous newspapers and magazines, including *Time*. Today he writes op-eds for newspapers across the political spectrum (from the liberal *Guardian* in the United Kingdom to the conservative *Washington Times,* from the *Canberra Times* in Australia to Johannesburg's *Business Day*). He is a regular pundit on military affairs for BBC TV and radio, Sky, Al-Jazeera, and others. He is the former editor of a number of UK security and foreign policy magazines including *Defence Review* and *Defence International.*

Paul Moorcraft has lectured full time at ten major international universities in the United States, Europe, Africa, and Australasia on journalism, politics, and international relations. He was a Distinguished Radford Visiting Professor in Journalism at Baylor University in Waco, Texas.

Moorcraft is the author of a wide range of books on military history, politics, journalism, and crime as well as an award-winning novel. His most recent coauthored book is *Axis of Evil: The War on Terror* (2005); the updated American edition is *The New Wars of the West: Anglo-American Voices on the War on Terror* (2006). His well-known coauthored work on counterinsurgency, *Chimurenga* (1982), will be republished in 2008 in an updated edition, as *The Rhodesian War: A Military History*.

A former senior instructor at the Royal Military Academy, Sandhurst (1973–75), Moorcraft was a member of the directing staff at the UK Joint

Services Command and Staff College (1997–2000). He also worked in corporate communications in the Ministry of Defence in Whitehall as well as in media operations in the field. He lives in the Surrey Hills, near London.

**Philip M. Taylor** is professor of international communications in the Institute of Communications Studies at the University of Leeds. Trained as an historian, he is the author of numerous works, including *The Projection of Britain: British Overseas Publicity and Propaganda, 1919–1939* (Cambridge University Press, 1982), *Munitions of the Mind: A History of Propaganda from the Ancient World to the Present Era* (Manchester University Press, third edition 2003), *War and the Media: Publicity and Propaganda During the Gulf War* (Manchester University Press, second edition 1997), *Global Communications, International Affairs and the Media Since 1945* (Routledge, 1997), and *British Propaganda in the Twentieth Century: Selling Democracy* (Edinburgh University Press, 1999).

Professor Taylor has lectured all over the world, especially to military establishments, including at the Supreme Headquarters Allied Powers Europe near Mons, Belgium; on NATO strategic courses at the Polish Land Forces Headquarters in Warsaw; and in Paris, Bratislava (Slovakia), and Tallinn (Estonia). In Germany, he has lectured at Church House, at the NATO School at Oberammergau, to the 1st Armored Division at Herford, and to the Allied Rapid Reaction Corps (ARRC) at Rheindahlen. He has also spoken at the Norwegian Defense and Security School (NORDISS) and at the Norwegian Staff Defense College in Oslo, the Swedish Defense College in Stockholm, and the Italian Air Force Academy in Naples. In North America, he has addressed the Canadian Armed Forces at Montreal Garrison and the Canadian Department of National Defence in Ottawa, and he has also spoken at the US Army War College in Pennsylvania. He has also lectured for the past fifteen years at the United States Air Force Special Operations School (USAFSOS, now a university) in Hurlburt Field, Florida.

Philip Taylor was also consulted on Serbian propaganda by the prosecution team of the Slobodan Milosevic trial at the International War Crimes Tribunal in The Hague in 2002. He also served for many years as executive secretary or chairman of the Inter-University History Film Consortium. He was made a fellow of the Royal Historical Society in 1982, is a fellow of the Center on Public Diplomacy at the University of Southern California, and was adjunct professor at the Universiti Teknologi Mara, Shah Alam, Malaysia. He lives near Leeds in the United Kingdom.